To Dick . . . MENTOR, COLLEAGUE, FRIEND,
who continuously encouraged us
to demystify group process

Critical Incidents in Group Therapy

SECOND EDITION

JEREMIAH DONIGIAN
State University of New York
College at Brockport

DIANA HULSE-KILLACKY
University of New Orleans

Brooks/Cole • Wadsworth

I⟨T⟩P® An International Thomson Publishing Company

Belmont • Albany, NY • Bonn • Boston • Cincinnati • Johannesburg • London • Madrid • Melbourne
Mexico City • New York • Pacific Grove, CA • Scottsdale, AZ • Singapore • Tokyo • Toronto

Sponsoring Editor: *Eileen Murphy*
Marketing Team: *Liz Poulsen, Christine Davis*
Editorial Assistant: *Julie Martinez*
Production Editor: *Keith Faivre*

Manuscript Editor: *Betty Duncan*
Interior and Cover Design: *Laurie Albrecht*
Typesetting: *Scratchgravel Publishing Services*
Printing and Binding: *Webcom Limited*

For more information, contact Wadsworth Publishing Company, 10 Davis Drive, Belmont, CA
94002, or electronically at http://www.wadsworth.com

International Thomson Publishing Europe
Berkshire House 168–173
High Holborn
London WC1V 7AA
England

Thomas Nelson Australia
102 Dodds Street
South Melbourne, 3205
Victoria, Australia

Nelson Canada
1120 Birchmount Road
Scarborough, Ontario
Canada M1K 5G4

International Thomson Editores
Seneca 53
Col. Polanco
11560 México, D. F., México

International Thomson Publishing GmbH
Königswinterer Strasse 418
53227 Bonn
Germany

International Thomson Publishing Asia
60 Albert Street
#15-01 Albert Complex
Singapore 189969

International Thomson Publishing Japan
Hirakawacho Kyowa Building, 3F
2-2-1 Hirakawacho
Chiyoda-ku, Tokyo 102
Japan

International Thomson Publishing Southern
Africa
Building 18, Constantia Square
138 Sixteenth Road, P.O. Box 2459
Halfway House, 1685 South Africa

Printed in Canada

10 9 8 7 6 5 4 3 2 1

Library of Congress Cataloging-in-Publication Data

Donigian, Jeremiah [date]
    Critical incidents in group therapy / Jeremiah Donigian, Diana
Hulse-Killacky. — 2nd ed.
        p.   cm.
    Includes bibliographical references and index.
    ISBN 0-534-35727-X
    1. Group psychotherapy.   2. Critical incident technique.
3. Solution-focused therapy.   4. Cogntive therapy.   I. Hulse-
Killacky, Diana [date]   II. Title.
RC488.D66   1999
616.89'152—dc21   98-46018
                                                    CIP

C O N T E N T S

CHAPTER FIFTEEN
Mass Group Denial

FOREWORD

Shortly before Jerry Donigian and Dick Malnati published the first edition of *Critical Incidents in Group Therapy* in 1987, I received a phone call from Dick Malnati. I was editor of the newsletter for the Association for Specialists in Group Work (ASGW) at the time, and Dick wondered if I could publicize the book in the newsletter.

"I can't," I replied.

"Why not?" he inquired.

"Well," I said, "if I do it for you, than I have to do it for everyone who writes a book on group therapy."

"But," he responded, "there are no other books in the world like ours."

Although I adhered to the no-publicity policy, Dick's words have stayed with me through the years. He was right. What Jerry and Dick produced in 1987 was a small masterpiece of a text on group therapy. It was different from what had come before it, mainly theoretical texts plugging one or more approaches to working with groups. It also influenced what came after it—specifically, books primarily having a wider scope in dealing with the universal problems of conducting group therapy.

The long-awaited second edition of *Critical Incidents in Group Therapy* was delayed by Dick Malnati's untimely and tragic early death. His passing broke up a team and a way of working. Thankfully, amid death has come life, as Jerry Donigian and Diana Hulse-Killacky have now paired to enlarge and enhance the original work that Jerry and Dick began. This second edition of *Critical Incidents in Group Therapy* stays true to the spirit and the style of the first edition, but it does more, much more. In this edition, the 6 theories originally examined have doubled to 12 theories. New experts have been consulted, and the critical incidents covered have grown in breadth and depth. Such an expansion is a welcomed addition. There are literally no mainstream group therapy models not addressed in these pages.

In addition, students are challenged more in the second edition of *Critical Incidents* to respond in writing—as well as mentally and orally—to events in the group process. The Theory Evaluation Form included in this text should go a long way toward helping would-be group therapists gain a greater understanding of themselves, as well as the theories involved in leading groups. The comparisons of theories in Chapter 19 and considerations for developing one's theory in Chapter 20 are two outstanding features of this text.

Jerry Donigian and Diana Hulse-Killacky are polished and accomplished professionals. They are skilled in organizing and summarizing group therapy approaches. They are concise and clear in addressing the strengths and limitations of theories and theorists. Their writing style is easy to follow and interesting. The professional practitioners they have included in this text are noted authorities who in honest and direct ways let readers experience how they conceptualize therapy groups and the crises that are a part of them. Readers of this text cannot help but be impressed with the material included in these pages, which is unmatched in any other text on group therapy.

Dick Malnati was right in 1987 that his coauthored book was unique. He would be pleased to see it now as well. Jerry and Diana show that from unfulfilled endings can come productive new beginnings that expand on what came forth originally. Although the second edition of *Critical Incidents in Group Therapy* is its own book, its ancestry is strong. Students, as well as seasoned professionals, have much to glean from this thorough and thought-provoking work. I have learned much in reading Jerry and Diana's manuscript. Like pioneers of yesterday, these authors have blazed a new and wide trail to help group therapists think about their actions and create innovative ways of responding to difficulties from a theoretical basis. By reading and responding to the chapters and situations contained herein, group therapists at all levels may enlarge their repertoire of what is possible and what is appropriate during times of stress in groups. They may also come to see a link between themselves and certain theoretical approaches that both binds them with others of like mind-sets and helps them get beyond a rigid parroting of techniques to genuine growth in how they operate.

Samuel T. Gladding
Wake Forest University

P R E F A C E

In 1997 Donigian and Malnati wrote that the antecedents to group therapy, for the most part, were in individual theories of psychotherapy. Implied, but not fully stated in the first edition of this book, was the fact that each of the six theories were representative of individual psychotherapy models that were adopted for and applied to group therapy. In Chapter 15 of the first edition, Donigian and Malnati suggested that in order for a modality to be considered truly reflecting group therapy it needed to view the group as consisting of the member, the leader, and the group as a whole. These three elements, or subsystems, were seen as being *isomorphically* related. They referred to this as *systemic–interactive group therapy.* None of the modalities in the first edition considered the triadic interaction of the elements. A theory considered either the leader and the member, the leader and the group as a whole, the member and the group as a whole, or the group as a whole and the member. Thus, it became clear to us that, although groups were being formed in whichever therapy was to be conducted, they still were conducted under a theory of individual therapy. With the exception of systems-centered® theory* and perhaps interpersonal psychotherapy, this second edition also includes at least three additional theories whose roots are in individual therapy—solution-focused, psychodynamic (psychoanalytic), and cognitive–behavioral therapy. Family-centered therapy is an amalgam of a number of theories, with group and family theories receiving a greater emphasis. So, as the reader embarks on the journey through this second edition, we urge that it be taken with a cautionary eye because, of the 12 therapeutic models presented here (all of which are applied to groups), at least 9, if not 10, are drawn from individual theories of psychotherapy. This is not meant to be an

*Trademark is owned by Y. Agazarian

indictment but more an attempt to raise awareness that just because therapy is *conducted in* a group, it does not mean that it is model-based *group* theory. Having said that, we want again to explain, as we did in 1987, how and why we saw the need to write this book.

This text grew out of our shared concerns as teachers of group therapists. Its earliest roots were grounded in the observations we made of our students as they struggled with their own evolution from students to group therapists. As they faced their first group sessions, we noted the anxiety students experienced as they encountered the variety of events that occurred during the therapy sessions. The personal effect such occurrences had on students would prove to present barriers to their own personal growth, which could be lifted only after they had gained a greater understanding of the theoretical assumptions that could guide them through each new situation. The most frequently asked questions pertained to what the students could do to understand their roles, as group therapists, to support them through these critical moments.

These inquiries underscored the value for therapists having a sound theoretical understanding of the dynamics of therapy groups. Understanding these dynamics quite naturally led to a study of the thought processes that proponents of different theoretical orientations undertake while they approach critical moments in the group's process. It is our view that the pivotal moment in the therapeutic process occurred at the juncture where the therapist's creative, scientific, and learned knowledge united. This happened when a connection between the therapist's knowledge gained from experience combined with the therapist's intellectual inquiry and study. Such a connection is often viewed by students of group therapy to be a spontaneous, creative response. Although the more experienced, theoretically grounded therapists will appear to respond to such occurrences without much hesitation, it is at this moment that students tend to question their abilities. This questioning may lead to a crisis for students; the experienced therapist, however, will move to a greater level of therapeutic effect.

This text was written in response to students' needs to develop a theoretical rationale that will sustain and guide them as they perform their work with therapy groups. We have chosen six incidents, which can occur in a group therapy session, that raise a number of theoretical issues and a variety of possible resolutions for the therapist. The order of these incidents by no means implies that they supersede others in importance. We chose those incidents that occurred most frequently in the groups we and our students faced over the years as we worked as group therapists and teachers of group therapists.

After we identified the six incidents, we presented them to experienced group therapists, each of whom was a proponent of a different theoretical orientation. We asked them to respond to each critical incident and explain the thought processes they went through that determined their particular responses to the incident. The therapists have presented their explanations in a here-and-now fashion that gives the effect of immediacy. In this way, students will have the feeling of being right there with the therapists as their mentors, permitting them to be privy to the therapists' innermost thoughts. The ultimate purpose of this approach is not to ascertain which intervention is the best one

but to help students (1) see, from the vantage point of experienced group therapists, the rationale that supported their action; (2) understand why they chose
the particular intervention; and (3) gain insight into how experienced group
therapists project the anticipated consequences of their choices.

New to this edition is the addition of 6 theories and 7 theoretical practitioners who represent them, bringing the number of theories to 12, doubling those
that were in the first edition. Other significant changes from the first edition include expansion of the section that addresses the degree to which the therapists
were congruent with their respective theories. We listened to the suggestions
made by our students and colleagues who have used the text in their classes,
and we followed their recommendations. We have moved this section from appearing as a separate chapter in Part 3 in the first edition to presenting it at the
end of each of the critical incident chapters (Chapters 13–18). This move also
serves to provide a summary to the critical incident chapters. We also expanded
Chapter 19 in which the theoretical practitioners' responses to each of the critical incidents are compared and contrasted. The first-edition chapter on rational–emotive therapy was submitted to Albert Ellis for revision; it now reflects
his rational–emotive–behavioral therapy. Finally, in Chapter 20, we have drawn
from systemic group therapy a triadic model (Donigian & Malnati, 1997) that
encourages readers to think systemically as they consider developing their own
theory of group therapy.

Authors' Reflections

Jeremiah Donigian

Over 10 years have passed since Dick Malnati and I wrote the first edition of
this book. Much has happened to me since then, including the passing of my
coauthor, colleague, and very dear friend. However, I have learned to believe in
divine providence; in what seemed to have been the blink of an eye, I was
blessed to find Diana Hulse-Killacky. She is not a replacement for Dick. She, in
her own unique and inimitable way, has become my colleague, friend, and coauthor. I have even experienced her as a coleader. How fortunate for me to have
her agree to join with me to write this second edition. By adding six new theories and seven therapists, we have increased the book to more than twice its
original size. Along with a number of other significant modifications, this edition is the product of our joint efforts. Trying to convince Diana of this has been
a hard sell for me. I can understand why she may feel this way, especially when
one feels as though she is the stepparent. And yet, taking the child into its ado-
lescence has its own challenges and rewards. For me, it has meant that our relationship has continued to deepen and grow as we shared this joint venture. I
am most grateful for that.

For over 35 years of marriage, I have had a wonderful partner, coleader, and
friend who did more than coparent our two daughters, Melissa and Rebecca.
Anna has understood my idiosyncrasies, managing to step back and encourage

me to "leave her" as the compulsive side of me took over each time I set about to writing. Without her understanding, support, and belief in herself, this book would have been an even more formidable undertaking. Divine providence intervened that many years ago, and for that I am eternally grateful.

DIANA HULSE-KILLACKY

Joining with Jerry Donigian on the second edition of *Critical Incidents in Group Therapy* was a most gratifying experience, personally and professionally. When I first met Jerry and Dick Malnati over 10 years ago, I was immediately attracted to their styles and impressed by their influence on group work training and practice. Their frequent presentations and the first edition of this book reflected a long-term, well-respected, and nationally recognized collaboration. Dick Malnati's untimely death left a deep void in the field of group work and ended this special relationship.

Jerry's great generosity, his openness to making connections, and his willingness to put his time and energy into fostering a new partnership set the stage for our work together, which has included presentations at professional meetings and various writing projects. Jerry is an inspiring mentor who has patiently guided me through my first experience as a book author. That journey has resulted in this publication, which blends our two voices with those of our distinguished contributors, and has allowed for the deepening of our friendship and the expression of our collective passion for the power of groups and the group process.

My contributions to this edition were further enhanced by the constant support and encouragement from my partner in life, Jim Killacky, who responded to my occasional compulsive moments with great wisdom and understanding. His presence was essential to the success of my work.

Acknowledgments

We are most grateful to Eileen Murphy, whose wonderful support helped us through the writing of this second edition. It was always there when we needed it. Thank you, Eileen, for helping us feel that no one else was more important than us each time we reached out to you.

Of course, a book such as this cannot be written without the contributors who were willing to place themselves on the line and respond to the critical incidents. Each of them was most willing and cooperative. So, thank you, Yvonne Agazarian, John V. Flowers, Rebecca LaFountain, Mary Jean Paris, James P. Trotzer, and Victor Yalom for your willingness to share yourselves.

We also wish to thank the following reviewers for their valuable suggestions: Cheryl Bartholomew, George Mason University; Dorothy J. Blum, George Mason University; Nick Colangelo, University of Iowa; Samuel T. Gladding, Wake Forest University; Bill Kline, Idaho State University; and David Mitchell, University of Central Oklahoma.

Our special thanks to Faye Cavalier, Katherine Keene, and Sola Kippers, graduate students at the University of New Orleans, whose research was of immense help in the preparation of this expanded second edition.

Finally, once again, our deepest appreciation and sincere gratitude is extended to Dottie Reed, who over the years has typed and edited the rough drafts that eventually and miraculously were shaped into books. No less can be said for this one.

Contributors

Yvonne Agazarian
Private Practice
Philadelphia, Pennsylvania

Thomas E. Bratter
Counselor/Therapist
John Dewey Academy
Great Barrington, Massachusetts

William R. Coulson

Albert Ellis
Institute for Rational–Emotive Therapy
New York, New York

John V. Flowers
Chapman College
Orange, California

Herbert Hampshire
Bel Air, California

Rebecca LaFountain
Shippensburg University
Shippensburg, Pennsylvania

Guy J. Manaster
University of Texas
Austin, Texas

Mary Jean Paris
Private Practice
San Francisco, California

Mirriam F. Polster
Private Practice
La Jolla, California

J. Scott Rutan
Private Practice .
Chestnut Hill, Massachusetts

James P. Trotzer
Rivier College and Private Practice
Neshua, New Hampshire

Victor Yalom
Private Practice
San Francisco, California

INTRODUCTION

Historically, most group therapy models grew out of individual psychotherapy. It was not until the influence of Yalom's (1995) work and those who introduced systems theory and thinking (H. Durkin, Agazarian, Donigian and Malnati, and others) that the interpersonal and systemic arrangement of therapy groups gained focus and group therapy models evolved. Therefore, we need to be careful not to confuse *theories of individual therapy*, which are applied to group therapy, with *theories of group therapy*. Because all of these theories are being practiced in group therapy settings today, we have included them in this book, which emphasizes the translation of theory into practice. We begin with an examination of the value and role of theoretical background for group therapists in their practice. We hope that as students gain a knowledge of differing theoretical approaches they will develop their own rationale of group leadership and group therapy.

During the life of a therapy group, there are moments when critical incidents evolve as natural consequences of group development. These incidents can present either potential barriers or potential opportunities for the group's growth. In this way, the incidents are viewed as *critical*. The manner in which group leaders—the therapists—choose to manage such critical incidents will determine the extent to which the incidents affect group development. These moments (which often appear unannounced) can prove to be true tests even for experienced group leaders who have a firm theoretical base from which to operate. For neophyte group trainees, these moments can generate enough anxiety to immobilize them as they face the situation with uncertainty and trepidation. It is at such critical moments that group therapist trainees most frequently question their supervisors about what action they should take and what rationale should support their intervention. These inquiries arise as students attempt to bring about an integration of theory with practice.

Other writers have grappled with the relationship of theory and practice. Howard Kiefer (1980) addressed the question in this way:

> Nothing is true in theory and false in practice, or vice versa; however coherent and free from self contradiction, no theory is adequate which fails to account for what happens in practice, unless it somehow is theoretically explained, understood, or fitted into a larger context, (it) remains a faculty mystery. Davey is right on insisting that the final test of any theory is whether it works in the sense that its implications and predictions are consistent with events. But completely unexplained events, completely unaccounted for facts, or what might be called raw data must be as meaningless to a man as to a rabbit—without the context of theory, they are at best, things processed by the senses, not grasped by the mind. This means that theory is the intellectual twin of practice, not its opponent; its verbal description and explanation not something separate and wholly other.

In his effort to pinpoint the origin and purpose of theory, Charles Clevenger (1982) allows that theory serves a very functional purpose. It provides a vehicle for bringing together independent observations and placing them in a systematic relationship that permits them to gain a significant and utilitarian value. Still further, Samuel Osipow (1973, pp. 2–3) offers that the role of theory "permits, by deduction, predictions to be made about other events in the framework under observation." He adds that "a good theory clarifies events and leads to further predictions about related events."

Clearly, we have evidence supporting the need for group therapists to have experienced group participation and to be intellectually aware of the various events (the whats) occurring in the group and to note the ways they evolve. Therapists must organize observed events into some systematic order, thereby developing an explanation for the predictability of their occurrence. With this knowledge, therapists will not find the group process a mystery, and they will be able to develop leadership styles consistent with desired therapeutic outcomes.

Some students of group therapy will develop their own personal theories; others will develop a rationale supporting their approach to group therapy. Such a rationale should address the role and technique of the therapist, the therapy process, and the nature of group therapy. For example, Irvin Yalom (1995, p. xii) prefaces his book by describing what he perceives as the front from the "core" of group therapy. The front is much like a facade; it is the "trappings, the form, the techniques, the specialized language, and the aura surrounding each of the schools of therapy." He adds that "the core consists of those aspects of the experiences which are intrinsic to the therapeutic process—that is, the bare boned mechanisms of change." Yalom believes that the front has a significant part to play (e.g., the charismatic quality of the therapist) in the initial stages of the group; but in the absence or neglect of the core of therapy, the therapeutic process is without substance and change is superficial. It is this core to which we address our thoughts.

This book results from our belief that students need to develop their core. They must first realize that effective group leadership demands that they have an intellectual support base from which to function and that this base be composed of general guidelines to assist them as they practice group therapy. These guidelines should be sufficiently broad and flexible to accommodate the dynamic process of group therapy. If the guidelines are too rigid, they will limit the variety of intervention strategies available to the therapist.

It is our position that students of group therapy can gain a great deal by studying, observing, and experiencing various approaches to group therapy— whether the models are based on theories of individual therapy or group therapy. In so doing, students can begin to recognize how they are affected emotionally and intellectually by each therapist's technique and methodology as well as by accompanying theory. The foundation for one's rationale for leadership style and group development evolves from such experiences. In fact, as students read the chapters on theory, they will discover that all theoretical models presented have some other theory as their antecedent. Perhaps students will be motivated to do as Yalom has done: to separate the *front* from the *core* of each of the theories presented in this text and begin to develop a rationale that will guide them as they assume their role as group therapists.

The text is designed to illustrate how theory is translated into practice by the proponents of those theories. Its uniqueness in this regard, however, relies heavily on the emphasis we place on how the theoretical practitioners manage each of the critical incidents they encounter.

In its broadest perspective, this text provides the student of group leadership with comparative approaches for dealing with critical incidents that arise in group therapy. Students will find they are not forced to extrapolate how the theoretical approach might be applied but will be able to follow the actual thought processes of the theorists as the incident is confronted.

The text shows the amount of variability or license practitioners have in interpreting the theoretical principles they follow as they encounter specific situations. This text also reverses a trend that depicts competitiveness among various theoretical approaches, which can make students look for the "right" or a "wrong" approach. It is our belief that students will instead find a variety of ways to deal effectively with critical incidents that occur in a therapy group. Thus, for aspiring practitioners, effectiveness will be shown to be a matter of *choice* and *blend* and not an issue of which theory is best.

Finally, and perhaps in a more idealistic sense, this text provides students the learning derived from experiencing various theories, which ultimately could provide the impetus to develop a theoretical approach most effective for themselves.

The text is organized into three parts. Part 1 describes each of the selected theories used throughout the text. Each chapter follows a relatively simple format. Brief explanations of the background of the theoretical development of its proponents, or founder, open each chapter. This is followed by an examination of the fundamental principles that undergird the theory, its key concepts, the role of the therapist, and the rationale for the techniques used, and finally, group processes. We have made no analysis or interpretation of the theories presented in each chapter. Our primary purpose in Part 1 is to provide readers with a common base of understanding and a referral source as they undertake Part 2.

Part 2 provides the central core of the text. Each chapter presents a hypothetical critical incident occurring in a group therapy session. This is followed by responses from each theoretical practitioner. Because it is generally accepted that theoretical principles are subject to the individual interpretation of the practitioner, we encouraged each of our theoretical practitioners to engage in that liberty. The response process to each incident was structured to ensure a certain amount of continuity in the way each theoretical practitioner dealt with the issue. The procedures they followed asked them to

1. Explain the thought processes they used to guide them as they selected their particular response, including what aspects about the incident prompted them to take the action they did.
2. Explain why they chose one particular intervention method over any other they may have considered.
3. State what consequences they anticipated from their action.
4. Point out what was the most glaring or outstanding condition of the incident, which they in turn identified as lending itself most readily to the theory (or its principle) they espoused.

If a therapist believed that the incident would not fit into or would not occur in one of the theoretical frameworks, he or she was asked to explain this position and show why an issue was not expected to occur.

A significant change from the first edition is to close each critical incident chapter with an examination of how congruent our theoretical practitioners were with their theories. Part 2 also initiates the students' direct participation in becoming aware of their theory of group therapy. Students respond to the same sequence of questions addressed by the theoretical practitioners and, at the end of each section, complete a "Theory Evaluation Form" designed to further highlight their evolving theory of group therapy.

Part 3 integrates the first two parts of the text, similar to the "capping" process of a typical group therapy session. We compare and contrast the interventions made by each theoretical practitioner, to highlight the similarities and differences of the approaches. We conclude by offering students guidelines by which they may begin to develop their own theory of group therapy.

PART ONE

SELECTED THEORIES APPLIED TO GROUP THERAPY

Introduction

The first part of this book, Chapters 1–12, provides the student with the primary principles that undergird each of the theories used by their respective theoretical practitioners in dealing with the critical situations in Part 2. Our purpose is not to teach theory per se but to offer its essence that guides its proponent as a group therapist. This introduction to theory examines the theorists' beliefs about the nature of human conflict and its sources, the role of the therapist, the therapist's use of techniques, the role of group members upon each other, and a sense of the group process that occurs.

Students interested in acquiring a broader knowledge of one or more of the theoretical perspectives should consult the "references" at the back of this book for further reading.

CHAPTER ONE

Client-Centered Therapy

Background

The name most synonymous with client-centered group therapy is Carl Rogers. In 1942 Rogers published *Counseling and Psychotherapy*, which contained the elements of a theory that was later to be more fully developed in his book, *Client-Centered Therapy* (1951). Client-centered therapy is an approach that grew from Rogers's experiences as a therapist. In 1946 Rogers, along with his associates at the counseling center at the University of Chicago, applied the principles of their individual therapy to individuals together in a group (Rogers, 1951). It was at this moment that client-centered *group* therapy began. By the early 1960s Rogers was devoting more of his clinical efforts and time to group therapy. In 1970 he wrote that group therapy has supplanted individual therapy as the primary focus of his professional life.

Client-centered group therapy is also known as *basic encounter group therapy* and *intensive experiential group therapy* (Rogers, 1967); in this book, we will use client-centered group therapy to avoid any confusion with other forms of encounter groups.

Searching for a theory of client-centered group therapy per se is a futile exercise. Rogers (1959) stated that he is "not attempting to build a high level abstract theory." However, in 1959 he extensively delineated his theory regarding individual therapy, personality, and interpersonal relationships. These formulations provide the threads supporting Rogers's rationale for client-centered group therapy. Actually, Rogers (1970) went so far as to say that his approach to group therapy does not differ in any fundamental philosophical way from his approach to individual therapy.

7

Rogers's client-centered approach to therapy grew out of his experiences as a therapist and an amalgam of thoughts distilled from theorists such as Rank, Buber, Lewin, Maslow, Combs, and Snygg. This unique blend of personal experiences and thoughts appears as a reflection of humanistic, existential–experiential, and phenomenological thinking. To appreciate how this translated into Rogers's brand of group therapy, we will examine the critical constructs that Rogers identified as the guidance system for his work as a therapist.

NATURE OF HUMAN BEINGS

Rogers holds that all human beings have the tendency to move toward actualization. It is the motivating force that urges humans toward activities of maintenance and growth. This belief in the inherent capacity of individuals to take charge of their lives is crucial to Rogers's form of therapy. He asserts that trusting in a client's basic ability to care for self is an extension of his position that people are much wiser than they think. It is society that has to be faulted for creating the barriers that keep individuals from realizing their full capabilities. Therefore, through therapy, people can learn to regain trust in themselves and to take responsibility for their lives. Consequently, Rogers tries to keep a very low profile in the therapeutic relationship; he works only to facilitate the release of the already existing growth potential in his clients.

SELF-CONCEPT

In most therapeutic modalities, understanding the nature of self-concept plays a significant role. In no other does it play a more important part than in client-centered therapy. Rogers (1959) devoted much thought to explaining how the self develops and how it ultimately affects human behavior. He went to great lengths to describe it and the constructs that reflect it.

Self-concept, according to Rogers, is a person's ability to perceive and differentiate the personal "I" from an internal frame of reference and to recognize the "I" as experienced from interpersonal relationships. Rogers refers to the development of a self-concept as a "fluid process." It is the way individuals differentiate themselves from others in their social relationships.

Rogers's constructs of congruence and incongruence related to the way the self is perceived and the way it is experienced in social relationships. If one's internal perception of self is consistent with the way in which projected self is *experienced* within interpersonal relationships, then a person is referred to as being *congruent.* However, should a discrepancy exist between the *idea* of one's self-perception and the projected experience (self-perception gained from social interactions), then it is said that this person is experiencing incongruency, or is *incongruent.*

Rogers offered that there are a number of ways by which an individual's self-concept is realized and, subsequently, the way a person functions. These constructs function much like needs. The way in which a person chooses to meet them determines the extent of the individual's growth and health. We will highlight four of the constructs to further explain Rogers's theories.

Rogers (1959, p. 208) stated that early in an individual's development the individual acquires the desire for a form of affirmation, labeled *positive regard*. This construct consists of "such attitudes as warmth, liking, respect, sympathy, and acceptance." Positive regard is a bilateral process; there is both a receiver and a giver. If a person experiences any of these attitudes coming from someone, then the individual is said to be in a state or condition of positive regard. Conversely, should a person experience liking or accepting of another person, then the individual experiences what it is like to perceive another in positive regard.

Should a person state "I accept you as a worthwhile human being without reservation or hesitation," it would be a demonstration of *unconditional positive regard*. The significance of this construct rests in its communication of total acceptance of an individual's strengths and limitations, never emphasizing one over the other.

With the first two constructs, the primary sources for determining one's self-worth are external—that is, socially derived and dependent on another person. Rogers believes there are also internal frames of reference from which an individual may draw feelings or perceptions of self-worth. The first of these, *positive self-regard*, is the ability of an individual to refer to internal resources for feelings of warmth, acceptance, and respect, without relying on sources external to the self for positive attitudes.

Finally, individuals also have the capacity to hold themselves in a state of *unconditional self-regard*. For this process, individuals do not discriminate between their own strengths and weaknesses, nor do they dwell on one over the other. In effect, this construct explains what is often referred to as self-acceptance.

These constructs provide a crucial aspect of the theory. Rogers believes that individuals who are fully functioning can rely on internal sources of self-reinforcement; they are less dependent on others for determining self-worth and self-acceptance. It is only when they lose sight of these internal support systems and become totally dependent on others that an unhealthy state of affairs exists. For example, if I am dependent solely on receiving positive feelings about myself from those around me, then I will focus my energies on trying to meet their expectations. This creates an imbalance in the self-system in which states of conditional positive regard and conditional self-regard exist.

Turning inwardly for support will not help me either, because what exists within me are feelings of unworthiness. Thus begins a vicious cycle that could have me depending on others for self-worth. Not receiving their positive regard, I will then turn inwardly for positive self-regard, but not having that within my self-system, I can find myself again turning outwardly. The resulting image that I project to others, however, may more than likely be one lacking in self-respect. Others, then, will have nothing to respond to other than my behavior, which reflects these nonpositive feelings toward myself. They in turn may have no reason to hold me in positive regard, thereby sending me behavioral messages that reaffirm how I already see myself.

Conversely, should I realize that I cannot please everybody by meeting all their expectations all the time and should I accept both my strengths and limitations, as well as feel free to be selective of the feedback from others, without dwelling on either the positive or negative, then what exists is a state of unconditional positive self-regard. As I project this image of myself outwardly through behaviors, the likelihood is strong that others will see me this way and thus respond in a way that says that they hold me in *unconditional regard.*

Key Concepts

The key concepts that support or guide client-centered group therapy can be viewed through three variables: (1) external variables, (2) group member variables, and (3) therapist variables.

EXTERNAL VARIABLES

Rogers (1970) first recognized that most encounter groups have *external variables* that separate them from other forms of group therapy. For example, the number of members generally involved in a client-centered group is not less than 8 or more than 18. Structure is very limited; allowance is made for the group to choose its own goals and personal directions. The group therapist works primarily to facilitate members to express their feelings and thoughts. Finally, there is a major emphasis for the therapist and members to pay attention to what is occurring at the moment of interpersonal interaction. This is referred to as *immediacy.*

GROUP MEMBER VARIABLES

Rogers (1970) developed eight hypotheses that are common to most encounter groups. We can refer to them simply as the ingredients that must exist in order for client-centered therapy to work.

1. The *need for safety* must be met before members will feel free to express themselves and lower their defenses. The leader should establish a psychological climate in which members can feel safe to interact intensively.
2. *Psychological and emotional intimacy* develops as a product of a safe psychological climate. This is evidenced as members begin to share and express their feelings about themselves and those they hold toward others.
3. *Mutual trust* evolves from the personal disclosures that have been made, and this may be evidenced in the form of each member's movement toward greater self-acceptance.
4. *Risk taking* develops as defenses give way. Personal attitudes, values, and behaviors are open to examination and possible change. Evidence of risk taking may be seen as traditional ways of thinking and behaving give way to new.
5. *Psychological openness* for individual differences (of self and others) develops. This is evidenced as members work to understand each other.
6. The process of *feedback* develops and becomes more evident. Members more openly share information regarding how they perceive each other. Feedback

contributes to self-knowledge by learning how one appears to others and the impact one has in interpersonal relationships.

7. Members become more *creative* and *imaginative* as a result of their newly found freedom. As a consequence, individuals find reinforcement for addressing their immediate social environment in new and different ways.
8. As a result of the social reinforcement received for the new behaviors, members can be expected, at least temporarily, to *transfer* these behaviors to their interpersonal relationships with others outside the immediate counseling group.

THERAPIST VARIABLES

The third and final level regards the therapist. Rogers (1970) believes that a therapist's attitudes and philosophy play a significant role as he or she leads a group.

First and foremost, a therapist must trust the group to develop its own potential and that of its individual members. Following closely is trust in the group process. Therefore, a role of the therapist, much as the therapist in individual therapy, is that of facilitator of the process.

The therapist must also believe that the group can set its own direction and thereby be capable of taking care of itself. This means that the group can recognize that there are barriers to movement or growth, which must be dealt with before the group can move toward a healthier state. But a group therapist should recognize the uniqueness of each group and understand that no two will begin or end the same way in their readiness to grow and move toward healthier states. Some groups will begin by being very resistant to expressing feelings and will thus move very slowly; others may be expressive from the outset and move rapidly.

The client-centered therapist should not enter into a group session with any specific goals for the group. The only thing that the therapist can expect to occur is that the process will always be the same; there will be movement, even though it may not be translated into a successful experience for the group.

Although there is much reliance on group process as being the primary force in the group, the way the client-centered group therapist facilitates that process is a key variable in the life of the group. To help move the group, the therapist must engage in a variety of behaviors, including empathic listening, disclosure of feelings, a willingness to share personal issues that are distressing, facilitating rather than directing the group, and maintaining a low profile in the role of therapist. To this latter point, Rogers stated that he sees himself more as a participant in the group and therefore tries to avoid emphasizing his role as its therapist. He believes that by so doing the group will be more inclined to take responsibility for its own growth and development and rely less on him as the force for doing so.

Rogers added that he wants the *whole* person to be present in the group. By this he means that members should bring both their cognitive and affective dimensions to the group so that he, as a facilitator, can work to help them express and grow their ideas and feelings.

Therapist Roles and Techniques

The category of therapist roles and techniques is difficult to address directly because Rogers has long been on record that he prefers not to use techniques or gimmickry in his work as a group therapist. Robert Coulson, in his book *Groups, Gimmicks, and Instant Gurus* (1972), addressed this area directly. However, if it can be said that whatever a group therapist does can be viewed as being a technique, then, by definition, the very act of employing any technique, in and of itself, is a technique (to do nothing is to do something). The client-centered group therapist performs certain functions in helping the group move toward a state of self-awareness.

SETTING THE CLIMATE

The way group therapists proceed to establish the emotional climate is most critical. By being transparent—that is, allowing for their own feelings and thoughts to be shared with the group and trying to remain flexible, receptive, and relaxed—therapists hope to convey to members that it is okay to feel free to be one's self. This modeling activity is also carried over to the way the group therapist *listens* to the members. The therapist tries to convey to group members that each is important and that what each has to say is significant. Rogers (1970) referred to this as *validating* the person. During this listening process, the group therapist is less inclined to be listening to the story line of the presenter and is more likely to seek out the meaning behind the words and identify the feelings the speaker is trying to convey.

By listening in this manner, the group therapist communicates to each member that—regardless of what is said, how emotionally deep or ridiculous—this is a safe place to say it and at least one person (the therapist) respects the person and acknowledges that what was said had significant meaning to the person who said it.

Psychological and emotional safety is provided in another way. Deep emotional disclosures or unspoken feelings can be painful and freeing experiences. Client-centered group therapists try to communicate to the member that they are psychologically with the group member during this critical moment. It is important that group members feel that someone is there who is psychologically and emotionally strong enough to support them when they face a crisis in the group.

ACCEPTANCE OF THE GROUP

Acceptance of the group communicates to its members that the therapist indeed trusts them to come up with their own direction. Such acceptance even takes into consideration whether or not they are at a point in their own individual readiness to deal with emotional issues. By not imposing expectations on the group, the therapist also facilitates the members to experience freedom to be creative and expressive. The end product can be a discovery of new and different ways to cope effectively with themselves and others, thereby developing a sense of personal independence and self-reliance.

ACCEPTANCE OF THE INDIVIDUAL

Acceptance of the individual is the therapist's way of communicating a readiness to accept the members as they are, with no hidden expectations. This granting of permission from the therapist to the members to choose whatever level of active commitment to the group they want is the first step toward facilitating self-acceptance. It therefore follows that as self-acceptance increases, greater risking behavior will be demonstrated, along with acceptance of individual differences as each person's unique qualities surface. Acceptance of the individual also helps facilitate members to develop their *whole* selves. Accepting the members where they are (e.g., intellectually involved or emotionally distant) reassures members and allows them to feel free to enter the group, eventually at an emotional level, should they choose.

EMPATHIC UNDERSTANDING

Rogers (1970) acknowledged empathic understanding to be his most significant and most frequently used activity as a group therapist. By trying to grasp the specific meaning of what a member of the group is saying, the therapist will facilitate member-to-member understanding. What one member *intends* to communicate is made clear for the others, thereby avoiding misunderstandings. By illuminating the interactive process, the therapist helps avoid the confusion that often arises: Participants on both sides of the interaction become so invested in their side of an issue that they fail to state clearly their position. In some ways then, empathic understanding can be viewed as the means by which the therapist helps the group stay focused on the issues at hand and develop a sense of congruency.

USE OF FEELINGS, OR THERAPIST SELF -DISCLOSURE

To achieve the objective of helping participants develop a wholeness about their person, a therapist can demonstrate, through modeling, the way to be expressive of one's feelings and how to trust them. Therapists should be responsive to both negative and positive affective states that exist within themselves. There is spontaneity or immediacy attached to this way of behaving. Rogers referred to it as an intuitive feeling, not consciously derived. By behaving in this manner, the therapist is also helping the group move toward a level of psychological and emotional intimacy. It is as though permission is being granted to share aloud the feelings that one is experiencing at that moment within the group. There is also an underlying assumption that there is trust in the group and, therefore, that the group will also hold in positive regard the person expressing the feelings.

CONFRONTATION AND FEEDBACK

Confrontation and feedback help participants learn about themselves, their self-concept, by communicating the way a member's behavior(s) are experienced by the therapist. The focus clearly must be on behavior that can be changed by the participants, and not an attack upon their personhood or the defenses over which they may have little control. Feedback can also provide information about how a participant's behavior presents a self-image to the other persons in the interactive exchange.

The leader can anticipate that feedback will facilitate group process. It may induce interaction. It may also precipitate distress in the person receiving feedback. In some cases, if the person receiving feedback appears to be overwhelmed by the process, the leader should allow the person to break emotional contact by acknowledging the fact that he or she may need to withdraw from the encounter.

THERAPIST EXPRESSION OF PERSONAL PROBLEMS

To function maximally as a facilitator of group process, Rogers believes he must divest himself of those stressful personal issues to which he may be attending while he is leading the group. Rogers believes that, unless he does so, such personal material will interfere with his ability to listen effectively. He cautions that the group therapist must be careful not to use the group to meet the therapist's own personal needs. However, there may be times when it would help the group to know that the therapist is experiencing difficulties and that it is not the group's fault.

AVOIDANCE OF INTERPRETIVE OR PROCESS COMMENTS

It is Rogers's belief that observations made by the therapist about the group process tend to make the group self-conscious and slow it down because the members feel as though they are being examined. Observations also tend to separate the group therapist from the members. Making process commentary works counter to Rogers's efforts to maintain a low profile and to allow group members to develop their own sense of responsibility and direction.

It follows that Rogers also avoids attempts to interpret the reasons behind an individual's behaviors. He submits that, at best, it would be an educated guess. Furthermore, such behavior on the part of the therapist has elements of authoritativeness, something Rogers wants to avoid projecting.

AVOIDANCE OF PLANNING AND EXERCISES

Rogers emphasized the need for the group to evolve naturally and to let the facilitative processes occur spontaneously. He views the use of preplanned activities or exercises as a resource of last resort. If role playing, body contact, or psychodrama are used, they should evolve naturally from the group and be designed to meet the needs of the members at that moment in time. In fact,

Rogers submitted that an exercise that may be truly spontaneous in one group might not be in another, because it may not work or have the same desired effect.

Group Processes

A client-centered group session is highly interactive, with great reliance on the members to provide the group's motivation and direction. Furthermore, the group therapist is very conscious of and dependent on the process of the group. On the surface it may appear as though the group therapist is very passive and doing very little. Nothing could be further from the truth. The therapist is in fact actively listening and observing the group's process patterns. Rogers (1967) identified 15 developmental patterns or stages that a group can be expected to go through, each with its own unique characteristic and effect upon the group's growth and development. These stages are presented next in the order they usually occur.

MILLING AROUND

Milling around usually occurs immediately upon the leader's disclosure that this group is unique, that members can expect virtually no direction from the therapist, and that they have some very unusual freedoms. The characteristics of this stage are awkward silence, confusion, cocktail-party conversation, politeness, some expression of frustration about what is expected or what the members should do, and a great lack of continuity between member-to-member statements. Usually during this period, members will try to identify roles, determine who the leader is, establish the group's purpose, and explore norms.

RESISTANCE TO PERSONAL EXPRESSION OR EXPLORATION

Members will generally present their public selves during the milling period. However, as some individuals begin to disclose personal material, others can be expected to respond with mixed feelings. Their own sense of insecurity may direct them to behave in ways that would mask the fear they experience as pressure mounts for them to disclose their own deep feelings. Such fear may manifest itself through questions regarding group trust, the reality of the group situation versus that of the real world, or by presenting an image of being all knowing or emotionally distant from that which is occurring in the group.

DESCRIPTION OF PAST FEELINGS

As time moves on, the expression of personal feelings tends to become the predominant issue. However, unresolved ambivalence between the group's trustworthiness and risk of self-disclosure is still present. Usually, a safer route will be taken. Members will often move toward discussing their feelings at an intellectual level by examining encounters they have had with individuals outside the group. This reference to emotional experiences occurring in the past are current at an intellectual level but truly exemplify feelings that exist in the *there and then*, as opposed to the *here and now* of the group.

EXPRESSION OF NEGATIVE FEELINGS

Generally, expect that group members will attack, criticize, or present nonsupportive statements to one another. This behavior may manifest itself in a way that reflects anger toward a member for remaining aloof or distant (i.e., not adhering to group norms). It may also be reflected in an attack upon the leader for not measuring up to the group's role expectations. Whatever the case, the astute observer will readily recognize that these feelings are very genuine and have a here-and-now quality. The feelings are personal and current as they occur in the group. Rogers theorized that either the members are testing the trustworthiness of the group and their freedom of expression or they are finding it easier to express negative feelings out of fear that positive ones, such as "I have warm feelings toward you," could be dangerous because they could leave them vulnerable and open to rejection.

EXPRESSION AND EXPLORATION OF PERSONALLY MEANINGFUL MATERIAL

The developmental sequence continues with some members beginning to disclose personally significant material to the others. Rogers believes that this disclosure may result from members' growing view of the group as their own, in which they can have some say in what they want to make of it. Another variable, which to Rogers facilitates the occurrence of this dynamic, is the development of a climate of trust, leaving individuals free to take some risk. This evolves, in part, from having earlier experienced and expressed negative feelings without dire consequences.

EXPRESSION OF IMMEDIATE INTERPERSONAL FEELINGS IN THE GROUP

Sooner or later, member-to-member interaction will lead to the expression of feelings one has for the other. The immediacy, the here and now, of the expression of feelings usually is the end result of an increasing climate of trust. The feelings can be positive or negative. For example: "I didn't like you at first because you reminded me of my ex-spouse," or "Your openness allows me to feel very close to you, and I like that."

THE DEVELOPMENT OF A HEALING CAPACITY IN THE GROUP

Certain group members will naturally and quite spontaneously demonstrate abilities to be helpful to other members who have been expressing their own difficulties. Rogers believes that group members are a valuable source of assistance in the therapeutic process for other members.

SELF-ACCEPTANCE AND THE BEGINNING OF CHANGE

The early stages of change are characterized by the demonstration of self-acceptance. In this phase of the group's development, members begin to make statements about themselves that reflect awareness of their own personal attitudes, values, behaviors, and role perceptions and their willingness to come to terms with them.

THE CRACKING OF FACADES

The group will reach a point where being open, genuine, and honest is the most important group norm. As the group reaches this point, members become intolerant of members who do not conform. Their disdain for superficial and intellectual approaches to interpersonal relating is evidenced by behaviors that can range from sensitive recognition and nudging of a reluctant member to outright attacks, which often appear violent in their effect.

THE INDIVIDUAL RECEIVES FEEDBACK

During the life of the group, group members are given information about the way they are perceived by each other. Such information usually leads to new and deeper levels of self-awareness. Feedback can be warm and supportive, conveying positive messages about the way a person is perceived. Feedback can also be nonsupportive, conveying a negative message to the individual.

CONFRONTATION

Confrontation is an extension, or added dimension, of the feedback process that is addressed to a member's incongruent behavior. It generally is directed at individuals demonstrating feelings or thoughts that are not consistent with their demonstrated behavior. This phase of the process will usually occur later in the life of the group, not in its earlier periods. The interpersonal transactions that illustrate this stage occur as one member offers a statement that is straightforward and on the level (often called "leveling") about a fellow member's unappreciated behavior or about behavior that is not consistent with the member's expressed intended messages. Confrontation is often an unsettling experience for the persons involved and at times for the group as a whole, but it is a necessary part of the group's process.

HELPING RELATIONSHIPS OUTSIDE THE GROUP SESSIONS

Group process does not stop the moment a group session ends. Members will often form subgroups that meet outside the regularly scheduled sessions. Frequently, such subgroups, composed of two or more members, will meet to provide help and support to one another as they experience the advent of new self-perceptions that evolve from being in the regular group. Often it is through such subgroups that individuals can come to personal acceptance and actualization of themselves.

The Basic Encounter

The intensity of the interaction among members over a period of time eventually leads to deeper emotional levels in their relationships with one another. The extraordinarily close and direct contact, which normally is not attained in everyday life, contributes to the change-producing dimensions of the group experience. The emotional tone of the group is heavy and often interspersed with both fears and expressions of attachment to one another, which usually are qualified by statements that they have never felt this way toward another person before.

Expression of Positive Feelings and Closeness

One can expect that as the group's life continues feelings of warmth, unity, group spirit, and trust evolve. These are manifestations of the realness of the members, which includes the expression of negative and positive feelings.

Behavior Changes in the Group

Some definitive behavior changes occur as the group matures or moves towards termination. Physical gestures are altered, and individuals present themselves as relaxed, open physically, and able to deal with each other in ways that reflect acceptance of other members. Voice tones are congruent and express feeling. Word choices are carefully made in order to express thoughtfulness and straight messages, as well as to offer help. Individuals also appear to listen intently in ways that reflect interest in understanding the other person accurately. There also appears to be a spontaneity in the way members respond to one another, as though it were a demonstration of being free from the intellectual inhibitions that blocked them during the very early stages of the group.

Summary

In client-centered group therapy, the therapist's primary objective is to help members become aware of themselves and to translate this awareness into behavior that reflects self-responsibility, instead of feeling controlled by the environment. This objective is achieved largely through what has been referred to as the basic encounter.

The client-centered group is highly interactive, with much reliance on the members to provide its motivation and direction. In striking contrast to other approaches to group therapy, the therapist maintains a very low profile and will be a participant-member. By so doing, the leader places an additional burden on the members to take responsibility for the group's movement.

By adhering to the belief that *group process* remains the same regardless of the group's composition, the therapist can be effective and in fact remain different from the other members. By trusting and understanding that a group must go through various developmental stages, the therapist can actively participate as a member while working as a facilitator of that process. By attending to the *way* things are happening in the group, the therapist helps members deal with resistance and feedback and contend with confrontation, provides empathic understanding, and models such qualities as vulnerability, transparency, and genuine and trusting feelings. These important qualities reflect the realness of being human and are the means through which the client-centered therapist helps members experience behaving in new ways. By providing for such experiences within the group, members will learn the behaviors that will enable them to deal effectively with their lives.

CHAPTER TWO

Cognitive–Behavioral Theory

Background

In the 1960s behavioral therapists recognized that the group could be used as an important context for behavioral treatment. Sheldon Rose (1993) demonstrated how behavioral principles of reinforcement and modeling could be applied to group treatment. The use of behavioral interventions in group settings extended the use of these interventions to a broader context.

In the late 1970s and early 1980s, behavioral therapy groups began to include cognitive restructuring, coping skills training, and relaxation training. The inclusion of cognitive processes paved the way for an integration of cognitive and behavioral approaches to psychotherapy (Mahoney, 1977). Based on the principles of Albert Bandura's (1977) social-learning theory, exposure methods were added to reinforcement and modeling as major intervention strategies.

The cognitive-learning perspective, as discussed by Mahoney (1977), consists of four fundamental assertions:

1. The human organism responds primarily to cognitive representations of its environments rather than to those environments per se.
2. These cognitive representations are functionally related to the processes and parameters of learning.
3. Most human learning is cognitively mediated.
4. Thoughts, feelings, and behaviors are casually interactive (pp. 7–8).

Since the beginnings of the cognitive–behavioral interface, this approach has gained prominence; many of its interventions have been successfully applied in group settings to treat a wide variety of presenting problems including depression, anxiety, parenting skills, divorce, and pain management (Rose, 1993). Whereas social skills training was the major form of group therapy in the 1970s, stress and anger management became the focus of group therapy in the 1980s.

From the mid-1980s to the present, interest in the role of group processes in the cognitive–behavioral approach has increased, indicating the continued recognition that members can benefit from interactions with others. Many problems discussed in cognitive–behavioral groups are social-interactional ones; thus, the presence of other clients provides an opportunity for the leader to observe and for the clients to practice new social-interactional skills with peers in a protected setting (Rose, 1993).

Key Concepts

COGNITIONS

As already noted, the relationship between thoughts and behavior is central to a cognitive–behavioral approach. In the practice of cognitive–behavioral theory (CBT), certain cognitive concepts are emphasized and have been explored by a number of theorists. For example, Ellis (1962) focused on irrational beliefs that contribute to one's emotional distress. Beck (1976) explored the impact of certain automatic thoughts on helplessness and depression. Meichenbaum (1977) introduced the notion of maladaptive self-talk that can greatly influence one's actions and feelings. In all these formulations it is believed that one's thoughts play a major role in determining a person's actions.

THE HERE AND NOW

In CBT approaches the therapist is primarily interested in understanding the presenting problems in the present. Although attention to past social-learning history can be helpful, the therapist is likely to emphasize the current environment and other variables in understanding what variables are functionally related to the client's present behavior. When extended to groups the concept of the here and now facilitates the learning for all members.

LEARNING

In the CBT approach all behavior is learned. Clients learn adaptive and maladaptive behaviors, and cognitive–behavorial therapists believe that through the use of CBT principles clients can relearn more helpful and adaptive ways of behaving in the world. The cognitive-behavior therapist will need to identify the events that precede and follow the client's behavior in order to conduct a functional analysis. The variety of variables that contribute to the development of a certain behavior include environmental circumstances, thoughts, beliefs, assumptions, and attitudes.

SELF-EFFICACY

The construct of self-efficacy is important to the assessment and treatment of problems within the CBT framework and key to the process of change. Bandura (1977) proposed that people develop expectations for their success in performing certain behaviors. He believed that the expectations that people carry around with them influence their decisions to try new behaviors and to change. Therefore, believing that as people gain more self-efficacy they will likely increase their effort to change behavior in a variety of situations, the cognitive–behavioral therapist attempts to increase client self-efficacy.

Therapist Roles and Techniques

Rose (1993) identifies nine major categories of therapist behaviors that can be observed in CBT groups. These categories, summarized next, reflect movement of the group over time.

ORGANIZING A GROUP

The therapist focuses on such issues as the type of group and the logistics of when and where the group meets, for how long, and whether the group will be open or closed. Intensive therapy groups tend to operate for 14–18 weeks, whereas short-term training groups are usually 6–12 sessions in length. Time-limited groups tend to be theme focused (e.g., stress reduction, anger management).

ORIENTATION

In the CBT approach, contracts are often used to help members clarify purpose and content issues. Members also discuss with the therapist responsibility of membership in the group. Through dialogue the therapist and members negotiate goals and content while attending to process concerns.

BUILDING GROUP COHESION

The cognitive–behavioral therapist is interested in establishing a climate in which group cohesion can develop. Therefore, the therapist is likely to provide refreshments to promote member-to-member positive contact. For the therapist to successfully implement a variety of techniques in the group setting, a climate of respect, connection, and communication, needs to be present.

ASSESSMENT

In the CBT approach, assessment may begin in the pregroup interview and is likely to continue throughout the life of the group as members clarify their concerns. The therapist encourages members to identify areas of concern and the resources they bring to the group endeavor. Throughout the assessment process the therapist instructs members in how to frame their concerns in behavioral terms. In addition, members are asked to identify thinking and feeling responses to specific situations.

MONITORING

This concept is important to the cognitive–behavioral group therapy change process. Observation is a key means of data collection. The therapist observes behaviors and the situations in which they occur, prior to developing a plan for change. Once the plan is set the therapist monitors the ongoing data collection in order to identify evidence of member change.

EVALUATION

Similar to assessment, evaluation in the CBT group is ongoing. The therapist constantly gathers and monitors data related to member goals. This information is evaluated after sessions and at the end of the group experience.

THERAPEUTIC PLANNING

The therapist utilizes the group as a whole to identify common skill deficits and to uncover social and psychological resources. During this time the therapist and group members make plans that are implemented through group exercises. These individual plans are consistent with the group's purposes and may include a focus on systematic problem solving, social skills training, cognitive restructuring, and coping skills training.

GROUP PROCEDURES

Group instructions for interactive or cooperative activities distinguish group procedures from individual interventions. In the group setting the therapist encourages member-to-member discussions in place of therapist-to-member discussions, more characteristic of individual therapy. Member-to-member interaction, the most commonly used intervention technique, is used with other procedures such as "recapitulation, subgrouping, fishbowl, leadership training, group exercises, and the buddy system" (Rose, 1993). This interactive nature of member-to-member discussion is further illustrated through modeling, rehearsals, coaching, problem solving, and brainstorming activities as members are invited to share their particular experiences, information, skills, and ideas.

Group procedures can be used to strengthen equal member participation by modifying the group structure. For example, if a few members speak most of the time, while others are usually quiet, the therapist might share these observations and invite the members to develop a structure by which more equal participation can occur. In the case cited by Rose (1993), the vocal members agreed to recap the previous speaker's comments before stating their points, and the quiet members agreed to write down those thoughts that they did not share verbally in the group. The therapist called upon the quietest members first. This particular strategy was used until the participation evened out and demonstrated the use of problem solving, rehearsal, leader cueing, and recapitulation of the previous speaker's statement. Group procedures can also be used to modify level of group cohesion and agreement to certain group norms.

Transfer and Maintenance of Behavioral Change

A goal of group therapy is to help members transfer learning in the group to life outside the group. In the CBT group, this transfer is facilitated by intragroup procedures and extragroup procedures. Members engage in intragroup procedures when they rehearse events in the group that they are likely to face in their everyday lives. When members practice behavioral assignments in their own environment, they engage in extragroup procedures.

To assist further in the transfer and maintenance objectives, the therapist is likely to reduce the frequency of reward and to take time at the end of a session to review cognitive strategies. The aim of these and other interventions is to help members strengthen the maintenance of new skills long after the group therapy experience has ended (Rose, 1993).

Finally, the therapist encourages members to identify and develop networks of support to help them continue their learning beyond the therapy group. These networks can exist in the members' social network or can take the form of nontherapeutic groups. The point is to maximize the chances that the skills and behaviors learned in the therapy group will generalize to the real world (Rose, 1993).

Group Processes

In CBT group settings, members take advantage of many opportunities to learn and practice behaviors and to modify their cognitions. In these groups, members benefit from giving and receiving both feedback and advice. Helping others takes on therapeutic value as members not only provide assistance to other members but also help themselves. This phenomenon of altruism is an important curative factor in group therapy (Yalom, 1995).

The concept of reinforcement, central to cognitive–behavioral group therapy, comes to life in multiple ways when members are given opportunities, instructions, and rewards for reinforcing other group members (Rose, 1993). As members engage in feedback, they help one another confront distorted or self-defeating perceptions as well as learn which behaviors or attitudes are attractive or annoying to others. Rose (1993) underscores the belief that members will benefit from member feedback. In the group setting the numbers and variety of potential models, coaches, monitors, role players, and general resources are increased.

Summary

Cognitive–behavioral groups are short term in duration and are widely used to address a range of presenting problems for adults and children. Increasingly, this approach emphasizes the role of interpersonal learning and the value of using all members as resources in the therapeutic encounter. Within a homogeneous setting, some groups offer members a chance to develop specific skills related to work and daily life situations. Other groups, organized more heterogeneously, can be designed to address broader applications of social skills. The link between research and practice is a particularly impressive feature of the CBT approach.

Group therapists within this framework, which emphasizes participation and information, believe that pregroup preparation is essential in order for members to prepare for a successful group experience. Pretraining helps members make informed decisions about their willingness to join a group. Because voluntary participation is seen as crucial to success, it is important for members to embrace the concept of collaboration and involvement. CBT groups will tend to follow certain stages and principles, irregardless of focus (Rose, 1977). These include the forming of the group, which precedes the stage of developing group attraction and identity. Here, the pregroup-preparation interviews set the stage for members to explore their goals and learn that member interaction is an important part of the learning process. Through modeling and helping members become acquainted with one another, the leader further promotes a climate of openness and sharing in the group. The working stage begins with helping members learn the behavioral frame of reference—that all behavior is purposeful. This understanding of the antecedent–response–consequence model of behaviorism is necessary for members to assess and monitor their actions and ultimately learn to recognize any behavior change in the group or outside in their daily lives. Later in the course of the group, members move into a problem-solving process whereby they specify what they want to change, monitor the changes they make, and assess the success of their actions. As noted earlier, the cognitive–behavioral therapist uses many techniques to help members reach their goals. These include modeling, reinforcement, contracts, behavioral rehearsal, coping skills training, cognitive restructuring, and coaching. The active, present, voluntary, and collaborative participation of group members is the key to success in these groups.

CHAPTER THREE

Family-Centered Therapy

Background

Family-centered group therapy is a blending of family therapy theory and group dynamics theory and applying them to group therapy. In 1989 Trotzer wrote to the interface of "group and family counseling." Ostensibly, he views family theory as a "resource in group counseling" and therapy. The value of using family theory in group therapy lies with "understanding and helping individuals in groups" (p. 455). Thus, family-centered group therapists draw upon family theory to explain individual member problems and to help them determine the interventions they will employ.

Practitioners of family-centered group therapy need prior knowledge and training in family therapy and group therapy. Theirs is more of an integrated approach that, in addition to family theory, draws understandings, concepts, and methodology from psychodynamic, individual and developmental psychology, and group therapy. All form the basis from which techniques of family-centered group psychotherapy evolve.

Family-centered group therapists see the family as the first group in which individuals learn how to interact. It is within the family that individuals initially develop human relations skills, learn the rules that guide individuals in interacting with others, learn how to manage conflict, learn how to deal with authority, learn how to become responsible, and so forth. These skills and knowledge are what individuals bring to group therapy. Family theory helps explain and develop an understanding of how and why individuals behave as they do from the context of their family of origin. Thus, the contribution of family theory to family-centered group therapy will include but not be limited to intergenerational affects on members, family-of-origin issues (e.g., divorce) birth order, only child, parent–child relationships, sibling relationships, authority, intimacy, boundaries, conflict management, enmeshment and disengagement, and so on. For example, Trotzer (1989) uses these two latter concepts, which had been formulated by Minuchin (1974) as possible explanations for why some individuals might be hesitant to make a full commitment to the group early on because they would be betraying their loyalty to the family (emotionally enmeshed family of origin). Then there are others who might eagerly embrace the group early on but not remain as committed in later stages of the group (disengaged family of origin).

Psychodynamic, individual, and developmental psychology provide references to intrapsychic issues of the individual, stages of individual development such as early-childhood concerns, the needs of a group of adolescents versus those of a group of 40-year-olds and so on. Concepts drawn from group dynamics theory are group stages, group process, group as a whole, group cohesiveness, norm setting, member and leader roles, goals, homogeneity versus heterogeneity, here-and-now versus there-and-then focus, and subgrouping, to name some.

Key Concepts

GROUP STAGES

Group stages—security, acceptance, responsibility, work, and termination—are sequentially presented in developmental order. The stages are fluid and interdependent. Each has its own characteristic (much as can be found in human developmental stages). It is possible for groups to evolve naturally along this developmental path after meeting the needs and accomplishing the developmental tasks of each stage. Likewise, it is possible (as in human development) for a group to become arrested at a stage in its development. Finally, and most important, stages also define group process.

SELF-CORRECTING AND SELF-MONITORING PROCESSES

Self-correcting and *self-monitoring processes* exist in all groups. These processes are activated when any of the following occurs: A member appears to be ostracized from the group, the group as a whole becomes enmeshed, or the group as a whole seems to be in flight. If a member attempts to disengage or separate (ostracize) from the group, other members will attempt to draw the person back. When the group as a whole is experiencing extended intense emotional tension, members will eventually engage in behaviors to relieve the tension. At times the group as a whole will engage in intellectually safe material, focus on issues that clearly avoid the more significant and relevant issues (emotionally disengaged), or do both. At such times certain members will reveal their frustration and redirect the focus back to the group's primary goals.

THE GROUP AS POWER

The *group as power* refers to the collective impact of members (i.e., group as a whole) upon individual members. This can take the form of imposing a system of rewards and punishments to effect conformity and consensual validation that is in the form of feedback drawn from the members. It is a means of helping member(s) maintain congruency, move toward problem resolution, and so forth.

CURATIVE FACTORS

Curative factors, as identified by Yalom (1995), explain the therapeutic effect of groups. There are 12 such factors: interpersonal input, catharsis, cohesiveness, self-understanding, interpersonal output, existential factors, universality, instillation of hope, altruism, family reenactment, guidance, and identification.

ESSENTIAL THERAPEUTIC RELATIONSHIP QUALITIES

Essential therapeutic relationship qualities consist of seven ingredients:

Trust includes trusting others and being trustworthy for the establishment of a safe and secure environment that fosters risk taking; it also includes maintaining confidentiality.

Acceptance means that regardless of one's fallibilities one is allowed to freely be.

Respect is similar to Yalom's (1995) curative factor—universality. It means that there exists a willingness to relate to "the uniqueness and inherent dignity of each person and the commonality of humanness we share" (Trotzer, 1989).

Warmth refers to the ability to give and receive unconditional positive regard to and from another.

Communication is a relational factor that allows for meaningful interactions to take place between and among members of the group.

Understanding is the ability to provide empathy. It involves setting aside one's own personal biases and ways of viewing the world in order to understand the other person from his or her frame of reference.

Feedback is a means used for helping group members learn if their behaviors are consistent with their intentions. It is information intended for use by the receiver to assist in self-regulation of behaviors, just as a gyroscope is used to help keep a ship on its path.

Therapist Roles and Techniques

ROLES

Family-centered group therapists draw upon group therapy and family therapy to determine their roles. Trotzer (1989) offers that the group leader's role consists of a number of subroles:

Director: In this role, leaders actively determine "the nature and focus of group interaction." Of primary value is attention to processes that will assist in meeting individual member needs or encourage group interaction. Leaders need to be careful to not develop an overreliance on individual members or the group as a whole for self-determination.

Facilitator: Once the group is up and going, leaders take their cues from what is already occurring in the group. There is an allowance for the group as a whole to take its direction from individual members. Interventions are intended to help members and the group as a whole maintain focus on goals. Leaders need to be careful not to take a laissez-faire position in the group; theirs is an active and involved role. They need to be ready to intervene whenever members or the group become stuck or seem to have lost direction.

Participator: The intention here is for leaders to not appear emotionally detached and separate from the members. Yalom (1995) has identified that the personal quality of the leader is what distinguishes leader effectiveness more so than theoretical orientation. Knowing when, how, and to what extent to participate in the group is a delicate matter. On the one hand, leaders need to be sensitive to when members truly wish to have leaders share their views and experiences and to when they may actually be intruding. Leaders must keep in mind that the purpose of the group is for the members.

Observer: In this role, leaders are most like Yalom's (1995) process observer. The primary mission here is for leaders to provide commentary on how (or the way) they see the evolution or occurrence of transactions that are related to member-to-member interactions or to the group-as-a-whole interactions.

Expert: Leaders are seen here as the source of knowledge and wisdom. It is a tenuous role, for it places leaders in an omniscient and omnipotent position within the group. Making the group leader centered can actually detract from the very purpose of forming a group, which is based on member-to-member interaction. Once this occurs, leaders will have a difficult time disengaging from that position. However, the education, enlightenment, or information which the leader can provide at strategic moments can be most helpful and useful for members and the group.

Besides using group therapy, Trotzer (1989) turns to Zuk (1981) for adding the family therapist's dimension to the role of group leader. The roles of celebrant, go-between, and side taker—according to Zuk—were developed because he believes that family therapists unavoidably are drawn into the intensity of the interaction between family members. Therefore, these roles help therapists work effectively, even though they may become emotionally engaged in the family system. Trotzer (1989) sees the parallel effect occurring with group leaders when emotionally charged interactions occur in the group. He believes that the therapist roles identified by Zuk will also help group therapists.

Celebrant: This role sets up the therapist as the "official" who is in the position to (1) define what the problem is, (2) confirm that it has basis in fact, and (3) attempt to normalize it.

Go-between: Here, the therapist is a mediator. The nature of this role is much like the facilitator. The therapist makes efforts to bring oppositional viewpoints to a place of understanding. Moreover, he or she facilitates the occurrence of communication between members and serves as the individual through whom conflicting points of view are reframed to bring about understanding.

Sidetaker: In this role, the therapist will actually take sides with the intention to foster therapeutic change and problem resolution. It is the time when the leader's influence plays a significant part in the therapeutic process.

TECHNIQUES

For the family-centered group therapist, techniques are framed as group leadership skills. The skills, according to Trotzer (1989), fall into three categories, with each having subareas.

Reaction skills have the leader being responsive to interactions occurring in the group by being receptive to individual members and the group as a whole. Five subcategories comprise this skill area:

Listening actively communicates acceptance, respect, empathy, and caring. This is the primary subskill.

Restatement repeats back the content of the members' communication much in the same way it was presented.

Reflection provides meaning to the message of the members' communication. This allows the sender to feel understood by the leader.

Clarifying actually attempts to make clear vague or confusing messages. This can be achieved simply by asking the member to explain what was meant, for the leader to better understand the member.

Summarizing encapsulates all that has been said in a form that brings seemingly disparate messages together into a meaningful whole.

Interaction skills provide for the mediating function of the group. Here, leaders "control and guide the group interaction and facilitate therapeutic impact" (Trotzer, 1989, p. 200). Eight subcategories comprise this skill area:

Moderating ensures that all members are being heard, makes certain that fairness prevails, and encourages group interaction.

Interpreting attempts to explain member or group-as-a-whole behavior and gives it meaning that may not, at that particular moment, be clear to any except the leader.

Linking ties together similar points that are presented between members in an attempt to facilitate cohesiveness. It is akin to using Yalom's (1995) universality factor.

Blocking is the act of intervening when countertherapeutic behavior on the part of members has taken place or is about to take place.

Supporting is behavior that a leader offers when wishing to reinforce and encourage desired behaviors. When withheld it can work equally as effectively to extinguish undesirable or nonfacilitative behaviors.

Limiting involves those behaviors a leader uses to build norms and develop the culture of the group. Generally, these behaviors convey what is allowable and tolerable.

Protecting insulates individual members or subgroups from countertherapeutic actions-behaviors being imposed by other members or the group as a whole.

Consensus taking seeks a common ground and identifies where loyalties and splits lie within the group. The intention is to help members understand where they stand in relation to each other on issues.

Action skills are the means available to the leader to activate group process. They lead to moving the group to deeper and more meaningful interaction. Six subcategories comprise this skill area:

Questioning: Few questions are real; more frequently, they are inverted statements that hold the hidden agenda of the sender. In its truest form, a question asks for clarification, can help members or the group as a whole to examine motives for behaviors, can lead to insight, and so on.

Probing: Probing helps members become introspective and reach deeper levels of awareness.

Tone setting: Tone setting is the effort on the leader's part to establish a climate or an atmosphere that is conducive to member interaction. It includes the physical arrangement of seating, the décor of the room, the leader's voice tone, how the leader begins the session, and how the leader knows when a serious situation may finally need to be abated.

Confronting: Confronting helps members or the group as a whole face matters that are too difficult or that are being avoided. Also, confrontation is useful when members and the group as a whole are not behaving congruently.

Personal sharing: Personal sharing refers to a leader making self-disclosures. The intention is to join with the members in a way that allows for the leader to be viewed as being human and not emotionally distant. This skill has to be used judiciously and with care. The danger is turning it into a therapy session for the leader. On the other hand, personal sharing can also provide an example for the members to follow.

Modeling: Modeling involves those behaviors that the leader wants to teach group members, by demonstrating through example. This can take the form of how to offer feedback, how to confront, how to self-disclose, and how to be an active listener.

Integrating family therapy techniques into the group can be most effective in facilitating intrapersonal exploration and interpersonal interaction. Yalom (1995) offered that family reenactment is one of the curative factors. After all, the first group experience most people have is with their families. It is therefore one of the possible areas that members can share in common. However, with the issues of diversity, culture, and family structure that exist today, family-centered therapists need to be sensitive and not employ biased and culturally insensitive techniques, even though the temptation may be there to do so. On the other hand, some techniques, which are drawn from family therapy and are also sensitive to the diversity of group members, can be used by the family-centered group therapist. Trotzer advocates the use of structured, family-based group techniques such as "Rules I Grew Up With" and "Sibling Position" (ordinal) (1989, pp. 462–464). The first technique can be used to help form therapeutic ground rules that lead to appropriate group norms. The second technique helps establish cohesiveness and does so without the risk of engaging in deep self-disclosure.

Trotzer adds that a number of precautions need to be taken when employing such techniques and includes the concern members have for maintaining *family loyalties*. Some cultures would not allow disclosures. The intention is to "seek resources and not skeletons." Leaders need to make certain that meddling in family affairs is avoided at all costs. This means that only material that bears directly on how members interact with fellow members is relevant. He urges that leaders avoid doing "long distance family therapy" or turning group members into therapists for their own families. Members need to *feel free from threat* of what is being asked of them. Private family matters are to remain private. The purpose and intention of the technique has to be made clear. Family techniques need to *avoid drawing out toxic emotional disclosures*. For most members, disclosure of highly traumatic family events and issues can be devastating. Again, the sensitivity to take precautions against this happening means that leaders should not select techniques that have the potential for leading members into such highly sensitive areas.

Group Processes

At the base of family-centered group therapy is an existential philosophy for explaining the process of interpersonal change and growth. Trotzer (1989) in fact refers to Maslow's hierarchy of needs. He adds that "an effective group process depends on having members at a point where they are ready to work on meeting their higher order needs" (p. 68). Accordingly then, group process begins with meeting physiological needs progressing through safety, love and belonging, esteem, and self-actualization. It therefore follows that family group therapists would attend first to meeting the *physical needs* of group members (e.g., the environment in which therapy is to take place). *Safety needs* include trust in self and others and by others. The safety need can only be met as social interaction is promoted. Family-centered group therapists will work toward encouraging group interaction. They will frequently rely on structured exercises designed to facilitate group interaction that leads to establishing trust. Such efforts will attend to building norms, risk taking, and developing a group culture that tolerates and allows for expression of individual differences. Creating an atmosphere that fosters the development of emotional and psychological intimacy will help meet the needs for *love and belonging*. "Whereas trust is the foundation of the group process, acceptance is the framework around which it is built" (Trotzer, 1989, p. 72). Once again, it would be very likely for family-centered group therapists to employ structured exercises emanating out of family theory to facilitate members achieving a sense of belongingness and acceptance.

The need to feel significant and worthy describes *self-esteem*. This need is that which can only be met through social interaction. As with the preceding two needs, leaders encourage group members to interact with one another. The focus is helping individual members recognize and take responsibility for their strengths. This is achieved by having the group as a whole provide reinforcement and support through feedback and consensual validation. As individual members gain in self-confidence, they are more able to also face their limitations (i.e., problems) and feel encouraged to work through them.

As the sense of responsibility for taking care of oneself develops through the course of growth in self-esteem, group members are in a position to begin to attempt working through their problems. In a sense, they have achieved a form of *self-actualization* when they have acquired the basic knowledge for addressing intrapersonal and interpersonal issues.

These skills are practiced in the group and are generally in the here and now. The whole atmosphere in which the group functions is a balanced blend of cognitive and emotional sharing. Member-to-member interaction tends to be very authentic. Group leaders are likely to maintain a lower profile as members assume more effective responsibility for their interactions.

Summary

Family-centered group therapists are more likely to view the group as a family with its hierarchical organization of authority and influence resting with the leaders and the power for affecting change being with members. The task of family-centered group therapists is to help release the power for change that is within the group. This is done in a way that helps individual members become self-reliant and develop the skills to effectively deal with intrapersonal and interpersonal problems. In family-centered group therapy, therapists are very active in the early stages of the group's life. The primary focus is on meeting the basic needs of each member. Therapists would likely draw on family theory to help explain and understand member behavior—for instance, addressing how a member's ordinal position in the family may be effecting his or her behavior in the group or noting how certain family rules are playing themselves out as a member struggles with issues of intimacy in the group. Therapists use themselves as models to help members develop skills such as feedback, confrontation, or self-disclosure. All along, therapists strive to help members reach that stage in the group where they can work on individual issues freely. This means that they have reached a stage of self-actualization within the group. To facilitate members reaching this stage, the roles that family-centered therapists assume take any number of forms: director, celebrant, go-between, side taker, facilitator, participant, observer, and so on. Any or all will be engaged in, according to the discretion of the therapist. Moreover, family-centered group therapists attempt to model the actualized state in their efforts to be spontaneous. They resist being rubberized, and this can be evidenced in their eclecticism and integration. They are not hesitant to draw on individual and developmental psychology, psychodynamic theory, family theory, group theory, and existential philosophy. Ostensibly, they will bring all the knowledge and resources necessary to facilitate change and growth in group members. One is inclined to conclude: If it is helpful, a family-centered group therapist will use it.

CHAPTER FOUR

Gestalt Therapy

Background

A discussion of Gestalt therapy accurately begins with an introduction to Frederick Perls, the founder and developer of its basic principles. The history and evolution of Gestalt therapy is well documented and has received considerable attention. Perls received his M.D. in 1921 and went on to receive further training in psychoanalysis. In 1926 he worked with Kurt Goldstein and received his first exposure to Gestalt psychology. In 1942 his formalized theories on applying the principles of Gestalt psychology to personality development and psychotherapy were published in a manuscript titled *Ego, Hunger, and Aggression* (later in book form, 1947/1969c).

Gestalt therapy differs from Gestalt psychology, developed originally by Wolfgang Kohler and Kurt Wertheimer. These classical Gestalt psychologists developed a theory of perception that attempted to explain an individual's perceptual process by understanding the interrelationships between the *form* of the object being observed and the way in which the person was *perceiving* it. It was a conscious effort to show that the perceiver was not only reacting to situations but had partial responsibility for how such situations were perceived (their form). These perceptions in turn affected how the observer dealt with the situations. Wallen explained that the significant difference between Gestalt psychology and Gestalt therapy was that "the academic Gestalt psychologist never attempted to employ the various principles of Gestalt formation . . . to organic perceptions, to the perceptions of one's own feelings, emotions, and bodily sensations. He never really managed to integrate the facts of motivation with the facts of perception" (1970, p. 8).

Gestalt therapy was also a movement away from the psychoanalytical and behavioristic approaches to therapy. When Perls, Ralph Hefferline, and Paul Goodman, published *Gestalt Therapy* (1951) it marked their attempt to construct a unique blend of certain psychoanalytic principles with those of existential and phenomenological thought with a humanistic orientation. The cultural and social aspects of the 1960s allowed for the addition of a humanistic flavor to clinical and counseling psychology and marked the period when Perls's work received its greatest acceptance and popularity. His book *Gestalt Therapy Verbatim* (1969b) has become the pillar upon which Gestalt therapy has developed.

Perls referred to group psychotherapy sessions as workshops. The Gestalt workshop group typically consists of a therapist and 5 to 8 group members meeting on a weekly basis. Meeting times are usually 1½ hours but may range from 1 to 3 hours. Some weekend workshops are conducted for as long as 20 hours. It is not unusual for a single therapist to work with a group of 16 people, but two therapists usually lead groups numbering 8 or more. Workshop sessions tend to be longer in duration as the size of the group increases.

Key Concepts

Fundamental to Gestalt therapy is the belief that people are striving for *completeness* or *perfection*. Translated, this means that

> There are values in living that persons know from their own experiences or from their observations of others to be valuable and enhancing: spontaneity, sensory awareness, freedom of movement, emotional responsiveness and expressiveness, enjoyment, ease, flexibility in relating, direct contact and emotional closeness with others, intimacy, competency, immediacy and presence, self-support, and creativity. (Fagan & Shepherd, 1970, pp. 1–2)

It is the way in which people view the world that blocks or impedes achievement of such growth and "experiencing of life." The objective of therapy is to free a person from these barriers to effective living.

Critical to the process of helping clients remove these barriers are the concepts of *here and now*. Gestalt therapy does not concern itself with personal histories. It holds disdain for the "should's, could's, and ought-to-be's," which are brought about through attempting to meet expectations of societal roles and norms. Perls has often referred to this as top-dog and underdog aspects of the personality. The top dog is the moralizer: Its specialty is telling individuals what they should or ought to do; it is the boss and also condemns. The underdog tries to counter the top dog by excuses, apologies, and defensive behavior. For the Gestalt therapist, the way to resolve the dispute between the top dog and the underdog is referred to as *integration*. The therapist attempts to get the two arguing sides to cease striving for control. Bridging the gap, or unifying the two sides of the personality, is intended to overcome the split caused by these two struggling sides and make the person whole. Gestalt therapy urges individuals to experience the present, while developing a self-support system and avoiding manipulative behaviors designed to gain environmental support.

The existential dimension of Gestalt therapy is emphasized here. The therapist's role is to create a "continuum of awareness" (Perls, 1969b, p. 51). It is through this moment-to-moment awareness that the member realizes there is some unfinished business (i.e., recognizes incompleteness). The tendency, according to Perls, is for individuals to mask this incompleteness by intellectualizing. He writes that this flight away from the present may be seen as "jumping like a grasshopper from experience to experience" (1969b, p. 51). Thus, one never stays long enough to complete the business at hand. Gestalt therapists therefore minimize the *why* of behavior and emphasize the *what, how,* and *now.* Perls's famous statement "lose your mind and come to your senses" (1969b, p. 9) tries to get members to focus on the *now* of their experience.

Conceptually, *focusing* plays a significant role in Gestalt therapy. Focusing means the therapist is attending to members' behaviors at the moment, including voice modulations and changes in body posture. The focusing process involves the therapist's search for the inconsistencies in the members' verbal and nonverbal behaviors that prevent achievement of completeness. This process requires the therapist to confront members when incongruencies are noted in the therapeutic situation. By "cutting through the garbage" (Perls, 1969a), the therapist forces members to deal with the immediacy of the problem. Member denial or avoidance of exhibited discrepancies of verbal and nonverbal behavior is usually futile, because the therapist continually focuses members on the very moment the encounter is being experienced. In short, members are forced to face themselves squarely and are not allowed to escape, short of withdrawing (Perls, 1969b).

Closely related to the focusing process is the concept of *responsibility*. This is exemplified by insisting that members make I-statements, that they take ownership for their behavior in dealing with life and not blame others for the way they act. Learning to be responsible rids members of the temptation to lean on role expectations set forth by society.

RISK TAKING

Taking ownership and responsibility for one's behavior can present risks to the individual. This element of *risk taking* is another important concept in Gestalt therapy. To take a risk requires a willingness to take chances, to experiment in order to move toward understanding one's self more fully. How the therapist allows for members' risk taking and what it means is best explained by Joseph Zinker:

> Even though I respect the validity of his [the member's] experience, I am tempted to whet his appetite toward a formulation of new visual or cognitive or motoric perspectives of himself. The new perspective or dimension does not have to be dramatic; it merely needs to move the existing system into a highly fresher view of itself. (1977, p. 18)

There is some anxiety in this, for members are being asked to view the experience of self from a novel perspective, a break from the comfort of old ways. It becomes a task of the therapist to help the members recognize that anxiety is a part of life (Levitsky & Simkin, 1972). The way toward becoming whole is to face anxiety (which often is in the form of resistance to change) rather than take flight from it.

Finally, for people to be totally integrated, they must be willing to accept themselves as who they are in order to be *authentic*. It is important for members to become aware of their thoughts and feelings and ways of experiencing the environment. Zinker expresses best what Gestalt therapy means when he states,

> It stands for all that is in front of me, for all that promises completeness of experiencing, for the things to come which are awesome, frightening, tearful, moving, unfamiliar, archetypical, growthful. . . . One needs "juice" to make creations and if the juice is not in the person's feelings or language, then it is surely somewhere in his body. (1977, p. 19)

It is the communicating of being alive and just *being*, rather than playing at life, to which authenticity refers. In other words, a person must feel free to be angry, sad, and happy and to fully experience the complete range of living.

Therapist Roles and Techniques

A fundamental concern of Gestalt therapy is to identify "the nature of complete functioning and completed experience . . . which suggests an underlying question which the therapist asks both himself and the patient: 'What is the nature of complete living?' " (Levitsky & Simkin, 1972, p. 245). Attending to this primary issue creates the basis for Gestalt therapy's method and techniques. From the viewpoint of the Gestalt therapist, however, techniques are simply that. They are to be viewed "merely as convenient means, useful tools for our purposes but having no sacrosanct qualities" (Levitsky & Perls, 1970, p. 140).

Clearly then, techniques are not the focus of the therapist. Instead, what is important are the purposes that techniques serve. Thus, the emphasis of Gestalt therapy falls on the therapist's ability to be creative, to work freely, and to utilize "his prime instrument—himself" (Polster & Polster, 1973, p. 21). Similarly, Zinker viewed Gestalt as being "Creative Therapy" (1977, p. 17).

It would be a contradiction to impose upon Gestalt therapists the techniques they "should employ in therapy." However, Levitsky and Perls (1970, p. 140) have identified techniques that are centered around two sets of guidelines, referred to as "rules" and "games." Although there are a limited number of rules, there is no definitive limit to the list of games.

Close examination indicates that these techniques are extensions of the basic concepts of Gestalt therapy, thus giving them a valid reason for existing. Besides the basic rules discussed earlier of now, I-language, and the awareness continuum—or the *how* of experiencing—there are three additional rules: (1) I and thou, (2) no gossiping, and (3) asking questions (Levitsky & Perls, 1970).

The *I and thou* rule is intended to state emphatically that communication involves two people, the sender and the receiver. Members are made aware that they are to be *talking to* and not *talking at* the listener.

The purpose of the *no gossiping* rule is to help members recognize their feelings. It insists that the person speak directly to an individual who is present and not about a member who is not.

The *asking questions* rule, is grounded in the belief that behind nearly every question is a statement. The therapist is therefore urged to help members recognize the difference between a manipulative type of question that is not truly seeking an answer versus questions that are genuine or legitimate, such as inquiring how a person may be feeling at a given moment.

The forum in which the basic techniques of Gestalt therapy are utilized is called the *experiment*. The experiment in Gestalt therapy is designed to facilitate members' effective dealing with barriers "without sacrificing the immediacy of experience" (Polster & Polster, 1973, p. 234). The members are allowed to act out unresolved feelings in a relatively safe environment, which supports risk-taking behavior. During this period of experimenting, the therapist relies on creative processes to select the techniques that for that moment seem to offer the most help to the individual members in dealing with unfinished business (such as anger toward another person).

As stated earlier, there are an indefinite number of games in Gestalt therapy. The following sections illustrate only a limited sampling of the type of games a Gestalt therapist may employ.

MAKING THE ROUNDS

Making the rounds often functions as an ice breaker in Gestalt groups. The event that usually precipitates the use of this technique is a statement by a member that he or she does not like anyone in the group. Such individuals may in fact be avoiding facing feelings they are experiencing right at the moment, regarding themselves. The therapist may direct members to express how they feel about each of the other members and what it is about these other members that affects them that way. By so doing, the members are *focusing* on the experience right then and there at the moment of confrontation. In this way, they can gain insight into their own feelings, as well as how they perceive others.

GAMES OF DIALOGUE

Earlier we presented the theory of top dog and underdog. These are the dualities within individuals that tell them what they should do (top dog) and that make excuses for why they did not get the job done (underdog). This split within individuals manifests itself in a variety of ways. It is the therapist's task to identify the behavior when it occurs. At that moment the therapist will direct members to actually engage in dialogue between these two parts of themselves. If the conflict is between a group member and a person outside the group, the individual may be instructed to engage in a dialogue between himself or herself and the other person, by imagining the other person is actually there. The member would address the person, imagine the received response, and then reply to the response. The game does not have to rely on dialogue between persons; it can also involve various parts of the body, such as right hand versus left hand.

THE HOT SEAT

Perhaps the hot seat is the technique for which Gestalt therapy is best known. The term *hot seat* is derived from a situation in which a chair is placed directly in front of and facing the therapist, who in turn invites any group member choosing to "work" to sit in the chair. The objective is to get group members to face their problems as they are presently experiencing them. They are not allowed to talk about them (intellectualize). By revealing their personal material in front of the group, there is an added intensity of experiencing something that cannot be discounted, thereby increasing self-awareness. Furthermore, the therapist focuses the members on the unfinished business by interacting with them directly. Almost appearing unmerciful at times, the therapist will aggressively confront members to deal with their problems.

Polster and Polster (1973) have developed an additional dimension to the concept of the hot seat. They refer to it as the "floating hot seat." It is designed to take advantage of the phenomenon of universality by encouraging group members to participate spontaneously in the sharing and disclosing begun by the member who is in the hot seat. The net result is that group member participation is increased.

ROLE REVERSALS

The use of role reversals encourages group members to play out roles they generally suppress. Perls believes that often individuals' overt behaviors actually represent just the opposite of what are underlying tendencies. For example, members may say they do not like to get angry. Their present behaviors show them to be timid and nonassertive, and they complain people do not respect them. The therapist, in this case, may ask members to behave in just the opposite of the way they have in the past—that is, to express their anger and their feelings about not being respected. It is through risking this experience, which has been so marked by anxiety, that members come in contact with a dimension of their being that they have long suppressed.

Group Processes

Although the Gestalt workshop group is more therapist centered than client centered, the therapist makes it immediately apparent that group members must take responsibility for their own behavior. There is less reliance, formally, on the interactive behavior of and between members than on the therapist for directing a member's actions. There is no prearranged plot, instead, the therapist observes and detects the specific behaviors in which members are engaged. The therapist then points out the behaviors to the members, who can choose to work or not work. It is at this point that the therapist's creative skills are needed to select the technique that will enable members to experience the meaning of their behaviors. The therapist, relying heavily on intuition, may choose to disregard the presence of other members momentarily and work one to one with the individual whose behavior is currently being dealt with. Or, the therapist may choose to direct one participant to turn and work directly with each group member through the use of experiments or exercises designed to emphasize those behaviors that have been blocking the member from functioning fully.

The Gestalt therapist believes that an inextricable relationship exists between the working member and other group members. Through their identifications and projections with the working member, other members gain from observing their peers' experiences. Similarly, for the person in the hot seat, the presence of the group provides an implied support that facilitates risk taking. As a result, the heightened experience leads to personal growth for the individual and other members. The therapist is aware of this dynamic and employs it fully by helping the client to stay in the here and now by confronting individuals about incongruencies and by pointing out ineffective ways in which they have chosen to deal with their lives.

The therapist makes no effort to interpret "discoveries" made by group members. Interpretation is appealing to the rational side of participants and could help them avoid taking responsibility for their behavior. Instead, the therapist attempts to help members learn how to take full ownership for their actions and gain greater self-trust and self-reliance through the process of confrontation or by employing the rules or games of Gestalt therapy.

Summary

Taking responsibility for one's self is a primary task for each member in a Gestalt therapy group. There is little reliance on member-to-member interaction, unless it is directed by the therapist. Usually, group members are expected to volunteer the problem on which they wish to work. From that point on, the relationship is between each member and the therapist. The therapist employs a variety of techniques to assist the member in resolving unfinished business.

As working members present unfinished business, other members will often vicariously experience, through identification, segments of their own unfinished business. Thus, the group lends itself to being a forum for therapy, where support is provided for members to carry out their own individual experiments.

During the experimentation process, the therapist attends very carefully to members' physical and verbal cues. The therapist actively confronts members' incongruencies. The members are forced to communicate in the here and now. Staying in the present does not allow the participants to talk about the past or search for the why of their behavior. Energy is directed toward experiencing in the present. The therapist continually works to help participants accept that reality is now and that it is counterproductive to establish controls over the present to regulate the future.

Because change (like aging) is inevitable, the participant is encouraged to accept what *is* as opposed to what *should be*. As a consequence, each member will realize that nothing is permanent and that there are things for which one can be responsible and things for which one is not.

CHAPTER FIVE

Individual Psychology

Background

Alfred Adler, who like many others broke away from Sigmund Freud, developed an approach to human behavior that stresses the social aspects of living as they relate to mental health. The heavy emphasis on social involvement may seem in conflict with the term *individual psychology* until we realize that the origin of the term is German and meant to convey the concepts of the uniqueness and indivisibility of the human organism, not separateness or isolation from other people. In fact, one of the most persistent areas of disagreement between Adler and Freud stemmed from their beliefs about the basic motivation of people. Do sexual instincts determine social behavior, for instance, or does social interest determine sexual responses?

Adler believed that social interest is the primary force that influences not only sexual behavior but also all other human behavior. Infants are born into a social atmosphere and become increasingly aware, as they grow and develop, that their survival demands certain kinds of social behavior and that they are in fact totally dependent for many years on the adults who surround them. As time passes, they devise and revise the *way* they view their worlds, and their behavioral responses are attempts at effectively coping with such interpretations. These unique views about the nature of life and its meanings both result from and contribute to each individual's self-appraisal, in a never-ending cycle of evaluation and interpretation.

The worldly environment seems so overwhelming to individuals at birth that a profound feeling of inadequacy and inferiority must inevitably develop. From that day on, according to Adlerians, people become goal oriented, both physically and psychologically. So, if as adults they want to know what causes them to act in a certain way, they must focus on their current objectives, rather than on some historical events. This does not of course mean that people always reach their objectives or that their objectives are always productive ones. Nor does it negate the premise that their early recollections of childhood and their ordinal position within the family constellation do not affect their achievement levels. If these past experiences have been very painful, their current outlook, and therefore their social responses, may be twisted and warped.

Because human beings tend to define self-concept in terms of their perceptions of and comparisons with others, the most significant parts of their environment are the people who provide models for them. That is, all human behavior is socially motivated by the basic task of striving to find a satisfactory niche among fellow humans. The nature of that niche depends in turn on perceptions individuals have of those humans and of the environment in which they all function. That sought-after niche, and those perceptions, though continually in a state of some flux, acquire a basic stability that becomes the model and guide by which individuals conduct their lives.

Even so, Adler maintained that the human personality is much more than a passive recipient and responder to external influences. The outlook individuals have on life is the result of their unique and idiosyncratic *interpretation* of their environment, and two people under the same environmental influences may create substantially different interpretations. To this extent, Adler said individuals are the creators of their worldview and their lifestyle and therefore capable of changing and developing their own destiny. For individuals who are motivated toward making productive modifications in their attitudes and behaviors, this approach is an obviously optimistic one.

The Adlerian emphasis on social interest and the necessity for harmonious social living indicates a high priority for group work, even though Adler himself wrote little about group potentialities. His death in 1937 preceded the tremendous group therapy movement that began after World War II. However, a large number of his disciples, such as Rudolph Dreikurs, Helene Papanek, Donald Dinkmeyer, and Heinz and Rowena Ansbacher, have made substantial use of group processes in their writings and practices.

Much of Adlerian group therapy is preventive, educational, and developmental in nature, as maladjustment is usually considered to be closely related to faulty interpretations of one's environment, misguided or distorted forms of compensation for feelings of inferiority, and goals inappropriate to social living. Because individuals can have conscious control over all of these phenomena, the therapeutic process is largely one of cognitive examination of their attitudes, values, goals, lifestyle, and self-esteem. Emotions are viewed as tools that people create in order to reach certain social goals and are therefore *not* the primary focus in Adlerian groups.

Key Concepts

SOCIAL INTEREST

Social interest connotes a feeling of identity with humanity, a sense of belongingness believed to exist innately in every human being but which needs to be developed and nurtured. The ideas of social interest, social feeling, and social cooperation are both practical and idealistic and both desirable and realistic.

Like most members of the animal kingdom, humans, as a species, naturally strive for self-preservation. In addition, humans have cognitive powers that encourage them beyond mere self-preservation; they want to *advance* themselves. By virtue of their intelligence, humans have a choice: They can strive for their goals in a "survival of the fittest" manner, or they can behave cooperatively in a community effort. To use the former method is both painful and destructive and totally illusory because of its self-defeating consequences. When individuals correct the faulty thinking that leads to destructive attitudes and actions and instead encourage the emergence of a feeling of intimate belongingness to each other, they will greatly diminish the feelings of alienation and loneliness that engulf them and lead to maladjustment and unhappiness. They will then emphasize the importance of sharing, equality, interest in others, responsibility, and cooperation.

Dreikurs wrote that "the social interest has no fixed objective. Much more truly may it be said to create an attitude of life, a desire to cooperate with others in some way and to master the situations of life. Social interest is the expression of our capacity for give and take" (1950, p. 9).

HOLISM

Adlerians perceive the human psyche to be an integrated whole, and any attempts at factoring out self-contained, separate parts for study are erroneous methods of investigation. Even though human beings may often *appear* to be inconsistent and incongruent, they really are quite constant and congruent in terms of their intentions and in the behaviors they believe will lead to the fulfillment of those intentions. Because therapists as observers are by definition outside the human psyche (or individual system), it is their lack of understanding of how that system is operating at a given point in time that causes confusion.

This holistic approach also applies to Adlerian groups. When some part of the group undergoes changes, the whole group system is forced to adjust itself in order to regain its own sense of consistency and congruency. "We consider the group an open system which is different from the sum of its units, the individual members," Helene Papanek wrote (1964, p. 43). Any change in the group is followed by a change in its units, the individual patients, and vice versa; each member can influence and change the group.

SELF-DETERMINATION

Individual psychology has a firm belief in the strength and in the creative powers of individuals to determine their own destiny. People make choices and act on those choices in accordance with their own subjectively determined goals, and they must take responsibility for their choices. This is an awesome challenge, but it also provides individuals with continuing opportunities to make new and different choices, thus altering the outcomes of their existence.

In a group setting the concept of self-determination becomes very important. With such an outlook the group therapist can encourage members to examine, with the help of each other, their goals, choices, and convictions, including their origins and potential revisions. But the decisions must always remain with each member and must be based not on past causality but on future goals.

GOAL ORIENTATION

Dreikurs (1950, p. 11) wrote that, according to Adler, all living things seek a goal. With regard to humans in particular, Adler declared that it is impossible for us to understand their behavior and actions unless we know their goals. The Adlerians believe that cognitive power (as opposed to emotional power) dominates the human system and makes individuals' conscious determination of goals a priority in all therapeutic endeavors. Whereas past and present behaviors are necessarily goal oriented, the *understanding* of those goals may not always be conscious. Rather, the goals may have been developed as a response to childhood experiences and somewhat habitually continued into adulthood even though inappropriate.

Dreikurs describes two fundamental kinds of goals. The first is a *lifestyle goal* that develops in early childhood and emanates from significant childhood experiences, primarily related to family interactions. This goal results in a general pattern of thinking and behaving, whereby the individual begins to live life according to certain subjectively developed principles. Within this general pattern, the second form of goals, *situational goals*, are created and acted on daily. Though sometimes difficult for an observer to discern, these situational goals fit somehow into the lifestyle goal, according to the "private logics" of the individual (Dreikurs, 1971, p. 52).

In an Adlerian group, identifying the goal orientation of members is an underlying task of the therapist and helps members understand both their present behavior and their future conduct. The emphasis is placed on the *purpose* that behavior serves rather than on the causes from which it developed. In other words, to find the causes of behavior, Adlerians look to the results of that behavior. The desire for that result (the goal) is the real cause of the behavior.

FAMILY CONSTELLATION

Individual psychology puts significant emphasis on early childhood recollections as a major factor in the attitudes individuals acquire and the goals they seek. Because the family is the focal point for most such experiences, the nature of the family system and how individuals view their role in that system is pertinent to an adequate understanding of current functioning. Adlerians believe, for example, that different ordinal positions in family births can have significant influences on individual development. Sibling rivalry, for the purpose of gaining parental and environmental support and approval, for example, is a common phenomenon, especially among successively born children close in age. These early family experiences then tend to exert much influence on the manner in which life is perceived and lived by each person.

Accurate perceptions of the family constellation can be therapeutic to members of a therapy group. Becoming cognitively aware of how one is currently influenced by past relationships can help participants resist those influences if they so choose. In addition, the group members may perceive helpful similarities between their family constellation and the group setting of which they are now a part.

INFERIORITY FEELINGS

Born with total dependence into a world of overwhelming size and power, young children soon become aware of their relative inferiority to the environment. To survive, appropriate coping behaviors must be learned, which are responses derived from the way children perceive their environment. Adlerians believe that the nature and quality of such responses are largely influenced by the kind of parenting that is provided. Thus, there is a heavy emphasis on parent education. Even so, with societal reinforcement of feelings of inferiority and the general lack of parenting skills in the public domain, many children grow up with feelings of inadequacy and behaviors that are highly self-defeating as responses to those feelings.

These responses are often mistaken attempts to equalize the balance of power—to prove to oneself and significant others that one is indeed not inferior but rather *belongs* in an integral way to the social milieu. The tendency, however, is to overcompensate: "Whenever an attempt is made to compensate for an inferiority feeling, this is never done merely by actual compensation, but always leads to overcompensation" (Dreikurs, 1950, pp. 30–31).

Often, because of inadequate adult responses to such behavior in childhood, children grow up clutching the same kinds of responses that enabled them to survive an earlier age but that are inappropriate in adulthood. The inferiority feelings may persist, even while feelings of equality or superiority may be communicated. These feelings of inadequacy about oneself can have harsh social consequences.

> The behavior of all children and all adults establishes the general validity of the following law: The natural social interest of every human being reaches its limits when feelings of inferiority arise. . . . As soon as an individual inferiority feeling is established, development of the social interest becomes impaired. One cannot develop a feeling of belonging if one considers oneself looked down upon. (Dreikurs, 1950, p. 20)

The impact of this concept on Adlerian group functioning is important. Because, to some degree at least, there seems to be a universal feeling of inadequacy in people, it may be that the recognition of this common characteristic tends to act as a unifying principle for group participants. From this cohesive force, members would be encouraged to provide the mutual help that will in fact exhibit their social interest while also improving their self-concepts. According to Adler, these two facets are inseparable.

LIFESTYLE

As individuals develop, they create perceptions of both themselves and the world outside. They then respond according to their unique interpretations of those perceptions. The consistent, purposeful direction of these responses defines their lifestyle:

> It is a set of ideas, schemata, and, not as in common parlance, habitual modes of behaving. Schematically, the life style may be seen as a syllogism: "I am . . ." "The world is . . . " "Therefore . . . " And whatever the case may be, it is in terms of the proposition which follows the "therefore" that the person thinks, feels, perceives, dreams, recollects, emotes, behaves, etc. (Allen 1971a, p. 5)

The lifestyle, then, evolves from a goal-oriented cognitive process and gives each individual's life some stability and consistent direction. This is true even though the person at times appears to act incongruently. In such cases, Adler believed that the observer is inadequately comprehending the individual's Gestalt, not that the individual is behaving or thinking inconsistently.

Seeing one's lifestyle clearly is often difficult, whether you are that person or an observer. "As long as a person is in a favorable situation, we cannot see his style of life clearly. In new situations, however, where he is confronted with difficulties, the style of life appears clearly and distinctly" (Adler, 1956, p. 173). Because group counseling situations tend to be strange and anxiety producing for most people, the lifestyle, along with its characteristic modes of behavior and attitudes, becomes readily apparent to the skilled Adlerian group leader. Because it is thoroughly ingrained from childhood, it is also very resistant to change. Nevertheless, a basic understanding of one's lifestyle, along with group encouragement and personal motivation, can provide an individual with all the tools needed to make significant modifications.

Therapist Roles and Techniques

Adlerian group therapists are both models of effective living and strategists and technicians. They are highly involved both in and with the group and strive to be appropriately creative and spontaneous. They are free to use whatever methods seem to be in the best interests of the group's basic goal: the improvement of members' self-esteem and the simultaneous enhancement of their social interest and value. As such, therapists' basic *attitudes* are of primary importance.

Thus, therapists must approach the group in a genuine spirit of equality and, in every way possible, encourage each group member to follow suit. They must communicate a high degree of empathy and respect, as well as honesty, openness, and congruency. Adlerian group therapists believe that their actions do indeed speak more influentially than words, but when both are employed congruently the impact is infinitely greater. Therefore, although their attitudes, behaviors, and communication skills are basic to adequate modeling, they are usually insufficient for the therapeutic needs of the group. Other more technical and professional competencies are required as well.

Donald Dinkmeyer, W. L. Pew, and Donald Dinkmeyer, Jr. (1979) have described several such competencies. They involve an understanding of group development and processes, a comprehension of human nature and behavior from an Adlerian point of view, and the possession of a variety of specific techniques and strategies to further the goals of the group.

Initially, the group must gain structure in some way and acquire some purposes for its existence. Adlerian therapists usually take a substantial amount of responsibility for encouraging the development of a structure that they believe will facilitate the attainment of the group's goals. These goals may be more specific than improvement of self-esteem and enhancement of social interest, but these more basic goals are always kept in mind and never knowingly violated. Within this broad framework, therapists often allow group members to determine subgoals that are meaningful to members. In both cases, therapists help members attain a facilitative structure and meaningful goals by both showing and telling them facilitative aspects of the communication process and encouraging them to act likewise. They may use verbal and nonverbal exercises to accomplish this goal, or they may wish to use the natural unfolding of the group's interaction to point out helpful approaches, behaviors, and responses.

Because social interest is a primary focus of Adlerian groups, the therapist's early role must also stress the building of positive relationships between the therapist and members and among members themselves. The therapist tries to help the participants identify their human similarities and develop a cohesive bond that will encourage the open sharing of lifestyles, feelings, and individual goals, as well as development of the skills and courage necessary to give helpful feedback.

Adlerian group therapists do not have a specific methodology common to all Adlerians and are therefore free to be spontaneous and creative, but their responses must be preceded by certain learned skills and abilities, such as thematic listening and behavioral interpretation. Therapists must be able to confront individuals emphatically, head off destructive elements, recognize and focus on group assets and positive feedback, paraphrase and clarify issues, and summarize group content and processes. They must also be astute observers and interpreters of nonverbal behavior and adequate diagnosticians. Belief in the holistic and goal-oriented purposes of all behavior and in the human ability and necessity of self-determination and decision making guides therapists in their verbal and cognitive interventions.

Group Processes

The Adlerian philosophy, dominated as it is by concepts such as social interest, lifestyle, goal orientation, holism, human worth and dignity, and self-determination, mandates the development of certain group processes. Such groups must be expected to stress the development of a social climate wherein social interest could be positively expressed. But Adler also believed that social interest, although inherent and innate in all of us, needs to be environmentally nurtured or it may remain forever dormant. Thus, the initial thrust of an Adlerian group is not only to develop a structure conducive to such nurturing but also to help, in every way possible, the participants experience their innate interests in social cooperation. This may be accomplished through didactic instruction, group exercises, or the therapist's interpretations to the group of their own interactive behaviors; often, some unique combination of all of these methods is employed.

Many individuals have learned faulty behaviors and made faulty assumptions about themselves and the world as a result of early childhood and family experiences, so an adequate feeling of self-esteem and social interest cannot be expected at the start of a group. In the process of developing that self-esteem and social interest, each participant's current lifestyle will eventually emerge amid the interaction and becomes important resource material for subsequent sessions. As group cohesion is developed, members will begin to take more and more risks, in accordance with the model set by the therapist. Honest and caring feedback results.

> The whole process can be described as a cycle that is being set in motion and in which (a) perceptions and beliefs change, (b) courage and belonging enable one to try on new behaviors, (c) involvement and risking are rewarded by acceptance and belonging, (d) fear of making a mistake is replaced by the courage to be imperfect, which reduces anxiety and insecurity, and (e) as self-esteem and feeling of worth develop, the person is able to try additional change. (Dinkmeyer et al., 1979, p. 141)

The social interest that is deliberately developed in the group is the sine qua non (the essential factor) around which the group becomes and remains therapeutic. Feelings of belongingness, acceptance, support, and worthiness are basic to action; before individuals can adequately test out the reality of old and new behavior, they must feel a basic sense of security and self-esteem.

Adlerian group members are continually urged to investigate the meanings of behaviors, to become aware of their own motivations, and to guess at the motivations of others. Such investigations bring some insights, which can then be tested either within the group or with group support. "There are four phases to Adlerian Group Counseling: (1) the establishment and maintenance of an appropriate counseling relationship; (2) psychological investigation or analysis; (3) insight; (4) reorientation of goals" (Hansen, Warner, & Smith 1976, p. 59).

Adlerian group therapists are free to create their own evaluative instruments to assess the progress of group participants, but much of the assessment is subjective and pragmatic. Adler contended that significant progress occurs as each participant continues to gain more self-confidence and simultaneously reaches out to help others. These goals represent the self-esteem and social interest concerns of the Adlerian viewpoint. Group feedback to each member, and the results of each member's "reality-testing" efforts both within and outside the group, help provide the validation by which both individual and group progress can be assessed.

Summary

Like many other approaches to group counseling, the relationships of group members to each other, and of each to the therapist, are highly significant in individual psychology. For some participants, a strong attachment to the group is enough to stimulate both their thought processes and desired behavioral changes; for others, additional activities are necessary, and the leader may incorporate didactic instruction, group exercises, and specific homework assignments into the process.

It is the end result that is important, not the particular methodology used. This does not mean that "anything goes" but that it is the basic and general *attitude* of group therapists that is crucial. Therapists must be models for behavior that is to be encouraged by the participants—models of positive self-esteem and of social interest and social caring. *How* they behave when they present themselves is much more important than *what* they specifically do.

Initially, group therapists must somehow try to influence the direction of the group toward a cooperative, caring social climate that acts as both its own reward and as the basis for risk taking and reality testing for the participants. During this continuous process, the material focuses primarily on the goals and lifestyles of the participants, with the aim of acquiring insights and understandings that will stimulate productive actions. These actions may result in the modification either of goals or of some aspect of a self-defeating lifestyle.

Although group therapists may use special techniques, such as group exercises, to help them accomplish their goals, Adlerian principles stress the cognitive domain as the controlling force in life. Early and continuously as individuals develop, they intellectually interpret their environment and cognitively create a lifestyle designed to further their goals. In the process, their emotions become tools that further these goals and are thus generated in time with their intentions. Such often heard comments as "I can't help it; that's the way I feel" would likely be challenged in an Adlerian group, possibly with a didactic explanation such as "Emotions cannot make one do something that one does not want to do." This lack of emphasis on the basic significance of emotions, in and of themselves, is a major distinguishing difference between Adlerian group therapy and many other common approaches.

CHAPTER SIX

Interpersonal Psychotherapy

Background

Interpersonal group psychotherapy (IGP) joins with other group psychothera-pies by focusing on interpersonal issues; however, IGP is anchored in the inter-personal theory of psychopathology, which assumes that client problems result to a large extent from maladaptive interpersonal beliefs and behaviors. IPG has its roots in the works of neo-Freudians like Karen Horney, Harry Stack Sullivan, and Erich Fromm, who recognized the effects of social forces on personality de-velopment and psychopathology (I. Yalom, 1995).

Harry Stack Sullivan's formulations were especially influential to IGP because he believed that the personality was developed from interactions with significant others and that the appraisals from others affect the development of a person's self-concept. Sullivan's (1955) term *parataxic distortion* is central to IGP. These dis-tortions lead to maladaptive beliefs that in turn extend to behaviors. For ex-ample, if individuals learn from early childhood interactions that they must ask to have their needs met, then they will engender anger or rejection from others. Thus, these individuals are unlikely to express their needs in a way that gives them any gratification (V. Yalom & Venogradov, 1993). This example is one of many that clients might bring to group psychotherapy settings. In IGP, with its emphasis on interpersonal learning as the basic curative factor, members are helped to achieve satisfactory relationships through the use of such a technique as consensual validation, which comes about from the exchange of feedback in a group atmosphere that addresses members' here-and-now group behavior.

The interpersonal factors so crucial to IGP were integrated by Irvin Yalom (1995), who recognized their contributions to the group process and who later developed a comprehensive approach to IGP, along with leadership techniques to increase interpersonal learning. Central to Yalom's approach was the identification of a number of curative or therapeutic factors that are both the "actual mechanisms of change" and "conditions of change" (1995, p. 4). These therapeutic factors are, universality, instillation of hope, imparting of information, altruism, corrective recapitulation of the primary family group, development of socializing techniques, imitative behavior, interpersonal learning, group cohesiveness, catharsis, and existential factors. (See I. Yalom, 1995, for a detailed description of these factors.)

Irvin Yalom's approach and his exploration into these curative factors were enhanced by the research orientation of the National Training Laboratories and the statement of its founder, Kurt Lewin: "No research without action, no action with research" (V. Yalom & Venogradov, 1993, p. 186). This statement propelled Irvin Yalom and his colleagues, Lieberman and Miles, to engage in the pioneering Stanford University encounter group study (Lieberman, Yalom, & Miles, 1973) and other investigations. The findings from their studies supported the notion that interpersonal learning is an important curative factor in groups. Influenced also by the National Training Laboratories' focus on other disciplines, group leaders began to move beyond the examination of models developed for individual psychopathology and therapy to an examination of the role of interpersonal and social forces in understanding group phenomena (V. Yalom & Venogradov, 1993). Finally, the impact of processing events in the here and now in T-groups showed such a positive impact in these groups, that the here-and-now approach was adapted for the IGP framework.

Key Concepts

INTERPERSONAL LEARNING

As noted earlier, the primary emphasis on interpersonal learning in IGP is what distinguishes IGP from other types of group psychotherapy. Interpersonal learning is both a curative factor and a goal of IGP. The focus on interpersonal learning allows a diversity of goals to emerge that range from finding ways to sustain an intimate relationship to developing strategies to better relate to people in daily work and living situations (V. Yalom & Venogradov, 1993). Attention to these goals helps members take their learning beyond an increased understanding of their relationships in the psychotherapy group setting to a mastery of interpersonal skills in their daily lives outside the group setting. The premise behind this strong focus on interpersonal learning is that through feedback from others—feedback that includes positive, encouraging statements as well as behavioral suggestions for the receiver to reflect on or to try—recipients can gain information about how they come across to others. As the feedback is processed in the group, the members become aware of their thoughts and feelings about their interactions in the group, and they become much more tuned in to how others react to them. This valuable knowledge obtained in the group setting then becomes the mechanism to propel the interpersonal learning that is so vital for successful interpersonal encounters in everyday life.

THE GROUP AS A SOCIAL MICROCOSM

Group psychotherapy provides a setting where people are likely to display their interpersonal behavioral patterns; as V. Yalom and Vinogradov suggested, "Given enough time, the group will become a miniaturized, somewhat artificial, but ultimately accurate representation of each patient's social and interpersonal world" (1993, p. 186). Thus, the issues that bring people to group psychotherapy are likely to get played out in the group meetings. In short, the interpersonal patterns that are impeding the group member's success with interpersonal relationships outside the group will become evident in the group and provide the leader and members grist for the therapy mill.

There are many issues to address in any type of group setting; however, the IGP leader will seek to frame goals in terms of interpersonal issues. This focus is at the crux of this approach. In fact, Irvin Yalom has noted the struggle he sometimes felt when facing the choice between a focus on interpersonal issues and a patient's interpersonal concerns:

> Much as I love to do group therapy, the format has one important drawback for me; it often does not permit the exploration of deeper existential issues. Time and again, in a group, I gaze longingly at a beautiful trail that would lead me deep into the interior of a person, but must content myself with the practical (and more helpful) task of clearing away the interpersonal underbrush. (1989, p. 162)

It is exactly the clearing away of the interpersonal underbrush that is at the heart of IGP. In fact, Irvin Yalom's (1983) groups in inpatient settings are designed to help members select a goal for the session that can be framed in interpersonal terms. In these groups, which are short in duration (i.e., 1 hour) and which have changing memberships in each session, Yalom invites members to pick something they can do in the group that is possible to accomplish in the time frame available and that uses the resources of others in the group. He is likely then to keep the attention on issues that can be addressed in the here and now of the group setting.

THE HERE AND NOW

This concept is intertwined with the concepts of interpersonal learning and the group as a social microcosm. By attending to the here-and-now events that are occurring in a group session, the leader and members begin to uncover how these events are contributing to the development and presence of each person's social microcosm (I. Yalom, 1995). Once identified, the leader must help *illuminate the process*. This means that members are helped to examine, understand, and reflect on what just happened in the group. As members reflect and develop more understanding of these events, they are likely to experience a carryover of these learnings to life outside the group.

INTERPERSONAL FEEDBACK AND CHANGE

These concepts form the core of group psychotherapy. In such groups, members have the opportunity to become a more accurate perceiver of self and others. It is hoped that as IGP members learn about themselves in relation to others they will make changes that will improve their lives outside the group therapy setting. Feedback becomes a potent vehicle for promoting such learning. Irvin Yalom (1995) presents a four-step sequence that members follow:

1. Members learn through feedback and self-observations how their behavior is perceived by others.
2. Members learn how their behavior makes other people feel.
3. Members learn that their behavior influences other's opinions of them. These opinions take the form of positive reactions, like respect, to negative reactions, like avoidance.
4. Members take all the information gathered in steps 1–3 and reflect on how that information influences their opinions of themselves.

Therapist Roles and Techniques

CULTURE BUILDING

Creating and convening a group are central tasks for the IGP therapist. The selection and preparation of members are contributing factors to the success of IGP. As members join a group, they turn to the leader, and their relationships to one another occur through their early encounters with the leader. Thus, the leader's job is to recognize that the group is the agent of change. The therapeutic factors of support, universality, advice, interpersonal learning, altruism, and hope are enhanced by member-to-member interactions (I. Yalom, 1995).

How the leader conceptualizes his or her role determines whether the leader operates as the agent of change or whether the group is the agent of change. Irvin Yalom provided a clear definition: *"If it is the group members who, in their interactions set into motion the many therapeutic factors, then it is the group therapist's task to create a group culture maximally conducive to effective group interaction"* (1995, p. 110).

In all groups, norms will develop, whether healthy and constructive or unhealthy and damaging, for members and the group as a whole. The leader's task is to work with group members to establish norms that will encourage therapeutic factors to emerge and to help members see that they have an important responsibility to make the group work effectively.

ACTIVATING THE HERE AND NOW

Attention to the here and now is important for identifying the immediate events that are occurring in a group session. The IGP therapist cannot stop with the actual here-and-now events, however helpful they may be to the facilitation of meaningful feedback and self-disclosure; rather, the therapist must additionally attend to the illumination of process. This means that the IGP therapist helps members identify and understand the process and the group's transactions. With this understanding and reflection, members will make stronger links between experiences in the group to life experiences outside the group.

First, the IGP therapist helps members experience the present events; second, he or she helps members reflect on what just happened. In this way, members can retain the power of the moment while developing a cognitive framework for remembering the experience in a way that can help them generalize the learning to relationships in their daily lives. This second part is facilitated through the *self-reflective loop,* or process commentary (I. Yalom, 1995).

ATTENDING TO PROCESS

The IGP therapist is always aware of process. Process concerns the how and why of a person's verbal content. To illustrate, Irvin Yalom provided an example:

> During a lecture, a student raised her hand and asked, what was the date of Freud's death? The lecturer replied, "1938" only to have the student inquire, "But, sir, wasn't it 1939?" The student asked a question whose answer she already knew. Obviously her motivation was not a quest for information. (A question ain't a question if you know the answer). The "process" of this transaction? Most likely that the student wished to demonstrate her knowledge or wished to humiliate or defeat the lecturer. (p. 131)

This example provides a scenario of many that might occur in a group. The leader will have to decide whether to tuck away the event for future reference or respond to it in the moment. The event might be isolated or reflective of a series of statements that this member has made in the group before.

It is important to remember that the search for process is not limited to one statement but can include a sequence of statements. IGP therapists consider their choices of how and when to respond to the process by considering the needs of the group. Member statements can be considered as critical incidents for the IGP therapist to address in order to move the group along in a direction that reflects the group's needs at that moment.

The IGP therapist can respond appropriately and therapeutically, by following three steps:

1. Think here and now. In this way the IGP therapist is ever vigilant about moving issues by members into the here and now of the group experience.
2. Move the focus of conversation and interaction away from abstract, intellectual, general, and outside issues to a focus on the specifics, the personal, and what is happening in the group at that moment.
3. Encourage responses from other members. This is often facilitated by helping members talk directly to one another using I-statements.

Group Processes

As noted earlier and frequently throughout this chapter, attention to group processes is the major tool employed by the IGP therapist. From the beginning the therapist considers how to engage members and how to hook them into seeing that this group experience will be therapeutically helpful and relevant for their needs. The therapist works with the members to set norms that will promote interaction and member responsibility and that will set in motion the therapeutic factors that are the mechanisms and conditions of change.

To this end the IGP therapist helps members frame their concerns or issues into interpersonal goals. Ever mindful of the role of process, the IGP therapist uses here-and-now events in the group and the process observations associated with those events to further the members' awareness of their transactions and how these transactions are related to their own struggles with their particular relationships outside the group.

The IGP therapist teaches through modeling the skills of process commentary and feedback exchange. Although the therapist does make statements directed to specific individuals in the group, there is likely to be more emphasis on member-to-member interactions and comments made by the therapist to the group as a whole. In this framework the past and the intrapersonal focus have a place; however, the primary focus is at the interpersonal and group levels.

Interpersonal psychotherapy groups move through a developmental sequence that includes orientation, conflict, and cohesiveness. IGP therapists are knowledgeable and skilled in recognizing group development issues, and they use their knowledge to understand the difference between favorable and flawed development. These distinctions are important and offer the therapist clues about what to do and where to go with specific interventions. To "work the process" effectively, leaders must have a conceptual map to guide their behavior. The ultimate goal of these groups is to develop and nurture a group climate that will allow the unfolding of curative factors that lead to interpersonal and intrapersonal insight and change. This change becomes evident as members acquire increasingly higher levels of interpersonal competence.

Summary

Interpersonal group psychotherapy is based on the notion that (1) the group is the agent of change and that (2) within a setting that supports and promotes therapeutic factors and where members can interact freely with one another, interpersonal blocks or deficits can be identified and addressed. Once acknowledged and addressed, members can be helped to make changes in their behaviors that lead to more satisfying relationships in and outside the group setting. Irvin Yalom was the first to pull together the therapeutic factors and create a comprehensive approach to IGP.

The emphasis on culture building, the recognition of the group as a social microcosm, the belief that process is the "power cell" of the group, and the therapist's skill of working the process by identifying and illuminating here-and-now events all lead to the likelihood that members will develop cognitive and experiential skills for improving and strengthening their interpersonal relationships (I. Yalom, 1995). Through the vigilant focus on process and interpersonal feedback, members learn more about how they perceive others and how others perceive and respond to them.

CHAPTER SEVEN

Psychodynamic Therapy

Background

For the uninitiated, thinking of psychodynamic (or psychoanalytic) group therapy might naturally have a corollary thought of believing Sigmund Freud as its founder. However, Alexander Wolf (1949) is credited for being the first to apply psychoanalytic principles to therapy groups, and Wilford Bion (1959) is viewed as being the first to have developed a theory of psychodynamic group therapy. Freud's contributions to group therapy lie with his important book, *Group Psychology and the Analysis of the Ego* (1921). Much of Freud's theory was based on his own self-analysis; the same can be said about his theory of group psychology. He wrote of crowd behavior and two primary elements that governed it: *regression,* which refers to the willingness of the individual to succumb to the attraction of the crowd's contagious affect by joining it; and the *loss of individual identity,* which refers to absorbing the group's identity and simultaneously relinquishing autonomy to the group leader. At the time he wrote this book, his critical concepts of transference and countertransference had not yet been applied to groups. Roth wrote of Freud the group leader and presented him at his various stages of development as having "his first organized experience with a working group in which he was a leader" and that occurred when the first analytic study group was formed (1993, p. 12). It included, among its more noted members, Adler, Jung, and Rank, all of whom were to later disassociate themselves from Freud. As time went on, key concepts such as transference and countertransference were introduced; all along, central to the group's functioning was the role and position of the leader (Freud) who remained the omniscient father figure.

It remained for later-day psychodynamically oriented therapists to take Freud's central principles and revise and refine them to apply to group therapy. For example, contemporary psychodynamic group therapy according to Durkin (1964) holds that

- The leader is not necessarily held up as the ego-ideal by members.
- Members are not expected to be passive or dependent.
- Leaders are not solely responsible for establishing group standards.
- Not all members react to the leader and the group in the same way.
- Members do not repress their aggression out of the need to be obedient to the leader.

Contemporary psychodynamic group therapy infuses psychoanalytic principles within a group therapy format:

> Psychoanalysts in groups emphasize harmony growing out of disharmony, reciprocity growing out of antagonism, ego growth through persistent emphasis on supporting the suppressed ego, self respect and respect for others in the course of the struggle, the appreciation of differences, and a sense of mutual regard as treatment goes on. (Kutash & Wolf, 1993, p. 126)

Accordingly, all psychodynamic groups are premised on the fact that all behavior and thought have purpose and are connected. Even the most outlandish behaviors are traceable to insulating the person from pain, and the objective of therapy is to facilitate empowering the individual through insight to more effectively manage the unconscious conflict between id, ego, and superego (Rutan, 1993).

Rutan offers the following five principles that undergird psychoanalytic theory: "(1) There is psychological determination, (2) there are unconscious processes, (3) human behavior is dynamic and goal directed, (4) human development is epigenetic, and (5) functions of the mind are at work at any given point in time" (1993, p. 141). He adds that, while contemporary psychoanalytic group therapy has and is going through significant modification, a crucial emphasis still remains that is "on the interpersonal factors involved in personality and pathology and the effects of interpersonal factors on cure" (p. 145).

Key Concepts

Transference

Historically, transference means that a member would project emotions only onto the leader that were based on unresolved past experiences with authority figures—for example, parents. Contemporary psychodynamic therapists say it also occurs with peers or fellow group members (Rutan, 1993).

Countertransference

Formerly, countertransference was viewed solely as "an unconscious pathological distortion by the therapist because of unresolved conflicts. . . . [It is now] . . . broadened to include the therapist's entire conscious and unconscious affective responses to the interpersonal field of the patient therapist interaction" (Rutan, 1993, p. 145). Tuttman has expanded the application of countertransference to include "leader and the group as a whole, between peer members within the group, and between the leader and each group member" (1993, p. 99).

RESISTANCE

Resistance, viewed as among Freud's primary discoveries (Rosenthal, 1993), is the overt or covert means by which a member or the group responds in opposition to other group members or the leader. It is a way that the individual member and group defends against exposure and change (Greenson, 1978). Resistance can take a variety of forms: absence, late arrival, monopolization, scapegoating, subgrouping, and attack on the leader, to name some.

REGRESSION

Regression is a primary defense mechanism by which the individual unconsciously insulates the self-system against "events, feelings and traumas that threaten to overwhelm the personality" (Rutan, 1993, p. 140).

Therapist Roles and Techniques

"The psychoanalyst faces a fundamental technical problem—an ignorant patient" (Rutan, 1993, p. 141); that is, group members are unaware of the unconscious processes at work, and the psychoanalyst's objective is to help members gain insights into themselves. However, members employ defense mechanisms at an unconscious level in order to insulate themselves from the pain that awareness will bring them, so therapists need to employ techniques that will help members feel secure and safe enough to examine the unconscious—that is, bring it to a conscious level of awareness. Foremost for the group therapist is to join with members, to establish a rapport that leads to a good working relationship. Once rapport is established, psychodynamic group therapists then can move members from the unconscious to the conscious through such traditional means as free association, slips of the tongue, analysis of transference, dreams, character style, dream analysis, interpretation, resistance, transference, and working through.

Rutan and Stone (1993) have identified that leader behavior falls into two categories: role (or style) and focus, each of which have several continua (Figure 1).

According to Rutan (1993), the therapist-role dimensions are explained as follows:

1. **Activity** ⟷ **Nonactivity**   The primary emphasis here is to facilitate the emergence of transference, which then is to be analyzed. Analytic group therapists tend to keep a low profile. They tend to be less verbally and physically active, although they are, at a subvocal level, listening, feeling, hypothesizing, and empathizing. The objective is to have the members take the initiative and set their own agenda for therapy. The therapist focuses more on the process

PSYCHODYNAMIC GROUP PSYCHOTHERAPY

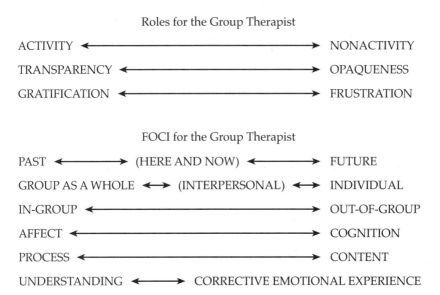

Roles for the Group Therapist

ACTIVITY ←————————————————————→ NONACTIVITY

TRANSPARENCY ←——————————————————→ OPAQUENESS

GRATIFICATION ←——————————————————→ FRUSTRATION

FOCI for the Group Therapist

PAST ←————→ (HERE AND NOW) ←————→ FUTURE

GROUP AS A WHOLE ←——→ (INTERPERSONAL) ←——→ INDIVIDUAL

IN-GROUP ←————————————————————→ OUT-OF-GROUP

AFFECT ←————————————————————→ COGNITION

PROCESS ←————————————————————→ CONTENT

UNDERSTANDING ←————→ CORRECTIVE EMOTIONAL EXPERIENCE

F I G U R E   1   *Leadership dimensions of the group therapist* Note: From *Psychodynamic Group Psychotherapy* (p. 128), by J. S. Rutan and W. N. Stone, 1993, New York: Guilford Press. Reprinted with permission.

than the content of the members' deliberations. This apparently ambiguous setting is deliberately designed—for it draws, rather than reduces, the symptoms needing to be addressed that the members' character traits produce.

2. **Transparency ↔ Opaqueness**   Here, the group therapist resists as much as possible self-disclosing personal material in the belief that this time is for group members to examine their own projections and inner convictions. However, Rutan (1993) cautions that opaqueness should not be confused with remaining emotionally aloof and avoiding personal warmth. "Strict traditionalists rarely give much hint about their own inner feelings while practitioners with an object relations point of view often find it useful to share an emotional reaction to a patient or the group in order to facilitate exploration of projective identification" (Rutan & Stone, 1993, p. 130).

3. **Gratification ↔ Frustration**   The role of the therapist is to foster frustration, not minimize it. It is believed that frustration, when intensified, will develop into regression, which in turn will generate primitive feelings that have been guarded in the unconscious by various defense mechanisms. By surfacing the maladaptive feelings to the conscious, the member will be made aware that these feelings are compromise formations and contain invalid, defensive emotional responses. However, the group therapist must be careful not (a) to foster too much anxiety (frustration) so that the building of trust is stifled or (b) to provide too much gratification so that sufficient anxiety to foster change is absent. Likewise, the therapist must avoid (a) succumbing to the temptation to

become too central (gratifying countertransference needs) so that the group becomes leader dependent or (b) being overly frustrating so that the members become discouraged to take initiative (Rutan & Stone, 1993).

Where the leader focuses attention is the other piece of a leader's role and function. Moreover, each area of the focus dimension is important, and areas are not mutually exclusive (Rutan & Stone, 1993). Regarding focus, Rutan (1993) offers the following:

1. **Past ←→ Here and Now ←→ Future**   This focus debunks the view that traditional psychoanalytic group therapy centers primarily on the past. It is argued that "transference for example is a here-and-now phenomenon" (Rutan, 1993, p. 142). However, the present often can be unclear without using the past as context. Rutan and Stone (1993) suggest that therapists can also call upon their emotional experiences of the moment to explore the past or remain in the present. For instance, how therapists may feel at the very moment of the group's interaction could mean that members are engaging in defensive behaviors. Such behaviors could represent for therapists "a response to unattended group conflict, a product of individual character styles (roles), or newly emerging transferences. The past, either near or remote, may then shed light on the present conflict" (p. 134). Rutan and Stone (1993) add that therapists can use their own anxiety as a signal or guide about whether to continue on a given course or to change. If anxiety is attendant with remaining in the here-and-now experience, then that is the signal to remain; similarly, if it is experienced when attempting to link the present with the past, then the therapist is to trust that it is the thing to do.

What of the future? It is "always present" (Rutan & Stone, 1993). Members are continually testing new behaviors as a means for determining ways of interacting in future social situations. A goal of psychodynamic group therapy is to help prepare members to effectively manage their lives once they leave the group.

2. **Group as a Whole ←→ Interpersonal ←→ Individual**   Psychodynamic therapists must continually move from "observing the group as a whole, attending to the interpersonal interactions within it and analyzing individuals" (Rutan & Stone, 1993, p. 135). However, for psychodynamic group therapists, groups are merely the means for assisting individuals.

3. **In-Group ←→ Out of Group**   Though in-group relationships are primary, member relationships are not limited to them. In fact, psychodynamic therapists find that out-of-group relationships can provide valuable information. Significant out-of-group events can only affect members, and sharing their responses and ways of managing them can be useful. However, whenever possible, psychodynamic therapists will encourage focusing on in-group relationships and events. But as with the past–here and now–future continuum, therapists need to keep in mind that the exclusive norm of counting only in-group events is restrictive and could eliminate access to valuable information.

4. **Affect ←→ Cognition**   This dimension means that insight (cognition) in and of itself is insufficient; it must be accompanied with an emotional experience or understanding. In essence, for learning to occur, attention must be

given to both the cognitive and affective dimension. Psychodynamic therapists must realize that a balance needs to be struck or a connection made between intellectual and feeling (catharsis) awareness.

5. **Process ←→ Content**   According to Rutan, "Group process is the corollary of free association in dyadic analysis . . . " (1993, p. 142). Psychodynamic group therapists need to consistently attend to the two levels of communicating: that which is being vocalized and that which is occurring at the subvocal level (i.e., at a conscious and unconscious level). On the surface, what is being voiced (content) needs to be connected to the process (underlying meaning). They are associated; through the use of free association, all seemingly random events are found to be connected. Thus, all content is to be seen as potential process that leads to revealing uncovering unconscious material.

6. **Understanding ←→ Corrective Emotional Experience**   Here the emphasis is for providing both cognitive and emotional awareness or insight with the opportunity to practice newly acquired behaviors in the group. Members need the opportunity to practice the newly acquired insights so that the group understands the meaning of healthy relationships.

The psychodynamically oriented group therapist may employ a number of methodologies or techniques, all of which are intended to help bring the unconscious to conscious awareness. Among them are free association, interpretation, resistance, dream analysis, transference, and working through.

Free association is considered to be among the primary techniques used by psychoanalytically oriented group therapists. Formerly, they were more concerned about helping individual members bring forth repressed issues to their conscious level of awareness. By helping members reduce ego control and encouraging them to feel free to express their thoughts, feelings, and fantasies, therapists could then strive to make connections between the associations, in an effort to bring about insight. Such free associations were often referred to as the content of the associations. However, contemporary psychodynamic group therapists place equal importance on the process—that is, to understand the motives that lie underneath the associations. Thus, how a group member responds (i.e., reacts) when unconscious material is brought to the conscious is interpreted. The content provides the context in which the process is placed, this helps the therapist understand the sequence in which a member's pain is experienced and repressed and when it subsequently manifests itself in symptomological behavior (Rutan & Stone, 1993).

Interpretation in psychodynamic groups generally means to make conscious and repressed (unconscious) feelings, thoughts, and fantasies and to attach meaning to them. The objective is to help a member develop an understanding of the underlying motives of his or her behavior (Rutan & Stone, 1993). There is not widespread agreement among the different psychodynamic groups regarding what is to be selected for interpretation or how interpretations are to be made, but a general consensus is that interpretations are best made and have most value when they address feelings and behaviors that are demonstrated in the present but are not part of the member's conscious awareness. For interpretations to have value, leaders need to avoid making them too intellectual or offering them when a member is in an extreme emotional state.

Resistance usually takes a variety of overt forms such as silence, scapegoating, and arriving late and shows up in other more covert ways—for example, silence. It is the means employed to avoid facing repressed, painful feelings or events that are part of the member's unconscious, for to raise them to the conscious level of awareness will mean having to face them. Considered another of the "windows into the unconscious" (Rutan & Stone, 1993), it can be used by the group therapist. Resistances are seen as opportunities to help lead members to insight. This is achieved through the group therapist's interpretation of the resistance at both the content and process levels.

Dream analysis in psychotherapy groups can have even greater value than in individual analysis because members can freely associate their own unconscious material with those of the dreamer and other members (Kutash & Wolf, 1993). Moreover, through the use of group-as-a-whole free association, members are encouraged to avoid interpreting an individual member's dream but to associate it as though it were their own (Kutash & Wolf, 1993; Rutan & Stone, 1993). The task for therapists is to encourage the individual dreamer and the other members to develop their own associations and interpretations of the dream(s).

Transference is another one of those windows to the unconscious (Rutan & Stone, 1993). Its discovery and analysis is considered to be the most important work a group therapist can do (Kutash & Wolf, 1993). The transferring of family members' qualities onto the therapist or other member(s) can effectively block the establishing of healthy and functional relationships in the group, which can in turn impede an individual's or the group's progress. As was discussed earlier, the group therapist's task is to help uncover not only the content of the transference but also the process—that is, the reason behind its occurrence. The advantage group therapists have over individual therapists is that the group provides a variety of opportunities for transference to occur, given the number of personalities that comprise the group. The member then can transfer his or her own transferational feelings onto the group therapist, other members, or the group as a whole. By enjoining members to help one another give and receive feedback on those behaviors that are seen or experienced as counterproductive, the therapist helps the member address his or her own associations and work through them.

The purpose of *working through* is to make insight effective (Rosenthal, 1993). Considered to be a most significant part of the therapeutic process, it is, however, the one frequently neglected. Rutan and Stone offer that "it is a slow and incompletely understood process" (1993, p. 78). It is very time-consuming, for it requires recognizing the many forms that pathological behavior takes on. A member may have believed he or she has worked through an issue, but it may reappear in another way. This is why the group format lends itself as a means for helping individual members work through their issues more so than individual therapy. For them, the group provides a social microcosm in which to act out their counterproductive behaviors and from which group-as-a-whole feedback can help them realize when they have actually employed more effective coping behaviors. Ultimately, working through will be achieved when a member can apply insights gained from group therapy to out-of-group social experiences.

Group Processes

Psychodynamic therapy expects its members to release themselves from their defense mechanisms in order to bring their unconscious (repressed) feelings and thoughts to conscious awareness. Establishing rapport between the group therapist and each member is critical, so a climate of safety to risk must be put in place. However, a basic premise is that anxiety will prevail, so the group therapist must always observe the various behaviors that members employ to manage it. There is also an awareness of the group as a whole and how members collectively cope, at both the individual and group level. What will be revealed are early-life defense mechanisms. However, the relatively unstructured nature of the group and the low profile of the therapist tends to create an ambiguity designed to heighten anxiety. It is a deliberate means for stimulating regression (Rutan & Stone, 1993) and to learn how members will manage anxiety.

Conscious of the stages of group development, the therapist employs techniques that help members do work that is stage appropriate. For instance, in the initial stage, the therapist plays a significant role in helping members develop group norms and culture—that is, to help members expand upon what behaviors and issues are to be tolerated and allowed to be addressed. The therapist engages in techniques that foster transferal behaviors from member to leader or member to member; thus, a psychodynamic group therapist commonly encourages interaction among members and simultaneously employs clarification, confrontation, interpretation, and working through techniques, with the objective of helping members gain insight. Believing such techniques have therapeutic value, the group therapist also helps members employ these very same techniques. The ultimate objective of psychodynamic group therapy is for individuals to acquire skills that will help them function effectively in their other social world.

Summary

The uniqueness of psychodynamic group therapy lies in the fact that it promotes "the exploration and working through of unconscious processes" (Kutash & Wolf, 1993). Through free association, slips of the tongue, dream analysis, analysis of transference, interpretation, and working through, the therapist fosters the exploration of unconscious processes.

A psychodynamic group is more likely to be heterogeneous; that composition not only reflects a microcosm of society but also creates the semblance of a family on which group members can place transferential feelings. At times, psychodynamic group therapists will be less inclined to include their self-disclosures; this behavior heightens member anxiety and increases the chances that members will transfer their unconscious feelings onto the therapist. However, it is just as likely that psychodynamic group therapists will disclose their personal reactions to members. Rutan offers that seeing the therapist as being human "does not diminish the power of transference" (1993, p. 145). Furthermore, group therapy is a very interactive and intense interpersonal (and intrapersonal) experience, and a therapist who remains emotionally detached from it actually can inhibit the attainment of therapeutic outcomes. Such detachment also underscores the fact that transference in psychodynamic groups is no longer seen as solely a vertical process but that it also occurs horizontally between members.

Maintaining a here-and-now focus is important; however, understanding the influence of history and events of the past and how they distort one's current way of managing life can free a person to apply this self-knowledge gained from insight to present interpersonal interactions. That remains as the primary goal of psychodynamic therapy.

CHAPTER EIGHT

Rational–Emotive–Behavioral Therapy

Background

In the mid-1950s, Albert Ellis formulated a new approach to personality change, which he termed rational–emotive therapy (RET). Trained in psychoanalytic procedures, Ellis had become increasingly disenchanted with the inefficiency and general ineffectiveness of psychoanalysis and began searching for a more efficient and helpful approach. RET was an outgrowth of this search and the result of his previous training, clinical experiences, and logical and scientific thinking. In 1993 Ellis announced that he was changing the name of his approach to rational–emotive–behavioral therapy (REBT) because RET had always stressed the reciprocal interactions among cognitions, emotion, *and* behavior. By adding the *B* to RET, Ellis more clearly illuminated the behavioral procedures that had historically been a central feature of his approach (Ellis, 1993).

According to this approach, people have an innate tendency to pursue happiness and pleasure, but they also have a strong predisposition to engage in self-defeating behaviors. The words *tendency* and *predisposition* are significant in that they do not represent a deterministic philosophy. Rather, they indicate that, though we may be pulled in these directions by our biological inheritance, it is possible—with desire and hard work—to overcome such psychological gravity. Thus, some people seem passively to accept an existence of unhappiness and pain, whereas others are motivated to overcome their self-defeating tendencies and to behave primarily in self-enhancing ways.

Whichever choice is made though, it is reached through a highly cognitive process whereby individuals *condition themselves* to think and act and emote according to their idiosyncratic belief systems, that is, whatever individuals *believe* to be true about a certain event or condition governs their emotional reaction to that situation. Such beliefs may in fact be rational, that is, reality based and provable—or irrational, fantasized, and unprovable.

Because our goals tend to be rational but our means of achieving them often irrational and self-defeating, we become frustrated and inappropriately emotional when presented with such a situation, that is, not only do we become frustrated about a given situation, but we also overreact and become frustrated about our frustration, eventually engaging in what Ellis terms "awfulizing" behavior. We blow things way out of proportion; we tell ourselves we "just can't take anymore." At this point we become emotionally disturbed, not because of what others have done to us or because the situation is truly horrendous, but because we have talked ourselves into such a state that we have become emotionally immobilized.

Ellis sees this self-talk (a cognitive process) as the culprit when it is insane and irrational, but as the antidote when it is sane and rational; that is, since people talk themselves *into* emotional disturbances, they can also talk themselves *out* of them. However, because we have a strong predisposition to think crookedly and to create our own misery, the antidote is often most effectively applied with outside help.

This help can be given in the form of group activities, and REBT practitioners are often quite involved in leading such groups. Ellis has described four kinds of groups available to REBT participants: family groups, regular weekly group therapy sessions, marathon sessions, and workshops (1974a, p. 17). Though the format may vary in each setting, the basic principles of REBT remain the unifying force. These principles stress that "significant personality changes . . . come about when the individual clearly sees, acknowledges, and works very hard at surrendering or minimizing his (or her) puerile demandingness. . . ." (Ellis 1974a, p. 15). In a very real sense, that often means a radical change in an individual's philosophy about life itself, as what was once "terrible" now becomes "inconvenient" and what was once "intolerable" now becomes "unpleasant."

Thus, as situations are perceived in less upsetting ways and with less upsetting words, the individual perceiving the situations becomes correspondingly less upset. Then, as this new perception of life pervades more and more of one's life situations, it becomes a permanent fixture in the individual's life, resulting in basic personality change.

As noted earlier, however, the tendency toward self-defeating behavior is strong and not easily overcome. Besides this biological predisposition, cultural and educational influences can likewise encourage unhealthy beliefs, feelings, and actions. These influences too often foster and model irrational ideas and belief systems, especially in the immature young child who is understandably gullible and suggestible. Once these ideas take hold, they become very resistant to change because our natural tendency is to reindoctrinate ourselves with these ideas as we grow older. And, even if we *do* modify our philosophies and our irrational belief systems at a cognitive and emotive level, behavioral change can be exceedingly difficult. Therefore, homework assignments are commonly given in REBT so that a congruence will emerge between the thinking and feeling processes and behavioral activities.

The general goal of this cognitive–emotive–behavioral approach to philosophical reorientation and personality change is "to internalize a rational philosophy of life just as he [the client] originally learned and internalized the irrational views of his parents and his community" (Ellis, 1962, p. 95). More specifically, this means creating a way of life that affords us a reasonable degree of happiness and enjoyment. The REBT therapist thus tries to help clients accept and accomplish the following objectives (Ellis & Whiteley, 1979, pp. 54–57):

1. A healthy outlook toward *oneself*. Ellis uses the terms *self-acceptance, self-interest,* and *self-direction*. According to his view, people open themselves up to irrational conclusions when they rate their self-worth according to their earthly achievements. People are worthy because they are alive; and because they are unique and separate individuals, they are interested primarily in themselves. Rational thinking would therefore induce them to take responsibility for the direction of their own lives.

2. A healthy outlook toward *others*. Even though rational people are basically self-oriented, there is also a strong predisposition to live in a group atmosphere. Therefore, if people completely ignore others' self-interests, irresolvable conflicts are likely to arise, some of which will result in a defeat of *our own* self-interests. Some degree of help and cooperation with others is therefore in our best interests—healthy and rational. This often calls for an attitude of tolerance and flexibility whereby we accept others' rights and behaviors precisely because we accept our own. We allow both others and ourselves the leeway to make mistakes and to learn from them, and we do not insist on such rigid rules that we become immobilized and self-defeating.

3. A healthy outlook toward *reality*. There are few guarantees in life. We live in an uncertain world, full of both tragedy and pleasure, much of it not under our control. Mature and healthy people accept this reality—and make the best of it by choosing to view life as adventuresome and creative rather than as fearsome and routine. These individuals know that risk taking is a part of life and that mistakes sometimes result. Yet this does not deter them; in fact, it spurs them forward. They attack life and thereby control what they can, instead of letting life attack them and thereby controlling very little.

4. A healthy outlook toward the *future*. Emotionally and rationally secure people are committed to life and to the preservation of happiness. They are absorbed in daily living and are optimistic about their future. At the same time, they are aware that life is a struggle, sometimes requiring exhaustive work and striving just to stay even. Since they are both optimistic and realistic, they do not have expectations that are impossible to attain, but they do recognize the possible rewards of diligence and commitment. Thus, they can act objectively, rationally, and systematically when this behavior is called for. They do not negate their emotions but tend to exhibit control over them when they are appropriate to the situation.

Key Concepts

A-B-C-D-E Construct

This construct is REBT's best-known and most basic precept. The letters *A* through *E* represent both a theory of human behavior and personality change and a basic cognitive method of clinical practice. The first letter, *A*, symbolizes an *activating event* or *experience* of some significant stimulus that triggers an emotional reaction or *consequence* (represented by the letter C).

According to REBT, it is inaccurate to say that *A causes* C because it is unlikely that everyone would react the same way to that activating event. Rather, it must be how a given individual *perceives A* that causes a specific reaction; that is, what a person *believes* about the occurrence of *A* is really what causes C. This *belief* is represented by the letter B. When this belief system is based on irrational and unprovable ideas and thoughts on a given subject, it can lead to inappropriate and dysfunctional emotions and behaviors.

When this happens, REBT therapists must help their group members to actively and forcefully *dispute (D)* these irrational beliefs about *A*. The therapist accomplishes this by (1) vigorously challenging the client to prove the validity of those beliefs, (2) serving as a model for other group members to do the same for each other, and (3) teaching members how to challenge their own belief systems to help sort out facts from unrealistic hypotheses.

This disputing process will eventually lead to a new and more realistic understanding of one's self-defeating tendencies and behaviors and will result in new cognitive insights that represent the *effects (E)* of this disputation.

Homework

Assignments for work done outside the counseling session are common in REBT. These assignments maybe cognitive, emotive, behavioral, or a combination of these. For example, group members may be asked to utilize the Self-Help Report Form that helps them to go through the A-B-C-D-E cognitive process described earlier; they may then be asked to explain how they used this process to help themselves when the group reconvenes the following session.

Or members may be assigned an emotive task such as rational–emotive imagery. This kind of assignment may first be practiced in the group with the expectation that further practice be tried between sessions. This technique might involve closing one's eyes and imagining oneself encountering an emotional situation and then consciously working at changing the original inappropriate feelings to more appropriate ones that befit the situation.

The therapist may also recommend a behavioral assignment. For example, the therapist may suggest that the member perform an observable action outside the session, such as a shy member initiating a conversation with intimates, acquaintances, or strangers, determined by the individual's idiosyncratic problem area.

In theory there is no limit to the amounts and kinds of homework that can be given to group members. Assignments outside the group are important in helping irrational ideas, inappropriate emotions, and self-defeating behaviors that may be temporarily changed during the group sessions and become more permanent through the reinforcement of continuous and successful practice outside the group setting.

THREE BASIC "MUSTS"

In some of Ellis's early writings, he listed numerous irrational beliefs that led in varying ways to emotional disturbances. These have more recently been consolidated into three basic "musts" with which individuals indoctrinate themselves:

> (1) "I *must* (or *should* or *ought*) perform well and / or be approved by significant others. It is *awful* (or *horrible* or *terrible*) if I don't! I can't *stand it*. I am a pretty rotten person when I fail in this respect!" (2) "You *must* treat me considerately and fairly. It is horrible if you don't! When you fail me, you are a bad individual, and I can't bear you and your crummy behavior!" (3) "Conditions must be the way I want them to be, and it is *terrible* when they are not! I *can't stand* living in such an awful world. It is an utterly abominable place!" (Ellis & Whiteley 1979, p. 46)

According to Ellis, it is this childish and unrealistic demandingness—this *must*abatory thinking—that is at the root of virtually every emotional disturbance. Obviously, these three "musts" have many derivatives and subcategories with which the group leader and group members may work.

RATIONALITY AND IRRATIONALITY

REBT defines "rationality" essentially as goal-enhancing behavior and "irrationality" as goal-defeating behavior. More specifically, "the term *rational,* as used in REBT, refers to people's (1) setting up or choosing for themselves certain basic values, purposes, goals, or ideals, and then (2) using efficient, flexible, scientific logico-empirical ways of attempting to achieve such values and goals and to avoid contradictory or self-defeating results" (Ellis & Whiteley, 1979, p. 40).

It is significant to note that these goals are not chosen by the therapist but by the members themselves. The degree of rationality is then determined by the extent to which group members' behaviors move them most effectively and efficiently in the direction they want to go. Even so, at the most basic "want" level, Ellis sees almost universal similarities among people, even though their specific goals may differ greatly: Most people desire to live a long life, to engage in some form of intimacy with others, to be socially productive, to become involved in some forms of recreational activities, and to be generally happy in all the above pursuits.

Rational thinking, emoting, and behaving, then, represent a process through which such pursuits can be attained, whereas irrational behaviors, thoughts, and emotions lead to a defeat of such pursuits. The practice of REBT emphasizes the use of scientific methodological thinking to challenge those belief systems that lead to goal-defeating results. "The essence of the scientific method is exactly this: to set up a series of hypotheses, to see what results they lead to, and then to debate or challenge these hypotheses if the results seem to be poor" (Ellis & Whiteley, 1979, p. 69).

HEDONISM

As mentioned above, nearly all humans are basically hedonistic; that is, they seek pleasure and happiness. Unfortunately, however, occasions often arise when we have to choose between short-term pleasure and long-term happiness. REBT perceives most people as striving for long-term happiness, but many of these people seem to *demand* short-term pleasure as well. When these goals are incompatible, the end result can only be varying degrees of frustration, often culminating in irrational behavior and inappropriate emoting.

If individuals consciously choose short-term pleasure in a given circumstance and are willing to take the probable long-term consequences without whining and moaning, then their behavior and thinking may well be termed *rational*. However, the desire to attain both long-range happiness and short-range pleasure is very strong, and although our basic values usually favor the long-term principle, our behavior leans toward the short-term pleasure.

According to Ellis, the low frustration tolerance that is often at the root of this self-defeating behavior inhibits people from reaching their long-range goals. This desire to avoid immediate pain and discomfort comes from our wishes to take the easiest way out, which may well have its basis in our biological predisposition toward self-defeating behavior. This is why people must be vigorously challenged and taught to challenge themselves and each other, to overcome their various forms of irrationality. Individuals can in this way work to change their philosophy and emotional states as well as their behavior so that this tendency to defeat themselves will be intensely combated on all fronts.

Therapist Roles and Techniques

The therapist's role in REBT groups is active, directive, and authoritative; there is little question about who is in charge. The REBT therapist's main goal is to assist group members in minimizing their emotional disturbances and self-defeating behaviors by acquiring a more realistic and workable philosophy of life. REBT therapists actively teach group members that self-condemnation is one of the main courses of emotional disturbance, that it is possible to stop rating themselves on their performances, and that through behavioral homework assignments they can reduce the occurrence of irrational thinking that leads to disturbances in feeling and behaving. In varying ways and at different times, therapists act as teacher, catalyst, confronter, efficiency expert, model, observer, and scientist. They must have a great deal of common sense, understand and be able to use the principles of logic and of human behavior, be well versed in the REBT approach, and be unafraid of debating, disputing, confronting, and challenging group members. Therapists' attitudes must reflect an unconditional acceptance of each and every member and a willingness to communicate respect by being open, honest, straightforward, and genuine in relationships with the group. Yet relationship building is only a means to an end, a way for therapists to get their foot in the door and a way of showing their care so that group members will open themselves up to the therapists' influence, which comes in the form of interventions, interruptions, and modeling. The real therapeutic value lies in the technique through which group members learn to challenge their irrational assumptions and beliefs and to engage in alternative behaviors that are goal enhancing rather than goal defeating.

REBT breaks down these techniques or methods into three rather distinct classifications—cognitive, emotive, and behavioral. The cognitive methods used in REBT most distinguish it from other forms of therapy. Ellis has written that "all told, REBT therapists tend to use perhaps 40 or 50 regular techniques and theoretically, cognitive-oriented therapists have a dozen or more major procedures at their disposal" (Ellis & Whiteley, 1979, pp. 66–67). When broken down into subcategories and specific treatment forms, more than 200 types of interventions could be labeled cognitive. And, since REBT is highly eclectic, pragmatic, and individualistically oriented, therapists and group leaders are free to create and experiment with techniques, as long as they remain generally consistent with the basic theoretical and philosophic outlook of REBT.

The most fundamental cognitive method stems from the *A-B-C-D-E construct* discussed earlier. Through this technique, group members are taught how to challenge and dispute their irrational beliefs and assumptions. Therapists are of course the primary teachers and may engage in some very didactic activities in so doing. In addition, therapists may work one on one with some or all group members and, in the process, model what they want members to learn. Then, as members begin to challenge and dispute themselves and each other, therapists act as supervisors to this process.

Often some form of *cognitive homework* is given to specific group members, as deemed appropriate. In an effort to help members gain greater understanding of the constructs they are learning, such homework may include the use of books, recordings, and films, or it may be a creative endeavor that addresses the idiosyncratic situation of each of the members. One of the more common and formal methods involves the DIBS technique (disputing irrational beliefs), in which members work on one particular irrational belief at a time and learn how to dispute it. Then, they continue such disputing—a few minutes a day, over several weeks, for example—at home, until the message is sufficiently internalized.

Other cognitive techniques favored by Ellis include the use of mental imagery, bibliotherapy, and teaching as learning; all can be employed in numerous ways in group counseling. Because our minds are involved in the creation of illogical assumptions, employing *mental imagery* to block out these self-defeating thoughts and pictures by creating or strengthening more self-enhancing ones is often highly useful. Reading relevant books and articles, bibliotherapy as a cognitive tool is often used to help group members gain a deeper understanding of the cognitive concepts they are learning. Another technique, *teaching as learning,* can be most useful in a group setting. As indicated above, one of the goals of REBT is to teach the group members to help each other so that, in the process, members will learn how to help themselves more effectively and efficiently.

REBT uses several emotive techniques designed to elicit feelings among group members. Perhaps the most basic, though ambiguous, technique is that of *unconditional acceptance*. This attitude must be conveyed to members at a feeling level; to merely say it does not communicate it. Therapists must be able to separate persons from their behaviors, to accept individuals totally precisely because they are human, while still being able to attack the irrational beliefs that are causing individual's problems.

Role playing is another technique that can be used to evoke feelings. The therapist (or any member) may suggest such an activity in order to give members some corrective practice before they go out and try it on their own. The ways in which role playing can be effectively utilized are limited only by the creativity of the group participants.

The process of *therapist modeling* can also be highly effective in producing a feeling of fairness and congruence. Asking members to accomplish what their therapists are unable or unwilling to do is seldom therapeutic. But when therapists show that they can and do effectively use those principles they have espoused, it encourages members to work even harder and more productively.

Sometimes emotions can be stirred by suggesting that a member make new self-statements that are more rational. Or the emotional intensity of old but basically rational self-statements can be increased by challenging the process the member(s) used to arrive at such self-statements. By making these statements more affective, they appear more believable and can be more easily internalized. In a similar vein, verbalizing self-statements in a less affective manner decreases their believability and internalization.

Imagery is used as both a cognitive technique and an emotive one. By asking members to create in their minds a very emotional picture, the participant can develop a highly emotional state that the therapist can then work with in the immediate moment. In addition, members can be taught to bring themselves to such a state so that they might practice gaining control of these emotions.

Finally, Ellis has developed *shame-attacking exercises* whereby members are assigned tasks, to be performed either in or outside the group, to combat feelings of shame and humiliation that often accompany other feelings of inadequacy and serve only needlessly to heighten their anxieties. Members are asked to do something ridiculous or shameful and then evaluate the results— which are inevitably less horrifying than they had been telling themselves. Thus, members learn to put themselves into a more rational perspective, to laugh at themselves, and to take themselves less seriously, thereby decreasing their anxieties and disturbances.

The behavioral techniques of REBT represent the third mode of therapist influence. Even if the cognitive and emotive methods are working well, the forces against rationality are so strong that individuals will likely revert back to old illogical behavior—unless they are induced to frequently practice the new behavior.

Most of the methods common to behavioral therapy are useful in REBT. Often they are given in the form of work outside the group, after having been initiated and practiced in the safer atmosphere of the group, for it is unlikely that permanent change will occur otherwise. The suggested behaviors are always put into a cognitive framework, usually involving the REBT concepts of irrationality, demandingness, and *must*abatory thinking. What is likely to work, and for whom, is usually the criterion for the use of behavioral techniques. As with the cognitive methods, the number of possible assignments is virtually limitless.

However, because some of these assignments can be quite uncomfortable and frightening, the use of *operant conditioning* is sometimes employed. The principle behind this technique suggests that in order for a desired or teamed behavior to continue to occur it must be followed by a satisfactory experience. REBT therapists therefore encourage members whose anxieties make assignments difficult to carry out to reward themselves—*after* they have carried out their specified tasks. And if further encouragement is needed, some equally distasteful punishments can be effected if their tasks are not completed within a specified time.

Group Processes

As mentioned earlier, Ellis described four types of groups that REBT theorists utilize: workshops, family groups, marathons, and general weekly sessions. Though obviously some procedural variations result from differences in makeup and structure, the general principles of REBT encompass them all. We will examine the latter two groups, with an emphasis on general weekly sessions, because they correspond most closely to the groups discussed in this book.

There is no set procedure that every REBT group therapist must use, but it is fair to assume that therapists will be quite active and directive from the beginning. For example, after a general welcome and basic orientation at the beginning of the first session, therapists ask members to introduce themselves and to state their goals. Follow-up questions are asked, with ever-increasing challenges toward more personalized and risking information. For marathon sessions, REBT therapists might ask such questions as "What bothers you most right now?" or "What are you most ashamed of at present?" or "Think of something risky you can do at this moment and do it."

REBT therapists do not necessarily wait for volunteers to respond. They may call upon particular individuals or ask silent ones why they did not speak or act. For those who seem shy, ashamed, or embarrassed, this may signal the need for some shame-attacking exercises at a later time.

The point is that therapists do not usually sit silently by and allow the group to grope and drift while searching for something meaningful to talk about. Instead, they are likely to direct and structure the process in an effort to make the group as therapeutic and efficient as possible. If therapists feel that relationship-building activities or exercises are warranted, they will suggest them—

knowing that the most significant therapy will occur when the members start dealing with their irrational thoughts and behaviors.

During these early hours of therapy, the questions and activities initiated by therapists encourage interaction among members. However, therapists are usually careful to limit any given transaction to a few minutes in order neither to allow anyone to monopolize the group nor to forget the main purpose of the group, which is to attack and replace irrationality with goal-enhancing thoughts and behaviors. During these early moments, group members learn many things about each other that are useful in the more meaningful activities occurring later on.

Thus, though therapists are usually quite active in *structuring* group activities, these activities are designed to encourage group interaction. To utilize the principles of REBT on each other's behalfs, group members must learn these principles first. Therapists can help members accomplish this task by assigning outside reading, films, and demonstrations and through didactic instructions and modeling. As has been suggested earlier, *how* individual REBT therapists accomplish this task is much less important than *that* they accomplish it.

Whatever methods or combinations of methods therapists choose to aid members' awareness of the REBT approach, they will inevitably model its use within the group. As members learn through cognition, observation, and experiences, they are encouraged to use these REBT principles with each other. This peer assistance often arises spontaneously; if it does not, therapists can initiate activities to stimulate it. For example, a therapist might ask a member to specify someone in the group in need of help and to join that member in the center of the group by applying REBT helping principles in a one-to-one confrontation. If or when the pair begins to stumble, the therapist can ask other group members to help out.

In such situations, therapists maintain control over the process and act as supervisors to the helpers. When members' attempts at helping become ineffective or inefficient, the therapist can interrupt, intervene, and influence the process and direction of the interactions. Such interventions are necessary precisely because the group *helpers* are, at any given moment, subject to the same irrational beliefs and inappropriate emotions and behaving as those they are trying to help. Thus, out of ignorance or misapplication of principles or unrecognized self-defeating thoughts, group members can sometimes lead each other astray, even though their intentions are quite the opposite. As they practice and gain experience session after session, their ability to help can be expected to improve considerably. This allows the therapist to become less directly active as therapist and more indirectly active as teacher, reinforcer, and monitor of the helping process.

As mentioned earlier, assigning homework activities is common in REBT groups. Members are encouraged to create and suggest such assignments for their peers. Usually, the therapist discusses with the members appropriate kinds of homework. Correction or discussion of homework also occurs in subsequent sessions. Weekly REBT sessions usually last from 2 to 2½ hours. The percentage of time spent discussing, correcting, and suggesting homework assignments will vary considerably, according to the members' stage of development.

Summary

People are born with strong tendencies toward both rational, self-enhancing behavior and thought processes and irrational, self-defeating behavior and thought processes. Humans' wishes, desires, and goals tend to be pleasure oriented and rational, but their means of achieving them often takes them further away from those goals. To gain long-term happiness, we are often impatient and unwilling to endure short-term discomfort. Believing we can always have both is an unreasonable and unrealistic belief but one that is often reinforced through our culture and educational process.

To desire complete and everlasting joy and happiness is not irrational; it is merely human. However, to expect and *demand* such a perpetual outcome is not only irrational but also can lead to tremendous emotional trouble and inappropriate behavior when that demand is not fulfilled. This childish demandingness arises out of a self-defeating belief system that REBT seeks to challenge.

Ellis has categorized 12 irrational ideas, which he believes to be the basis for nearly all emotional disturbances, into three major *musts:* (1) I must be totally competent and approved of; (2) others must treat me fairly, or they are bad people; (3) living conditions must be the way I want them to be. These demands and their derivatives and corollaries set the stage for such immobilizing feelings as hate, depression, anxiety, and guilt. And, because these feelings are largely nonproductive, people commonly feel guilty about feeling guilty, depressed about feeling depressed, and so on. In other words, we continually reindoctrinate ourselves with our own irrational thoughts, feelings, and behaviors.

REBT approaches this problem at all three levels but emphasizes cognition. Thus, the irrational beliefs of an individual are recognized, challenged, and attacked in a logical, scientific manner. Rather than accepting the common argument that a certain experience or event *causes* an emotional reaction, the REBT practitioner would try to persuade an individual that the event was only a catalyst that awakened an irrational belief *about* the event. It is that belief that truly causes the emotional reaction; thus, that belief must be challenged and seen for what it is, if the reaction is to subside and change. In this way, REBT promotes a whole new outlook on life, a new approach to emotional dysfunctioning, and a new philosophy for everyday living.

REBT is suited to the group work setting because members are taught to apply its principles in the group, to practice new behaviors that involve taking risks, and to receive group feedback on homework assignments conducted outside the group setting. Members learn to recognize irrational ideas and to connect them to dysfunctional emotions and inappropriate behaviors. Group therapists are usually active in structuring and directing group interactions and activities in the most effective and efficient manner. Their methods of teaching the approach may vary according to style, but members must learn the A-B-C-D-E model if the group is to be minimally effective.

The use of homework assignments is also part of the REBT group process. These assignments are created by members and the therapist to fit the particular needs of each individual and may be cognitive, emotive, or behavioral. In this way, the REBT approach is very eclectic and quite pragmatic, utilizing its own specific theory of personality change but also using methods often associated with many other approaches. Members can experience assertiveness training, role playing, and other structured activities that help foster a radical philosophical change.

CHAPTER NINE

Reality Therapy

Background

The principal proponent and founder of reality therapy is William Glasser. A psychiatrist, Glasser took issue with the basic concepts of psychoanalytic counseling and in 1965 outlined six primary ways in which his approach to therapy differed from traditional therapy. Much like other systems of psychotherapy, reality therapy was born out of individual therapy, with its principles later applied to group situations.

Reality therapy has a very rational appeal, and no small wonder that it should. It avoids dealing with history, feelings, and attitudes; instead, it deals directly with behaviors. It emphasizes what is happening in the present and demands that group members learn how to take responsibility for their actions. There is a great emphasis on the teacher–learner, or pedagogical, relationship that exists between group member and therapist. The primary objective of reality therapy is to *teach* members to behave in responsible ways. The ultimate consequence of such action, it is believed, leads to successful living.

Key Concepts

The fundamental premise underlying reality therapy is that people who suffer personal, psychological, or irrational problems have not adequately met their basic needs. These fundamental needs are to love, to be loved, and to feel worthwhile. Glasser believes that a person who is in need of help has *chosen inappropriate ways* to satisfy his or her needs. The consequence of this leads to symptoms that reflect the degree to which these needs are not met. Conversely, as needs are satisfied through appropriate behaviors, the tension they created is reduced.

INVOLVEMENT

Involvement represents a crucial component to reality therapy. It is, according to Glasser, a process whereby a client or member finds another "person with whom he can become emotionally involved, someone he can care about and who he can be convinced cares about him" (1965, p. 26). This relationship with at least one other person represents the process by which love needs are met. Without this significant person, one's basic needs will not be fulfilled. It is very important that this other person be in touch with reality and be able to fulfill his or her own needs within the world.

According to Glasser, learning to fulfill one's needs appropriately begins in early infancy: "A person who does not learn as a little child to give and receive love may spend the rest of his life unsuccessfully trying to love" (1965, p. 13). For Glasser, love is synonymous with involvement. The extent to which individuals involve themselves in loving ways with others is a reflection of the degree to which their need for love is fulfilled. Generally, individuals who become involved with others will be successful, whereas those who remain uninvolved will feel alienated, experience anguish, and see themselves as unsuccessful or as failures.

FEELING WORTHWHILE

Just as significant as giving and receiving love is the need to feel worthwhile. Individuals who hold themselves as being worthy believe that what they do with their life is worthwhile and that their very existence does make the difference. This is an inner-care belief system that is projected behaviorally in actions that reflect self-respect. It is not the stereotypical, conceited, egotistical, or narcissistic self-involvement that is referred to here. It is in fact just the opposite. Persons whose needs are filled in regard to their own self-worth will generally be capable of extending respect toward others and engaging in loving relationships.

According to Glasser, the key to gaining self-worth is to abide by the norms of society. For example, behavior that reflects meeting the standards of morality and expectations of others' productive work are the means by which the needs for self-worth and love are met.

Glasser contends that both needs must be met in order for a person to be free from others. Individuals can have strong feelings of self-worth, but not have their love need fulfilled. This would mean they would still be in pain and discomfort. In essence, the two needs (love and worthiness), though independent of each other, must both be fulfilled if individuals are to function free of anguish.

RESPONSIBILITY

A critical factor in meeting the basic needs of individuals is responsibility. Glasser believes that it plays a significant role in personality development and that it is the parents' task to demonstrate to their children how to be responsible. By so doing, children will develop their own sense of self-worth. This ultimately leads to what Glasser refers to as "success identity." It results from learning effective ways to satisfy basic needs. The parents of such children not only allowed their offspring to experience activities on their own but also demonstrated love and care through disciplining their children, teaching them right from wrong, and, in effect, providing them with appropriate role models. This form of involvement helps to develop *success identity.*

Conversely, a child's feelings of being unloved and unworthy leads to irresponsible behavior and creates a *failure identity.* Parents of children who have developed a failure identity have acted irresponsibly themselves because they have not become involved with their children. Perhaps they choose the "easy way out" when faced with disciplining their children. They tended to "give in" to their children's every wish, rather than taking stands that may not have immediately pleased their children. Individuals with failure identities manifest them in a variety of unrealistic ways in an effort to reduce their pain or discomfort. These behaviors range from emotional disturbances, such as mild depression, to full-blown psychotic episodes. They may take the form of behavior problems that are antisocial (alcoholism, drug abuse, etc.) and physical responses manifested as illness (e.g., ulcers, hypertension, headaches, backaches).

DENIAL

Glasser refers to such behaviors or symptoms as denial. It is believed that although these symptoms may hold validity for the group member they are in fact excuses for not facing the reality of the individual's situation. Responsible and involved behavior would not lead to these conditions or, at the very least, would allow a person with a success identity to face these afflictions responsibly and not use them as excuses for behaving irresponsibly.

Reality therapy draws its name from its effort to help group members quit denying the reality of their world and to help them realize that they must learn to meet their needs within the norms of society. However, therapy extends beyond helping group members accept the reality of their environment. It also helps them learn behaviors that will enable them to fulfill their needs in the real world, thereby reducing stress. The objective of therapy is to get group members to eliminate established but inappropriate coping behaviors from their responses and add new, more effective ones.

Therapist Roles and Techniques

It is peculiar to reality therapy that the group leader's role and therapist techniques are synonymous with group process. Glasser has identified seven developmental stages of therapy. These same stages are reflective of the roles and techniques that the therapist must employ in order to facilitate members' growth to responsible living. Consequently, the therapist's roles, group techniques, and group processes will be presented simultaneously.

To be effective, the therapist must employ these techniques in a developmental sequence. To ignore them is to doom the therapeutic process to failure.

Group Processes

STAGE 1: THERAPIST INVOLVEMENT

The most significant ingredient in reality therapy for therapists is to develop a warm, intimate, and emotional relationship with each group member. It is the lack of such involvement with another person that has brought the group member to seek help. This is the most difficult and trying period in therapy. Therapists must demonstrate their emotional regard for group members and be willing to suffer through their difficulties with them. The objective is to get each member to move away from self-involvement and self-focus to involvement with another.

Members are encouraged to trust that someone does care about them and feel they are important. The therapist helps members accomplish this by acknowledging that whatever feelings or thoughts individual members choose to disclose are significant and of interest to the therapist. Two things are accomplished in this process. First, members feel validated through involvement with significant others, and, second, through modeling, the therapist demonstrates to other group members the way to move outside of self-involvement to involvement with another. It is the immediacy of this interaction between group member and therapist that allows the member to experience involvement with another in a warm, accepting, and nonpunitive atmosphere. The conditions present maximize the chance for success in developing responsible behavior. By so doing, the member is given the opportunity to develop a sense of self-worth.

STAGE 2: FOCUS ON PRESENT BEHAVIOR

Reality therapy holds little value in delving into history. Though it may make for an interesting story line, it provides excuses for members to avoid taking responsibility for their present situation. Instead, the therapist works to get members to focus on their present behavior. The effort here is to help members recognize that their current lot in life is the consequence of their behaviors.

Although members may press to discuss the feelings that are attendant with their behaviors, the therapist's task is to downplay them as much as possible, short of denying their significance, and to attempt to focus members' attention on their behavior. It is only through the altering of behaviors that members can achieve success identity. Therefore, the therapist makes efforts to help members develop responsible behaviors and recognize the consequences of their actions. It is important to remember that one of the objectives of reality therapy is to help members assume responsibility for their behaviors. The underlying premise is that members have developed a repertoire of behaviors that have allowed them to avoid their responsibilities and that this has evolved as a matter of choice; that is, members have *chosen* to engage in self-defeating behaviors. It is even possible that they no longer consciously realize that they have made the decision to behave as they do. Therefore, the therapist must work to focus members on what they are presently doing, as opposed to why they are doing it. This helps members become *aware* of the control they do have over their behaviors and that ultimately the consequences of such responsible action are not as painful as those of irresponsible behaviors. Within the group setting, members can practice the new responsible behaviors that lead to involvement with others.

Stage 3: Evaluation of Behaviors

In the process of helping members develop responsibility, there comes a moment when they must examine and evaluate their behavior in terms of its effectiveness for meeting their needs. How responsible are their behaviors? It would be counterproductive if the therapist made that determination. It is the therapist's task, however, to keep members focused on the fact that they have made behavioral choices and to realize that the resulting consequences of their acts is their responsibility.

Stage 4: Developing Positive, Responsible Behavior

After members have evaluated their behaviors and accepted them as irresponsible, they must take the responsibility to want to change. Then they must develop, with help from the group, a positive plan of action. This plan should be realistic. Members who have had failure identities often do not know how to plan effective ways for coping with life. The therapist and the group therefore help the member develop a step-by-step program of action, with each step maximizing the chance for success. By ensuring the achievement of each subgoal, the member is provided the opportunity to experience success. This experience helps the member avoid fear of rejection and does not allow a confirmation of a low sense of self-worth.

Stage 5: Commitment

The next step in the process requires members to develop a commitment to their plan of action. This is often not an easy task, for each member's identity with failure is strong. Commitment is in the form of a pronouncement (much like a contract) that members have made out loud to the therapist or the group and from which it becomes hard to back out. It necessitates an involvement with another that heretofore was missing. Therapists are aware that members' failure identity had kept them in self-central positions; however, a commitment to change, through implementing a plan of action, creates pressure to move away from an inner-directed self-focus to an outer-directed other-focus. Achieving success can be enhanced because quitting (failing) on a plan of action that has been announced to others would be difficult. It is through commitment, then, that one can reverse the failure identity process and develop a success identity.

STAGE 6: NO EXCUSES ACCEPTED

On the face of it, it would be easy to believe that members may fail to meet their commitment. This is especially so because members have lived failure identities, where commitments and involvement with others were virtually nonexistent. Yet, it is precisely the type of reasoning that could defeat the efforts of the therapist. The therapist must develop a very hard line. Once a commitment is made, no excuse is valid. The members must not be allowed to explore why they have not fulfilled their commitments. Instead, the therapist's actions must state to the members, "I care about you, believe in you, and value you enough that I am not going to buy into allowing you to experience failure again." The objective is not to reduce the tension but to maintain it, so members will learn that the only relief is through positive action. Further, it is precisely at such times that the therapist may say, "Okay, your plan failed, what do you want to do about it now?" In the therapist's response, no acknowledgment was made to explore the excuses or reasons why the plan failed.

If individual members have failed a plan of action, they may need to reassess it to see if it is still realistic. If it is, the plan may require a renewed commitment. If it is not, then an alternate plan, oriented to achieving the same objective, may be needed. Again, the therapist avoids delving into why the first plan did not work but helps members recommit themselves to the new one.

STAGE 7: AVOID PUNISHMENT

Group members who have developed a failure identity have learned to accept punishment. In fact, it might be said that they expect it. It is virtually a form of negative reinforcement, confirming their sense of worthlessness and the belief that no one cares. Therefore, it moves members to avoid involvement with others. The purpose of this stage is to allow members to experience the consequences of failure in order to accomplish their plan of action, learn to take responsibility for it, and learn how to reevaluate the situation free from punitive measure imposed from another.

Glasser wrote about the process of facing reality through this kind of therapy:

> Our basic job as therapists is to become involved with the patient and then get him to face reality. When confronted with reality by the therapist with whom he is involved, he is forced again and again to decide whether or not he wishes to take the responsible path. Reality may be painful, and may be harsh, it may be dangerous, but it changes slowly. All any man can hope to do is to struggle with it in a responsible way by doing right and enjoying the pleasure or suffering the pain that may follow. (1965, p. 50)

Summary

A reality therapy session appears to be more akin to a discussion group than a therapy group. Whereas Gestalt therapy focuses on here-and-now behaviors and client-centered therapy attends to the group's present experiencing, reality therapy attends more to the progress of each group member's efforts to work toward achieving a success identity, by overcoming actions affiliated with non-involvement and low self-worth. The group session is used as an opportunity for each member to move outside and away from a self-centered focus, toward a focus on another. The group therapist acts both as a role model for and facilitator of members to experience a realistic caring involvement with other persons. Through mutual caring and continual focus on developing responsible behaviors, group members are encouraged to assist each other to avoid irresponsible behavior. The group therapist engages in a pedagogical relationship with members, directing discussion and using the influence of the group to help members adhere to group norms (the lack of which was one of the very reasons for a person's difficulty).

By identifying their denial, the group therapist also directly confronts members if they are avoiding responsibility for their behaviors. Again, this therapist action acts as a model for members to involve themselves with another person in a responsible way. The ultimate goal of reality therapy is to help members take what they have learned from their group experience and apply it to other parts of their life.

CHAPTER TEN

Solution-Focused Therapy

Background

Solution-focused therapy (SFT), based originally on the work of Milton Erickson, is an approach that has been traditionally used with individuals and families. This method emphasizes solutions instead of problems and identifies client competencies. The recognition that clients are already using successful solutions conveys an optimistic view of individuals who seek counseling.

As the SFT approach has developed, practitioners, like De Shazer (1985), have found that when clients are asked purposeful questions, when they focus on solutions and what they are doing well, they have success in designing workable solutions. In addition, because the SFT model emphasizes solutions, it tends to be brief in the group setting (LaFountain & Garner, 1996b).

SFT strategies are combined with therapeutic factors to provide positive group experiences whereby clients struggling with a range of issues can gain the assistance they seek. The heterogeneity of client concerns in SFT groups is considered an asset and offers therapists a means to easily place their individual clients into groups, without having to struggle with the logistical problems involved in organizing single-issue groups.

Key Concepts

PRESCREENING

Prescreening is central to SFT groups. During prescreening, clients are introduced to the language of solution-oriented talk. The therapist begins by asking, "What is it you would like to change?" As prospective members respond, the therapist pays close attention to the language used because members will present their beliefs about their situation through language. By engaging in this dialogue, members receive the necessary information to make an informed consent about participating in the group. In addition, prescreening helps the therapist better select members who will gain the most benefit from the group experience. The two major characteristics for inclusion into SFT groups are being amenable to changing themselves (rather than attempting to change others) and being able to articulate an attainable goal for themselves.

During prescreening, members may present a variety of issues or complaints. The therapist looks for such unifying themes as the desire to maintain a more satisfying and enriching life and the need for emotional relief. With these unifying themes present, the therapist can gather together people with a wide range of issues. This view—that there are underlying unifying themes across presenting issues—is basic to the SFT framework. In summary, there are two major tasks in the prescreening process: (1) assessing a member's suitability for working within the solution-focused paradigm and (2) identifying underlying and potentially unifying themes.

SCHEDULING

Scheduling is addressed more easily for SFT groups because the therapist is not trying to organize single-theme groups. In the solution-focused approach, the only logistical challenge is to locate a common time when all people can meet, unlike theme groups where the therapist is trying to search for common times for each population.

MEMBER STRENGTHS

In solution-focused groups, the therapist constantly emphasizes the strengths that each member possesses. Identifying and reinforcing these strengths occur throughout the life of a group. LaFountain and Garner (1996a) believe that by focusing on strengths they minimize the occurrence of such obstacles as labeling of participants, lack of role models, and member confusion or misunderstanding about the group process.

PROCESS GOALS

Process goals are emphasized in solution-focused counseling. There are four criteria for developing process goals: (1) positive expressions of what the member will be doing; (2) statements reflecting the active voice ("I will walk daily"); (3) statements that are realistic and within the member's control; and (4) statements that reflect the member's language.

KEYS

Keys refer to solutions or strategies that members discover and use to address the changes they want to make. In a group setting, members eventually realize through member-to-member discussions that one person's key or strategy can be applied to a variety of situations. When discussing keys the focus is always on what members can use to promote positive change, rather than on what is not working for them individually or in the group setting. *Looking for exceptions* is a key or strategy designed to help members identify exceptions—those times when the member does not experience a particular problem or difficulty. For example, rather than discussing the occasions that do not work for group members, members are asked to state an event or occasion they wish to see continue. This shift from a negative focus to a positive, workable focus becomes a tool for individuals to use in the future. Looking for exceptions can become *skeleton keys*, which are transferable tasks that can be applied to a range of situations.

Therapist Roles and Techniques

In the SFT model, the therapist begins to teach concepts in the prescreening session. Through questions directed at what the individual would like to change, the therapist assesses the individual's willingness to share information in the group and the individual's appropriateness for membership in the group. The therapist engages each prospective member in a dialogue that sets the stage for the nature of exchanges that follow in the actual group setting. Similar to many other group models, SFT groups follow a developmental sequence that mirrors the stages described by Irvin Yalom (1995). These stages are summarized next.

INITIAL STAGE

The first session in this stage extends the discussion that begins in the prescreening interview by asking participants to describe what they wish to change. The therapist points out that although situations may differ across individuals there are many similarities. By addressing the differences and linking together the similarities, participants find that they are not alone. This universality of member experience promotes group cohesiveness (LaFountain & Garner, 1996a).

Besides to the focus on commonalities, the therapist teaches participants how to change language that conveys helplessness to language that is more productive and potent. For example, the participant who states "I'm an overeater" can be helped to rephrase that statement to "I tend to eat too much at times" (Walter & Peller, 1992).

The first session concludes with attention to encouragement and task (De Shazer, 1988). Therapists reinforce members who employ useful and effective statements. Members leave with a task to complete that is directed toward change. In session 2 of this stage, members report on their homework assignments, and through the use of hypothetical questioning they develop process goals.

The initial stage, then, is a time for the therapist to focus on introductions and ground rules, while encouraging and promoting member-to-member interactions and relationships. During this stage, attention is also given to helping members establish their goals for change.

SECOND STAGE

This stage is characterized by conflict and hostility. The hostility can surface when those members who are clear about goals become impatient with those who are more hesitant in identifying or stating their goals. The therapist is likely at this point to pose a question addressed to the group as a whole: "What is occurring in this group that you would like to see happen more?" (LaFountain & Garner, 1996, p. 130). Responses to this question lead members to solutions or keys. As a result, members learn to focus on what they want to continue in the group, rather than on what they do not like. During this stage, the therapist continues to work the group process by making statements directed to the group as a whole and by helping members talk directly to each other.

THIRD STAGE

In this stage, members learn that their individual keys are really common strategies that can be applied to a variety of situations. Through the exchange of solutions or keys, members increase intermember support and cohesiveness.

At this point in the group, members continue maintaining progress toward their goals and providing assistance to those members who are stuck. Action-oriented and specific homework assignments are linked to content covered in the group sessions. In this stage, the therapist works with the group members to determine if subsequent sessions are necessary to address the needs of group members.

Termination is indicated when members make changes that seem durable and when they believe they can operate well on their own (Huber & Backlund, 1991). During termination, group members are asked to share their progress as it relates to their goals and to provide feedback to the leader and to other members.

In summary, the therapist works with the content and process to help members develop connections and resources in the group, while attending to tasks that help them meet their personal and group goals. These groups are brief in nature, and members are encouraged to terminate the group when their goals have been reached. LaFountain and Garner (1996a) note that SFT groups may not reach the intensity of work that Yalom writes about for more mature groups. The structure of SFT groups and the ongoing attention given to the relationships and interactions in the group, however, do promote many of the therapeutic factors presented by Irwin Yalom (1995), including universality, instillation of hope, interpersonal learning, and cohesiveness.

Group Processes

In the SFT group model, strong emphasis is on group process from the beginning of the encounter between therapist and members. The therapist encourages member-to-member interaction through such tasks as introductions, discussions about group norms, and get-acquainted activities. Members share their goals, and the therapist helps members clarify goals while providing commentary on similarities and differences that surface as members interact with each other. Concepts of universality, instillation of hope, and cohesiveness are important to member success in the group. Therefore, the therapist takes an active and intentional role in helping shape an atmosphere where members feel safe and trusting enough to offer their ideas and feedback.

As the group matures, the therapist continues to utilize leader-to-member and leader-to-group statements, which encourage member-to-member interaction. Blockages to work are addressed. For example, the use of exceptions facilitates the group process by the act of naming the problem and then rephrasing it into positive, attainable goals. When members do not like what is happening in the group, the therapist and other members help the disgruntled ones reframe a dislike into a focus on what is working in the group. This strategy has the effect of reducing the incidence of advice giving and the accompanying frustration, which can occur when members want to speed up another member's goal-setting progress.

Homework assignments provide members the opportunity to practice outside the group setting and to bring content to the group for discussion. The therapist is always acknowledging the here-and-now experiences in the group and inviting and encouraging members to give and receive feedback on their behaviors as they seek ways to reach their goals for being in the group. The attention to clear language, to the giving and receiving of feedback, and to the here-and-now actions in the group all promote a constant recognition that how things happen in the group are intertwined with the content. The giving and receiving of feedback is crucial to helping members recognize the generalizability of their keys or solutions to broader issues—for themselves and for others in the group.

Encouragement is promoted throughout the life of the group. For those who are successful in meeting their goals, the therapist acknowledges members' efforts and encourages members to continue their efforts. The therapist asks members who are stuck to focus on aspects of their lives that will help them to continue building on their successes. For members who find themselves in a rut, the therapist encourages them to try something different. Members who have difficulty controlling temptations or urges are invited to pay attention to themselves as they meet up with temptations or urges that interfere with their goal attainment. In all these examples, encouragement is balanced with suggestions. This counseling approach reinforces that all members have strengths to utilize, even when they are struggling.

As SFT groups prepare for termination, the therapist once again enlists the resources in the group. Members are encouraged to review and share their progress toward meeting their goals. They offer feedback to one another and celebrate the changes they have made. As members prepare to depart the group, they reflect on the positive changes they have made as well as obstacles that may face them in the future. In these groups the therapist commonly encourages members to serve as support systems to each other.

Summary

Solution-focused therapy represents a belief that people change through the process of identifying what they are already doing well and building on those strengths and successes (LaFountain, Garner, & Eliason, 1996). Purposeful questioning is one of the strategies used to help people design and develop workable solutions to the problems in their lives. In the group setting, members recognize an action-focused agenda that is intended to promote new ways of thinking about their problems and challenges.

Group work within this approach is action oriented and brief. Groups are formed around multiple issues because this approach believes that the nature of the presenting problem is not a concern for participation in the group. Rather, therapists share the assumption that members' needs for emotional relief and the desire to live a more satisfying and rewarding life are the important and unifying concepts to consider when forming a group. Within this approach then, these multi-issue groups overcome the types of scheduling obstacles found in groups designed around single themes (LaFountain & Garner, 1996b).

Basic to the success of SFT is the attention to solution-oriented talk, hypothetical questioning, and the practice of doing something different. Attending to the here-and-now behavior in the group, encouraging member-to-member interactions, and giving and receiving of support and corrective feedback teach members to use one another as resources and discover ways to generalize their specific solutions to a range of life issues.

These groups tend to be brief, but the focus on group process strengthens the power of the learning possibilities. From the beginning the therapist helps members learn the language and the protocol so that their chances for success are maximized. One strong and consistent theme is the need to teach members about the content of what the group is about as well as the process skills likely to maximize each member's chance of success in the group. SFT counseling has been traditionally used with families and individuals; such groups are being formed increasingly in schools with children and adolescents (LaFountain et al., 1996). As LaFountain and Garner point out, these groups are "a viable alternative for clients who could benefit from a brief model focusing on change and creating solutions" (1996a, p. 10). The attention to prescreening and the identification of potential members who are likely to benefit from this approach will continue to be important as therapists and researchers examine the benefits of SFT groups with a wide range of individuals and presenting concerns.

CHAPTER ELEVEN

Systems-Centered Therapy

Background

Systems-centered therapy (SCT) for groups grew out of an amalgam of Lewin's (1935) field theory, Howard and Scott's (1965) theory of stress, Durkin's (1981) infusion of systems thinking into group therapy (Agazarian, 1997a), and the general systems theory of von Bertalanffy (Agazarian & Janoff, 1993). It is from general systems theory (GST), however, that a large measure of SCT draws its formulation. Therefore, it makes sense for us to digress for a moment in order to present an overview of GST.

Systemic thinking in the social sciences can be traced to the work of Ludwig von Bertalanffy (1968), a biologist who opened the door to applying the laws that governed biological organisms to other broader, larger, and complex systems. His approach was viewed as a challenge to the scientific thinking of the day. He believed scientific investigation had become too reductionistic in its attempt to explain phenomena. He held disdain for the microapproach to scientific inquiry—that is, "the position that in order to understand phenomena, it was best to reduce them to their smallest parts and study those parts in isolation" (Donigian & Malnati, 1997, p. 2). To the contrary, he believed that for seemingly unrelated events to be understood they need to be placed in a context where they are seen as parts of a larger system with which they had interaction or relationship. This was the wellspring from which GST evolved.

It was von Bertalanffy's view of the way systems were organized that caught the attention of social scientists. It was his position that all systems are part of larger systems. Taking this concept further, systems are also structurally similar, albeit in their hierarchical arrangement they may be more complex. Therefore, whether a system is the size of an individual in a work group, the work group itself, or that of the whole corporation, all levels are systemically connected (subsystems within subsystems). Each level of the system (subsystems) is in dynamic interaction with the others, and each is organized in ways that make it similar to the other. This organization is known as the *principle of isomorphy*, and it is central to GST. To fully grasp how a system works, one must observe the *interactive process* taking place among the elements that comprise it. Systemic thinkers consider *how* systems are organized and *how* their parts are interdependently related. They consider all living systems as *open*, meaning they are continually interacting with their environment whether the system is exchanging information (sociological system) or oxygen and carbon dioxide (biological system). More important, adherents of GST are concerned with the *interactive patterns* formed by the relationship of the subsystems within the system and the system with its subsystems. It is the process of this pattern of interaction that becomes the focus of study (Donigian & Malnati, 1997).

Besides the principle of isomorphy, the concept that living systems had the capacity for self-maintenance and governance (regulation) was what truly separated von Bertalanffy's view from the more mechanistic view. This is known as the concept of *equifinality*: Living systems can arrive at a final goal from a variety of directions (i.e., There are many roads to Rome!). Equifinality introduces the notion that choice, empowerment, creative ability, unpredictability, and spontaneity rest within the system.

How to make the transition from GST to group therapy is the challenge that group therapists face. Agazarian (1997a) understood the task to be complex. She credits Helen Durkin's pioneering efforts for applying the principle of isomorphy to group psychotherapy. However, it is still not a group therapy theory; it only forms the "baseline from which to build a group theory" (Agazarian & Janoff, 1993, p. 37). Therefore, SCT intended to not only offer a new approach to group psychotherapy but also provide a new baseline. SCT's principles are designed to be generalizable to all systems. Agazarian holds that SCT serves as a metatheory and that the techniques drawn from it can be applied in other therapeutic approaches.

Agazarian has striven to bridge the gap between the individual system and the group-as-a-whole system. This bridging required to first develop a set of operational definitions of GST's concepts of isomorphy, hierarchy, structure, function, and dynamics that could then be generalizable to the hierarchy of all human systems and then made relevant to group psychotherapy (Agazarian & Janoff, 1993).

Following that, Agazarian (1997a) defined the hierarchy of group therapy, which includes the member system, the subgroup system, and the group-as-a-whole system. It is the isomorphic relationship of all three systems upon which SCT is predicated. She holds that their structures need to be defined in such a manner that to describe one would be to describe the others. And that, ostensibly, is a critical characteristic of isomorphic relationships: Bringing about change in any one of the subsystems will effect a change in all, and touching one subsystem is to touch them all. Therefore, according to Agazarian, in the hierarchical arrangement of the group, it is the subgroup system that plays a pivotal role between the individual-member system and the group-as-a-whole system. The subgroup becomes the "fulcrum for change" (Agazarian & Janoff, 1993, p. 39). When conflicts are raised at any of the system levels, subgroups are formed that relate to addressing either side of the issue. Containing the splits within the subgroups is what makes subgroups functional. Members are forced (by the leader) to choose which side of the issue they wish to explore (not defend). Thus, the focus of the subgroup is on members' similarities and not their differences. This focus leaves individual members free from enacting familiar defense mechanisms (e.g., scapegoating), and members are encouraged to understand one another in the fullest sense of empathy. Functional subgrouping also serves to contain the conflict within the group as a whole. Thus, the task of the group as a whole is made clear.

As each subgroup deepens its exploration of its side of the conflict, it becomes more differentiated, which results ultimately in seeing similarities it holds with the other side. The more this process of accepting differences and acknowledging similarities continues, a new integration evolves in the group as a whole (Agazarian, 1997a). The process also includes a strong pedagogical element at the individual-member-system level. Therapists help members learn the skills (driving forces) to bypass the (restraining) forces that deter them from moving forward to achieving their ultimate goal, which is to effectively live life interdependently with others.

Key Concepts

APPREHENSION

Apprehension is intuitive knowledge that is gained through experience, and it is affectively based. The way it is made known is to translate it into words. Such insight changes peoples' lives, for they have experienced risking to explore the unknown.

COMPREHENSION

Comprehension is cognitive knowledge that is arrived at through thinking and imagining. It is the world already known through words (Agazarian, 1997a, p. 18).

COMMON SENSE

A goal of SCT, common sense is the marriage of apprehension and comprehension, which are subsystems of the individual. It leads a person to live life effectively.

FORK IN THE ROAD

Not only is the fork in the road a major SCT concept, but it is also the primary technique of SCT therapists. (See "Fork in the Road" under "Therapist Roles and Techniques.")

Function

According to Agazarian, the function of all living systems is to survive, develop, and transform from simple to complex systems.

Functional Subgrouping

Functional subgrouping contains the splits within the conflict between that which is known (comprehension) and that which is unknown and yet to be explored (apprehension) within two subgroups, respectively. Such subgrouping allows individual members to fully experience exploration in their respective subgroups without needing to resort to defensive posturing. Because they choose the subgroup and thus the side of the conflict to explore, their initial experience involves exploring similarities with members whose responsibility is to listen empathetically.

Boundarying

Agazarian defines boundarying as "the application of the systems-centered methods and techniques that reduce the restraining forces to communication at the boundaries within, between, and among systems in the hierarchy and increase the probability that information (energy) will be transferred" (1997a, p. 300).

Phases of Group Development

SCT groups have the potential to go through three phases of group development, each of which has subphases. Each phase has its own defenses and provides the context in which each can be addressed. Only certain work can be done in each phase—that is, phase-appropriate work. Therefore, sequencing (tracking phases and subphases) and timing are important therapist tasks as subgroups and members undertake their work. The three primary phases are authority; intimacy; and interdependent love, work, and play (Table 1).

Centering

Agazarian defines centering as "vectoring energy toward the psychophysiological 'center' (physiologically, the diaphragm and lower abdomen), with the intention of accessing spontaneous, apprehensive understanding of the relationship of the self to the context and goals of the present. Centering increases boundary permeability between apprehension and comprehension" (1997a, p. 300).

Role-Lock Defenses

Agazarian defines role-lock defenses as

> module 2 defenses modified in the fight subphase of group development. Defensive projections and projective identifications into one-up-one-down role relationships

(e.g., identified patient and helper; scapegoat and scapegoater, victim and bully, and other defiant/compliant splits that repeat old roles). Symptoms generated: repetitive stereotypical interpersonal relationships at work and at home. (1997a, p. 307)

VECTORING

Vectoring is the directing of work-energy forces across the boundaries toward the goal (Agazarian, 1997a).

RESTRAINING FORCES

Restaining forces are those vectors that oppose or work against the driving forces and reduce boundary permeability to the driving life force. They take forms such as ambiguities, and "always-never" thinking (Agazarian, 1997a).

DRIVING FORCES

Driving forces are those vectors in the force field that direct the life force toward the primary goals of survival, development, and transformation. They take the forms of behaviors that have a positive, "can do" approach to life (Agazarian, 1997a).

PARTNERSHIP

In SCT groups the therapist governs the structure of therapy and confronts the member with a series of forced choices between exploring the defense itself or what is being defended against. Such choices are referred to as the *fork in the road*. The member determines which fork in the road he or she will take. The therapist does not make the choice for the member; the choice of whether or not to explore the known or unknown road is the member's. This process in which the therapist presents the choices and places the categorical decision to be made before the member; and then in turn leaves up to the member to decide which road to follow, is considered a partnership.

TREATMENT PLAN

SCT is a systematic approach to problem resolution. Therefore, the treatment plan is a systematic step-by-step process that works toward undoing defenses in the systemic hierarchy of the individual member by employing the functional subgroup technique.

RESONANCE/RESONATING

In some ways, resonance/resonating refers to the congruence of affective experience that exists (occurs) with each of the system levels—self with self, self with the subgroup, and self with the group as a whole. It is considered to be the criterion for joining a subgroup.

TABLE 1 **SCT modifications of restraining forces to group development**
From Agazarian (1997b).

Subphase issues	Restraining forces modified	Symptoms modified
	Phase one of group development: Authority	
	Social defenses (module one) Stereotypic social communication	Inauthenticity
Flight subphase The identified patient	**The triad of symptomatic defenses (module one)** 1. Cognitive distortions and worrying that divert attention from reality testing 2. Tension generating stress-related psychosomatic defenses, which avoid the experience of emotion	Anxiety Tension Psychosomatic symptoms
Transitional subphase between flight and fight Indirect scapegoating	3. Defending against the retaliatory impulse by constricting it in depression or discharging it in hostile acting-out	Masochistic depression Sadistic and hostile acting-out
Fight subphase Intermember scapegoating	**Role-lock defenses (module two)** Creating one-up/one-down role relationships	Reciprocal maladaptive role pairing
Transitional subphase between authority and intimacy Scapegoating authority Negative transference	**Resistance to change defenses (module three)** 1. Externalizing conflicts with authority: defensive stubbornness and suspicion from the righteous and complaining position 2. Disowning authority; defensive stubbornness and suspicion of self that blames personal incompetence	Role suction into interdependent roles of victim, victims' victim, and abuser Crisis of hatred Resistance to reality

TABLE 1 *(continued)*

Subphase issues	Restraining forces modified	Symptoms modified
	Phase two of group development: Intimacy	
Enchantment and hope subphase Idealized transference Cultism	**Defenses against separation (module four)** Enchantment, idealization, blind trust of others, merging, and love addiction as a defenses against differences	Idealization Cultism Dependency at the expense of interdependence and exploitability
Disenchantment and despair subphase Alienation Existential despair	**Defenses against individuation (module four)** Disenchantment and blind mistrust of self, others, and groups; alienation, contempt, and despair as a defense against similarities	Despair Independence at the expense of functional dependency and interdependence
	Phase three of group development: Interdependent love, work, and play	
Ongoing phases of work in the *experienced group* Interdependence	**Defenses against knowledge (module five)** Defenses against inner reality and comprehensive and apprehensive knowledge **Defenses against common sense (module five)** Defenses against outer reality and reality testing	Impairment of decision making and implementation abilities; loss of common sense and humor Self-centeredness at the expense of both self and the environment

Therapist Roles and Techniques

SCT group therapists are not shy and are expected to maintain a high profile. This is especially the case when a group is being formed for the first time. This may not be the same for a group that is being formed of persons who have had SCT group experience. Such groups can be expected to skip the early phases of group-as-a-whole development. Thus, the degree to which the therapist is visible can be expected to be less than when a group is composed of members with no SCT group experience.

Leaders are faced with three primary tasks that Agazarian (1997a) states as requisite during the first few minutes of SCT groups. Attending to these tasks will determine how the group will develop. They are as follows:

1. Drawing boundaries that will define the group
2. Directing the energy from outside the group into the group and focusing it on the goals
3. Developing systems-centered members, subgroups, and the systems-centered group as-a-whole, which will introduce the way of working that characterizes an SCT group (p. 53)

Agazarian (1997a) believes that those therapists who have been schooled to respect the defenses of each member may actually be doing so at the expense of the member. SCT therapists, on the other hand, are encouraged to "immediately bring defenses to their patients' attention while simultaneously teaching them the skills they need in order to modify the identified defenses" (p. 39). She found that defenses are sequentially ordered and modulized them (five modules) according to the phases of group development. Therapists need to not only contextualize the defense according to the phase of group development but also recognize the sequential order of the defense being presented and be consciously aware that the presented defense is one that the individual can change.

The roles of SCT group therapists include having them

> humanize, normalize, legitimize, and depathologize defenses; help patients learn to state the obvious, use common sense, discover reality, and contain the potential work energy in frustration rather than discharge it or constrict it; and insure that patients always recognize the fork in the road and understand the choices available to them. (Agazarian, 1997a, p. 39)

Interpreting individual psychology is frowned upon. Rather, therapists are to reframe and contextualize conflicts, helping SCT group members to see themselves and their human conflict as a system "that exists only in context of the here-and-now environment" (Agazarian, 1997a, p. 39).

When considering techniques that are available to the group therapist, we need to keep in mind that, perhaps more so in SCT groups than in any other, techniques are not the *sole* province of the therapist; members learn to implement immediately at the individual system level, subgroup system level, and the group-as-whole system level. Also important to remember is that the concept of isomorphy is ever present: The hierarchical arrangement of systems includes the individual member, subgroup, and group as a whole, which in turn is the paradigm SCT therapists follow.

FUNCTIONAL SUBGROUPING

Functional subgrouping

is a conflict resolution technique in which members are deliberately encouraged to form subgroups around two (or more) sides of a conflict. Conflict is thus split and contained in the group-as-a-whole rather than within its members. Subgroup members work together within their own subgroup, to explore their similarities (rather than to scapegoat group differences). As each subgroup works, members discover differences in the apparent similarities within their own subgroups, and then recognize similarities between the different subgroups. As similarities in the apparently different subgroups are recognized, integration takes place in the group-as-a-whole. (Agazarian, 1997b)

BOUNDARYING

Boundarying

is the application of the systems-centered methods and techniques that reduce the defensive restraining forces to communication at the boundaries within, between and among systems in the hierarchy, and increase the probability that information (energy) will be transferred. Boundarying is done by modifying defenses at the boundaries of space, time, reality, and role. Defense modification in SCT is a predetermined sequence of SCT methods and techniques which systemically undo defenses against the intrapersonal and interpersonal communications of experience in the context of the phases of group development. (Agazarian, 1997b)

VECTORING

Vectoring is the directing of

working energy across the boundaries towards the goal. A vector is like an arrow in flight, which has a direction, a force and a target or goal (point of application). Driving and restraining forces are vectors with opposing goals. When behavior is framed in terms of vectors, then all behavior is interpreted as a vectorial output of the system that diagnoses the direction in which the system is traveling, the amount of energy (motivation) for the journey and the goal direction that the system is traveling. (Agazarian, 1997b)

EYE CONTACT

Besides verbal transactions, visual transaction is elevated to a primary means for communication across the boundaries between systems. The intention is to require "individual members to cross the internal time boundaries from there and then to here and now" (Agazarian & Janoff, 1993, p. 41). Not only are members being asked to be aware of what is behind their own internal boundaries, but they also learn to develop an understanding (empathy) for what is behind the eyes of the other. Mind reading and psychologizing of others is avoided; as a result, members can learn how to be with one another in the fullest sense.

FORK IN THE ROAD

The fork in the road is the forced choice that SCT members are given at the direction of the therapist. The first choice is between explaining (comprehension) and exploring (apprehension). Finally, choice is made between exploring defenses against reality versus discovering the reality of experience, conflicts, or impulses that the member defends against. Agazarian (1997a) adds that the "journey is to be experienced rather than explained." The fork in the road is the major technique employed by SCT group therapists.

CONTEXTUALIZING

Contextualizing is the

> capacity to see more than one context at a time. In SCT, individuals experience themselves in the context of the member, subgroup, and group-as-a-whole systems. Contextualizing requires the vectoring of energy into the roles and goals that are appropriate to the different system of the hierarchy. (Agazarian, 1997a, p. 30)

CONTAINING

Containing occurs when members "increase their sense of self by staying in resonance with themselves until they can resonate with others" (Agazarian, 1997a, p. 35).

Group Processes

Perhaps the way to view the process of SCT groups is at first to witness the way therapists create the partnership between themselves and group members. This is a crucial moment in the life of the group. It is important for members to realize at the outset—that with the exception of governing the structure of therapy, which is the therapist's responsibility—that they each are responsible for the choices they make: whether to explore their defenses or what the defenses are defending against. This fork in the road is what therapists confront the individual members with early on. Members are faced with a forced choice; they *must* explore either one or the other side of the split.

Contextualizing therapeutic work to the appropriate subphase of system development is of paramount importance. Therapists need to ensure that each member's work is completed before moving on to the succeeding subphase (see Table 1). Because all new members (to SCT thinking) arrive to the group in their self-centered system, the therapist's task is to help members develop a member role. This role leads members to seeing or viewing themselves as part of a subgroup system. As members of a subgroup, they also learn to see how they and their subsystem are also part of the group-as-a-whole system. This awareness leads to "changing the context of experience for group members from the self-centered system to the self-centered system in the systems-centered context" (Agazarian, 1997a, pp. 33–34).

SCT therapists direct the focus and work of each system in the hierarchy throughout the three phases of group development (see Table 1). They employ the techniques of subgrouping, boundarying, and vectoring. Collectively, these techniques comprise the "blueprint" for building an SCT group. Therapists need to ensure that the work to be done is phase appropriate and need to follow the *four-step process* (presented in the following paragraphs) involved in developing an SCT group. The steps are sequentially ordered, and maintaining the sequence is critical to group development. To abort or not follow the four steps of the process would result in the SCT group not being formed or not being fully functional if formed.

1. **Structuring the Observing System From the Self-Centered System.** Agazarian (1997a) refers to the observing system as the "eye" of the self-centered system. As in most groups, members arrive viewing themselves as central, for they have not yet developed the perspective of simultaneously relating to the self and the group. Therefore, the therapist will help each member learn to observe the self from a systems-centered perspective. This involves learning to distinguish between comprehensive (cognitive) and apprehensive (intuitive/affective) knowledge. This is a most crucial skill for members to develop. It enables them to recognize the difference between their (spontaneous and intuitive) emotional responses to reality and those emotional responses resulting from their interpretation (intellectual/cognitive processing) of reality.

2. **Structuring the Member System from the Observing System.** The primary goal or task here is for members to increase the ability to resonate with their intrasystemic selves and the intersystem of the group. Resonating requires that they "(1) bring their member system into being by vectoring energy toward the emotional (apprehensive) part of the self and (2) contain the energy while they experience resonance, first with themselves and then with a subgroup" (Agazarian, 1997a, p. 34).

3. **Structuring the Subgroup System from the Member System.** Ostensibly, this means forming the functional subgroup, a central moment in the development of SCT groups. Unless each person experiences the process of developing or joining a *functional subgroup*, a systems-centered group will not be formed. The formation of the boundary between the *member system* and the *subgroup system* occurs at the moment when resonance is established between the individual member's emotions and those of the subgroup. This is when members realize the connection between experience and context; changing context affects the way one experiences.

This step also is pivotal because members begin emphasizing their similarities as opposed to their differences with others. Thus, through resonating, members are brought into contact with others who may form a potential subgroup. Through the formation of subgroups, a structure is presented for encouraging members to feel secure to not only maintain their sense of connection with their individuality but also feel connected to their subgroup, regardless of what else may be occurring in the group as a whole. The formation of this important structure is what creates the boundary of the subgroup. Ultimately, this formation leads to members feeling free to have differing experiences as they move from one context to another. This sense of empowerment occurs as a person learns the skills for leaving a self-centered world (Agazarian, 1997a).

4. **Structuring the Group-as-a-Whole System From the Subgroup System.** The subgroup systems comprise the group as a whole. The process of subgrouping brings group as a whole into existence. Individual-member conflict is transferred and contained in the group as a whole where integration of information takes place. It is here where members simultaneously experience a relatively conflict-free resonance between themselves and their subgroups, while working in the whole "group environment that explores and integrates what generated the conflicts rather than splitting them off and rejecting them" (Agazarian, 1997a, pp. 35–36).

We know this step has been achieved when individual members engage in behaviors that demonstrate they are transitioning from a self-centered to a system-centered focus. Members become more consciously aware of the context in which they exist and realize it is the context that determines what they can realistically achieve at any moment in time (Agazarian, 1997a).

The four-step structuring process is not to be confused with the three phases through which SCT groups develop. The former refers to construction of the group; the latter refers to the stages of group development, which are based on transitioning from authority to intimacy to interdependent love, work, and play. The process of SCT groups can be followed as the individual-member system faces the conflicts that are characteristic of the phase or subphase of group development. Once again, it is important to underscore that therapists must ensure that the issues members address are appropriate for the subphase and phase to which the group has developed.

As the group progresses through each phase, the methods and techniques for managing the defenses that occur are sequence specific (i.e., designed to modify the defenses that are presented for the phase or subphase at that moment). Agazarian (1997a) introduces a five module approach to defense modification. Therapists intentionally work to help members *explore* and *understand* the underlying motives of their defenses, as opposed to impulsively acting them out. To achieve this end, therapists make certain that each module of defense modification is phase specific, sequentially developing from simple to more complex defenses. By doing so, the group's equilibrium will be maintained.

The last point needs to be amplified. Unlike most other therapies, SCT does not encourage the heightening of anxiety and acting-out behaviors that are manifestations of defense mechanisms. The therapist is to help members recognize the split within their conflict, and the defense itself, and then force members to choose on which side of the split they wish to work. The fork-in-the-road choice then has a member joining with others who may hold a similar view; thus, the subgroups are formed within which the respective sides of the issue are explored. The ultimate goal is to lead members to a point where they can recognize and understand that how they experience their world is based on how they choose to view themselves in it. The world itself will not change; however, should they change the way they perceive themselves in it, not only will their way of experiencing it change but also their behavior. Considering this in a systemic context, we then can see how a change in one part of the system might then influence the system above it, and so on.

Perhaps the words of a Chasidic Rabbi (1970) on his death bed offers us another context from which to experience SCT:

> When I was young I set out to change the world. When I grew a little older I perceived that this was too ambitious so I set out to change my state. This, too, I realized as I grew older was too ambitious, so I set out to change my town. When I realized I could not even do this, I tried to change my family. Now as an old man I know that I should have started by changing myself. Had I started with myself, maybe then I would have succeeded in changing my family, the town, or even the state—and who knows, maybe even the world?!

Summary

Systems-centered therapy for groups is a very structured and systematic approach to helping individuals release the forces for change. Based on a theory of *living* human systems, the origins can be traced to general systems theory. The principle of isomorphy and the hierarchical arrangement of systems are central to SCT. It means that systems are structurally, functionally, and dynamically similar from the simplest to the most complex. Furthermore, an intrasystemic and intersystemic interdependence, which is arranged in a hierarchical order, allows each system to influence or to be influenced by the system immediately above it or below it. Accordingly, SCT groups develop along a three-phase path from authority and intimacy to interdependent love, work, and play. Each has its subphases and modules for tickling out the defenses to be explored, according to the phase of development. Exploration of defenses is conducted by members joining or creating functional subgroups. Members learn how to come together and explore their similarities on their respective sides of the issue (conflict/defense) rather than separating over their differences. Through the methods of boundarying and vectoring, members learn how to systematically dismantle their defenses and to redirect their energy in ways that ultimately lead to helping them reach their own and the group's goals.

SCT group members are encouraged to explore their impulses in their subgroups, rather than acting them out or explaining them. Thus, overt behaviors such as scapegoating are unlikely to occur in a group. Members learn to move from solely a self-centered orientation to a self-centered within-a-system orientation of the environment. By recontextualizing the self in this manner, one learns that the way one experiences the environment depends on how one perceives himself or herself in it. These perceptions of self place the power back to the individual. Having such choices leads to empowerment of the individual.

The role of the SCT therapist is active, directing, and controlling. The therapist is responsible for controlling the structure of therapy by bringing the defenses to the attention of each group member. At that moment, each member is faced with a fork in the road—to explore the defense itself or what is being defended against. The therapist helps each member learn the skills of subgrouping, boundarying, and vectoring (contextualizing) to effectively deal with the conflict. However, at no time does the therapist tell a member which choice to make; that responsibility remains with the member.

Ultimately, the goal of SCT is to help individuals "regain their common sense, their sense of proportion and their cosmic sense of humor, as well as their ability to access the joy (and the pain) of living in the here-and-now" (Agazarian, 1997a, p. 297).

CHAPTER TWELVE

Transactional Analysis

Background

At the moment of birth, infants automatically adopt a healthy attitude toward both themselves and others—an attitude of basic trust and worthiness, which transactional analysis (TA) describes as "I'm Okay—You're Okay." Thereafter, however, that view is continually modified according to their interactions (transactions) with others. Until approximately age 6—while children are in the initial stages of building this personal view of themselves and their world— their personality is most easily influenced. After that time, their energies are channeled primarily into activities and behavior designed to confirm and reinforce this learned viewpoint.

Such is the basic position taken by Eric Berne, generally agreed to be the creator of this approach to human development and change. Berne, a psychiatrist trained in analytic procedures, developed and organized his ideas in the early 1950s. With the help of interested colleagues in his home area of San Francisco, he refined and modified these ideas, which soon began to influence other mental health workers in other parts of the country and world. Finally, in 1966, four years before his untimely death, Berne formally applied his approach to the group mode in his book *Principles of Group Treatment.*

The success of TA is perhaps most attributable to its practical emphasis on actual behavior and applied concepts, in contrast to the more traditional psychiatric emphasis on the unconscious and inferential aspects of personality. What can be *seen* and *explained* in terms that are personally meaningful in day-to-day living is certainly more likely to be accepted by people than the more complicated and mysterious elements of psychoanalysis. The TA prcoess explains a large part of the general acceptance of this approach.

TA's approach to personality development stresses that growing children have both physiological and psychological needs, each of which requires transactions with others in order to be met. In their earliest years, when the development of their self-esteem and other-esteem is most pliable and easily influenced, these "others" are primarily adults, usually the parents. If their transactions with these adults are in keeping with the reinforcement of the "I'm Okay—You're Okay" life view, children develop into reasonably healthy adults, able to initiate and sustain productive relationships.

However, if the transactions are of a nature that suggests a more negative view of the self and the world, other life views may become dominant in a child's mind. Perhaps the most socially destructive view is "I'm Okay—You're Not Okay." This individual's earliest transactions with significant adults may have been so punishing that the outside world can only be seen in negative terms when compared with oneself. Some degree of obnoxious, antisocial, revengeful, and perhaps paranoid behavior can be the result of such an outlook.

A third life view, "I'm Not Okay—You're Not Okay," is a viewpoint centered in despair and hopelessness. Not only may one's earliest transactions have encouraged and reinforced an outlook of unworthiness about oneself, but also the whole rest of the world may in fact look lousy. Depression, boredom, and a general lack of energy and enthusiasm might well characterize someone with this life attitude.

The fourth life view, "I'm Not Okay—You're Okay," may well be the prevalent outlook in our social system and perhaps even most socially productive. Probably not as personally fulfilling or relaxing as the basic birth outlook of "We're All Okay," this view can create a competitive, striving personality, anxious to contribute to society in a way that gains the feeling of "Okayness" attributed to others but not oneself.

Unfortunately, to gain that feeling of worthiness in comparison to others, most of us resort to playing social "games" that are uniquely and idiosyncratically designed to give us the "strokes" we believe are needed for our psychological survival. The strokes we attempt to get, through manipulation and game playing in our transactions with others, are in accord with the view that we learned through our earliest transactions with others.

Strokes, in TA terms, are simply indications from outside sources that one is a unique human being, that one counts in some way, that one has an impact on his or her world, and that one's life has some individual meaning. If an individual has come to believe that he or she is basically "Not Okay," then the strokes that are sought may well be negative ones; that is, the games that are created and played will be programmed to reward the individual with a reinforcement of the existing feelings of unworthiness. The search for strokes is an essential aspect of everyone's makeup and can have positive, negative, or mixed elements. Because this search is action oriented, in that it requires transactions with others, it can be observed and analyzed so that one's basic life view may be identified by others who are aware of such processes. Both insight and actual behavior, then, are cornerstones of the TA model, and both are vital to the proper functioning of a TA group.

The need for outside sources of reinforcement to reaffirm one's basic life position necessitates the structuring of one's time to actively seek those strokes. TA identifies six basic avenues that are useful, though not necessarily healthy, in this endeavor.

1. *Withdrawal.* An individual may withdraw into his or her own fantasy world and thereby provide to oneself those strokes not found in the outside world. Such a withdrawal from transactions with others in favor of talking to and stroking oneself is tantamount to an isolationist position and hardly conducive to a healthy personality when carried to extremes.
2. *Rituals.* The use of rituals also provides us the means to gain strokes. Even such an automatic response as "How are you today?" indicates a real, though perhaps superficial, recognition of one's personhood; such rituals may take on even greater importance when they are withheld, as when one is snubbed. Unimportant as such transactions may first appear, they often represent highly significant strokes to people who structure their time largely in an effort to obtain such ritualistic responses.
3. *Pastimes.* Pastimes represent another significant avenue for gaining attention and recognition. "Passing the time of day" might be a way to paraphrase this method. It would include various types of discussion sessions about such external issues as politics, sports, and economics. Entering into such discussions may give one a sense of belonging, being cared about, being listened to, and being considered important enough to be talked with.
4. *Activities.* Another way of putting oneself in a position to gain strokes is through activities of various kinds. Our work is one such activity, but participation in sporting events or organizations may be even more valuable to some individuals. The transactions that take place while engaging in such activities may be vital to the affirmation of many and may be accomplished verbally, nonverbally, or paralinguistically (tone of voice, hesitation of speech, or emphasis of certain words).
5. *Games.* Perhaps the most discussed but least understood or recognized form of stroke getting is through the use of games, which Berne has often humorously but meaningfully detailed in *Games People Play* (1964). These games are designed by the participants to result in victories according to the basic life position of "Okayness" that each participant holds. For example, if an individual's series of transactions (which make up a game) conveys both direct and subtle messages of a controlling nature, then the recipients of such messages must desire to get *their* strokes by being controlled. If these recipients cannot get the strokes to match their perceptions of their life position in this way, they will cease to respond according to the rules of the sender's game, and that game will end. Those individuals who see game playing as their primary means for receiving strokes will then seek out other persons more willing to play by their rules, and for whom those rules will provide the strokes they deem necessary to continue their "racket" of basic life view. The recognition and analysis of such maneuvering—which takes place through transactions within the group—is a vital part of the therapeutic strategy of TA counseling.

6. *Intimacy.* The final avenue for receiving strokes is intimacy, which Berne sharply distinguishes from pseudointimacy (Berne, 1966, pp. 231–232). According to Berne, real intimacy is a game-free exchange of transactions, affective and spontaneous in nature. Such exchanges rarely occur in group settings, perhaps due to the inability of most participants to program themselves internally when they respond, as contrasted with considering how they will "look" in front of others. This tendency of individuals to inhibit themselves (which comes from socialization experiences) takes away from the authenticity of the transaction and thus becomes another game. Real intimacy is perhaps its own reward in that it provides strokes on an "I'm Okay—You're Okay" basis.

These six methods constitute the means by which individuals structure their time in order to put themselves in the most advantageous positions to receive the amounts and kinds of strokes they feel they need to reinforce and confirm their destiny and role in life. This life script (personality) in turn was prepared primarily in the first few years of life, through transactions of both a verbal and nonverbal nature with the external world. How individuals use their personalities to conduct transactions with others is explained in terms of ego-states.

All individuals contain three such ego-states: Child, Parent, and Adult. These ego-states represent the dominant forces affecting an individual's behaviors at any given moment. An understanding of these ego-states and how they function in transactions between group members, and between group members and the group leader, is necessary to the proper functioning of a TA group. Because transactions of individuals with the outside world (as represented by significant others in one's group) both determine and reinforce their lifestyle, as exhibited in behavior and personality, it is understandable why TA proponents put such a premium on group therapy, where here-and-now transactions can be immediately recognized and analyzed. The insight acquired through such group analysis enables each individual to make the desired behavior changes.

Key Concepts

Ego-States

According to TA principles, each of us is driven, at different times and in different places, by one of three internal command stations known as Child, Parent, and Adult. Although these ego-states may be aware of each other's existence, only one of them can be in charge at any given moment. The commands given by these ego states are also very different, and internal challenges will occasionally arise for dominance in a given situation.

The Child is the first ego-state to develop and is in fact inherent at birth in the form of the Natural Child. The Natural Child is a subpart of the Child ego-state and represents the uncontrolled, untrained, undisciplined, and nonsocialized part of the personality—the part that totally seeks its own spontaneous pleasure, without regard to social dictates. Soon after birth, however, the infant must begin to curb some of these natural tendencies and adapt to the demands of more powerful others. This develops into the Adapted Child—that part of the personality responding to training, learning, and authority. A third part of the Child ego-state, known as the Little Professor, begins to develop during the preschool years. The behavior of this aspect of the Child reflects the beginning of rational, logical, evaluative thinking and is the forerunner of such behavior in the Adult ego-state. According to TA, the Child ego-state is the most significant part of the personality because it is the foundation upon which self-esteem is built.

The Parent ego-state is well developed by the time a child enters school. It represents the assimilated dictates of right and wrong and appropriateness that all children acquire through messages from parents and other authority figures. It is sometimes all too recognizable by parents who see their own questionable behaviors and verbalizations mimicked by their young children. Such messages are internalized and often carried into adulthood, regardless of their objective accuracy. Prejudices and traditions are passed from generation to generation in this way because the Parent ego-state is nonperceptive and nonthinking. It assumes the truth of past mandates and judgments and acts similarly to a conscience. It is as if we have tape recordings being played over and over in our heads; to the extent to which these recordings shut out current, more accurate information, they may be destructive. Parent material contains elements from all three ego-states of one's own parents, as well as from other significant adults in our past—all of whom received *their* parental mandates from the three ego-states of important people in *their* background, and so on.

As indicated earlier, the Child's Little Professor is the earliest forerunner of the Adult ego-state. The Adult is that part of the personality that assimilates and evaluates information, makes decisions, and deals in facts, logic, questions, and outcomes. It is rational and bases its behavior on current data it has collected. Unlike the Parent and Child ego-states, which focus mostly on emotions and the past, the Adult's emphasis is cognitive and current. Because the most impersonal Adult ego-state is usually more acceptable to others in interpersonal transactions, the Child and Parent states sometimes try to disguise themselves as Adults in an attempt to deliver a message with as little risk as possible. For example, a teenager, upon arriving home late at night, might be asked this outwardly Adult question from his or her parents: "What time were you supposed to be home?" Chances are, however, that it is the parent's *Parent* ego-state doing the talking and that the real message is "You're late! And I want an explanation!" The receiver will likely see through the disguise, though, and the subsequent responses will indicate whether or not a game is about to be played.

All three ego-states are useful at different times; the appropriateness of their use, according to the situation, is the key criterion. Overuse of any one or two to the exclusion of another can be detrimental to interpersonal functioning.

EXCLUSION AND CONTAMINATION

The terms *exclusion* and *contamination* relate to the malformation and malfunction of the ego-states described above. In some cases, usually due to inadequate parenting, individuals get stuck in one or two ego-states and have great difficulty activating the other(s). The exclusion of an ego-state greatly increases the chances of such individuals being avoided, chastised, or patronized in situations where the activation of the excluded ego-state(s) would be appropriate. In other cases the ego-states may not be adequately separated within the personality structure, causing such rapid changes from one to another that an observer might question the stability of such an individual. Ideally, the ego state will be flexible enough be to called upon without too much delay but without being so fluid that it becomes difficult to distinguish one from another.

Contamination occurs when one ego-state gains too much influence over another. Usually, this happens when the Child or Parent intrudes upon the Adult. For example, contamination has occurred when it is appropriate for the Adult to assess a situation objectively, but objectivity is clouded by a bias that has been accepted as fact but which in reality represents a strong Parental prejudice.

TRANSACTIONS

As indicated earlier, transactions are attempts to gain the recognition and attention considered necessary for physiological survival. Such transactions begin at the moment of birth and continue thereafter as the desire for psychological stroking gains greater emphasis as persons approach adulthood. For the most part, however, adults desire strokes to confirm the life view of "Okayness" that they formed as very young children. Young children's transactions form the personality basis that they will attempt to confirm in adulthood. Therefore, individuals' earliest transactions are obviously much more significant to their development than are the later ones that may well serve as reinforcers of rigidity. When looked upon in this manner, it is not difficult to understand (1) why group members will go to great lengths to avoid change and (2) how game playing contributes to that avoidance behavior. The recognition and analysis of such games thus becomes the heart and soul of the process in a TA group.

The interactions, or transactions, that occur between people are three basic types: complementary, crossed, or ulterior (crooked). These transactions result from whichever ego-state is in control of a person's behavior at a given time.

When clear messages are emitted from an ego-state that is clearly recognized by both sender and receiver and when the receiver responds from the appropriate ego-state, the transaction is said to be *complementary*. For example, if person A makes an Adult remark to person B's Adult ego-state and the latter responds with an Adult remark (Adult ego-state to Adult ego-state), there has been a complementary transaction, and communication is likely to continue.

However, if person A sends a message from the Adult ego-state to person B's Adult ego-state, but B's Parent or Child ego-state responds, then there has been a *crossed* transaction, and communication is likely to deteriorate or end. In this case, at least one of the participants may become confused, angry, or suspicious, and because the transaction has produced strokes for only one of the players, the unrewarded person will desire to structure his or her time in different ways.

An *ulterior* transaction occurs when a significant message is being sent at a subtle or hidden level, alongside another message being sent at a clear and open level. In other words, the most important message is disguised to lessen the risk for the sender (and perhaps for the receiver, if both understand the game being played). If the sender's disguised message is uncovered and if it should prove to be embarrassing or somehow destructive, then the sender can always find a defense in that the *actual words spoken* clearly conveyed an innocent message. Often the hidden message is emitted through nonverbal gestures, facial expressions, or tone of voice, making it very difficult to "convict" one or both communicators in terms of their intentions.

GAMES

Though the concept of games was described in an earlier section, it needs further recognition here because it plays an important role in TA. Berne described a game as "a series of ulterior transactions with a gimmick, leading to a usually well-concealed but well-defined payoff" (1966, p. 207). Since the acquisition of strokes is a basic motivation of TA theory, games are only played when all players are receiving the strokes they need to confirm their accepted life position. "In effect, there are no real losers in games that people play with one another; both partners receive the payoff they seek" (Hansen, Warner, & Smith, 1976, p. 189). The importance of games and game analysis in TA groups has been further noted by Berne in his discussion of time-structuring options open to people in their quest for strokes: "Since the experienced transactional therapist will quickly break up rituals and pastimes to move on to games, and since, on the other hand, real intimacy rarely occurs in groups, most of the proceedings of transactional groups will consist of games and game-analysis" (1966, p. 231).

SCRIPT AND COUNTERSCRIPT

Once individuals have begun to solidify their life position (feelings of personal "Okayness" in comparison to the rest of the world), they make life plans to fit that perception. This script is similar to that of a play in which the actor knows how the play is to conclude and works diligently to behave throughout the play in a manner appropriate to that predetermined ending (life position). In real life, however, the script is usually an unconscious plan, although the individual may be just as diligent as the actor in making it come out according to the script. Unfortunately, such scripts are commonly written in early childhood, when the individual is quite incapable of making such serious and often tragic commitments.

If growing children are subjected to a significant number of important ulterior transactions, they may develop alternate scripts to use upon occasion. That is, if inconsistent, garbled, or misunderstood messages were received or if they were told one rule but saw an opposing rule modeled, a counterscript might result. At times, then, in trying to implement *everything* taught, individuals could take on a Jekyll-Hyde character that would permit the inclusion of contradictory parental mandates and injunctions.

Therapist Roles and Techniques

To function most effectively, the TA group therapist must be authentic, genuine, and a skillful diagnostician and analyzer. Neither by itself is enough.

Even though TA is a therapist-centered approach, therapists' authenticity must communicate humility, equality, and openness. They should be able to model behavior that they expect of members, such as a strong commitment and sense of responsibility to the group and to any contracts that have been agreed on. Within this basically democratic demeanor, therapists are free to be themselves. Though certain techniques have been found to be especially useful to many TA therapists, they are in no way restricted from creating their own techniques as well.

Besides the personal characteristics, therapists must be highly skilled in the collection and evaluation of group data; therefore, they must have well-developed powers of observation and interpretation. They must be astute and active listeners to the group's messages, as well as skilled at analyzing ego-states, transactions, games, and scripts; they must also be able to transmit those skills to group members so that the members can help each other, rather than rely solely on the therapist.

It is common for TA therapists to use a chalkboard as an aid in explaining the analytic concepts exhibited in group interactions. Using the chalkboard serves two purposes: It provides clarity to group transactions, and it helps the group achieve the Adult state by enabling members to rationally scrutinize their transactions as they appear on the board.

In one of his essays on group treatment, Berne (1966) devoted an entire chapter to "The First Three Minutes" of the group encounter, indicating his emphasis on setting an appropriate climate and direction. Berne believed that this time was the most important in the therapy process. And, because TA is highly therapist centered, it is the therapist's responsibility to develop a comfortable atmosphere and to determine a positive direction.

Berne wrote that, "for the group therapist to be the master of his own destiny requires a commitment which misses no opportunity to learn, uses every legitimate method to win, and permits no rest until every loss has been thoroughly analyzed so that no mistake will ever be repeated" (1966, p. 75).

Interrogation

At times the group leader needs more information from a member in order to analyze the member's feelings or behavior. The therapist then merely asks a straightforward question of the member's Adult ego-state and hopes for a clear, Adult response. Such questioning provides direction to the session, aids in data collection, and models Adult behavior. However, it is important *neither* to get more information than is immediately needed *nor* use this technique if the member's Child or Parent is likely to respond. Otherwise, the member may seize the therapist's questioning as an opportunity to play games.

SPECIFICATION

The object of specification, Berne wrote, "is to fix certain information in his [the therapist's] mind and in the patient's mind, so that it can be referred to later in more decisive therapeutic operations" (1966, p. 234). In other words, when therapists seem reasonably confident that a member will accept their statements about demonstrated behavior, the therapist can then verbally clarify and formalize that finding, for later use. It is important not to engage in such specification if the member is likely to deny it later or if it has not been sufficiently determined (in which case it might well lead to a sidetracking argument or to a psychoanalytic game).

CONFRONTATION

The therapist uses confrontation to point out inconsistencies between current behavior and behavior that has previously been analyzed and specified. Its objective is to stir the member and to gain a response from the uncontaminated Adult. If the confrontation has been well timed and worded well, the result will usually be a thoughtful pause or an insightful laugh, both of which are deemed therapeutic.

EXPLANATION

Explanation by the therapist to a member represents an effort to interact with and strengthen a member's Adult ego-state. Explanations should be brief and to the point; if previous transactions have properly prepared members to accept the explanation in their Adult ego-states, then some significant cognitive learning can transpire.

ILLUSTRATION

To loosen up the members while still transmitting an important message, the therapist uses illustration as a humorous follow-up to a successful confrontation. It is intended for the member's Adult consumption, while being certain that the Child is also listening and appreciative of the humor. In this process, the Parent must remain in the background and not interfere. The illustration can be a humorous anecdote dealing with issues external (but relevant) to the group, or it can be an internal focus of comparisons within the group. Illustrations can immediately follow a successful confrontation or can be brought up several weeks later, depending on the nature of the situation.

CONFIRMATION

Even though a member's Adult ego-state may have been strengthened and stabilized through confrontation and perhaps illustration, the Child does not give up inconsistent behavior and thoughts easily, and most will return at some point. When they do, they serve to confirm the therapist's earlier diagnosis and should lead to a new confrontation that will further strengthen and reinforce the Adult's position.

INTERPRETATION

Up to this point the therapist's strategy has been to stabilize, decontaminate, and strengthen the Adult ego-states of the members. Now the therapist's Adult needs to team up with the member's Adult in order to gain control over the team composed of the member's Child and Parent—a team often torn by internal fighting as well. Interpretation is made with the member's Child state, looking for past reasons for inappropriate behavior, much in the same mode as traditional psychoanalysis. The goal is to deconfuse the Child, making a more total recovery or cure possible. However, if the Adult is strong enough to remain in control of this still-confused Child and the member has gained enough symptomatic relief and social control to function well, this situation can be crystallized without going through the rigors of much interpretation.

CRYSTALLIZATION

Crystallization is a therapist-to-member, Adult-to-Adult transaction in which the message is conveyed that group members are perfectly capable of ending their psychological game playing if they wish. At this juncture the process of transactional analysis is completed, for the therapist's job has been to bring group members to the point of being able to choose between healthy and unhealthy behavior. Obviously, adequate preparation throughout the sessions has been necessary; the Adult has been strengthened, the Child has been modified, and hopefully the Parent's desires for control and dominance have been appropriately lessened.

Group Processes

According to Berne, "The object for group treatment is to fight the past in the present in order to assure the future" (1966, p. 250). The past is represented by the Child and Parent ego-states, and the "present" focus is guarded by a strong Adult. Effective and appropriate relationships among the three ego-states are essential for a productive future and necessitate an Adult predominance. To reach that goal, certain group processes are advocated toward strengthening the Adult.

THERAPEUTIC PROCESSES

Berne (1966) identified four therapeutic processes that are part of the group setting. Three of them are found in any social interaction: (1) the drive toward health, (2) the need for strokes, and (3) the corrective experiences found in all social relationships. The fourth process—the behaviors of the group leader—is different. Therapists are responsible for the preparation of the group members to engage productively in group processes through individual interviews or pre-group meetings. The purpose for such screenings is to discuss commitment, communicate procedures, and establish minimal comfort levels, one with another, and not to exclude certain types from the group (Berne, 1966).

Therapists' process objectives are primarily to focus on group work activities that involve Adult-to-Adult transactions. As therapists listen to and observe group interactions, they become aware of games being played and can interrupt members with their diagnoses and analyses, thereby helping members with insight into their behavior and giving them permission not to play games. At times, therapists may need to give strong support and reassurance or may need to persuade and demand, but these techniques should not be used frequently.

CONTRACTUAL AGREEMENTS

A well-known element in TA group therapy is the contractual agreement, usually made up of two parts. The first is the contract established between the therapist and member. This can be accomplished at preliminary individual interviews, where potential members can explain their desires and the therapist can help in the clarification process. If members are too confused to contractualize such wishes, numerous group sessions may be required to specify the contract. Members may also change the contract one or more times upon discovering new aspects of their selves; such changes, if based on significant learnings, are encouraged by the therapist.

The second kind of contract is a group contract in which all members agree to offer samples of their behavior with and toward other people, regardless of what that behavior might be. In this contract, the therapist agrees to say anything that might be helpful to a group member and not to withhold information that is relevant to the purpose of the group. Both contractual agreements lend purpose and direction to the group process.

GROUP STRUCTURE

The TA group structure is considered to have a very simple, two-pronged dimension. The *external boundary* separates the group from outside influences and varies according to the degree of cohesiveness found among members at any given time. The *internal boundary* is one that exists between the group therapist and group members. According to TA, therapists cannot become "just another group member" without relinquishing important leadership responsibilities. TA therapists would neither desire such an outcome nor be functional with it. Instead, they are primarily listeners, observers, diagnosticians, and analysts— and, secondarily, process facilitators.

ANALYSES

Analyses in TA are geared to four different levels, which depend on the nature and purpose of the group. To achieve the most complete treatment, all four need to be accomplished; each one is built upon the previous level and must be completed in order. However, some significant learning can accrue through understandings acquired at any of the levels without necessarily progressing through all four.

The first of these is *structural analysis.* At this level, group members examine the structure of their own ego-states. The goal is to develop an increasing awareness within members of how their ego-states function in reality and to encourage decontamination of the past.

The second level, *transactional analysis* (also the name usually given to this whole approach to therapy but here merely is another level of analysis) builds on structural analysis. At this level, the nature of both the major and minor transactions occurring within the group are analyzed. These transactions can be complementary, crossed, or ulterior. An understanding of the ego-state from which an individual is communicating and the responses received from another member can provide enormous insights into the transactional patterns in which one engages throughout life.

The third level is *game analysis* and necessitates knowledge both of ego-states and of transactions. A psychological game involves a series of ulterior transactions in which players all gain the kinds of strokes they feel they need. The communication may appear vague or innocent at a superficial level, but at a deeper level important messages are being given and received. Group therapists must carefully listen and observe to determine the games being played and the payoffs being received. When they expose both the games and the players, they end the secrecy and thereby make the payoffs less lucrative. In addition, the therapist gives permission to the players not to play the games anymore but to look for better and more meaningful ways to gain strokes and to structure their time.

The deepest level in TA is *script analysis,* which examines basic life plans, positions, and decisions, most of which individuals made as young children and are unconscious, though powerful, in the adult. Since these basic life plans are so deeply embedded in the adult, they are highly resistant to change—and any attempts require great leadership skills. The results of significant learning in this regard can be extremely disconcerting and depressing, especially in older adults who may feel they have little time to make changes. Script analysis represents a very difficult and demanding level of influence and should be attempted only by the most skilled TA therapists.

Summary

Infants are born with a positive view of themselves and their world but need both physiological and psychological nurturing to preserve it. Such nurturing comes through transactions with other people—primarily adults, the most significant of whom are parents. Our innate psychological hunger for recognition and attention compels us to seek strokes, the nature of which (in later life) depends upon the kind we received and became accustomed to in early childhood; thus, strokes may be pleasant or unpleasant.

Much of our energy goes into structuring our time to get the strokes we believe we need. There are several ways of getting these strokes, but the most significant, in terms of our psychological well-being, is by playing games. By definition, games are always rewarding to the players in some way, or they would not continue to be played. Often, however, they are self-defeating in more significant ways.

These games are developed in response to a life position of "Okayness," which comes from our early contacts and transactions with parents and other authorities and which determines the kinds of strokes we seek. This position is often solidified before the child begins school and leads to a premature life script that becomes more and more rigid in adulthood. When our transactions and life script become too unrewarding, group counseling may be sought. Such counseling may be at any of four levels, each one denoting greater depth and sophistication.

TA group therapists conceptualize their work by means of ego-states. Each person is considered to have three such ego-states (Child, Parent, Adult), only one of which can be in command of the personality at a given time. Depending on the level of counseling that has been contracted, the group process may focus on the structure of one's personality, the nature of the transactions between group members, the analysis of psychological games being played by group members, and life-script analysis. The basic goal of TA group therapy is to understand the ego states from which one is operating and their most effective and appropriate use in life situations.

The personal qualities of TA group therapists are considered vital to the attainment of group goals. They must be ethical, responsible, purposeful, respectful, and genuine, as well as intelligent enough to be able to use—and transmit to others—the conceptualizations of TA. Leaders must also be excellent listeners and observers and astute diagnosticians and analyzers. Finally, they must have an adequate sense of timing and the ability to use specific leadership techniques mentioned throughout this chapter.

PART TWO

Theoretical Practitioners' Responses to Specific Critical Incidents and Their Congruence With Theory

Part 1 introduced you to 12 selected theories of group therapy and explained how the theories developed, what constitutes their primary concepts, the techniques therapists utilize, and how the group therapy process is perceived in each. Now we want to see how theoretical practitioners, representing each theory presented earlier, approach specific critical incidents that might occur in group therapy. Each of the following six chapters presents a critical incident, which is followed by the responses of each theoretical practitioner (TP) to the situation and an analysis of each practitioner's congruence with his or her theory. Before moving on, however, we wish to make certain that our TPs are represented fairly and accurately. Therefore, we need to note that a number of them give voice to how and why one or more incidents might *not* occur in their therapy groups. For instance, Agazarian sees herself as more like a substitute leader in each of the incidents and offers us the following as a means for understanding her responses:

> Although the dynamics of a system-centered group are no different from any other kind of group, the way those dynamics are manifested are. SCT members are encouraged to explore their impulses in subgroups instead of explaining them or acting them out. Thus, many of the critical incidents discussed . . . may not have occurred in a systems-centered group in the ways described in this book. This presented a dilemma, which I resolved by imagining how I would intervene if I was a substitute leader in these groups.
>
> I discuss the technical and dynamic issues that are involved in the incidents from the SCT point of view. It will be seen that many of the responses to the incidents are quite long—this is not typical of systems-centered interventions except when the SCT leader considers it necessary to reframe the way the members are responding to the group. What is useful perhaps, is that these interventions are typical of the kind of

bridging that leaders can make when shifting their orientation from an individual-centered towards a group-as-a-whole or systems-centered point of view. (1997b)

A second purpose of Part 2 is to provide an analysis of the degree of congruence between theory and practice. We do this by interpreting the responses our TPs have made to the critical incidents, in light of their adherence to the various constructs that comprise their respective theories.

Our approach is to understand how the TPs determined the action they chose and to see if they anticipated the consequences of their intervention. Above all, we try to observe how the TPs' actions and thoughts relate to the primary principles undergirding the theories they espouse. We also try to see the amount of variability or license the TPs have taken in interpreting the theoretical principles as they encounter the critical incidents.

Students can be helped in developing their own rationale or theory of group therapy by, first, selecting the theoretical orientation they think they most likely would adopt and, second, selecting the theoretical orientation they think they least likely would adopt, and the reasons supporting both.

As students approach each incident, we encourage them to read it first and, before reading how each of the TPs responded to the incidents, answer the following questions:

1. How would you respond to the incident? Explain what thoughts you had as you determined your particular responses. Include what it is about the incident that prompted you to do what you did.
2. Explain why you chose the particular intervention you did, over any other you may have been considering.
3. Declare what consequences you anticipated from your action.
4. Explain which elements of your theory guided your interpretation of the incident and which subsequently led to your actions.

Finally, we have prepared a series of five questions that we believe will help you formalize your theory of group therapy. The questions comprise what we refer to as a Theory Evaluation Form. We suggest you try to respond to it after you complete reading each chapter in this part. After you finish reading all chapters, you can collate your responses to each question, and thereby develop a *profile* that describes your theoretical approach to group therapy.

CHAPTER THIRTEEN

The Initial Session

The initial session often can have a significant effect upon the future of the group. How a group therapist chooses to deal with it is important. In this incident, our theoretical practitioners will be entering a group of nine members meeting for the first time.

Critical Incident 1

You are a counselor at a university counseling center. You have been acutely aware of the difficulty a number of freshmen students have been having in adjusting to college life. You offer to organize a counseling group to help students contend more effectively with their new environment.

Your group consists of nine volunteers (five men and four women), whom you have screened. Each has expressed a willingness to participate in the group you are forming. It is meeting today for the first time. All nine members are present as you enter the room and sit down. You introduce yourself, and the members introduce themselves. Then they each turn and look at you expectantly. There is an initial period of silence.

Client-Centered Therapy

Implemented by William R. Coulson

Our La Jolla groups often begin in silence. We do not want anyone to take over and consequently offer no ground rules. We want a group experience that is not a repetition of what has happened before, including at La Jolla.

I do not want to know what is going to happen before we begin, or it would not be as good as it could be. If I were to guide the group, I would bring it to premature focus, reducing the number of solutions generated within the group to deal with our common, immediate problems, such as "Will I use my time well here? Will I get through this with integrity?" That problem, created by the act of bringing the group together, stands for and (if it is dealt with respectfully) includes the other problems that plague the members and the therapist in life. I hope for each individual to be stimulated to solve the group problem for himself or herself, including elements that might lie so deep as to make a member unable to explicate them. I hope for a therapy group that will provide what Michael Polanyi calls a "heuristic experience"—discovery, the full value of which will depend on maximum presence from us all and minimal cause to run through old routines, therapeutic or otherwise.

So there is often silence at the beginning. We do not yet know what we will do with ourselves. Finding solutions will be a struggle, one which, if we are honest, we often must return to waging in silence. In the early moments of the group, silence protects against takeover—by group members or the therapist. You might think it would *promote* takeover, by someone moving in to fill the vacuum. But that does not often happen. The therapist has a good deal of initial authority by virtue of title. If he or she does not take over in the silence, members seem unlikely to do it either. Once enough time has transpired for members to realize that the therapist's best qualifications may be that she or he is a person like themselves, they will also know that no one need dominate the group.

In the initial awkward silence, I might say something like, "This silence isn't easy for me, either."

Another possibility in the initial silence is just to wait. I believe that is what I would do here. I will assume that silence provides the group with the opportunity to learn to tolerate ambiguity. That would not be my initial goal. But, since the silence arose anyway, I would tell myself (in order to keep quiet) there could be a good lesson in it—maybe about ambiguity or maybe that interactions can go well between people, even when they are awkward at first.

When I am tempted to intervene too soon in the silence, it is because I am asking myself such panicky questions as "What if nobody talks the whole hour?" The answer I remember having given myself is, "Then at least it will be different." I have never been in a college counseling group where *nobody* talked for an hour—and I bet the members have not either. If this is the time it happens, it will surely have given us something to talk about later.

Cognitive–Behavioral Therapy

Implemented by John V. Flowers

Behavioral groups do not begin with silence but usually start with enthusiasm due to the pretherapy training. In my groups, before people attend their first behavioral group, they are given an assignment card (standard 3 × 5 card). Each client writes two problems he or she hopes to resolve in therapy: One should be easier to disclose, and one should be harder. This assignment usually translates into identifying a problem that is less severe and one that is more severe. These helpful "problem cards" are part of the therapy pretraining, which the literature has shown to be very effective in making the therapy process successful. Pretraining clients in what to expect and establishing group norms can avoid many pitfalls of the unstructured group.

The problem cards make disclosure a group norm before the first therapy session. Of course, clients are told they do not have to disclose either problem they have written and may choose to disclose something they have not written. This new problem should also be written on a card after the session to keep track of the client's disclosures in therapy. Writing these initial problems on a card provides choice within a structure; the client chooses what to disclose, but some level of disclosure quickly becomes the group norm. Records and potential assessment are embedded in the pretraining, making evaluation and therapy assessment normal rather than atypical for the clients. Because there is an ongoing record of what is discussed, the disclosures can be part of an outcome measurement package assessing the efficacy of the particular group for a specific client.

In an opening session of a group with problem cards, the question "Who would like to begin?" elicits only a momentary silence before a new member hesitatingly plunges in. The description "hesitatingly plunge" is a conflictual metaphor, as is the idea of a therapy group. Those few times when this question is greeted with silence (usually with therapy-training groups of professionals, interestingly enough), the instruction "Read back over your problem cards," followed by a short wait, and the question "Who would like to begin?" has never failed in my experience.

Silence in groups is perfectly all right, and certainly occurs in behavioral groups, but initial opening session silence is not particularly productive in a behavioral group and establishes an incorrect model in a therapy mode emphasizing participation and information.

In subsequent groups, members would have to rewrite the problem cards as their entry ticket to the group. Members often write them right before a group session but some, perhaps the more compulsive or the more disturbed, write them during the week between the group sessions. It is interesting and informative to review these cards to see how they change over the course of group therapy. For instance, in a recent social skills group, Joe's early cards were dominated by problems of depression, low energy, and lack of motivation. By the middle of the 16 sessions, Joe's cards changed to anxiety-based disclosures concerning social fear and the impact of the presumed evaluation of others. Although Joe's depression had not responded to the group's intervention, the group helped greatly with his anxiety problems, with a consequent lifting of the depression as well. It is also important for therapists to know what problems are written down but not disclosed. Our research has repeatedly shown that problems important enough to be written but not disclosed become more severe over the course of the group. Thus, the therapist should encourage a member to disclose a repeatedly written, nondisclosed problem. Such encouragement should occur in an individual meeting because overt encouragement in the group could trap the member into an unwanted disclosure. Disclosure is the norm that leads the group toward effectiveness, but the voluntary nature of the disclosure is essential for group ethics and group safety.

Family-Centered Therapy
Implemented by James P. Trotzer

As a group leader who uses family theory or the system's perspective as a resource in conducting counseling groups, I engage in a form of mental preparation that considers both group process dynamics and relevant systemic constructs apropos to the purpose of the group and the nature of its members. In anticipation of this initial session, my group dynamics thinking would incorporate information about the individual *person*, the interpersonal *process*, and the group's *purpose* (Trotzer, 1989). Each aspect is addressed in the form of a question: (1) How can I help this group account for and meet the unique and common individual needs of each group member? (2) How can I help this group develop an interactional and interpersonal process that is therapeutic? (3) How can I help this group address the purpose for which it is assembled—that is, in this case, help members address their difficulties in adjusting to college?

My system's perspective supplies me with a wealth of resources and constructs related to the aforementioned questions, thus giving me a kind of running start to the group process (Trotzer & Trotzer, 1986). Most group-counseling proponents, including Irwin Yalom (1995), note that all members of a therapy group carry scars from their membership and experience in their primary group—their family. This observation pertains directly to the content of group sessions that emerges over time. However, in the beginning phase of the group process and especially the initial session, I believe the impact of family dynamics is manifested in the predispositions members bring with them in the form of group expectations and their views of themselves as persons and participants. These predispositions evolving from their family-of-origin experience may enhance or inhibit group interaction and involvement in an active or reactive sense. Individual-member inclinations can be resources or impediments to group process. Therefore, I take them into account and bring them to the forefront as extremely useful facilitative data in the forming stage of the group process. When I raise and address these individual traits as the group forms, I acknowledge the personhood and uniqueness of each member and the critical importance of connecting these diverse individuals in such a way that a therapeutic group milieu emerges.

It is my view that family-of-origin experiences shape members' predispositions toward interacting within the group, which in turn affect group process. For example, a family's norms regarding self-disclosure will influence the degree to which one feels free to disclose in a group where disclosure is an accepted and established norm. Similarly, individuals whose families are enmeshed may, early in the group's life, feel conflicted to commit themselves fully to the other members out of loyalty to their families of origin. Conversely, individuals whose families are emotionally disengaged may enthusiastically invest themselves in the group early on but not be as emotionally committed during the middle and later stages of the group. One final example relates to conflict resolution. How conflicts were managed in families of origin can affect the way in which members resolve interpersonal conflicts within the group. For instance, if the family norm was to suppress or deny toxic interpersonal issues, then members from such families will likely experience difficulty engaging in feedback and confrontation.

At the beginning of the group, I use an agenda of four generic group tasks, addressing them either directly via structured intervention or indirectly via process evolution. These tasks are (1) getting acquainted—acquiring knowledge about one another; (2) interpersonal warm-up—moving affectively toward one another; (3) setting boundaries—establishing ground rules that identify expectations as to participation and focus; and (4) building trust—laying the foundation of trust that addresses individual security and facilitates the risk taking necessary to participate in the group.

Here again, family theory provides me with constructs that relate both to techniques and to content and that can be related to the developmental tasks noted above. For example, I often use the construct of ordinal position in the family constellation to enhance the get-acquainted process by having members include that information in their introductions. As each member provides that basic information without elaboration (e.g., "I'm the oldest of three with a younger brother and sister"), I invite the group to hypothesize on what they "know" about the person by brainstorming possible traits the person may have. Statements such as "What do you know about an 'oldest'?" and "How might that relate to dealing with going off to college?" solicit the desired information and its relationship to the group's focus. Following the brainstorming, I invite the focus member to comment on the accuracy or inaccuracy of the comments, modifying, clarifying, disregarding, or adding to the feedback as he or she feels appropriate. This activity conducted in a go-round format not only addresses the get-acquainted task but also introduces the group to the interpersonal processes of self-disclosure and feedback in a relatively nonthreatening manner.

The fact that this group is composed of college freshmen prompts me to consider another vital contextual assumption that can enhance the forming dynamics of the group process. I assume that the members are from families that are in the launching stage of the family life cycle and that each member is likely to be a "revolving door" family participant. Consequently, the members have a common ground on which they can identify and bond, even though each may have had different family-leaving experiences. Raising the umbrella of common ground from a family perspective addresses the interpersonal warm-up task as members move toward one another and become more comfortable with each other. For instance, a structured exercise, which may help achieve this, is to have each member share if they were the first to leave home,* how the family

---

*If not, then who left home ahead of them and how the family addressed each who left after that.

prepared for and managed that, and what the experience was like for each of them—that is, how hard, how easy, and what made it so; frequency of contact with family by phone, letters, visits; and the like.

I consider the construct of *boundaries* as one of the most pragmatic contributions of system's thinking to group work. This construct bears directly on the utility and necessity of formulating group ground rules. Every family teaches its members rules about relating. However, these rules may be either spoken (i.e., clearly verbalized with regard to expectation and consequences) or unspoken (i.e., never verbalized but affectively influential and powerful in the lives of the family members). I believe these internalized rules have a direct correlation to group boundaries.

The spoken form relates to the ground rules that govern the group (e.g., confidentiality), and the unspoken form relates to the norms that evolve over the course of the group's life span. If I were to choose to structure this group at the beginning, I would ask members to share the "rules they grew up with" as an excellent springboard to discussing group boundaries and ground rules.

I frequently use a structured group activity that combines trust building and boundary formation in groups during the initial session. One exercise that has worked particularly well with young adults is the Three Secrets Activity. I ask members to write three things they would not likely share with this group. I assure them that they will not be required, manipulated, or tricked into sharing these secrets. (This statement of mine raises the trust issue.) After they have finished writing, I instruct them to put their secrets away and then ask them to discuss why they would not share these things with this group. Although discussion tends to begin slowly (part of the distrust–trust dynamic), the eventual result is usually a very energetic and intense interaction that typically serves to ferret out members' concerns, fears, and anxieties about the group. The discussion also accentuates the members' need and desire for agreed-on ground rules in order for the group to be a safe place to risk discussing personal concerns.

My decision to use structured activities in this group of college freshmen will be predicated on the initial interaction of the members as the group assembles. If the group engages in interactions where the expected restraints, resistances, and obstacles are the norm for new social beginnings, I would take a facilitative posture and, if needed, would use structured activities as resources to the group. However, if the members lack the skills or resources to work their way to the connectedness necessary to become cohesive or if resistances appear to be detrimental to the members or the group as a whole, my leadership posture would be more directive in nature, and I would use one or more of the aforementioned structured activities to initiate interaction, direction, and focus. Because this is a group of young adults, a pregroup decision to structure is inappropriate. Therefore, the initial silence would be treated as a normal event typical of first meetings, and the group would be given time to address the initiative (getting started) issue. I would expect the first 20–30 minutes or so to provide me with some clues about the direction my leadership will take and whether and how I would use the systemic constructs and techniques I have previously described.

Gestalt Therapy

Implemented by Mirriam F. Polster

The purpose in forming this group is to help entering college students "contend more effectively with their new environment." Because these young people have gotten this far, it is reasonable to assume that they have, for the most part, been doing okay in their lives and it is this particular situation that presents them with difficulties. Although this is a reasonable assumption, there may be some more pervasive trouble for certain individuals, and bearing this in mind as the group starts is wise.

I am guessing that one of the most prevalent characteristics of this group is that each member secretly suspects that the troubles he or she is having are unique and, in some vague way, reflect badly on himself or herself. This uneasy suspicion is common at this age. Reinforcing this fear is everyone else's apparent success at dealing with this situation, making it too inconvenient or too risky to even air these doubts. It might mark them in the eyes of others and lead to a deeper sense of isolation.

Perls (1969b) has defined growth as the movement from environmental support to self-support. This is a relative and gradual progression; we are never fully free of our reliance on some form of external support, but we do change our balance of dependency. This realignment of the balance between environmental support and self-support may well be an underlying question faced by the people in this group.

These young people are in transition; for some, this is the first dramatic turning point in their lives. They stand between what they have been and what they want to become, what they are and what they feel they should be. Their lives at home may have had many familiar comforts. There was a built-in society—familial, academic, or religious—into which they were born and were gradually introduced with parental or sibling support. Here at the university, they have been dunked, all by themselves it must seem, into a fully functioning system with rules and customs already established (and in many cases unspecified), which they have to learn quickly. Everybody else, walking swiftly to classes with their friends, seems already to know the rules.

So here they are, their admonitions (to themselves) to keep quiet and not stand out are counterbalanced by the intensity of the stress they are experiencing. This is a common struggle and one that, when expressed and acknowledged, might serve as a unifying force in group formation. It is the dynamic of mutuality in the group that I, as leader, would foster at this stage. A common problem, expressed with feeling and seriously attended to, is probably the most potent basis for group cohesion. The uniquely individual form these problems may take for each person can be revealed from this mutual source of support. The leader, in supporting this development and attending to the ways in which this expression can be made even more poignantly, is setting in motion the very force these students need eventually to move out of this group into independent action. They need to learn to support themselves better and to perceive more sensitively how others may be feeling so that they can identify people whom they might want for colleagues and friends.

So, after introductions are made, I would ask each of them to make a statement about their experiences as beginners in this new community. What pleased them? Dismayed them? Puzzled them? Confused them? What did they miss? Whom did they miss?

As the group continued, I would pay particular attention to how they listen to each other and how they express themselves. I would work at sharpening their language so that it better expresses what they want to communicate. They may be relying on familiar phrases or expressions, shorthand ways that communicated quickly and well at home but that do not mean the same things to the people here. They need to learn to make it with the people here and cannot afford merely to repeat old behaviors and habits. To do this, they have to be actively and energetically open to differences as well as commonalities with each other. Lively appreciation of differences is important because these can then be experienced as inviting and fascinating rather than discouraging or intimidating.

An appreciation of these differences can provide support because members will have devised various ways of coping with some of the specific problems that bother them. One person may have answers to another's questions, although still troubled by a problem that another has resolved, and so on. Articulating these differences becomes a way of getting unstuck, of supporting fertility of mind. The energy that these students may be using to appear as if they fit in can be devoted instead to improvising behavior by taking examples from the group, trying them out elsewhere, and using the group to come back to and continue to work out what remains troublesome.

We could have role-playing sessions where the group enacts either the circumstance or a situation with an individual that is giving them trouble. The change of perspective that may come from playing an aloof professor or an arrogant and harried graduate assistant may lead them either to view these characters in a different light or to find new sources of energy and support within themselves to cope more effectively with them. Experiments in speaking directly and stating clearly what they want could change the nature of their contacts with other people on campus. It is within this group, balancing individual venturesomeness against the need for group support, that creative solutions may be invented and tried out. What the group members do in the campus situation would not be a carbon copy of the experimental action they have tried out in the group; indeed, it is better when it is not. The students need the experience of supported improvisation, which is, after all, what most actions are.

The group thus serves as the temporary environmental support that can bridge the gap, as accustomed support from a familiar environment diminishes and support from the individual and a new group grows.

Individual Psychology

Implemented by Guy J. Manaster

The premise in this situation: The university environment poses problems because it is different from and larger than the institutions with which the students have previously dealt, *and* they do not know what to do. A therapist must be aware, in entering a group such as this, that one or some of the volunteer group members may also have personal problems. These problems may be felt for the first time with greater intensity in the new, different environment of the university. Not living at home may allow, if not force, freshman students to examine themselves and realize that some help is needed. Thus, we would begin this group as if its task was evident—to assist in adjustment to a new environment—while staying sensitive to the possibility of more severe personal problems needing remediation within or outside the group.

At the critical, first moment in this situation, I would set the task-specific tone for the group with an introductory message such as "I offered to organize this group because I know how difficult it can be to get it together and get going in college. There are three basic life tasks—work and school, friends and community, and loved ones. When you come to college you want to make it in school and come out prepared to appreciate life and to get a fulfilling job you both enjoy and do well. You probably don't know many people here, if you know anyone. You want to make friends and have a good time. This may be the first time you have lived away from your family, and you may be lonesome. You may have been going out steadily with someone at home, but you probably want to go out with someone here. What you want really is to belong and to feel that you belong. Everyone wants to belong.

"However, there are things you don't know, or think you don't know, or can't do. Some concerns may seem trivial. I once knew a guy who left college when his clean clothes ran out. He was embarrassed to go to the laundry with them. Some concerns seem crucial, important, and immediate, but are they? Do you have an academic major area? Do you need one now? I think our job here is to find out what concerns we have, what we don't know or feel we can't do. I think between all of us we can figure this place out. Maybe we can start out by each of us telling the others what is bothering us most. Bill, would you tell us what's bugging or worrying you, what you want? Then we will go around the group and figure out how we want to proceed."

My intentions with this opening are very direct and are based in Adlerian theory. First, I would want us to get going in the group and would want to get all group members working out specific adjustment problems. The sooner they meet a challenge and deal with it successfully, the sooner they will feel confidence to go on to conquer other challenges.

Next, I would want the group to share concerns as quickly as possible. Each member will, in his or her own way, have notions of inferiority based at least in part on the idea that he or she is the only one with these kinds of concerns. In a homogeneous group such as this one, considerable commonality of concerns would no doubt be presented. If the problem areas are not clearly the same, the reasons for their being concerns may be similar among the group. I would try to show the similarities, such as the members' attempts to remain different, to avoid failure no matter how inconsequential, and to buoy themselves up by feeling homesick, dwelling on "back home" where they were loved and appreciated. Both group camaraderie and a greater feeling of commonness with other freshmen would, I hope, come from this sharing and interpreting.

After listening to everyone in the group, we would have a slate of problems, which together we would organize in order to solve. This might entail, over ensuing weeks, skill building in problem solving and information gathering and development of social skills through role playing or psychodrama. A good deal of value clarification may be needed, and some instance of specifically focused, mutually agreed-on behavioral goal setting would be valuable. The tools used, the counseling techniques, may not be strictly Adlerian (i.e., introduced and developed by Adler or his followers), but they would be used within the Adlerian framework of understanding the individual and group process.

Interpersonal Psychotherapy
Implemented by Victor Yalom and Mary Jean Paris

Prior to the initial group session, we would meet with each prospective member for a pregroup interview. This interview is a screening method for member selection as well as an opportunity to educate and prepare the potential member for the group. Naturally, we would obtain routine intake information such as motivation for therapy, ego strength, environmental stressors, and history. Although this basic information is important, the primary focus of the interview is to acquire interpersonal history and a sense of the individual's problematic interpersonal behaviors. Thus, we would explore in some detail the quality of their past and present relationships, including family members, friends, intimate partners, and co-workers. As we hone in on the purpose of the current group, we would focus on their social adjustment to college life: Are they making friends? Do they feel that they fit in? What efforts have they made to try to meet other students? Are they feeling lonely, anxious, or depressed? The information obtained would give us an idea of some of the possible issues that would eventually arise for each member in the group and the kind of support, experiences, and feedback that would be most useful to them.

During this interview, we would also explore their fears, concerns, and hopes regarding the group and would try to give them a realistic picture of how the group actually operates. We would explain key concepts of the interpersonal model of group therapy, including the value of interpersonal learning, the use of the here and now, and the conception of the group as a social microcosm. We would attempt to demonstrate how these principles can be used to address the client's presenting concerns. For example, if a student complained about the difficulty in making new friends, we would emphasize that the group is an ideal arena to obtain data that may help him better understand the difficulties he is encountering. Rather than spend an inordinate amount of time hearing about his frustrations in trying to meet other students in his dorm or classes—encounters that the group leader or other members cannot fully understand, not observing them firsthand—we would instead focus our efforts to a greater degree in observing how he interacts with other members in the group. This focus on the behaviors and interactions that occur among group members is what is referred to as the here and now. By providing feedback to this student on how he interacts in the therapy group, he would learn a great deal about his interpersonal skills and would start to sort out which of his behaviors draw people toward him and which behaviors are likely obstacles to forming friendships.

Interpersonal learning is a vital therapeutic factor of the group experience. The group experience is most useful when the relationships in the therapy group are used as a blueprint to learn more about interpersonal behaviors outside the group. As group leaders we realize the importance of keeping in mind that the purpose of forming this group is to help entering college students adjust to their new environment. As such, the students are not explicitly seeking membership in this group to deal with their interpersonal issues. We would need to actively work to help members translate their present difficulties into interpersonal problems. The group could also be helpful in many other ways, being an oasis of support for students feeling overwhelmed in a new environment.

After the initial introductions, silence ensues in the group, and the members look at the group leaders expectantly. We might attempt to plunge the group immediately into the here and now by asking the members how they are feeling about being in the group. If members acknowledge anxiety or discomfort, we would encourage them to expand on these feelings, to describe them in some detail if possible. What are they anxious about, what negative outcomes do they imagine? We would also try to relate these concerns to the challenges of adapting to their new college experience, as well as to other peer or family situations that come to mind. For example, if they are anxious about fitting in the group and being judged negatively by others or, conversely, if they are worried that other members will have problems more serious than theirs, we would explore whether these are familiar feelings. If so, where have they experienced these feelings before, and what was the result?

An intervention of this sort is aimed at generalizing the members' experiences in the group to their relationships out in the real world. This is an essential component of the here-and-now approach: Leaders must first help group members engage with each other, have a real emotional experience in the therapy room, and then understand as fully as possible the implications of that experience. To the extent the therapy group focuses on the here and now, it increases in power and effectiveness. But the goal is not simply catharsis or "encounter," it is to learn from the group setting about the nature of their interpersonal world.

Another option would be to encourage members to talk about why they are in the group and what they hope to get out of it. We would then listen to their responses with special attention to the areas of their expressed concerns that are interpersonal in nature. For example, if a student complained about feeling overwhelmed and hopeless by the academic demands, we would want to get a realistic picture of what these demands are and whether that student is really in over her head. But we would also want to explore the social component of this experience: What are the internalized expectations of this student? What is this student's definition of success? Is she carrying around unrealistic demands of her parents? How does she rate herself vis-à-vis other students? Thus, we could start to refocus what might seem to be (or might actually be) a problem for the academic advising department into a concern that can be dealt effectively in an interpersonally oriented psychotherapy group. The student could find support in the group, could find solace in discovering that she is not alone with her fears, but might also begin to rethink some of her assumptions about what percentile rank she needs to occupy in order to be an acceptable member of the student community. In the group she might initially feel intimidated because other members in the group seem more competent and intelligent. She might tend to isolate and not contribute much unless called on. We would assume that this is a reflection of what she is doing outside the group, further compounding her academic anxieties. This further expands the useful territory that we would hope to cover in the therapy—that is, helping her not to isolate but to use the group as a vehicle of support and, more important, as a way to develop a supportive network of friends in the campus environment.

Psychodynamic Therapy
Implemented by J. Scott Rutan

From a psychodynamic perspective, the initial group meeting offers an opportunity to view characteristic "hello" styles of the members. The anxiety of the new and strange situation would also allow us to observe the various defenses used by members to cope with this situation. Thus, the *content* that is discussed, though important, is ultimately less important than what it implies about how each member approaches this situation. The group task in a first meeting is to assess the safety of the situation. Typically, this includes members seeking common ground, things that they share with one another.

Whereas some leaders might attempt to lessen the anxiety in order to facilitate interaction and comfort, the dynamic leader is more interested in gaining access to unconscious data. Thus, I would not intervene and interrupt the silence. I would be more interested in observing how the members deal with the silence, who ultimately breaks it, and how the group roles begin to develop. In this particular group, the goal is to help individual members understand more about how they cope with new situations (specifically, college). The group becomes a laboratory for exploring how members cope with *this* new situation.

From a dynamic point of view, it is assumed that individuals do not create new behaviors just for the therapy group. Rather, we are privy to characteristic coping styles. Thus, the "helper" in the group was likely the "helper" in his or her family of origin. Dynamic therapy precedes from the assumption that insight and understanding lead to change. By helping members become curious about how they came to adopt the styles they used in this first group, the therapist is beginning the task of helping members think psychodynamically about their behaviors, feelings, expectations, and perceptions.

Toward the end of the meeting, I would likely say something like, "Everyone faced the difficult task of meeting strangers and determining whether this would be a safe place and I would be a safe leader." I would then point out some of the specific styles employed by members to accomplish this task.

One important consequence of my taking a quieter, less intrusive role is that it may enhance the opportunity for group members to begin developing transference; that is, lacking much data about who I am and what I am thinking, members will begin making *assumptions* about who I am. Dynamic theory posits that we can deduce a great deal about the past from these assumptions.

It is worth noting at this point that all psychodynamic groups form around a clear and mutually accepted set of group agreements (Rutan & Stone, 1993, pp. 117–126). These agreements include expected behavior regarding attendance, participation, and so on. Thus, if members vary from the agreements (e.g., coming late), there is an opportunity to explore what unconscious motivation might lay behind specific behaviors.

Rational–Emotive–Behavioral Therapy
Implemented by Albert Ellis

This is an ideal situation for the use of rational–emotive–behavioral therapy (REBT) because the group starts off from scratch and has not been allowed or encouraged to flounder in any nondirective manner, nor to acquire a prejudice in favor of becoming absorbed in its members' early history, in their "family" relationship to each other, in their attachment to the group leader, in their obsessive–compulsive interest in the group process itself, or in various other kinds of theories that are dear to the heart of most leaders and are therefore willy-nilly crammed down the gullible gullets of most therapy group members. For a change, the prejudices of REBT will be able to prevail! In my thinking about the group and what form I would like to see it take before I actually begin working with it, I would examine the general and specific goals of REBT and how they might best be implemented in this particular group.

Doing so, I see REBT as designed to help virtually all humans, and particularly intelligent ones, cope with their regular life problems and with their own tendencies to disturb themselves. I assume that virtually all college freshmen, in particular, are born and reared with a huge propensity to cause themselves needless emotional pain and turmoil, but they also have several significant innate healthy or rational tendencies, including the tendency to think, think about their thinking, be curious, learn, become aware of their own emotional disturbances, desire to change and actualize themselves, and be able to choose much of their future emotional and behavioral destiny. I therefore assume that just about all members of the present group will benefit from REBT and that some of them can be shown how to make profound changes in their thinking, emoting, and behaving by learning and practicing its principles.

I would open the first session of the group by stating my goals in forming the group and would try to discover whether all or most of the members are willing to go along with these goals. I would say something like, "Let me explain my main motives in forming this group. I think that all of you, as you have told me already in my individual talks with you, would like to contend more effectively with your new college environment and that you have the ability to learn to do so. As humans, you have some degree of free will, or choice, in the things you do—though let's not run this idea into the ground and piously claim that you are totally free! You, as humans, are somewhat limited by your heredity and your environment. You can't do anything you wish to do—even though you can do much of what you would like to carry out.

"One of your important limitations is that, in many ways, you often tend to think crookedly and behave dysfunctionally, and you do so mainly because that's the kind of creature you are—limited. Despite your intelligence and education, you still tend to think irrationally: to use absolutistic modes of thought; to believe in nonexistent magic; to observe poorly and often make antiempirical conclusions about your observations; to make fairly frequent use of illogical forms, such as nonsequiturs, arbitrary inference, and circular thinking; to defy and to 'devil-ify' yourself and other humans; and often to override your straight thinking with dogmas, overgeneralizations, bigotries, prejudices, and superstitions.

"In terms of the form of psychotherapy and group therapy that I am going to employ with you in our subsequent sessions, all of you, like virtually all the rest of the human race, strongly tend to be intense *musturbators.* You mistakenly—and quite self-defeatingly—often think that, first, you absolutely must do well and be approved by others; second, that you *should* and *must* be dealt with considerately and fairly by the other people with whom you closely associate; and, third, that the world *ought to* and *must* provide you with conditions that give you, fairly easily and quickly, whatever you dearly want and refrain from giving you the things and situations that you consider highly obnoxious.

"Perhaps you can manage, because some of you are talented in this respect, to upset yourself emotionally without any use of imperatives like *must, should, ought, got to, have to,* and *need.* Perhaps, but I doubt it. So far, whenever I have come across a disturbed person during the last quarter of a century, I have immediately been able to spot his or her *musts* that largely lead to this person's disturbance. And I have also found that the three main derivatives that people have as irrational ideas actually seem to stem from their basic *musts.* These derivatives are:

1. Since I *must* do well and be approved of by all the people I consider significant, it's *awful* if and when I don't!
2. I can't *stand* failing and being disapproved of by others, because I *must* not fail and *must* not be disapproved of!
3. Because I have failed and been disapproved of by my significant others, as I *must* not be, I am a *rotten person* who is not likely to do well at anything in the future and who really does not deserve good things.

"Now what we are going to do, in the course of these group therapy sessions, is to zero in on any or all of the things that bother you—or, in REBT terms, about which you choose to bother yourself. If you have problems in school, in your social affairs, in your love life, with your parents, or in any other area, I want you to bring them in—and we will work on them together. But, even more important, we will be interested in your problems *about* your problems. Thus, if you are doing poorly in your schoolwork, we will not only concern ourselves with ways in which you can do better but will also look at your feelings about this schoolwork—especially feelings of anxiety, depression, inadequacy, hostility, or apathy. In REBT we define such feelings as unhealthy—

meaning they do not help you to live happily and get more of what you want and less of what you don't want.

"This doesn't mean that we want you to be unfeeling and unemotional. Rational, in REBT, doesn't mean unemotional, calm, indifferent, or passive. It means, usually, quite emotional—that is, vitally concerned with your own and others' well-being and feeling keenly sorry, regretful, disappointed, annoyed, and irritated when things are not going well for you and those for whom you care. Rational also means strongly determined to change what you don't like in the world, including your own self-defeating feelings and acts; and it means willing to work for a happier, more fulfilled kind of existence."

I would stop at this point and give the group members a chance to speak up and express themselves: to argue with me, to bring up other ideas, and especially to say what they would like to get out of the group sessions. I would have all of them try to bring up at least one problem that seems to be bothering them most at the present time: something on which they would like to work. I would have them briefly tell something about themselves—where they are from, why they came to college, what some of their main goals in life are, and the like.

I would then ask a member who is particularly bothered about something now—such as the problem of being relatively alone and friendless in this new college situation—to bring this up for discussion. I would also ask how many of the others felt similarly bothered. I would illustrate REBT to the group members, largely using this first individual's problem: showing her, for example, that she felt lonely at point *C* (emotional and behavioral consequence) after being in a situation at point *A* (activating experience) and that her new college situation, *A*, did not *make* her feel lonely, although it may have *contributed* to this feeling. I would try to show her (and the other group members) that she mainly chooses to upset herself, at point *B* (her belief system about what is happening at *A*), by *demanding* and *commanding* that a better situation exists, rather than merely *preferring* and *wishing* that it be better.

As I revealed to this group this woman's own irrational beliefs (at point *B*) with which she was creating her inappropriate feelings (of self-downing, hostility, and self-pity) at point *C* (consequence), I would also quickly start challenging these ideas and disputing them, at point *D*. Thus, I might show her that she was telling herself, at *B*, "People *should* be more friendly to me in this new college environment! I *can't bear* their curtness and indifference! What a *terrible place* this is compared with the way things are at home!" I would try to help her dispute these irrational beliefs by asking her, "Where is the evidence that people *should be* as friendly as you'd *like* them to be? In what way can't you *bear* their curtness and indifference? Assuming that things really are more difficult here than at home, how does that difficulty make this a *terrible place*? And I would try to get her, at least temporarily, to give up these self-defeating ideas.

While doing this, I would try to involve the other group members in disputing and challenging the member who brought up a specific problem. In other words, I would get the group members immediately started on REBT problem solving, discussing both of its aspects. First is discussing one's problem *about* a problem, or one's feelings of emotional upset when one experiences this problem; trying to see how they arise from one's own thinking or attitude toward the problem; and then making some concerted attempt to change that attitude and eliminate or minimize the emotional disturbance. The second aspect is, as the disturbance seems to be getting under one's control, going back to the original practical problem and trying to see how it can be solved. Thus, in the young woman's case, once she began to stop hating herself, hating others, and thinking of the school as a terrible place, the group would discuss with her what she could do about making more friends and being alone less. For example, she could speak more to the other students in her dormitory, meet with some of those in her class to study together, join some of the college clubs, and the like.

Before session 1 ended, I would hope that I had presented the main elements of REBT, and some of its usual goals, and illustrated some of its techniques by applying them to at least one major problem brought up in the group. I would also suggest an activity-oriented homework assignment to the member(s) whose problems we are trying to resolve. Thus, our lonely members might take the homework assignment of opening a conversation with at least three new people in the course of the next week. All members of the group might also be given a shame-attacking assignment, such as doing something they consider foolish, shameful, or embarrassing, and working on their belief system so that they would not feel the usual degree of shame that they normally feel when doing this "embarrassing" thing.

In this manner, I will be setting the stage for the group to have an ongoing experience of rational–emotive–behavioral therapy. I would suggest that the members give it a chance for at least four or five sessions, to see what they can learn from it. However, if any members object seriously to the procedures that are used, they could discuss these objections from time to time and also choose to quit the group. If several of the group members want a quite different kind of group experience—such as a psychoanalytically oriented or an encounter-type experience—I would suggest that they still try this REBT group for awhile and, if they are still dissatisfied, that they then try to find a group more amenable to their desires. I would not fall into the trap of seriously modifying the procedure that I usually follow in an REBT group because I personally believe in the effectiveness of that procedure. And if several or most of the group members really want to do something else, I think they should work with a leader who believes in that alternate kind of procedure.

Reality Therapy
Implemented by Thomas E. Bratter

When the group convenes for the first time, I would attempt to arrive before the session is scheduled to begin so that I could greet the members individually and introduce them to one another. I would start precisely at the agreed-on time by suggesting that each take a few minutes to share with the group whatever he or she wished and briefly state some of the prominent reasons for wanting to join. In all probability, after the introductions are concluded, there would be an initial silence. I would welcome the opportunity to break the silence and set the ground rules.

"I'm pleased you decided to come because I've heard much sensitivity and intelligence in this room. It's funny because listening to you describe yourselves and concerns remind me of when I went away to college. Even though I was only twenty miles away from my family, the first night I can recall crying. I was frightened that I wouldn't make any friends . . . and that I wasn't as bright as everyone else. But, I guess my big fear was that I was different . . . strange . . . crazy. I wish I had been given the opportunity to meet with some people to discuss my fears because I think that would have helped. Actually, I think that is all we can do here: to share experiences . . . the good . . . the bad . . . the pleasant . . . the painful. I envy you because you are lucky that here you can be real . . . you can tell it like it is. But I do not expect you to begin to 'bare your heart and soul' because it will take some time before we begin to trust each other. I sincerely hope that whatever is said in here remains in here. Confidentiality is important because no one will want to talk. I wouldn't. I don't know what we can do if someone decides to publish what we say in the newspaper, but I hope this is not something that will occupy group time. The only thing that would insult me enormously is if anyone should come here 'high.' Again, that would be a group decision, but it would really annoy me because we are adults and here to relate honestly and openly. Obviously, when someone is talking, we can show them the respect he or she deserves and not interrupt. The final rule is of course no violence or threats of violence. We can become angry and show our rage, but we do not need to revert back to animals and threaten. I've spoken too long. Does anyone have any questions or comments?"

Solution-Focused Therapy

Implemented by Rebecca LaFountain

I see this initial group meeting as an extension of the prescreening process, where I meet individually with each of the potential group members and establish the tone of the group. In the prescreening meeting I would tell the participants that I expect them to be involved, that the group emphasizes a goal-oriented approach, and that I encourage solution-oriented talk as opposed to problem-oriented talk throughout the course of the group. After learning the expectations of the group, each candidate could make an informed decision about whether or not to join the group.

I would not be taken by surprise when the group members look to me for direction following their introductions. In fact, I would anticipate that they will look to the leader for guidance; therefore, I would attempt to structure the introductions so that we can build on them. I would start out by welcoming the students and asking them to introduce themselves by discussing such things as where they are from, their majors, how they spend their free time, and the like. After everyone has had a turn and they look to me as if to say "What's next?" I would help them build on the introductions by encouraging them to share with each other the commonalities they discover among themselves. They may find that two of them grew up in nearby towns or that several participants like the same kind of music. The purpose of this activity is to promote cohesiveness and interaction. If a participant attempts to speak *about* similarities among members, I would direct him or her to speak *to* the other members.

I would summarize the commonalities among some of the group members and make a transition to the second part of the session by stating, "You have some similarities among yourselves; another aspect that you share is that you all have something that you would like to change or do differently." In so doing, I would attempt to emphasize the solution-oriented language, which I had introduced in the prescreening meeting with the question "What is it you would like to change?" I would ask the students to share with group members that which they had discussed in the prescreening meeting with me. While group members focus on each others' presenting concerns, they often feel relief when they realize that they are not alone in their misery. This notion of universality, as described by Irvin Yalom (1995), promotes group cohesiveness.

Another goal of the exercise is to help students realize that, although they have different presenting difficulties, a common underlying theme links them together. Whereas some students may share that they are homesick, other students may be having difficulty adjusting to group-living situations, and others may be struggling to balance their newly found freedom and responsibility. That which the students share in common is a need for emotional relief and a desire to maintain a more satisfying and enriching life (Huber & Backlund, 1991).

While participants focus on each other's presenting difficulties, I would focus on the students' language because students present their beliefs about their situations by the language they use. For example, solution-focused counselors make a distinction between *problems* and *difficulties*. Difficulties become problems when people mishandle their difficulties and apply more of the "same solution" to their difficulty (Huber & Backlund, 1991). For example, a female student who is having trouble making new friends at college and chooses to avoid certain social activities that would make her feel most anxious is experiencing a difficulty. If she eventually begins to avoid all social activities, then her way of coping is becoming a problem for her. I particularly would listen to the students' use of labels and absolutes. For example, if a male student says, "I'm a procrastinator," I would respond by saying, "You tend to wait at times until the last minute." As long as the student sees himself as a procrastinator, he will remain helpless and stuck, but replacing the noun, *procrastinator,* with the verbs, *tend to wait,* opens the door to more possibilities. If the student "tends to wait *at times* until the last minute," then it is possible he could "begin earlier in other instances."

The students in this group would most likely respond to my question about what they would like to change, in one of four ways. The first type of response is for students to readily relate to other group members that which we discussed in the prescreening meeting. A second type of response is for students to minimize that which we talked about in the prescreening (often they do this out of anxiety). In this case I usually do not address the difference as long as the essence of the presenting difficulty is the same. For example, if a female student shares in the prescreening meeting that "she wants to lose weight" but then in front of the other group members she says that "she wants to think better about herself, " I would not point out the difference. A third type of response is for students to present a difficulty other than the one we discussed in the pre-screening. In this situation I will ask him or her (without revealing the specifics), "What about the concern you shared in the prescreening?" A final response is one of silence. In those cases I prompt the student by name and say, "Chris, can you share with the group what you came up with in the prescreening?"

I would conclude the first session with encouragement by expressing appreciation to the group members for their efforts in sharing that which they want to change. In addition, I would assign them a task that provides direction for constructing change. I would do this by asking the students to be "on the lookout" during the following week for situations that they would like to happen more often.

Solution-focused counselors believe that clients, for the most part, know what they need to do. The counseling process helps give them the courage and support to try a new solution. The structure imposed in solution-focused groups helps create a "safety net" for the group members as they take their first "baby step" toward change.

Systems-Centered Therapy
Implemented by Yvonne Agazarian

> *Our group is beginning its life in silence. Silence is ambiguous, ambiguity arouses anxiety in us human beings, and when we are anxious we are likely to explain the world based on our wishes and fears rather than on our direct experience. Being anxious, we are more likely to make negative predictions, rather than positive predictions, about what is going to happen. Negative predictions make us still more anxious. So, the group is at its first fork in the road, and exploring either fork will be useful to us. We can continue to sit in silence and notice if there are anxiety-provoking thoughts that are making the silence uncomfortable for us, or we can explore with each other the experience we are having as we sit in the uncertainty of here and now.*

The intervention opens by framing the context: silence in a new group. From a systems-centered therapy (SCT) perspective, silence typically introduces ambiguity. This is stated as a reality to the group and deliberately normalizes the typical responses to ambiguity.*

---

*Boundarying is the application of the systems-centered methods and techniques that (1) reduce the defensive restraining forces to communication at the boundaries within, between, and among systems in the hierarchy and (2) increase the probability that information (energy) will be transferred. This is done by modifying defenses at the boundaries of space, time, reality, and role. Defense modification in SCT is a predetermined sequence of SCT methods and techniques that systematically undo defenses against the intrapersonal and interpersonal communications of experience in the context of the phases of group development.

The sense of urgency that anxiety generates drives people to interpret reality (both their inner and outer reality) before they explore it. Establishing a reality-testing climate requires people to test reality before they interpret it. One of the major goals in SCT is to encourage members to become researchers of their own experience and to base their trust appropriately by testing their expectations in the group. In an SCT group, blind trust and mistrust is transformed into functional trust as members test the realities of their fears and wishes in the group.

One of the first things SCT members learn is the *fork in the road* between explaining and exploring their experience, discovering for themselves (1) how explaining experience leads to what one knows already and defends against uncertainty by explaining it away and (2) how exploring experience leads to discovering what one did not know (or what one did not know one knew!) about themselves, others, and the world. The fork-in-the-road method requires members to keep making choices about which side to explore first: their defenses against reality or the reality that they are defending against.

The most familiar leader intervention to silence at the beginning of a group is not to make an intervention and to join the group silence. An SCT therapist, however, keeps in mind the fact that silence in an unknown group is likely to trigger anxiety. The longer the silence, the greater is the anxiety; the greater the anxiety, the greater is the pressure to regress. When members do finally talk, they are likely to be defensive and stereotypic and will tend to introduce and establish flight basic assumption behavior in the group (Bion, 1959; Agazarian, 1997a). This is incompatible with the SCT goal of systematically weakening the defensive restraining forces to group development by deliberately reducing regressive and stereotypic communications.*

The expected consequences of the intervention would be to lower the group anxiety by reframing ambiguity as a stimulus that typically arouses anxiety. Reframing anxiety as an expected response to uncertainty provides an alternative "explanation" for experience; this tends to reduce the probability that members will make anxiety-driven, critical, or pathological interpretations of themselves and the group. Reframing of anxiety also provides a shared, here-and-now experience around which members can subgroup (which is the goal of most interventions in a beginning group).

These are three major intervention methods in SCT: structural interventions modify the permeability of the boundaries to communication within, between, and among the systems in the hierarchy; subgrouping modifies the functional ability of the system to discriminate and integrate differences; and vectoring di-

---

*SCT defines *apprehension at the edge of the unknown* as a normal form of "turbulence" at the boundary between the familiar and the unfamiliar that occurs in varying degrees of intensity. In SCT, *apprehension* is distinguished from *anxiety*: apprehension being a mixture of wariness and curiosity that potentiates exploration and discovery; anxiety being a defensive response that avoids uncertainty by interpreting it. When apprehension is contained, it is experienced as potential energy that keeps the person in a state of arousal and readiness, ready to explore and discover whatever reality will bring. When apprehension is not contained, the normal apprehension at the edge of the unknown is experienced as anxiety.

rects the system energy along the path to the goal.* Each intervention method tests a different hypothesis.†

The intervention above is initially a structural intervention in that it reduces the ambiguity by offering a normalizing explanation. Its intent is to make more likely the event that members be able to communicate within themselves and to each other with less defensiveness. The second part of the intervention contains both a functional and vectoring component. This part of the intervention makes a functional discrimination between the activities of explaining and exploring, and directs (vectors) the energy away from explaining and into exploring.

The most outstanding condition of this incident is that this is a new group. In SCT the work of the leader of a new group is to introduce the norms of universalizing, humanizing, legitimizing, depatholagizing, and normalizing human experience and dynamics.

Specific SCT methods make these ideas a reality in an SCT group. The first steps introduce subgrouping (to contain and resolve conflicts in the group),‡ boundarying (to modify the defenses that are generic to the different phases of group development), and vectoring (which orients group members to the goals of the group). The skills of subgrouping ensure that SCT members contribute to the group by exploring their own experience. They talk about themselves to each other. SCT members do not talk about other members, do not question them, or interpret them or encourage them into monologues. For example:

---

*In SCT, vectoring directs working energy across the boundaries toward the goal. A vector is like an arrow in flight, which has a direction, a force, and a target or goal (point of application). Driving and restraining forces are vectors with opposing goals. When behavior is framed in terms of vectors, then all behavior is interpreted as a vectorial output of the system that diagnoses the direction in which the system is traveling, the amount of energy (motivation) for the journey, and the goal direction that the system is traveling. This is done by using an adaptation of Lewin's force field (Agazarian, 1997a).

†The difference between boundarying and a boundary in systems-centered work is that the boundary is the threshold that marks the dividing line between one region and another in time, space, and reality. Boundarying is the action taken that influences the way that the boundary is crossed. In systems-centered work, the intention is to reduce the restraining forces at every boundary crossing. SCT assumes that driving forces are inherent in all living human systems toward the goals of survival, development, and transformation and are released when the counterbalancing restraining forces are weakened. SCT-boundarying techniques thus deliberately weaken the defensive restraining forces that inhibit the systems' innate drive. Boundarying is done in two different ways: through a systematic sequence of defense modifications that are related to the context of the specific phases of group development and through reframing.

The intervention above is a boundarying intervention, in that it modifies the permeability of the boundary between the member systems and the group as a whole by reducing ambiguity. It also reframes silence in terms that normalize, humanize, depathologize, and universalize member responses to context (thus increasing probability that there will be an acceptable common experience around which members can subgroup). It also introduces the major technique of vectoring (the fork in road) as preparation for understanding driving and restraining forces and defense modification.

‡Functional subgrouping is a conflict resolution technique in which members are deliberately encouraged to form subgroups around two (or more) sides of a conflict. Conflict is thus split and contained in the group as a whole rather than within its members. Subgroup members work together within their own subgroup, to explore their similarities (rather than to scapegoat group differences). As each subgroup works, members discover differences in the apparent similarities within their own subgroups and then recognize similarities between the different subgroups. As similarities in the apparently different are recognized, integration takes place in the group as a whole.

Asking "Why are you saying that?" or "Tell me more about that!" is a little like giving another member's boat a push out to sea.

Saying "I'm in your subgroup" is like an encouraging wave from the shore.

Working as a member of your subgroup is more than pushing another member's boat out to sea or waving encouragingly from the shore.

Working in a subgroup is getting into the boat and rowing, too!

Subgrouping requires members to "get into the boat and row" by sharing something of themselves in resonance with what other members are saying—keeping their input neither too light nor too heavy but just a little deeper than the last contribution, if possible. (This prevents moving the group toward the trivial, on the one hand, and a preemptive flood of emotion that no one can join, on the other).

When a member is distracted by anxiety, they (or the therapist) immediately ask the three SCT questions to locate the source of anxiety:

(1) "Are you having an anxiety-provoking thought? " (2) "Do you have a sensation or emotion that is making you anxious?" (3) "Are you uncertain about what is going to happen next? If so, you are at the edge of the unknown."

If the answer is the unknown, the leader continues:

"Everyone is apprehensive at the edge of the unknown, and it helps if you mobilize your curiosity."

SCT members are encouraged to notice (and discriminate between) what they think is real and what is real, by using their own common sense to check their data. For example:

A "mind-read" is checked out with a yes/no question like: "Do you think I am silly?" (Asking yes/no questions are often a difficult task in that it is embarrassing to make public the thoughts that engender painful self-consciousness.)

If the group answers yes, the leader asks, "How do you feel now that your worst fears have turned out to be true?"

If the group gives mixed reactions of both yes's and no's, the leader asks, "So your reality in this group is that x number of members do think you are silly, and y number of members do not. How is it for you working in a group where there are mixed reactions to you?"

If the group answers no, the leader asks the member whether or not he or she believes the answer. If the member answers no, the leader orients the member to reality by asking "So what is it like working in a group with a member you do not believe?" (Typically, a reality answer is a relief, even when it isn't the answer one wants!)

> *If the member does believe the answer, the leader asks, "How do you feel when you discover that the world isn't the way you thought it was?" (This question brings the member's attention to the cognitive dissonance that occurs when his or her picture of the world does not match with reality.) (Festinger, 1957)*

In this way, SCT members are encouraged to research their experience before they believe it. Trust, in an SCT group, is earned through the process of testing expectations.

Members are consistently encouraged to rely on their own common sense rather than on interpretations. The fork in the road between exploring and explaining requires reporting the physical and emotional experience that is occurring in the here and now, not talking about themselves or making interpretations of their experience. Insight occurs as part of the process—often without words.

Transactional Analysis
Implemented by Herbert Hampshire

A transactional analysis (TA) group would be likely to start out with each member having established a contract in a preliminary meeting with the therapist. There are occasions, however, when the therapist meets members for the first time at the initial session of the group. This is probable in university clinics or community centers where intake interviews are conducted by another clinician and an assignment to a group is made.

In this situation it is important to focus the group of students on establishing individual goals and articulation purposes at the outset. If the procedure is not followed, a group process is initiated that leaves members' individual dynamics in a position of lower priority than would naturally be the case. The task in a TA group is to effect a cure for the specific problem(s) identified by the individual so that he or she may move to another concern or leave the group until or unless some other problem is identified that prompts them to reenter treatment.

If I had met the group members previously, I would start the group by identifying a nonverbal response or by asking who wants to work on something. Introductions are then handled in whatever way they come up in the group. This intervention allows individuals to experience and demonstrate how they react to an absence of clear "rules" and how they solve the "problem" of not knowing each other's names. Very often, the way this procedure is handled reveals a great deal about group members' programming. One person will experience anxiety at the absence of directive leadership and resolve the conflict by "taking over," announcing that "we ought to start by introducing ourselves." Others will reveal their level of adaption by inquiring whether they "should" or whether they "can" introduce themselves. Individuals will often avoid the issue of names if the therapist does not focus on it and then insert it later in some parenthetical way that makes it appear to have little significance. No matter what form the transactions around introductions takes, it is useful for diagnostic and therapeutic purposes to let the process play itself out with as little structure being introduced by the therapist as possible.

If I had not met the group members previously, I would tell them my name and then "get to work." I might identify someone's apparent discomfort or agitation by inviting them to verbalize their feelings. The direction this interaction takes is toward establishing a contract. I would explain, essentially didactically, the importance of each person identifying which aspect of functioning she or he wants to change. The formation of effective contracts can often take a good deal of therapy and is a process that is continually sharpened and refined. It is important that members be clear at all times about what they are seeking from the treatment.

The process of contract negotiations is also therapeutic. Frequently, people come into therapy for reasons that are programmatic. They think "something is wrong" with them, or they have been pressured by others into concluding they "ought to" change. Students, for example, seek therapy for such problems as being "unable to study." The most obvious example of this pattern in other settings is the alcoholic who is trapped into treatment by a spouse who threatens to leave or a boss who threatens the loss of a job. The first task of treatment with these members is to help them recognize that they are not in group treatment because *they* want something and that they are defining their problem in a way that makes them their own enemy. Students who enter therapy because they "ought to" study more are essentially attacking themselves for their own behavior. In the process of establishing a contract, it may become clear that members want to disconnect from parental pressure to a degree that allows them to determine whether they even want to be in school. The student who "wants to change" very often has no sense that he or she can deal with their feelings and other people's in any way other than to adapt to external pressures.

It is a repeated clinical observation that treatment is not effective when a contract is made with a Parent, in opposition to a Natural Child, or both. Contracts opposing the Child are matters requiring control, not treatment. An effective therapeutic contract requires a goal that is defined by the person and that can be observably reached. The rule of thumb I suggest to members is to define their purpose for being in treatment so that it is apparent to *someone else* when achieved. The contract must be genuine in the sense that it also must include a recognition of what the "goal" is and what the therapist can contribute to the attainment of the goal.

Particularly at the outset of this group, but at other times as well, I would periodically digress from what someone is working on to do some didactic intervention. If the group is unfamiliar with TA, I would briefly explain the concepts of ego-states and transactions. This is likely to be one of the few times I would rely heavily on the language of TA. There is strikingly little use in my groups of "TA jargon" for precisely the reason that it is so easy to convert it into a jargon. The concepts are extraordinarily useful in producing clarity for both therapist and patient, but what needs to be talked about are feelings, problems, and people—not ego-state, game diagnoses, and the like. I am more likely to ask members how they think someone is likely to respond to what they just said than to identify that they are playing a game of "Now I Got You, You Son-of-a-Bitch." The purpose of TA treatment is to cure people and empower them to be autonomous and effective, not prove how clever the therapist is at being incisively analytical. Clients in TA therapy often read books on the subject and take workshops. These activities are encouraged because they provide members with the same tools for producing clarity and consciousness available to the therapist. These activities are not supported, however, when the language becomes something to hide behind while members are resisting change.

Theoretical Practitioners' Congruence With Their Theory

CLIENT-CENTERED THERAPY

If there is one approach to group therapy in which the therapist has the broadest interpretive range in applying theory to practice, it is client-centered therapy. Remember that Rogers himself said that he did not want to develop a theory of group therapy. He also told us that he made no effort to differentiate his approach to group therapy from that of individual therapy. With these criteria in mind, we approach the observation of our client-centered theoretical practitioner (TP). We want to see the extent to which the three key variables—external, group member, and group therapist—are considered and the degree to which our client-centered TP employs any or all of the 15 techniques (stages) identified by Rogers.

In this incident we have our first graphic illustration of the client-centered approach to group therapy. Our TP vigorously adheres to the basic tenets of the key concepts related to group member variables and group therapist variables. For example, he trusts the group to develop its own potential and to set its own direction; by offering no ground rules, he avoids taking over and tries to convey he is a person much like the members. He may employ self-disclosure or may simply remain silent, allowing group members to learn how to deal with ambiguity.

COGNITIVE–BEHAVIORAL THERAPY

This incident poses an interesting stimulus for our cognitive–behavioral therapy (CBT) TP. His initial response is to tell us that a behavioral group would in all likelihood not begin with silence. He then proceeds to restructure the group (reorganize) and *reorient* our way of viewing how behavioral groups are formed and begin, much of which is the type of *preliminary* pregroup work CBT therapists will have done.

In our case, he tells us that during pretherapy training, members will have identified two problems that they each wish to resolve. This addresses the concept of self-efficacy, which asks of each member to develop his or her expectations or goals. These problems are written on problem cards. As part of their pretraining, members learn that they will be asked to disclose what they have written or some other problem that they may have written during the session.

This pretraining sets the stage for avoiding the occurrence of such silence. Our TP, concerned with creating the correct CBT model, views the group silence as undermining that being achieved. Consequently, our TP would more likely have members refer to their problem cards and then respond to the question "Who would like to begin?" This intervention would generate the sharing of information and participation that CBT emphases as a requisite for its functioning.

FAMILY-CENTERED THERAPY

From the outset, our family-centered TP considers the phase of group development and takes into account the effect family dynamics has on the predisposition of members. He considers family norms that may affect the degree to which members are open (or closed), dependent, and independent and the extent to which such factors play out in the way members address personal problems in the group. He employs structured activities to address the above concerns and to establish boundaries and ground rules and to build trust and individual security that will lead to risk taking. The evidence clearly shows that our TP draws upon family theory to explain member behavior and to help him determine the intervention(s) he would employ.

GESTALT THERAPY

A crucial variable in Gestalt therapy is for the therapist to be a model of that which the theory espouses. In this case, as in each of the others, we need to ask ourselves, "Is our TP demonstrating spontaneity, emotional responsiveness, sensory awareness, and self-support; and is she expressing a 'juiciness' and freedom from barriers to effective living (i.e., "was she integrated?")?" In this incident our TP is not modeling the theory, but her way of addressing the incident clearly illustrates a congruency with theory. Her immediate interpretation of members' concerns is related to the barriers to effective independent living. Her approach includes the use of the here and now and having them "make a statement about their experiences as beginners in this new community." Her intention is to sharpen members' communication skills so that they can break from old habitual behaviors and to help them find what they hold in common with each other, as well as what differentiates them from one another. Highlighting differences leads members to feel free and encourages independence and self-support. These behaviors can be reinforced further through use of role playing that encourages experimenting with direct speaking and making clear statements about what members want from others. The desire is for role playing to lead to balancing individual venturesomeness (risk taking) against the need for group support, which in turn encourages testing out creative solutions to personal problems.

INDIVIDUAL PSYCHOLOGY

When we consider the behavior of our individual psychology (Adlerian) TP, we need to keep in mind how purposeful each of his behaviors is in helping group members achieve the primary concepts of individual psychology. We can also examine the extent to which he has exemplified being both a model of effective living and a creative and imaginative strategist and technician.

From the outset, our TP acknowledges reasoning and cognitive power over affective and emotional power. Such behavior is evidenced by his "critical introductory message," which explains the reason he formed the group. He not only adheres to Adlerian principles but also presents a subtle, different emphasis of the concept of lifestyle. He instructs members on the three basic life tasks and then tries to draw a commonality that members share, albeit their expressed concerns may appear at first glance to be the reason that gives them each a reason for feeling they are different. Once expressed, he sees members' problems being addressed by the group over the ensuing sessions.

Interpersonal Psychotherapy

What comes to our immediate attention when we witness our interpersonal psychotherapy TPs is how they adhere to keeping behaviors and interpersonal interactions in the here and now and move to establishing members' difficulties into interpersonal problems. These interventions tell us that our TPs are in keeping with the key concept of interpersonal learning. Thus, the reason for "plunging" the members immediately into discussing how they each feel about being in the group is to have them "learn from the group about the nature of their interpersonal world." By encouraging members to disclose in the group, they will find support in the group, as well as solace through the universalizing of their fears (similarity) with others, thus helping them avoid isolating themselves.

Psychodynamic Therapy

We learned earlier (Chapter 7) that anxiety and its creation play a crucial role in psychodynamic group therapy. We also learned that process (i.e., underlying/unconscious motives) is more important to understand than what (content) is being said. Furthermore, the therapist will also be inclined to encourage transferential feelings from the members. Our psychodynamic therapy TP without any doubt engages in behaviors and a role that encourages or fosters the foregoing concepts. He is more interested in understanding what is implied (process) by how each member approaches this new situation. He does not want to lessen the anxiety that the incident creates. In fact, he intensifies it by allowing it to deepen in order to gain access to unconscious data that may be reflected through member defenses and roles each assumes in dealing with silence. He also wants to help members begin thinking psychodynamically, (i.e., become more insightful) regarding their behaviors, feelings, expectations, and perceptions. To achieve this end, he would point out the behaviors members engage in as a means for managing the new situation, including how they deal with their concern for safety as it relates to the group as a whole and the leader.

Rational—Emotive—Behavioral Therapy

If there is any question whether our rational—emotive—behavioral (REBT) TP will adhere to the principles of his theory, they are removed immediately. From the outset, he is delighted to be the first to meet with this group in order to "prejudice" the members toward REBT. From the outset, he employs instruction in REBT principles. He also moves the group members (individually and as a group) to use REBT principles. He assigns homework and uses bibliotherapy, which he believes will appeal to and reinforce the rational side of group members.

REALITY THERAPY

As we learned in Chapter 9, group therapist roles and techniques are synonymous with group process, which in turn is identified by the seven stages a group must pass through. As we witness our reality therapy TP work in this incident (and later in the others), we try to see how extensively he adheres to acknowledging these seven stages. In addition, we examine how he integrates the key concepts that support reality therapy into his work. Finally, we look at the extent to which our TP appeals to our rationality, and if indeed he chooses to do this by engaging the group in some pedagogical dialogue.

In terms of style, our TP does not disappoint us. He does not allow the silence to settle into a moment of anxiety. He takes advantage of it to establish group norms. Using self-disclosure and I-statements, he demonstrates taking responsibility and establishing intimacy. He does not hesitate to take the initiative when he arrives early, greets and introduces each member, and starts exactly on time. By doing so, he further underscores the significance of responsible behavior. This action also conveys respect toward each member.

SOLUTION-FOCUSED THERAPY

Did our solution-focused therapy (SFT) TP follow the principles of the theory? If we were to judge on the basis of the way she reframes the incident, it is easy to say she certainly begins that way. The incident is viewed as to be expected and is part of the prescreening process. She wants to establish a climate of safety in order to encourage members to work. She achieves this objective by helping members share and find what they have in common. Upon establishing this common ground, she moves to introducing them to SFT language by asking them what they each would like to change. Such sharing leads to group cohesiveness, which is necessary for the group members to move forward. She continues to work at identifying unifying themes that link members together. This provides emotional relief.

She also focuses on each member's language in an attempt to make the distinction between *problems* and *difficulties*. Furthermore, she listens to discover if members use *labels* or *absolutes*. Again, she reframes members' language and ways of viewing themselves so that they can take a more opportunistic view of their difficulty. She also works to keep members specific about their presenting area of difficulty. These behaviors are all part of developing an SFT orientation. Finally, as she terminates the session, she assigns a task that provides a direction for constructing change. She has members focus on what they would like to have happen more often. Note that the emphasis is on the solution, not the difficulty.

Systems-Centered Therapy

Recall from Chapter 11 that systems-centered therapy (SCT) is a very structured and systematic approach to group therapy. SCT therapists maintain a high profile when a group is meeting for the first time, by attending to three primary tasks during the early moments of the group. SCT therapists are quick to bring member defenses to their attention, while teaching members the skills that will modify presenting defenses. Along with these actions, therapists also try to

> humanize, normalize, legitimize, and depathologize defenses; help patients learn to state the obvious, use common sense, discover reality, and contain the potential work energy in frustration rather than discharge it or constrict it; and insure patients always recognize the fork in the road and understand the choices available to them. (Agazarian, 1997a, p. 39)

Our SCT TP certainly does not disappoint us. We see this clearly by virtue of the way she responds to the incident. She is very structured and systematic in her approach. She attends to the three primary tasks of the group leader during the early moments of the session. Most evident are the SCT methods of boundarying, vectoring (resonance), and subgrouping (through facing the fork in the road), all of which tell us she was adhering to the primary tasks. Consistent with SCT theory, members are encouraged to test ("research") the reality of their experience, moving them from the cognitive experience to the affective, which in turn prepares them to resonate with one another.

Transactional Analysis

Because a critical dimension of transactional analysis (TA) therapy is the therapist's personhood, let us begin there. Does our TP model authenticity and genuineness? Does he demonstrate a strong commitment to individual members and the group? Is he being observant, quickly gathering and evaluating data?

He moves quickly to work, after simply introducing himself by name. This behavior helps establish an early norm in the group: Members are there not only to work but also to be authentic and genuine—that is, no game playing. His commitment to the group and individual members is evidenced immediately when he identifies a member's discomfort and encourages the member to verbalize his or her feelings, which has the intention of establishing a contract early on. This whole move also conveys how observant he is in gathering data, analyzing it, and acting on it. It appears the answers to all our questions are in the affirmative.

Moving on, our TA TP briefly engages in didactic work such as explaining constructs of ego-states and transactions and hastens members to talk about feelings, problems, and people. All of these activities are designed to help the group as a whole because this knowledge will prove to be useful. Such knowledge not only leads to members being clear about that they wish to change but also allows both the therapist and the group to observe the changed behavior when it occurs. We can conclude that our TA TP's approach to this critical incident is consistent with TA theory.

Theory Evaluation Form

1. Which theoretical practitioner do you most resemble? Why?

2. Which theoretical practitioner do you least resemble? Why?

3. What does your response to Question 1 tell you about yourself and your leadership styles as a potential or present group therapist?

4. What does your response to Question 2 tell you about yourself and your leadership style as a potential or present group therapist?

5. After rereading how the theoretical practitioner of your choice responded to the incident, how would you modify your response?

CHAPTER FOURTEEN

Group Attack of the Therapist

The following incident is one most therapists face in the life of a group. Sometime into session 3, the group turns and attacks you, the therapist.

Critical Incident 2

The group is made up of five couples. Initially, each couple had been seeing you separately. However, as you came to realize that their areas of concern had much in common, you asked each couple if they would be interested in joining a couples' group. You explained the rationale supporting your consideration for establishing the group, including the added value and benefits for recognizing behaviors that groups provide beyond meeting individually. They all volunteered to give it a try.

Briefly, the members are described as follows:

Couple 1 Nicholas and Laurie have been married for 15 years. They have two children, ages 10 and 13 years old. Nicholas is 35 years old, has a degree in engineering, and is employed as a design engineer. Laurie is 33 years old and has been a homemaker since they were married after graduating from high school. Laurie has expressed a desire to go to college and has stated that she is not sure she wants to remain being just a homemaker. Nicholas is confused over this sudden turn in events.

Couple 2 Larry and Pamela have been married for 2 years. They have no children. Larry is 26 years old, has an associate degree, and is an associate with an ophthalmologist. Pamela is 25 years old and is employed as a registered nurse at the local hospital. When they first came to you, they stated that they were unhappy with their marriage but were not sure why.

Couple 3   Paul and Joan have been married for 8 years. They have three children, ages 4, 6, and 7 years old. Paul is 34 years old, a high school graduate, and a self-employed plumber. Joan is 33 years old, has a master's degree in education, and teaches fourth grade at a local elementary school. Joan initiated their contact with you. When you first met them, the presenting issue was Joan's concern that Paul seemed to be avoiding her, and Paul had expressed that he was not happy.

Couple 4   John and Helen have been married for 10 years. This is Helen's second marriage. They have two children, ages 11 and 13 years old, both of whom are from Helen's first marriage. John is 40 years old, had attended college for three years, and now operates a printing company. Helen is 39 years old, a high school graduate, and is employed as a teacher's aide. She has stated that she wants to go to college. John has voiced opposition to this, and they have reached an impasse.

Couple 5   Peter and Doris have lived together for 10 years. They have two children, ages 4 and 6 years old. Peter is 31 years old and owns a florist shop. Doris is 31 years old, is a cosmetologist, and is employed by a department store. They came to you because they felt their relationship was not the same as it used to be.

The first two sessions had a great deal of activity. Member-to-member interaction seemed to develop easily. Early in session 2, the members engaged in a significant amount of disclosure and confrontation. It came about as a result of Nicholas's disclosure of his confusion about why his wife should want to go to school. He stated he felt that once she got a taste of it, she might want to go to work, and he questioned where this would all lead. As far as he was concerned, he felt their marriage was just fine the way it was, and he could not understand why it should change. As you listened to him, you observed how his wife was responding. She was sitting with her feet crossed in front of her and her arms and hands resting on her lap, with eyes looking toward her hands. Her face was expressionless. Your eyes shifted to the rest of the members. You could see John nodding as though he was agreeing with or understanding Nicholas's comments. His wife was looking at Laurie. Larry, Pamela, Paul, and Joan were listening intently to Nicholas. He no sooner had completed his statement, when Doris, with her voice sounding tense, stated, "That sounded just like a man! All they ever think about is that because their wives are working, they might end up running around!" Before she was able to continue, her statement drew responses from the rest of the group. You observed (to yourself) that Laurie had not participated in the ensuing interaction. You determined it was perhaps too early to make this observation known and that perhaps Laurie would, in her own time, present herself. The emotional level of the group was still relatively high as you moved the session to termination.

At session 3, you notice that the members are very jovial and quite verbal as they enter the room. As a matter of fact, they continue to discuss a number of issues such as dieting, politics, and sports throughout the first 15 minutes of the session. You finally offer that you think this level of discussion is not dealing with the issues or purposes of the group and ask the members if they are aware of the direction their discussion has undergone. There is a brief silence in the group. Then one of the members attacks you for seeming to appear cool, distant, and uncaring. With that, another states that she is beginning to question your qualifications as a therapist. The others join in the attack, each in turn questioning, in one form or another, your credibility as a therapist.

Client-Centered Therapy
Implemented by William R. Coulson

As a group begins, members grant the leader expertise, but I do not want it. My task, as I define it, is to work gradually into membership, to the point that I am not special. A major criterion of leadership will have been met when other members see me as a person like themselves.

I do not mean to be self-effacing. I also want members to see themselves as persons having all the power that comes with being the leader. When I am group leader, I feel like Superperson. The title does it for me. It permits me to be as sharp and attentive as I would like always to be—whether member or leader—but which as member ordinarily embarrasses me, lest someone accuse me of trying to be leader. I doubt that anyone would actually make such an accusation. Nonetheless, I often seem to need an initial role in order to drop my reserve and be as powerful as a person. I do not want to give up this power; I want to distribute it. Then all of us will be Superpersons.

As such, each of us will be different. Being persons includes our various backgrounds, the particular persons we have become. I do not want to pretend, for example, that I am not a professional psychologist. But I do not want special respect because group members have their own backgrounds, helping qualify them to contribute uniquely to the others. It is this distribution of unique perspectives within the group that I believe defines the power of group over individual therapy. The necessary resources are among us, not in only one. This is the client-centered hypotheses as applied to group work.

The present trouble in this group arose because the therapist failed to provide a personal perspective at a time when it was needed, and he or she now is being punished for it. One member calls the therapist detached ("cool, distant, and uncaring"). I doubt that the therapist is that way as a person. Yet one can see where the judgment of detachment originates. The leader seemingly has not participated except with unspoken or professional observations. My concern as the therapist now is that I not maintain this stance—in order to avoid a defense against the group's attack.

The incident offers an opportunity for rich personal learning, if the therapist will only take it. It requires the therapist to remain alert. For myself, I cannot envision a discrete picture of learning in this incident that could equal the latent possibilities in the actual interaction. The best of these possibilities will be quite unknown until the moment of their arrival at the next turn of the conversation. To take advantage of this opportunity, the therapist only need avoid shutting down.

The greatest danger in being under attack is to become psychological, seeing the group's aggression as *solely* the sign of members' own minor (and major) pathologies. Granted, therapists must not wilt under the attack by taking it too personally; they must therefore maintain an ability to see the attack as having as much to do with the group as with the therapist. To get full benefit from the criticism, however, they must listen to it openly. When it is offered, they cannot be thinking, "I know where *that* comes from." They have to acknowledge that others can tell them important things about themselves that they cannot know of their own. In the simplest terms, group members can *see* them; that's something they cannot do for themselves. The final decision about the importance of what group members tell therapists about themselves will and must remain with them, but they must not censor it through psychologizing about their critics. There is more than one kind of defensiveness. Therapists are unlikely to display the blatant, argumentative kind. If they become defensive under the pressure they now receive from the group, it is likely to be in an unwarranted extension of professional form, namely, psychologism (Buber, 1967).

I see the therapist as having made two errors in this situation. One occurred at the end of session 2, and the other just preceded the group's criticism.

The first mistake occurred when the trauma in session 2 was ignored. Doris rebuked Nicholas, seemingly out of the blue. She made an outrageous generalization about the husbands of working women. She must have been talking about her own relationship, but she did not get to finish. The group took off like a covey of quail, beating wings, banging against the ceiling, bouncing off the walls. That's how session 2 ended, with "the emotional level of the group still relatively high." Fright continued to affect the group at the next session. Members gravitated to small talk to protect themselves against the possible further trauma of examining or even acknowledging what had happened the last time.

Any trauma will cause a hole in the group unless someone has the nerve to point to it. As therapist, I would have done so myself if no one else had, just out of self-protection. If the disruption of session 2 was not explicitly noted in the group, I know it would have come back to haunt us later. Each person would carry a private opinion about what had happened, but there would be no common acceptance and readiness to move to a deeper level unless the incident was discussed in the group.

It is safe to guess that the individual couples talked about the incident when they got home after session 2—and that they talked *about* the therapist. I have sensitivity for the therapist being involved in a couples' group without being part of a couple. One knows that husbands and wives are going to talk about the session as they drive home. That is one of the benefits of couples' groups: Therapy goes on into the night. The therapist who works alone runs the risk of becoming a handy target when things become difficult for the group. So I bring protection with me when I do couple's groups: My wife becomes a member with me.

I hope she doesn't tell on me, tell the group the bad things I do at home. But I hope for the same direction (and intuitive sense of what is truly helpful in therapy) among the other couples, too. It is a waste of time when they bring stories of home life with them. There is little one can do to help. They have all the data. Someone will make a suggestion for improvement, and they will say, "We've tried that." There is little virtue in exchanging suggestions in therapy groups of any kind. It is far more interesting and effective when members react to one another as persons in the moment. Couples have the advantage in therapy of living together and taking the session home with them if they wish. But they cannot constructively bring home life to the group. They make themselves experts when they do, but experts only on their private histories. We need no experts. We do far better dealing with what we all can see, and that means what is happening in the group itself.

There was a big happening in this group, and nobody mentioned it. That's too much like life to suit me. The therapist should have said something at the end of session 2, even at the risk of running overtime.

The second mistake was scolding the group for making small talk at the start of session 3. *Of course* they made small talk. The group had ended in an uproar the last time they met, and they were afraid to go near it again. The therapist must have known what they were avoiding. Rather than accuse them of "not dealing with the issues or purposes of the group" (a phrase that, if actually used in group, surely would sound superior and coldly professional), the therapist should have admitted knowing that there was a hole in the group or even confess—if it were so—a personal desire to avoid it, too.

The therapist should now suffer the consequences in this instance and listen to what the group has to say. The therapist should realize that some of the group's criticism will be overdetermined (I would not be far off to say that they are scapegoating the therapist), but to learn from it, too. Hearing criticism directly (rather than hearing of it having been spoken behind one's back) is a rare enough opportunity that one ought to get all he or she can out of it.

For myself, I would probably blow the opportunity to learn from criticism, particularly if the group were unanimous in condemning me, but I would want to learn from it. Somewhere at the back of my mind, so far back that it might be unreachable when I was under pressure, I would have the idea that I needed to hear from people about myself, including, and especially, my mistakes. I would really *want* to treat these people as colleagues who, if I could listen to them (and perhaps if they could speak a little more gently), would help me gain perspective. Our therapist has been "observing" his or her "subjects" and has indeed been "critical." But the tables have turned; the subjects have now become critical themselves. We should have expected it. Any attempt to limit therapeutic judgment to the therapist alone would distort the obvious: Human intelligence, experience, and insight are widely distributed. The therapist has no corner on wisdom. Not only will group members exercise judgment of their own, but they also will surpass the therapist.

Cognitive–Behavioral Therapy
Implemented by John V. Flowers

I only conduct behavioral groups with two group leaders. For me, this absolute requirement is a result of my understanding of the principles of perception. Effective therapy requires the therapist to process complex information and cast it into a pattern that makes conceptual sense and generates possible interventions. The information generated in a therapy group is too complex for a single therapist to perceive and process, especially considering the paramount responsibility of doing no harm while ethically attempting to help people change their lives.

Group therapists (and everyone else) perceive what is across the room better than what is happening off to the side. This alone indicates that two therapists are needed to obtain a balanced perceptual view of the group. Much of the necessary information in the group is nonverbal, requiring active perception that is too difficult for one person to do effectively. Two therapists also allow for a reliability check on perceptions and interpretations about the meaning of data. These are compelling arguments for dual leaders in the complexity of the group.

The attack on a poor, lonely therapist battling the tides of irrational members simply does not happen when there are two group leaders. Leaders, especially if sitting somewhat across from each other, are rarely attacked simultaneously. Those times one therapist is attacked, the other therapist becomes more verbally active, while the attacked therapist is usually more silent. The leaders, especially the attacked leader, do not try to defend or explain but can express appropriate feelings of hurt or disappointment. The leaders generally try to avoid fueling the therapeutic fire unless there is a clear therapeutic goal for doing so. The rule for the attacked therapist is "if unsure, wait," which is possible if another therapist is in the room. Thus, the attacked therapist is not responsible for personal feelings and for conducting the group.

In behavioral group therapy, the group is participatory, but it is not fully democratic. The therapists have ethical responsibilities the clients do not share. The therapists are not free to totally be themselves and should act in their clients' best interests, which are not always their own. A lone therapist may want to withdraw when attacked, but that will leave the group leaderless. The assertion that the best interest of client and therapist is always the same is a deception of monumental proportions. The way to solve the problem of the group therapist with conflicted personal interests and group responsibilities is not to assert there is no problem but to prepare for it in a manner most beneficial to everyone's interests.

When there is group–leader conflict, the presence of two leaders makes ethical and effective resolution of the conflict easier and usually faster. The other leader often plays traffic cop, making helpful statements such as "Let's slow down and let 'Bill' reply to these concerns," or "Can you say that in another way which 'Bill' could hear this more easily." These statements help diffuse the worst aspects of attacks. An attack on a leader can also hurt the group when the attack is like an avalanche, becoming an almost mass contagion. Any leader behavior that slows the process almost invariably helps the group not be damaged, which is the first concern, and can help the attacked leader not be damaged, which is the second concern. After the do-no-harm criterion has been satisfied, the therapeutic meaning of the attack can be attended to and learning can occur.

Family-Centered Therapy
Implemented by James P. Trotzer

As a family-systems-oriented group leader, my initial thought about this group is that it is not a group composed of individuals but a group composed of systems. Each couple represents a system that maintains relational proximity between group sessions where they function together as a couple and (in four of the five cases) as a subsystem of a family system. Consequently, I must be aware that what happens in group goes home with them, which is vital for me to be aware of in this particular critical incident. My second realization is that a transition in my role as therapist is involved. Since each couple was initially engaged by me for marital therapy, my role as a professional is going through a transformation process from marital therapist to group therapist. As the group leader, I must be cognizant of this particular dynamic because very likely that transformation will set the tone for the group process and the work the couples will do in the group. As such, this shift in my role is a metaphor for the change process endemic in the work of this couples' group. The way I address and resolve the role change will influence the couples' change processes.

My observation of the group itself is that it is composed of couples who share a common developmental characteristic despite their differences (e.g., married for different lengths of time, different family life-cycle stages, and different family forms—i.e., nuclear family, blended family, cohabiting family). The commonality is that each couple is in some form of a dissatisfied relational state. Therefore, each couple is faced with the task of reorganizing its relationship toward greater complexity to enhance its functionality or have it face deterioration into disillusionment or dysfunction. In addition, each couple is experiencing the dynamic reality that relationships must either grow or atrophy. (Marriages can either get better or worse, and they usually do.) As such, each couple is sensing a prevalent tension between the need for change (morphogenetic force) and the fear of or resistance to change (homeostatic force). Each pair is on the brink of transition either in terms of the family life cycle (e.g., school-age family to adolescent family), gender-role change (e.g., wives wanting to go to college), or marital disenchantment (e.g., personal or relational dissatisfaction). "What's next?" is a primary concern for all the couples.

I believe the system's dynamics described above set the stage for the group process dynamics that culminate in the attack on the therapist—a situation that I think I would have anticipated and addressed in session 2 by the use of a common marital therapy intervention adapted to the group modality. The narrative of the incident indicates the leader is aware of the intensity of the group's involvement and the withdrawn state of Laurie, the spouse of Nicholas, who is disclosing his confusion about his wife's desire to go to school. The diverse and polarizing responses of group members are also evident, as is the observation that the emotional level is high as the group session moves toward closure. Given the systemic observation that couples take the group home with them, coupled with the observed dynamics, I would have made the following intervention at the close of session 2: "We are coming to the end of our session. I have noticed that the interest, intensity, and involvement has been very high during this session. Since each of you as couples have been involved, I would like to ask you to do something between now and next session. My experience is that intense discussions in couples' groups carry over into life between sessions. So, I would like each of you to observe and keep track of any ramifications of our work today that may appear during the week and report your observations next time."

By making a general request emphasizing observations rather than experience or affect, I set the tone that creates some detachment from the emotionality but maintains a connection to the focus. This request is based on the premise that change in marital relationships typically manifests itself in some form of gender-role conflict. I would present the task as a request rather than an assignment, thus providing the couples with a tool they can choose to use rather than a task they are required to perform. This task will help the group keep on track for either one of the following reasons. (1) As the leader, I made them take stuff home that may still result in an attack on me but remain within the context of the group focus. (2) Because it facilitates recognition of the *group impact dynamics* on couples regarding changes that are needed or that are already occurring in their relationships, I suspect this type of ending request would change an "out of the blue" attack into a therapeutic encounter that advances progress.

However, let's address the incident as it is actually described, considering first the dynamics that generated the attack and then several options available for my response. The intensity of session 2 served notice that individual members of each couple were identifying with the disclosure of Nicholas in some way. As this identification occurred, energy was mobilized, shifting the process away from the dynamics of triangulation (present when each couple was in marital therapy with me) to dynamics of connection (necessary for the group process to work). When the group resumed interaction, the connection with each other was retained, indicating some group cohesion and connection had occurred, but the attachment to the focus or content generating that connection was discarded. Thus, when I attempted to reconnect the group to relevant content, a coalescing process was promulgated where participants banded together as individuals to respond to my incendiary intervention that threatened to bring couple dynamics to the surface. This shift from a couple–therapist bond to a group allegiance signaled the emergence of cohesion in the group, albeit by default—that is, through the couples' attack on me as the leader.

The nature of the attack is instructive of the underlying systemic dynamics related to my therapist-role change. The attack reflects a mourning of losing me as each couple's personal marital therapist. (I am accused of being "cool, distant, and uncaring.") The attack also partially raises the members' anxieties about my role as a group therapist. (My qualifications and credibility are questioned.) Finally, the attack affirms the metaphoric enactment that relates to the gender-role issues in each couple.

Consequently, I see this event as pivotal for the group process. How I handle it is critical to whether the group will progress to a therapeutic work milieu or set in motion splitting dynamics that will undermine the cohesion of the group and immobilize the vital resources contained in each individual and couple. If I am immobilized or become reactively defensive, the group will likely turn on each other because a norm of viewing causes of problems as outside themselves as couples will be set. Like a symptom in a distressed system, I as the leader appear to be the problem. Attacking me represents the system's effort to maintain itself without changing. In this case multiple systems (five) are channeling their resistance into the attack on me as the leader. The objective of my response is therefore to dissolve the attack by flowing with it and turning it back toward the couples and the group in a therapeutic form.

In this session the couples' initial, friendly camaraderie while avoiding their issues is likely the work of homeostatic resistance. However, I believe an underlying residual tension promoted by the morphogenetic need for change is present as well. When I prompt group members to focus on their issues, this tension produces an immediate cathexis in the form of an attack on me. The message is, "He doesn't know what he is doing, which is why we are distressed." This is an accurate observation about their own dynamics, which is temporarily displaced on to the leader. A plausible reframe is, "We (as couples) don't know what we are doing or where we are going, which is why we are distressed."

The attack on me produces cohesion in the group but also generates a crisis. This crisis provides an opportunity (not without risk or danger) for me to help the group work through their tension and focus on the issues in the various relationships that the group can help resolve.

The following are three possible interventions that I could implement:

1. Acknowledge the coalescing phenomenon: I would shift the focus from me as the object and subject of the group focus to the process of group cohesion that made it possible. I would express a sincere acknowledgment of the way the group banded together into a cohesive unit. This would be done in a straightforward manner, or with a strategic, paradoxical twist; that is, "I have never experienced a couples' group that has come together so quickly. The strength of your togetherness is very impressive though disconcerting because it is focused on me."

2. Raise an "I wonder . . . " observation: "When we ended last time, there was an intense involvement that was personal and poignant. Today, the group was very jovial as we started but seemed to be avoiding things of a serious nature. I wonder what happened? You seem to think it has something to do with me. I'm open to that possibility, but is there more to it than that?"

3. Make a role differentiation statement: "As you confronted me, I realized that I'm the only one here who is not part of a couple. You go home from group with each other, taking with you what you experienced. I just go home and then

come to the next group session. What happens in-between is different for me than for you."

These interventions invite group members to attend to its process as a means of getting back to themselves. Because all couples are faced with coping with change and reorganizing their relationships in some manner, dealing with me as the leader is a useful springboard to try out the group influence process before applying it to themselves. This incident has high potential for propelling the group into the work stage of the group process. My inclination is to use the third option because it is closely related to the closing intervention I hope I would have made at the end of session 2.

Gestalt Therapy
Implemented by Mirriam F. Polster

This scene does not sound like one I would have gotten into. I do not mean that I might never be attacked or criticized. Rather, I would have behaved differently both at the end of session 2 and at the beginning of this one.

Doris's denunciation of men occurs in stereotypic terms near the end of session 2 and gets lost in what the rest of the group says afterward. An opportunity for dialogue has been missed. Her statement is an abstraction, dealing only in generalities. It would have been important in session 2 to bring it into the present circumstances by attaching it to the specifics of what Nicholas has just said. As it did end, Doris's energy is left constricted, tense, and deflected (Polster & Polster, 1973), and a chance for vital confrontation and contact is not supported. I would ask Doris to tell Nicholas more about her experience with "all men" and what it is in particular that she finds objectionable in what he has just said. Is she saying he is like all the rest? How? What does she know about him that suggested this? How does she want to respond to what the other group members have said?

Nicholas, too, has been vague and general. His statement requires more time to develop into specific revelations about his fears. What is it about Laurie's return to school that makes him apprehensive? If he is confused about why she wants to go back, why doesn't he ask her? If he is fearful about the consequences of her returning to school, what prevents him from telling her of his worries in a way that respects her needs and still honors his own uncertainty? What actual experiences has Nicholas had when this subject has come up between him and Laurie? Has he felt that there were things he had not told her, that remained unsaid and unfinished between them? Our situation presents an opportunity for the dialogue that is essential between them. Instead, Nicholas is allowed to remain vague, and Laurie sits there, staring at her hands, saying nothing. Is this a reenactment of how things go at home when this subject is broached, or has it previously led to such painful or unresolved feelings that a fresh discussion is to be avoided at all costs?

In responding to these events in session 2, I would try to heighten the possibilities for dialogue by sharpening the participants' awareness of particular feelings and complaints and also by body postures. The way Laurie is sitting, even though silent, is saying something. Can she put this into words? Would it then express hopelessness or resentment? How does Nicholas feel about her silence? How do the others respond to it? Addressing each other directly is a step toward resolution. How well Nicholas, Doris, Laurie, and the others can support strong contact, or flee from it, could then become more apparent and more workable. Right now, much of their energy goes into deflection; Nicholas gets confused and does not know how to ask the questions dealing specifically with his fears; Doris's complaints are off-target and stereotypically bitter; Laurie remains silent; and the group focus is allowed to dissolve into diffuse comment with little follow-up.

At the beginning of session 3, I would not have done what the group leader did—I would not have interpreted the group's behavior as avoidant. The traditional definition of resistance ignores the energy and creativity that may be expressed—in this case, the small talk—and moves instead to what is *not* being expressed, the last session's confrontation. Although a valid perspective, it emphasizes the opinion of the group leader, who decides what is important and tells everybody else that *they* are resisting. We could say that the group leader is resisting also—resisting the joviality and talkativeness of the group and taking a stand slightly lower than the angels, telling the mortals to get down to business. To regard the group's behavior as merely resistant is to disrespect their self-regulatory capacity to learn how to pace themselves. If I were interested in some other topic, I would simply put it out. I might say that I am eager to pick up where we left off last time—are they?

If we view what is happening at the beginning of session 3 as expressive rather than resistant behavior (Polster & Polster, 1973), we see different results. The group is interacting with energy and excitement. The members are talking about something other than their marital difficulties, it is true, but I will observe to see if they are listening to each other more attentively and taking each other's reactions and opinions more seriously than before. Perhaps learning how someone else goes about dieting is a preface to getting back to a deeper issue where that person's opinion will also be taken more seriously. Perhaps the group is warming up to get back to the loaded discussion of the previous session and is testing the atmosphere to see if grudges or sore feelings remain. Their self-regulation needs room to operate; if they feel driven back into confronting an issue, then I have changed the issue; they are no longer responding to Nicholas, Doris, and Laurie but also to me *compelling* them to respond. In a way, I have deflected them from the topic.

People in a group often need to determine the stability and trustworthiness of the group response. Although they can be overly careful about this on occasion, this is nevertheless a self-supportive action before heading into new emotional territory. They are exploring the balance between discretion, wariness, passion, bitterness, apprehension, directness, hopelessness, and the whole spectrum of feelings that can either muddy up or enliven the interaction of people, married to each other or not.

So I might wait out what appears to be small talk and look for an opening to bring it around to more familiarly therapeutic concerns. I avoided using the words *more serious concerns.* Humor and joviality *are* often deflections, but deflection can sometimes serve a useful purpose. People may need to skirt an issue, to buy time and perspective in a situation in which they might otherwise feel pushed beyond their present capacity to support themselves. Gradual descent into hot water is important for more than getting into bathtubs.

The opening could come directly from what one person may say or from another's response. For example, Doris, in talking about dieting, might say something about how unfair it is that women have to worry more about their appearance than men; someone talking about politics might express an opinion about the feminist movement; and so on. I could, instead of this approach, raise the issue directly by saying, "When we stopped last time we were in the middle of a hot discussion. Does anyone have some unfinished business left from that time?" Or I could ask some of the more vocal people from last time if there was something more they wanted to say now. Had they gotten their views across, or did they feel misunderstood and want to add something? I would make sure this time that Laurie did not remain a cipher. This was her husband talking; what were her reactions to his position? I might also ask John how he felt about Nicholas's speech. And certainly Helen.

Most important, though, I would be responding to the energy level and excitement of the group. These assets are too valuable to be scolded out of existence because at the moment they are not being applied to what I consider to be the central focus.

This is a group of people whose excitement customarily does not work *for* them. They convert it into anxiety, watchfulness, and confusion. These individuals need to experience trusting their excitement and learning how to support clarity and enthusiasm in their relationships. By staying aware of the specifics of their experience as it is occurring, and not complying with someone else's "shoulds" (even the therapist's), they will learn to support their actions in the present moment. Their sensations and feelings can then become orienting and arousing rather than distracting. Their experience of themselves can root them in the present instead of catapulting them into a future made scary, perpetually vaguely worded in impersonal clichés where they have all the painful sensations of arousal without the opportunity for interaction and resolution that exist only in the present.

Individual Psychology

Implemented by Guy J. Manaster

This situation is a beauty. It holds great potential for development of the group as a whole and of individuals. This presents an opportunity for group members to reveal themselves and their goals in interpersonal interaction and for interpretation of their goals in the group. It also gives me a chance to learn about myself and how I come across as group leader.

My previous tendency in this type of situation was to feel defensive; I had to fight my inclination to defend myself and do battle. I cannot remember ever giving in to that inclination, but I surely remember feeling like doing so. Maybe it is just maturity, but I prefer to think that I have internalized Adlerian theory over the years and gained both confidence in my adequacy and awareness of my imperfections. Openness to new options for thinking and behaving are the result. The response that immediately comes to mind in this situation is, "You may be right. What do you think I should be doing? What would a *real* therapist be doing?"

This response, I hope, would first make the point that I do not always have to be right, all knowing, and supremely confident, but rather that I am interested in learning and growing while still feeling adequate. This point would be particularly important for Nicholas and John, and probably Doris, all of whom appear to want things to be and therefore see things as clear, black or white, and definite.

My response also would be intended to indicate respect for the group's opinion. The group leader's interjection in session 3 that led to this attack can be read as, and may well have been taken by the group as, a put-down. If the group reaction has arisen because the leader had conveyed an attitude of "enough of this silly talk—let's get down to business—don't you know that you've been avoiding the issues," then an indirect, if not a direct, apology by the leader is called for. The leader may have inadvertently given that impression and should try to counter it. As leader, even if I had not transmitted this holier-than-thou attitude, which I know I would not have felt, I would want to show my respect for the group members as worthy people. Central to positive mental health in Adlerian theory is the feeling of equality with others. Equality and mutual respect are important in this group, where the difficulty inherent in marriage partners living as equals is compounded by traditional notions of differential status and value accorded by sex and credentials.

It is presumptuous to suppose that "You may be right" actually communicates all of these meanings, but from our previous contact and with follow-up, I would try to convey these points.

What was the purpose of the rest of my response? First, I want to know what they want. Second, I have set up a straw man, "a *real* therapist," the perfect therapist, in order to again present opportunities to emphasize personal and general fallibility, equality, and a spirit of working together.

I have two hunches. The first, mentioned above, is that I started this by putting down the group and they are saying "It's your fault we are off the mark. If you were a good therapist, we would be a good group." I have already stated how and why I would try to counter and make use of this theme.

My second hunch is that many in the group want *the* answer to their problems. By asking what they want of me, or of someone competent in another therapeutic approach, I can find out if this is true. If they answer that a *real* therapist would give more direction, tell them who is right, what to do, and the like, then my hunch would be confirmed. The discussion to follow would then have to turn to questions of values—what Adler called "the common sense of social living"—is there a right way, *an answer?* And I would have to confess that I do not know the answer. My task, as I see it and would explain it, is to assist in the development of processes based on social interest that foster equality of responsibility and satisfaction within the couple.

My hunches may be wrong. If they are, my response should, in any event, open the way for a new level of group process with some improvement in the ability of the group leader.

Interpersonal Psychotherapy
Implemented by Victor Yalom and Mary Jean Paris

In a group situation such as this, it would initially be hard for the therapist being attacked not to be defensive and thus be tempted to offer an "interpretation" that really serves as an attempt to put himself or herself in the all-knowing, authority role. We would try to resist this temptation and instead express genuine interest in the nature of the criticisms hurled at us. One fundamental way in which members benefit from the group experience is that they receive constructive feedback from other members and from the leader(s) that they can consider, assess, and utilize both inside and outside the group. The therapist under attack will want to model this behavior and listen intently to the group's feedback. At this point, the group leader will want to check in with herself or himself regarding the validity of the feedback from the therapy group. When one of the group members attacks one of the leaders for being "cool, distant, and uncaring," the first thing we hope that we would do is to honestly assess how we were actually feeling during the 15 minutes when the members were talking about nongroup issues. Was the feedback consistent with our internal appraisal?

If one of us realizes that in fact we were feeling bored and impatient with the group, then we would certainly understand why the group interpreted our behavior as uncaring and distant. In this case, we would frankly acknowledge being frustrated and would convey our understanding of how they could interpret our behavior as being uncaring. We try to model to patients how to be open to feedback without responding impulsively in a defensive fashion and that we too have blind spots and areas for growth. Parenthetically, when coleading groups, it is quite useful when one therapist is being attacked or challenged for the coleader to facilitate the exchange. Then the therapist who is the object of the attack can focus his or her energies on responding authentically and nondefensively without being distracted at having to manage the group at the same time.

The coleader could also elicit reactions from other group members: How do they feel about the therapist admitting feeling frustrated? Do they feel let down, angry, or grateful about the frank response? Besides simply acknowledging our feelings, we would also attempt to explain the source of frustration—that is, the group was discussing concerns that were not likely to be helpful or therapeutic, and we felt stymied in our efforts to get the group "on task." These interventions serve to reinforce the norms of the group we are trying to cultivate.

After looking at "our part" of the equation, we would then turn to having members explore whether any other unstated elements were feeding their attacks. If we have a strong hunch about this, we will usually offer it to the group as a possibility—but not as a proclamation! In this example, directing strong, angry emotions at one of the leaders could possibly be a way to deflect away from members' anger at each other. But, before we offer this observation, we would first encourage the members themselves to think about not only the cause of the flare-up but also their experience in getting angry: Was it uncomfortable for those expressing criticism? How about observing others do the same? Was there a point at which any of them were afraid? Did it feel good to get this off their chest? Was this a new or familiar experience for them? Is there a lot of expressed anger or criticism in their marriages?

An attack on the therapist is inevitable in the life sequence of a group. The therapeutic use of conflict, like all other behaviors in the here and now, can be extremely helpful for the members of the therapy group if the leader not only encourages the expression of angry emotions but also helps the members understand the experience. However, with the expression of anger, therapists have a particular duty to maintain a sense of safety—this is the framework that allows a full exploration of thoughts and feelings.

Psychodynamic Therapy
Implemented by J. Scott Rutan

Couples' groups represent a unique challenge and a unique opportunity because each couple represents a working system. From a dynamic perspective, the goal is to help each individual own and question his or her contribution to the couple's problems.

As in Critical Incident 1, the early stages of this group are dedicated to determining safety and common ground. Rather quickly, Laurie and Helen have determined that their wish to advance themselves represents a problem in the marriage.

My understanding of the dynamics of this meeting is that the leader erred when making the comment that "this level of discussion was not dealing with the issues or purposes of the group. . . ."

From a psychodynamic perspective, the group is *always* dealing with the important issues—either by addressing them directly, by addressing them in derivative material, or by resisting dealing with them. If the latter is the case, the goal is not to puncture the resistance but to *understand* it. (Remember, clients do not resist treatment or change, they resist expected pain.)

Thus, the anger at the leader serves at least two purposes. First, it is a defense against hurt feelings (because the leader had accused them of not working properly). Second, it is a move toward cohesiveness (circling the wagons against the leader is not an unusual way for a group to begin to bond together). As group therapists, we should remember that an attack on the leader is usually a good sign in that it indicates that the group has at least decided that the members are strong enough to not be destroyed by anger.

Rather than accusing the group of not working properly, I may have commented, "The group seems to be experimenting with somewhat safer subjects this evening. Perhaps this tells us that there are some leftover feelings from what was discussed last week." This is a dynamic intervention because it *implies* that groups never "change the subject." We operate on the principle that there is a continuous unconscious stream of associations. Whereas it may *appear* to the members that this week is discreet and disconnected from the past session, dynamic therapists always assume there is a connection. Part of the goal of this approach is to help our clients understand that the feelings they have are not random or chaotic but reasonable and understandable.

In this particular case, group members may or may not make a connection to the previous session. If they do, then they will proceed to talk about the residual feelings from the previous session in a more forthright manner. If not, we would assume there is resistance to returning to the feelings from the previous session. Again, in the dynamic tradition we would not attack the resistance but would attempt to understand it.

Rational–Emotive–Behavioral Therapy
Implemented by Albert Ellis

In terms of rational–emotive–behavioral therapy (REBT), the situation is partly that of a cop-out: The members of the group are probably doing what they naturally and easily do—avoiding difficult problems and avoiding the issues or purposes of the group, for two reasons. First, it takes less effort on their part, and second, it is easier for them to discuss whatever comes up and not get down to business. REBT sees this as the normal tendency of humans to have low frustration tolerance and to go for immediate satisfactions rather than long-range gains.

Therefore, as a group leader I expect this kind of thing to occur and to keep occurring. By luck, and probably not because I was doing very well myself as a leader during the first two sessions, Nicholas got to something important in his relations with his wife and showed that he was confused; and by luck, Doris reacted emotionally to Nicholas and showed her strong feeling about men dominating women in marriage and being overconcerned about their wives running around, rather than concerned about what their wives really want to do in life. This issue was not fully discussed, however, because time ran out, so I would raise it again at session 3. More than one couple has expressed a problem with the wife's career goals conflicting with the husband's desire for the woman to stay with the old ways.

By session 3, I would realize that I had not structured the group process sufficiently and explained to the members that we are neither merely interested in their expression of feelings nor are we too interested in their discussing unimportant topics or questions irrelevant to therapy, such as politics and sports. I would therefore explain to the members the basic purpose of an REBT group: The group is here to bring out practical problems and emotional problems about these practical problems. I would also explain that the goal usually is to understand and resolve the emotional problems first and then to work, simultaneously, on the resolution of the practical marital and personal problems of the participants.

I would emphasize that one of the main purposes of the group is to help the members solve their marital difficulties as well as their personal difficulties and that, because they all have somewhat similar problems in this respect, we will try to explore those difficulties common to most of them and see what general, as well as individual, solutions can be arrived at. I would emphasize that this is an REBT-oriented group and that, as leader, I expect to help all group members see that when they have practical marital problems, they almost always have an emotional problem or problem *about* the practical problem. The goal of group REBT is to help them see that they have some basic irrational beliefs directly causing or creating their disturbed emotional reactions. I would hope, therefore, that they disclose their emotional problems, look for the irrational beliefs that lie behind these problems, and dispute and surrender these beliefs.

I would then address the specific member who has attacked me for appearing cool, distant, and uncaring in the following manner: "Yes, John, you may well be right in accusing me of appearing cool, distant, and uncaring. I think that I definitely care about your and the other group members' problems and disturbances, and I am very concerned about helping you with these difficulties. But that doesn't mean that I care, personally, about *you*—that I like you or love you or would want to have you as one of my close friends. Actually, with some of your pretty abominable behavior—such as your hostility toward your wife and your business associates, which you have already spoken about—I'm not sure that I would want to be friendly with you at all, if I met you under social circumstances. I think I would find you bright and interesting and might well want to discuss certain issues with you—but, I doubt if I would find you very friendly! If you worked on and got rid of that hostility of yours—yes, perhaps then I would. But right now, with the hostility you show toward others and even with the tone of voice you are now displaying toward me, about my supposed coolness—no, I don't think I would feel very friendly toward you.

"Besides, the purpose of group REBT is not to display friendship, love, or warmth from the therapist to the group members, nor even from the group members to each other. If such warmth arises, as it sometimes does, fine. But love and warmth are not exactly group therapy and they are in fact often the reverse. One of the main things that people think they need—and I believe you are well in this class right now—is the undying and near-perfect approval of others. Well, they don't—they only *think* they do. Not that love and approval aren't nice; they definitely are! But *nice* doesn't mean *necessary!* If you want approval and you get it from others, great! That adds to your life. But if you think you *need*, you absolutely *must* have it, you are really in trouble. You feel marvelous, of course, when you do get it and very upset and angry—as you and the group members seem to be showing right now—when you don't.

"One of the fundamental propositions of REBT is that people do not *need* what they *want*. Almost all their desires and preferences, however great, are legitimate; and almost all their *needs* and *necessities* lead to trouble. For if you want something very much and don't get it, you are merely keenly disappointed and sorry. But if you think you absolutely need it and don't get it, you are destroyed: depressed, anxious, self-hating. So in REBT, we deliberately don't give therapeutic love, for that might encourage you to become a bigger baby than you already are! Unconditional acceptance, full respect for you as an individual, no matter how badly you may perform, is what we do try to give in

REBT and also what we try to help individuals to give themselves and to all other humans.

"I am trying to help you—and all the other group members—to unconditionally, fully accept and respect *yourself*. And if I succeed, in spite of or even because of my 'coolness,' I will encourage you to accept yourself *whether or not* I approve of you and *whether or not* you act very competently during your life. If I can help you see things that way, you'll really have it made! And the question of whether or not I approve of you or like you will be important, perhaps, but hardly vital."

If John wanted to talk more about this, I would welcome his doing so. I would try to show him that his anger at me comes not from his desire for me to be a better therapist and not from his feeling sorry and frustrated that I am not—but from his demanding and commanding that I *must* be the kind of good therapist that he wants and that it is *terrible* and I am a *rotten person* if I am not.

At the same time, I would try to draw the other members of the group into his discussion and would attempt to show all of them (1) that I might well be right about my leadership of the group because I have been following, quite deliberately, an REBT pattern of group therapy that usually brings about excellent results with most group members; (2) that I might be wrong about my leadership because I really am an uncaring person and have been missing the boat in several important respects; (3) that, even if I am wrong and uncaring, they do not have to put themselves down and make themselves panicked and depressed about my shortcomings as a group leader; and (4) that, even if I am wrong and inept, they do not have to anger themselves at me for having these failings but can instead regretfully decide that I am not the kind of leader they want and look elsewhere for another type of therapy or another type of REBT leader.

I might possibly, in the course of my talking to the members of the group, deliberately feign anger at and strongly criticize one of them for "wrongly" being opposed to me. Then I would suddenly stop my verbal attack, especially if the person I picked on became upset and started to attack me back, and show that I had feigned anger as an emotive exercise, to draw out the attacked person's (and the other group members') reactions. We would then explore some of these reactions in detail, see whether various members had felt very hurt or angry at my tirade, show them exactly what they had been telling themselves to create these disturbed feelings, and indicate what they could do to dispute and challenge their irrational beliefs and to rid themselves of these feelings.

I would also try to give some or all of the group members a homework assignment—perhaps one in which they deliberately courted the companionship of a cold, distant, uncaring person, letting themselves feel anxious, depressed, self-pitying, or angry when in this person's presence and then work on these disturbed feelings and try to change them into more healthy negative feelings of sorrow, disappointment, frustration, and annoyance.

In the above way, I would try to show the group what the REBT version of group therapy is and how it differs from some other forms of treatment. I would try to show them that, as REBT firmly posits, *A* (activating experiences) does not directly lead to or cause *C* (disturbed emotional consequences). The more direct and important cause or contribution to C is B (people's belief systems about what is happening to them at A).

I would illustrate to them, moreover, in general, and from the events and feelings occurring to them in the group, that their beliefs, at B, almost invariably are of two kinds when they feel disturbed at C. First, they have a set of rational beliefs (rBs), which consists of preferences or desires. For example: "I don't like the leader's behavior! I wish he didn't act that way! What a pain in the neck!" These rBs tend to lead them to feel healthy consequences (aCs), such as feelings of sorrow, regret, disappointment, and annoyance. Second, they have a set of irrational beliefs (iBs), which consists of commands or demands. For example: "The leader *must* not behave the way that he does! How *awful!* I *can't stand* his behaving in that manner! What a horrible leader and a *terrible person* he is!" These iBs tend to lead them to feel unhealthy consequences (iCs), such as hurt, self-downing, hostility, or self-pity.

I would then show the group members what I had neglected to show them previously: Their irrational, self-defeating beliefs are only hypotheses and not facts, and they can actively and vigorously dispute these hypotheses at point D. D, or disputing of irrational beliefs, is the scientific method of asking themselves such questions as "Where is the evidence that the leader *must* not behave the way he does? Prove that it is *awful* if he acts badly or inefficiently. In what way can't I *stand* his behaving poorly, against my and the group's interest? Where is it written that he, because he acts badly, is a terrible person?"

Asking these questions, they would then arrive at E, a new effective philosophy. E is a realistic acceptance of the way the world (or at least, the group member's world) is. If they would correctly answer their own disputational questions at D, they would usually arrive at E, along these lines: "Yes, the leader of this group has probably behaved in an ineffectual, incorrect manner—as fallible humans often behave; consequently, he will sometimes continue to act that badly and to lead the group poorly in the future. Too bad! Although I'll never like being inconvenienced by him and his actions, I definitely can stand them and can continue to live and to be relatively happy despite his incompetent performances."

Notice that the REBT assumptions—like those of most other psychotherapies, but perhaps a little more honestly and openly—are that no matter what goes on in the group (or in the lives of the members when they are outside the group) and no matter how poorly and foolishly the leader acts in the course of the group process, the members still *upset themselves* not by taking something seriously or making it important but by taking it too seriously and making it *all* important or *sacred*. Virtually everything, therefore, that happens inside or outside the group can be used as a focal point to show any individual member or all the members that they are irrationally creating their own feelings of anxiety, depression, hostility, worthlessness, apathy, and self-pity and that they can choose to think, feel, and behave much more effectively, in accordance with their own personal goals and values.

Once this idea of people's *self*-conditioning and the *self*-choosing of the way they react to "obnoxious" stimuli is accepted by group members, they can then be helped to go back to *A*, their activating experiences, and either see them differently (with less prejudice) or try to change them. In this present instance, once I help John and the others see that, however badly I behaved, they do not have to upset themselves about my performance, they will be in a position to see more accurately whether I really did behave that poorly. If I had not acted badly, then they could look into their own hearts and change their own feelings about my "bad" leadership. And if I had, they could determinedly and undisturbedly try to show me the error of my ways and to get me to change. Or, finally, they could decide that staying in the group was hardly worth their while and could individually or collectively quit.

REBT, then, attempts to help the group members identify their own disturbed thoughts, emotions, and behaviors and to change them and *then* to consider changing the situation they are in. It does not *merely* focus on one of these two goals but on both of them. It stresses the constructivist view that people are largely self-disturbers and have the ability to creatively undisturb themselves and also solve their practical life problems.

Reality Therapy
Implemented by Thomas E. Bratter

The group leader in this situation appears to have assumed a more traditional analytical–passive orientation. Not surprisingly, because of their own fears and resistance, the group members have decided to challenge the leader and his or her qualifications.

I believe those people with whom I work certainly are entitled to ask questions about my values and credentials. Rather than play therapeutic games, I would respond to such a request forthrightly and outline my professional credentials and experience in counseling.

In the group situation described, however, the timing of the disclosure reveals that the group has been frustrated and angered by the "cool, distant, and uncaring" therapeutic stance of the psychotherapist. Most assuredly, believing as I do, I would have avoided placing myself in a position where either my credentials or the therapeutic distance would have become legitimate issues. Let us assume, however, that I acted as the group leader has, and now the group has begun to demand some sort of explanation.

I would begin by saying, "I hear your anger and criticism, which I admit, in part, are valid. I can contribute more. I will make a commitment to do so. Yet, I am curious why the group wants me to run the show. I am impressed with the energy and intelligence in this room. No one has risked much by talking about themselves. There have been times when I hoped that someone would have related to what was being said, but for whatever reason it failed to materialize. Perhaps this would be a good time for us to reevaluate what we want from the group experience. I would appreciate learning why no one has wanted to discuss a personal issue for the first fifteen minutes." In so doing I would accept some of the responsibility for the slow start but then subtly suggest that everyone could have assumed a more active role and risked more personally. By heeding the criticism and then changing my behavior, I would have become a responsible role model. It is important to note that I would have agreed to change my behavior because I believe the comments are valid. If I disagreed with the suggestion, I would explain my rationale and would not change.

Solution-Focused Therapy
Implemented by Rebecca LaFountain

I begin each group meeting with a review of the assignment given in the previous session. Because of the structure, it is unlikely that this scenario, where the group members chit-chat for 15 minutes, would occur. This does not rule out the possibility of an attack on me, the group leader. In fact, group members may attack leaders for the structure imposed on the group.

Structure is meant to provide clients with a framework to take "baby steps" toward their goals. When clients are aggressive toward the leader, I hypothesize that they are fearful about the next step. I do not interpret this behavior as resistant but as an indicator that I must choose another intervention. Solution-focused counselors believe that by asking the appropriate questions, clients can create solutions.

One intervention I might attempt is to "do something different" from the members' perspective. For example, in this scenario if I were to ask couples what they did this past week that they would like to do more of, some of the members might perceive my structuring as pressure to change in a direction or at a rate they are not ready for. If Nicholas were to ask, "What does this have to do with Laurie wanting to go to school?" I might answer, "What would be helpful for you to talk about in the group today?" Although it may appear to the participants that I am turning the structure over to them, in my experience, the clients end up addressing the issue I initially attempted to introduce—only they have more ownership in the process.

Polyocularity, or the use of "many eyes," is another intervention to use when dissention toward the leader is apparent in the group. This term is one that De Shazer (1985) uses to describe the benefits clients derive when receiving counseling at his institute in Milwaukee. Behind the mirror are "experts" who provide valuable feedback to clients via the therapist. Likewise, in group, members benefit from the many viewpoints of each other. I rely on group members to provide one another with feedback when participants appear resentful of my confrontations. Group input is also invaluable for the purposes of support and encouragement.

A final area I want to address is first-order and second-order change. *First-order change* produces new behaviors without affecting the individual's underlying beliefs or rules. *Second-order change* involves a fundamental change in the client's rules. Clients may become angry if they feel restricted about what they can discuss in the group. Counselors new to the solution-focused model may limit discussion to the clients' specific process goals. However, counselors familiar with first-order and second-order change understand that most of the complaints that an individual presents stem from the same underlying beliefs or rules. Therefore, although the complaints may initially appear unrelated, they are most likely connected, and the counselor and other group members can help the individual understand the relationship between each presenting issue. For example, if I were to hypothesize that Nicholas's concern about his wife going back to school is based upon his belief that "as long as I control others around me, I do not have to deal with change," it would not be out of character for him to come into group one evening with a concern about a possible reorganization at work. Through polyocularity, the group members and I can help him relate the two complaints and apply the solution he is working on concerning his wife to the difficulty he is bringing up about work.

Movement from dependence on the leader to the expression of conflict toward the leader is normal and healthy in the group process. Just as solution-focused counselors help clients anticipate possible obstacles in their paths so that the clients do not become disillusioned, counselors need to be prepared for the likelihood that they will be the target of clients' hostility.

Systems-Centered Therapy

Implemented by Yvonne Agazarian

Confronted with this event and this group history, I hope I would say something like this:

> At this point in this group's life, it is very important for the group to question my competence to contain conflict and my ability to be caring toward members.
>
> Let's look at the context. The potential for conflict increased last session in this group. We raised the issue, from the husband's point of view, why wives could not be happy just staying at home, and we countered this from the wife's point of view as being "just like a man." We could probably all write the script of what comes next if we pick up from there.
>
> So I think I may have been clumsy just now in pointing out that the group was not dealing with this conflict. On second thought, I think the group, in its wisdom, is trying to do something more important _first_, and that is to check out whether or not I can help the group contain conflicts like this, if it comes out into the open.
>
> So I would propose we address this first. For the last two sessions, we have all had the experience of the realities of how I lead this group. We have data! I propose that we now pool our experience and identify the things that I do that you find helpful in addressing the issues that we have come here to address and the things that I do that seem to get in the way."

From a systems-centered therapy (SCT) perspective it is important to structure the group norms from the very beginning of the first session, specifically so that the group will not get into trouble before it is equipped to learn from it.*

By session 2 in this group, stereotypic subgrouping had split the group into a stereotypic wife subgroup (avoidant), a stereotypic husband subgroup (formed partly through nodding), and an "audience" subgroup. (This is typical of early flight-phase behavior; see Chapter 11, Table 1.) When Doris attacks the husband subgroup, she introduces the potential for active scapegoating. The group as a whole, however, intervenes to preserve the status quo (this is isomorphic: Laurie is preserving the status quo of her marriage by being an "audience" to her husband's complaints). After the threat of session 2, in session 3 the group-as-whole solution is indicated by the fact that the energy is high and the members verbal. When, after the first 15 minutes, the leader makes the intervention that the group is not dealing with the issues or purposes of the group, the group attacks the therapist.

The intervention that was made is negatively slanted. Negative interventions (telling the group what it is *not* doing) can be expected to arouse either compliance or defiance in relationship to the leader. In this group, it aroused defiance. However, the group has had no practice in bringing negative feelings into the *relationship* and exploring them with the leader and therefore have no alternative but to scapegoat the leader.

Scapegoating a leader before group members have learned how to support each other is likely to provoke reactions of guilt, depression (the sadistic impulses turned back in), and acting-out (perhaps in absenteeism or dropping out). Hence, the "taking back" of the intervention, owned as "clumsy," attempts to normalize and legitimize the group's anger with the therapist. The therapist's "proposal" reframes the group's response as a legitimate action in the service of the group and encourages the members to explore their experience rather than act it out. This influences the members to join on similarities rather than separate on differences, this discourages stereotypic subgrouping and encourages functional subgrouping.

SCT interventions take into account the phase of development that the group is in (Agazarian, 1994). All SCT interventions are phase specific and lay the

---

*Structural interventions test the hypothesis that by weakening the restraining forces to information (energy) at the boundaries of time, space, reality, and role, the strength of the inherent drive toward the goals of survival, development, and transformation will be increased. Because an inverse relationship exists between noise in the communication channel and the probability that the information it contains will be transferred across system boundaries (Shannon & Weaver, 1964), reducing ambiguity will increase the probability that information will be received and processed by the system.

Functional interventions test the hypothesis that systems survive, develop, and transform through the process of discriminating and integrating differences. Functional interventions influence the ability to discriminate and integrate differences in the apparently similar, and similarities in the apparently different is the information communicated by encouraging the communications to build on similarities rather than to diverge on differences (usually through the SCT conflict resolution technique of subgrouping).

Vectoring tests the hypothesis that when energy/information is deliberately directed away from defensive communications and toward nondefensive communications, both primary and secondary goal-directed activity will increase.

groundwork for later, more complex phases (see Chapter 11, Table 1; Agazarian, 1997a). This group is in the early flight phase, characterized by stereotypic communications. SCT leaders would not wish the group to attack the therapist until the fight phase, by which time the members will have acquired the ability to contain and explore, in subgroups, the hostile and blameful feelings toward the therapist that will generate impulses to attack.

The particular intervention made here is a *containing* intervention, directed to the group as a whole. Group-as-a-whole interventions are useful as transitional interventions and useful to SCT therapists when they are leading groups that are not systems oriented.

This particular intervention lays the groundwork for making a transition away from stereotypic subgrouping by encouraging the members to come together around their similarities. When members brought in their differences, they would be encouraged to form a counterbalancing subgroup. Introducing the SCT method of functional subgrouping provides an alternative to stereotypic subgrouping (which has occurred in this group around "men" and "women," "husbands" and "wives") and would enable members to explore the common experiences that are shared by married people.

The consequences anticipated (hoped for) are that the group members would subgroup around exploring the issue of trusting the leader (rather than acting-out scapegoating). The group would then have taken the first step in learning that trust in reality comes from testing expectations, which is fundamental to establishing the reality-testing climate that is the work of the flight phase. This in turn would lay the foundation for the group to explore, in subgroups, the issues of trust that exist for each of them in their marriages.

The most outstanding condition of this incident is that the group is scapegoating the therapist prematurely. SCT members are discouraged from doing the different levels of therapeutic work before they have developed the skills necessary to obtain a successful experience. Hence, in an SCT group, before members work with their scapegoating impulses toward the leader (their negative transference), they first learn to (1) recognize and undo the anxiety that is generated from anxiety-provoking thoughts; (2) identify the internal experience that is being constricted through tension; (3) undo depression by identifying the trigger episode in which their impulse to retaliate was aroused, denied, and turned back on the self; and (4) to explore the retaliatory impulse and ground themselves and to experience their own underlying aggression as a potentially nondestructive life force (see Chapter 11, Table 1). *

*The behavior in the episode is characteristic of the developmental phase in which members scapegoat authority. From a systems-centered perspective, it is premature behavior given that the group is in the first phase of development and in the subphase of flight. SCT leaders would not wish the group to attack the therapist until the fight phase, by which time the members will have acquired the ability to contain and explore, in subgroups, the hostile and blameful feelings toward the therapist that will generate impulses to attack.

Therefore, in an SCT group, session 1 would have encouraged members to come together around their similarities, thus taking the first step in learning how to form a subgroup. When a significant difference emerged in the group (as it probably would), those members who resonated with the difference would be encouraged to join this second subgroup. This *functional* subgrouping discourages *stereotypic* subgrouping (stereotypic subgrouping would come together around being "men" and "women" or "husbands" and "wives"). Through functional subgrouping, SCT group

SCT members learn to bring their sadistic scapegoating impulses first into the relationship with the leader (who will not take them personally) and only into relationship with other group members when they have learned not to take each other's communications "just" personally.

Transactional Analysis
Implemented by Herbert Hampshire

Working with couples is distinctly challenging as well as gratifying because one can examine not only individual scripts but the interlocking script that provides constant reinforcement and validation. Working with couples in groups has the added dimension of the group process. Members come into therapy for the paradoxical purposes of both changing the ways they function and maintaining their system against all assaults. These purposes become especially apparent when working with couples because the direction that the investment of energy often takes is toward changing the spouse rather than oneself.

The task with couples is always, to one degree or another, to undermine the existing symbiotic relationship and to produce what Murray Bowen (1977) calls "individuation" and Eric Berne calls "autonomy." In light of this goal, I would place emphasis at the outset on establishing a contract with *each* marital partner. Much of the "wheel spinning" in marital therapy occurs out of the omission of this stage. Nicholas and Laurie exemplify this point dramatically. When Nicholas says that "their marriage was just fine the way it was, and he could not understand why it should change," he demonstrates the fusion of the couple. Anything Laurie seeks to do in relation to herself is, within the context of the couple, perceived as something being done to the relationship. There is an illusion of shared purpose, with both of them "working on the marriage"; in fact, Laurie's purpose is to move away from allowing the context of the marriage to define her functioning and limit her behavior, and Nicholas seeks to maintain the primacy of their original contract. Because they were married at relatively young ages and had a child after only 2 years, Laurie probably now sees herself as having "sold out on herself" and as having "missed options" that she did not even recognize at the time. Within her programming, she has no apparent way to relate to her anger, resentment, and sadness. If her contract in therapy were related to developing the capacity to relate effectively to her own feelings, her movement in that direction, with Nicholas's growing cooperative participation, would be possible. If her purpose is kept at "something for herself"—that is, defined as outside the structure of their marriage relationship—therapy would unlikely proceed in any direction other than the escalation of antagonistic functioning.

Nicholas and Laurie are also classically illustrative of the game Berne saw as most often played out maritally—the game of "If It Weren't For You." The basic dynamics of the game revolve around a spouse—in this case, the wife—who is

members would be encouraged to come together to explore common experiences that are shared by people, whether they are men or women or whether they have roles as husbands and wives.

phobic in some way and the other spouse whose personal insecurity results in a "need to be needed," which takes the form of controlling rigidity. Thus, at the social level, Laurie wants to do something that Nicholas restricts her from doing. At the psychological level, she is afraid to do it, and he is afraid of having minimal worth or power. This example provides an illustration of the use of games in therapy. The value at the outset is to provide a direct and straightforward method of assessing the consequences of accepting at face value the stated motivation of the client. The therapist who agrees, simplistically, that Laurie's purpose is "merely" to get free of her husband's domination and to go to college runs the risk of using the power of his or her position to override Nicholas's very critical psychological value to her and to leave Laurie with little preparation in dealing with either her anxiety or her potential "failure." Game analysis also provides direct insight into the pattern of childhood, family, and functioning that existed for both partners—allowing the therapist to know the directions to move in, to elucidate for each partner the roots of their unconscious functioning.

It is always therapeutically dangerous to discount an emotional reaction as intense as Laurie's was in session 2. Her failure to verbalize her feelings merely serves to underscore the degree of conflict that has been engaged. In one sense, the pattern of interaction between Nicholas and Laurie is representative of their relationship. Ostensibly, he is in total control of what is taking place, and she is passively adapting—an indication of what has been going on throughout their marriage. Inevitably, when the submissive partner either has built up sufficient resentment or has become less phobic about responding, the system will be disturbed by a more active attempt to reorganize the balance of power.

The Child ego-state's emotional reactions are noticeable even when there appears to be a covert agreement to pretend it does not exist. Thus, all members of the group, even Nicholas, are responsive in some way to Laurie's communication of being the "victim." If the therapist allows that to go unnoticed, the entire group may perceive it unsafe to be weak or tentative and believe that the therapist cannot cope with or override the power of the programmatic responses of group members. This will typically lead to a retreat into a Parent ego-state that will critically attack the therapist or withdraw from the group.

The most important aspect of intervening with Laurie would be to eliminate the pattern of ignoring her responses. It would be sufficient to comment, "Laurie, I notice your discomfort; it would be good to put your reactions and feelings into words." It would matter less whether she accepted the invitation than that her difficulty in speaking had been acknowledged. Optimally, interventions would have shifted the pattern of the group to a more dynamically effective level.

When there is a great deal of interaction from the outset, it often indicates that individuals are able to "hide out" and avoid a level of self-revelation that would be anxiety provoking. Couples feel less vulnerable because they are not there as themselves at the outset but as a duo—which covers individual anxieties. All homogeneous groups have the potential for falling into patterns of pastiming that *appear* to be interactive but are in fact little different from what is engaged in at cocktail parties or bridge clubs.

From the beginning, reframing interactions so they may become more authentic is important. When Doris responds with "that sounded just like a man," I would be likely to ask her to speak directly to Nicholas and tell him how she felt about what he had been saying. Or I would ask her if she thought her partner had concerns about her "running around" and, if so, to talk directly about how she reacted to this. Or, I would point out that it sounded as if she were empathizing with Laurie and invite her to communicate that message directly to Laurie.

Moving interactions to a more authentic level becomes especially important when individuals in the group share dynamic issues and therefore have a tendency unconsciously to "protect" each other. There is much overlap among the couples in the group. Nicholas and Laurie as well as John and Helen are contending with the woman's redefinition of self and a desire to extend herself outside the home. Implicit are issues of control, domination, and submission. In some ways, Paul and Joan share the dynamic with a sex-role reversal. Joan is more educated and initiated the therapy contact, while Paul was apparently resisting being controlled by "avoiding her." Both Larry and Pamela and Peter and Doris are vague about what they want and what is "wrong" with their marriages. There is an underlying thread of helplessness and inability to achieve clarity and obtain gratification. In each of these couples, one would expect a strong pull toward relating to the therapist Parentally—as judge, decision maker, rescuer, and protector.

The continuation of pastiming when the therapist begins the group is a communication of anger at a therapist for "failing" in some way. It is as if the therapist has not demonstrated that he or she is "in charge of" the group, and the group therefore need not recognize any leadership. When this event becomes explicit, as in this case where the group members are openly attacking the therapist, it is easier to relate to. (To some degree, the group's response in this instance is provoked by the Parental observation of the therapist, which was probably experienced as critical and accusatory.)

One of the first concerns in the therapist's response to the expression of anger is to assess the degree to which there is Adult input contained in the members' reactions. Neglecting this assessment runs the risk of being hooked into a defensive, Parental reaction based on blaming the group members in some way. When a therapist does react in this way, it effectively undermines any potential therapeutic benefit for the group.

The key in responding to this situation is to allow the interaction to continue the process of revealing members' programming. I would likely move in the direction of asking people to define what it was they saw as "cool, distant, and uncaring." This intervention would lead to their identification that they were unwittingly seeking Parental rescuing—as they were accustomed to elicit in stress situations—or that they were protecting an internal Parent by not getting from others in the group what they saw the therapist failing to provide. As always, I would pursue the programming in the form of transactions with specific group members rather than talking to the group as a whole. In selecting the person to relate to directly, I would choose those with the greatest degree of affect associated with the conflict or those in whose scripts the issues were most salient. Because a great deal of the affect was generated from the previous session, I might ask Laurie to verbalize how she had felt about the therapist not rescuing or assisting her. For the same reason, I might work with Nicholas to get him to see that he in fact did not want Laurie "picked on" or discounted the previous week.

Theoretical Practitioners' Congruence With Their Theory

CLIENT-CENTERED THERAPY

Elements of client-centered theory abound throughout our theoretical practitioner's (TP) response to this incident. Most pronounced is his effort to reinstate himself as a member of the group; to accomplish this, he admits to his own imperfection as a person for not acknowledging the "hole" in group that had been created the week before. Added to this is his willingness to sit out the attack, paying attention to the messages being sent to him so that he may learn something about himself and from his mistakes. This behavior, as opposed to hiding behind the authoritative role that was readily available to him, would more likely lead to reestablishing himself as a member of the group. His ultimate desire is to encourage the collective wisdom that rests with the members, to be reinforced and validated.

COGNITIVE–BEHAVIORAL THERAPY

Once again, our cognitive–behavioral therapy (CBT) TP is quick to address how this group is *organized* and how he would *reorganize* it. We are also introduced to the importance of building group cohesion, group structure, and group norms.

Our TP informs us that he would not lead a group without a coleader, implying at the very least that he would organize the group differently. He introduces the ethical responsibility that leaders face. In this case, behaving freely and totally being themselves would be more self-serving and less in the best interests of the members. Furthermore, he suggests that under these circumstances a lone therapist might wish to withdraw, leaving the group leaderless. Thus, he presents for us a cogent argument for having a coleader. Furthermore, he is concerned about the principle of "do no harm." This principle is not representative solely of CBT groups but certainly is one of its foci because it leads to building group cohesiveness. Consequently, our TP would adhere to seeing that no damage would be brought to the group or the leaders, respectively, and in that order. Once this was ensured, then the CBT goal of understanding the meaning of the attacks to behavior can be addressed.

FAMILY-CENTERED THERAPY

Recall that earlier we said that family-centered group therapy (FCT) is more of an integrated approach that, in addition to family theory, draws understandings, concepts, and methodology from psychodynamic, individual, and developmental psychology and group therapy. This incident is the first example of how our FCT TP demonstrates the integration of all these modalities.

Early on he permits us to see how he views this couples' group from the context of family therapy (e.g., length of marriage; family life stages; nuclear family, blended family, cohabitating family; family norms). He introduces developmental and individual psychology related to the stage of development each member of the marital pairs has reached. He also informs us that he would have ended session 2 differently. Taking the position that he would have acknowledged the impact group dynamics had on the couples, he is still willing to address the incident as presented. He continues to draw on group therapy as he addresses the process of cohesion, underscoring that it is necessary if the group is to progress. However, he reluctantly admits the group manifested cohesion through its attack on him. He interprets this as member projection and displacement of unresolved interpersonal conflict onto him (a psychodynamic position). This form of transference is viewed as an opportunity (almost welcomed) because it, the crisis, was a symptom of resistance to change. In fact, he refers to the "underling systemic dynamics" related to his role change and that the couples partially "mourned" the loss of him as a personal therapist as the motives for the attack. Once again, we can view this as a psychodynamic interpretation. Each of his possible interventions, he concludes, has a group process focus, including attention to the stage of group development to which the group as a whole could be moved.

Gestalt Therapy

A number of Gestalt therapy constructs became immediately apparent as we listen to our Gestalt TP. Being in the here and now, or present; avoiding shoulds, oughts, and coulds; focusing on the part of the therapist; unifying the splits; encouraging responsibility taking; not following any prearranged plot; and dealing with unfinished business—all are but some of the constructs that evidence themselves.

From the very first, we learn our TP would have managed both the ending of session 2 and the beginning of session 3 differently. Implying that the incident itself might have occurred for very different reasons, she would have acknowledged Doris's denunciation of men but would have encouraged her to engage in a dialogue with Nicholas (and later Laurie), addressing how he affected her now, in the present. This leader intervention would also have reflected the Gestalt position of being specific rather than remaining general. She also focuses on (attends to) members' body movement and position (e.g., Laurie's silence).

Our TP is creative in the way she perceives the group. Rather than interpreting its behavior at the beginning of session 3 as avoidance, she outrightly states that the group was regulating itself (i.e., taking responsibility). The group was seen as being expressive, and she continues to focus on how members were relating to one another. By avoiding critical confrontation, she also does not tell them how they should or ought to act (according to her dictates). She respects the group members' need to take a break from the intensity of the previous session before they can immerse themselves in more intense work. She eventually does just that by encouraging members to address any unfinished business from the previous session.

INDIVIDUAL PSYCHOLOGY

Our individual psychology TP is, through his response, modeling the Adlerian approach. He is at once being instructive and informative by explaining how and why this incident "is a beauty" for the potential development it will offer to the group as a whole and individual members. He then models effective living, equalizing or leveling the playing field between himself and the members by virtue of his follow-up intervention that is intended to "foster equality of responsibility" within each couple.

His first response is one of internal reflection. He informs us that earlier in his career he might have reacted defensively but now sees himself as having grown and matured in confidence with his adequacy and acceptance of his imperfections. By doing so, the internal reflection enables him to see the different options for thinking and behaving as a therapist. This focus on options is the ultimate objective Adlerians wish for group members to achieve with regard to living. His overt response is the product of such reflection and is designed to level the playing field between himself and the members by immediately not accepting their "real therapist" and presenting himself as imperfect as they. This approach quickly diffuses the categorical way of living life that Nicholas, John, and Doris have taken. By reducing himself to being an equal to the others, he then can move the members to address the "common sense of social living" and establish his role as one who is there to facilitate each person in the couple to attain equality of responsibility. All these actions fit the characteristics of individual psychology.

INTERPERSONAL PSYCHOTHERAPY

A host of constructs related to interpersonal psychotherapy are brought into the open as our TPs address this incident. They include norm building, curative factors, imitative/modeling behavior, interpersonal learning, group cohesiveness, existential factors, coleadership, here and now, and process illumination.

Beginning with the value of working with a coleader, we see attention can be paid to group process illumination, while the leader under attack can focus more on modeling how one effectively receives and responds to feedback. We also learn that our TPs, initially, internally reflect on the feedback's accuracy, determining whether their inner feelings and thoughts are congruent with the feedback. Through process illumination, interpersonal learning is encouraged. Group cohesiveness is addressed by ensuring that safety needs are addressed (an existential factor). Members are encouraged to feel free to express their feelings, including those of anger. This norm building also contributes to establishing what can be tolerated in the group culture. Members are also encouraged to address the possibility of their *projecting* onto the attacked leader their unresolved issues with other members.

We also learn that conflict can be therapeutic, especially when dealt with in the present. This here-and-now experience, along with openly exploring with one another how members felt as they participated in the conflict, yields the opportunity for further interpersonal learning.

PSYCHODYNAMIC THERAPY

As we consider our psychodynamic therapy TP's approach to this incident, let us be mindful of some of the psychodynamic principles that we read about earlier. Among them are (1) members do not repress their aggression out of need to be obedient to the leader; (2) harmony will grow out of disharmony, and reciprocity will grow out of antagonism; (3) that all behavior and thought have purpose and are connected; and (4) no matter how outlandish, all behaviors are traceable to insulating a person from pain. Also, we need to see if key concepts are presented, such as resistance and the role of the therapist in dealing with it. In addition, we look for how interpretation is used in reframing the incident, which in turn determines the intervention used.

Our psychodynamic therapy TP once again addresses the fact that establishing safety and a common ground must receive initial attention. This is consistent with the psychodynamic approach. He then tells us that the therapist in the incident misread group behavior as not dealing with group issues; for as a psychodynamic therapy TP, he sees the group as always dealing with important issues (i.e., that all behavior and thought are connected). If the group is seen as being resistant, he does not chastise it for doing so. Instead, he wants to seize the moment as an opportunity to help members understand it. He interprets the attack as serving a dual purpose: (1) as means for insulating pain and (2) for establishing cohesiveness—both of which are welcomed signs. He also tries to help members make the connection to last week (principle of unbroken connection) and to normalize it. By doing so, he sets in motion an opportunity to revisit leftover, unfinished, feelings and to address the resistance to doing so (i.e., the pain) in order to understand it.

It is not outwardly clear whether our TP plans to address the concepts of transference or countertransference. Would you? If so, why?

RATIONAL–EMOTIVE–BEHAVIORAL THERAPY

Crucial to our witnessing our rational–emotive–behavioral therapy (REBT) TP is to understand that the group had received instruction in REBT, albeit it may have not been done well. Assuming that to be true, then what we observe him doing will make sense if we adopt the REBT frame of reference. This means we need to see if there is instruction in REBT principles, the assignment of homework, and the addressing of rationality and irrationality in behaviors. We also want to see if our TP is be active, directive, and authoritative in his role. In addition, we want to see if he employs his cognitive, emotive, and behavioral techniques in a way that ultimately encourages group techniques.

Our REBT confesses at the outset and admits that he may not have structured the group process sufficiently according to REBT principles. He would therefore instruct the group on REBT principles. He would include that the goal of therapy is to resolve emotional problems. Then he would simultaneously work on their practical marital and personal problems. We watch him as he confronts and becomes quite transparent with one of the members. This particular action typifies how our TP employs himself within the context of this situation. We get to see *him*. Disassociating technique from the person and person from the technique is difficult. The whole process deals with the immediacy of the incident. Our TP is unquestionably active, directive, and authoritative in his role. He appeals to the cognitive side of the member(s), and he frames the lesson to be learned within the context of the incident. He will use homework by prescribing the situation and having members work on the disturbed feelings they are having so that they will learn that their beliefs (*B*) about their experience (*A*) are what lead to disturbed feelings (*C*), not the experience itself. Does our TP model REBT? It is evidenced as he worked with John (and for the members to see and experience). Does he involve the others? It seems so, since he turns to them once John's work is through. Recall, he is going to "feign anger and strongly criticize" one of the other members for "wrongly opposing" him. That particular technique piques our interest and concern. How about yours? What buttons does that push in you? Approach your response from an REBT position. Get the point?

REALITY THERAPY

What leaps out first to get our attention are the concepts of involvement, responsibility, focus on present behavior, developing positive responsible behavior, commitment, and the avoidance of punishment. It seems all of these are in force as we read how our reality therapy TP responded.

We witness immediately that he would not play games and would be forthright in his response to the group. Moreover, assuming the group's observations of him are valid, he does not hesitate to model taking positive responsible behavior and to make the commitment to do so. He is just as quick to turn to the group members and lay before them whether they are going to do the same. This is done without scolding or punishing them. We also notice that his focus is on the here and now (i.e., present behaviors) and that he appeals to their worthwhileness by noting how they impress him with their energy and intelligence. Simultaneously, he asks them to assume responsibility for their behaviors by calling their attention to the fact that they appear to want him "to run the show."

SOLUTION-FOCUSED THERAPY

A crucial dimension of solution-focused therapy (SFT) is maintaining focus on process goals and the identification of keys, (i.e., the solutions to that which is to be changed). Another factor we need to keep in mind as we watch our SFT TP work in this session is the effect the group's life stage has upon her choice of intervention.

Although our TP does not deny that the group could attack her, it would not be due to her calling them for "chit chatting." Her group structure is such that each session begins by reviewing the previous session's assignment. Rather than seeing the attack as resistance, she reframes it as fear and then acknowledges that it is stage-appropriate behavior because there is movement from leader dependence to independence. She normalizes the event by telling us it is to be expected and as SFT leaders we should be prepared for it. We also learn that she would seek keys from the members by "doing something different." She would try to give the members more ownership of the process: "What did you do last week that you would like to do more of this week?"

She also attends to process, only here she introduces us to the concept of *polyocularity*, which refers to using the "many eyes" of the group. From this we can infer that the leader is never alone and can draw from the group members their take on the process (i.e., the way they see/saw things unfold) by offering feedback. The notion of first-order and second-order change also receives attention. We are made aware that SFT needs to get to those behaviors that affect the underlying beliefs or rules that govern client behaviors. These are second-order changes. There is an uncanny similarity to psychodynamic thinking here when she tells us that SFT holds that all complaints are most likely connected to a deeper belief or rule. Thus, the process of change requires attending to the process that goes beyond first-order change.

SYSTEMS-CENTERED THERAPY

As we stated in Chapter 11, we can expect to see a very systematic approach to this incident. We need to look for group processes that include partnering, contextualizing the work to be done, employing the fork-in-the-road technique, holding members responsible, knowing the phase of group development, boundarying and vectoring, and structuring the group through the four steps. We may also find that our systems-centered therapy (SCT) TP will help each member explore and understand the underlying motives of his or her behavior. Such exploration and understanding might be evidenced by attempts to lessen the emotional intensity of the group in order for members to focus on the individual system (themselves) and to first experience bringing change there.

Our TP admits she may well have been "clumsy." This initial act is intended to lessen the anxiety or emotional tension by normalizing the group's angry feeling toward her. By doing so, it also sets the stage for members to subgroup, through choosing one of the forks in the road. Let us take note here that this behavior may also be an act of partnering with the members on our TP's part. She joins with them, rather than reinforcing the split or scapegoating behavior. She is also cognizant that this behavior on the part of the members is symptomatic of the fight phase and therefore is not in the proper developmental order. It is necessary to return the group to the early flight phase because she views the group as scapegoating the therapist prematurely. She also draws boundaries by containing the members' responses to the group as a whole. She attempts to move the group members to come together around their similarities related to trusting her as the therapist. Thus, she structures the group by drawing boundaries that define it, collecting energy to focus it on its goals, and developing systems-centered members, subgroups, and a group as a whole, which characterize an SCT group's way of working.

TRANSACTIONAL ANALYSIS

This is session 3, so the question is whether this event would occur in a transactional analysis (TA) group at all. After all, contracts would be made, ego-states examined, and game playing would have been addressed. Yet, because it did happen, will our TP follow a TA path? Analysis and interpretation of each member's ego-state are among a TA therapist's primary techniques. How he attends to transactional ego-states and scripts and offers explanation are of interest to us.

We first learn why our TA TP would have headed off this type of incident before it got started. However, he does explain how he would view it: The *pastiming* activity in which members were engaged is the group's way of communicating how the therapist failed the members in some way. He offers that the Parental observation by the leader helped trigger the attack. However, his first analysis is to determine the ego-state in the members' responses. He tells us this will help avoid his engaging in blaming and Parental behavior. Thus, his response to sit back and allow the incident to play itself out also fits. The TA model for our TP will be to actively interpret member behavior as *unwittingly* attempting to engender a Parental rescuing response from him. By choosing to read member reaction as such, he is then in the position to pursue the programming he has set forth in the form of transactions with selected group members, as opposed to making a group-as-a-whole intervention.

Theory Evaluation Form

1. Which theoretical practitioner do you most resemble? Why?

2. Which theoretical practitioner do you least resemble? Why?

3. What does your response to Question 1 tell you about yourself and your leadership style as a potential or present group therapist?

4. What does your response to Question 2 tell you about yourself and your leadership style as a potential or present group therapist?

5. After rereading how the theoretical practitioner of your choice responded to the incident, how would you modify your response?

CHAPTER FIFTEEN

Mass Group Denial

In this incident the group faces a very significant moment, and it appears the members are engaged in mass denial. How the therapist chooses to interpret this incident will affect the way he or she intervenes and, ultimately, may have a direct bearing on the direction the group moves throughout the remainder of therapy.

Critical Incident 3

One of the head nurses from a large hospital in your community has contacted you. She informs you that a group of ten student nurses for whom she is responsible has expressed concern over personal difficulties in dealing with terminally ill patients and their families. She asks you to help. You agree to meet with the nurses as a group over a period of time.

This is session 4. Until now, the group has been dealing with a variety of issues that are not directly related to the primary purpose for coming together. Topics range from how they chose nursing as a career, complaints about the training schedule, insensitivity of some senior nurses, the rewarding experiences they had in the maternity wing, and the like. You observe that today Jean has been rather silent, and that when she does speak it is usually to agree with something one of the others has said. This is not her usual way of behaving; typically, she has been an initiator and very active contributor in group discussions. Suddenly, without warning, she blurts out that she does not think the group is truly aware of what nursing is really about and that what they have been dealing with is very safe and neat stuff. The other side, the real side, has a lot of sadness. Her voice is quivering, and she is shaking as she continues to relate to the group the incident she had faced today. A 10-year-old boy to whom she had been assigned, and for whom she had developed a great fondness, died from leukemia shortly before the meeting. Part of her responsibility is to report the youth's death and to be with the attending physician when he or she informs the child's parents. The group fell silent. This is the first time any of them had directly approached the topic of death.

As you observe the silence, your eyes search out each member. You can see that Jean's outpouring apparently has the effect of immobilizing the group. You are about to intervene with a comment about what you have just been observing, when Diane says that the doctor of one of her patients has informed her that the patient has been responding very positively to new treatment. With that, Tom says that he is glad he is having this experience because it helps him realize that he wants to specialize in pediatrics. Julie nods her head as though she were in agreement with Tom. It is not long before the group's discussion seems to be moving away from Jean's disclosure. It is obvious to you that Jean's statement presents an issue that poses a threat to them. You know it is an important topic that needs to be dealt with, but it is clear that the group is avoiding it.

Client-Centered Therapy
Implemented by William R. Coulson

I would be hopeful for this group. Ten nursing students who want to get together to deal with their feelings is a group with a lot of potential.

Maybe what they are facing now, however, is the sense that if they follow Jean's lead and move into their feelings, it will be artificial. When people are not used to speaking personally, they feel self-conscious about verbalizing feelings. Jean has had such a sad experience with the passing of her young friend that she cannot ignore her feelings; they are going to surface, if anyone will give them the slightest assistance. But the others, although they have talked initially of wanting to deal with feelings, now back away. I suspect they fear that if they let themselves feel Jean's sadness, and then express their fears, they will have been had—as with a brainwashing group when you give in to the conditioning regimen and start doing things unnatural for you.

One of the criticisms of feeling and expression groups like this one is that they are artificial. Members achieve a level of depth that is unreal, a level they can neither replicate in life nor even maintain with one another outside the group.

For the filtering process to occur from group to life outside the group, something worthwhile has to happen in the group. To have impact, it must be different than life. Usually, it has to do with feelings, the part of ourselves that ordinarily is withheld. In the group we *move into feelings* and thus create trauma. It is not real trauma. Nobody is even bruised. But members anticipate it as traumatic, and the nursing students' reaction to Jean's expression of feelings is to back away from it. They do not want to touch it. By experiencing a traumatic event together, members of a therapy group become close and begin to trust one another. If the nursing students continue to scatter because of Jean's expression of feelings, there will be no common experience. Jean's feelings will have divided them. If they are to succeed in pulling together in this crisis, they will have to talk about what they are now inclined to avoid.

In lieu of facing deeper feelings, members are acting as though the group experience is just another slice of life. Maybe they are protecting against the potential charge of artificiality ("She wouldn't say these things if it weren't for this meeting"). To help overcome this perception, I would move into Jean's feelings. I want to help members now reach that level of depth with one another that a critic might call unreal.

How would I proceed? First, I would realize that other members' lack of expression of their feelings does not mean they are not having them. If I am touched by Jean's account of the death of a little boy, that is a legitimate clue to the possibility that others are touched, too. Empathy works through identification.

Second, if I am going to be alert to my own reactions and listen attentively to Jean, I doubt I can be doing a third thing, looking around the room, observing the reactions of the members to what Jean is saying. I want to pay attention to Jean because I will not be able to feel with her if I am concentrating on the others. I disagree with the principle that the therapist is supposed to be alert to the behavioral clues his or her members provide: What they do with their hands, their eyes, and the like and believe that only in feeling *with* her can I know, except from memory, what sort of human experience this is.

Third, let us assume that I have been so absorbed in Jean's report that I start to cry. This could happen. The death of a small child is a sad thing. Then what should we do? Well, we'd have our trauma all right ("The therapist is crying. Now what?"). What if it turned out that Jean and I were the only ones who felt that badly about what she had experienced? Then, again, we would have something vital and immediate to talk about: How come we're so different? Maybe they would say, "Doc, you can't take these things so personally. You'd never survive in hospital work." They would say it with the intention of helping me; as I pointed out in the first incident, it could be helpful to them to help me. Then, too, we would at last be dealing with the subject we thought we wanted to talk about in the first place: our personal reactions to death.

So it might not be such a bad thing if I were moved to tears by Jean's story. I would not cry *in order to* let them help me or in order to finally get to the topic. But if the sadness arose, I would not resist it.

Fourth, let us say I have a cooler head and am not so deeply moved by Jean's account that I become emotional and miss the fact that others want to change the subject. Would I point out to them that they are avoiding Jean's theme? No. The most important thing to do is talk to Jean. If group members could not do it, I would begin myself, hoping they would take over, or at least join in, when they saw that Jean's sadness was not going to destroy them. I would ask her if she could say more. I would try to accompany her into her feelings and hope to bring the group along. I take it on faith that to be alive is to have deep feelings. Many people have trouble letting feelings out and, consequently, those feelings become barriers to personal development. I would now pursue the feelings, convinced that afterward someone would say, or want to say, "Thanks, I needed that."

Fifth, what if I noticed that although he was making brave noises, Tom's chin was trembling, too? Would I say, "I notice your chin is trembling, Tom"? No. I find it distracts people to describe their behavior. What needs to be highlighted is the *meaning* a person intends to express, not the clues by which you read it.

The purpose of sharing what I would and would not do is to help the group move toward a deep and feeling-centered experience. Too often, people express their feelings only in the closet. Group therapy brings them into the open. Openness about previously private matters gives group work its potential to help a person start growing again—especially in the professions related to medicine, where people have learned to keep their feelings under wraps.

The problem posed for members of the nurses' group (or by any other therapy group) is an existential one: how to find our way through our hours together without an agenda. The solution is not a technical or expert one, nor one known in advance. It is, I believe, an artistic one. In the process of creating it—and in many cases finding the process more satisfying than if the problem and its solution were more focused—members gain confidence about developing the same kind of artistic mastery in their own lives.

My guess is that Diane, Tom, Julie, and the others are backing away from Jean's approach to her sorrow because they feel like they are still in public. Her story invites them to yield to their feelings. Quite possibly, this is frightening to them, as the prospect of any important new behavior might be frightening. A sense of the isolation of the group experience from daily life can make letting go more possible, but this psychological isolation is probably what has not yet developed in the nurses' group.

As a group leader, I try to make success more likely by not giving guidance, a situation that by itself sets up a sharp difference between the group and the many settings in which members are expected to follow instructions. They may want instructions now. But I would rather see the group as a struggle, in which all of us will have to work hard, and maybe even be wildly inventive at times in order to find what we need.

Finding one's way successfully through the near-cultivated diffuseness of a good therapy group can lead to a real sense of achievement—and a confidence that a similar kind of artistic power is possible in life and work.

Cognitive–Behavioral Therapy
Implemented by John V. Flowers

Mass denial is obviously more prevalent in a group of clients with similar problems than in groups of heterogeneous composition. Such homogeneous groups are more common in behavioral group therapy than in most other modalities. Many behavioral groups are psychoeducational, involving clients with similar problems in a group and focusing on the specific problem area in common. There are behavioral groups for assertion, social skills, depression, agoraphobia, weight control, alcohol addiction, sexual deviation, AIDS-risk reduction, and a host of other problem-specific areas. Psychoeducational groups are probably the most substantial contribution that behavioral therapy has made in the general group therapy area. Despite the fact that behavioral group therapists encounter group denial frequently, this is not the important problem posed by this incident. The larger problem in this incident for the behaviorist concerns ethics. This group was formed for the purpose of dealing with the very behavior being avoided, but this agenda belongs to the head nurse, not necessarily the group. First, we need to know whether this group has mandatory or coerced attendance? Total group resistance is far more common in a nonvoluntary group, and nonvoluntary participation poses ethical dilemmas for group leaders. As a behaviorist, I always try to keep my contract with clients as clear as possible and would normally have covered the intent of the group in the introductory session. In many psychoeducational homogeneous groups, an introductory sheet addressing norms, confidentiality, and other group rules and goals is handed out at the beginning of session 1. Members who do not wish to participate are encouraged to leave. In the incident posed, it appears that the "client" (i.e., the person who wants the group to accomplish a task) is the head nurse who is not in the group.

Because the group could easily have mandatory or at least coerced attendance, even a clear contract of the group's purpose does not solve the problem. Clients have the right to avoid, just as therapists have the obligation to explain, the potential consequences of the avoidance. Although it might be "better" for the nurse trainees to confront their feelings about death and the power to help, that choice belongs to each member, not the missing head nurse.

There is a client at risk here, so I would have to address the avoidance as potentially hurtful to Jean, who asked for the group's help, which was then denied. After acknowledging that the group was formed to deal with the difficult feelings surrounding deaths of patients, I would also acknowledge that this might not be each member's agenda and that no one has the right to impose this on anyone who has not agreed to it. If there were enough time left, I would say I wished to address Jean's disclosure and am willing to excuse members who wish to leave for the rest of this session. It is my experience that most group members not only stay when avoidance is addressed in this way but also feel that remaining is their own decision. If there were not enough time to deal with the avoidance of Jean's disclosure in the group, I would meet with her individually at first opportunity to ensure that she was not a potential group casualty.

Next I would encourage members to address this issue on the next week's problem card, even if tangentially. Examples of various types of problems that might be written are (1) "I resent the fact I was asked to attend a group dealing with a problem I don't wish to discuss," (2) "I am uncomfortable dealing with Jean's feelings about her patient's death," and (3) "I don't know if this profession is correct for me, given how hard it is to deal with a patient's death."

An obvious therapeutic issue here is, Is the group ready for the discussion that is being avoided? Avoidance behavior is the bread and butter of behavioral therapy, and many strategies can be employed to reduce avoidance, including cured relaxation, graded approaches, and flooding, to name just a few. How far the group can safely go down this road is a therapeutic judgment of the two therapists working collaboratively.

The incident as presented is actually not the hardest avoidance problem that faces the group therapist. Jean's disclosure has opened the topic, and the leader can move back to it and either ask Jean how she feels about the groups obvious avoidance or ask other members how they feel about Jean's disclosure and the subsequent discussion. The more difficult scenario is when the entire group avoids what has to be discussed. A sexual deviation group whose members talk about everything but sex or a post–cardiac surgery group that avoids all references to death are examples. The problem card assignment helps, but in some cases group therapy can be ethically impossible; when this is obvious, group leaders should acknowledge this to themselves and to whomever contracted for the group. Behavioral therapy is a voluntary collaboration and does not work well when imposed on unwilling clients.

Family-Centered Therapy
Implemented by James P. Trotzer

My first thought regarding this group and this incident is that death always raises existential issues for each group member and reminds each member of past experiences with death. Both possibilities have tendencies to raise resistance in the form of avoidance of addressing the issue of death. For many group leaders, direct confrontation may seem to be the obvious approach to breaking through or working through the mass group avoidance. However, because of my systemic orientation, I believe many dynamics beyond the existential and the experiential are likely to be involved. Therefore, rather than confront the group, I would attempt to reframe the incident in a manner the group finds more palatable and that facilitates appropriate interaction.

My perception is that the group dynamic of denial emerges from the disclosure of Jean's personal emotive state, which produces a group emotive state expressed first by silence and then by denial. The silence is so loud that individual defense mechanisms kick into gear, producing a diverting response by Diane. This is followed by a cumulative group response that shifts the focus away from Jean's intense affect in response to loss (i.e., the death of her 10-year-old patient). My role and response at this juncture is critical because the group has demonstrated its tendency to cope by avoiding.

Reframing in systemic terminology means taking a current situation or circumstance with certain obvious implications, characteristics, or conclusions and giving it a different perspective by adding or shifting the context so that members have another set of response options. In this case the group response is silence and distraction. My reframing intervention is intended to raise alternate response possibilities. Several potential reframing suggestions and their systemic derivatives come to mind as I think about this incident. I will describe three possible responses and a specific structured intervention derived from family theory that will not only assist the group in addressing its purpose and focus but also extend the group's knowledge of the use of system's dynamics in responding to a dying patient or the death of a patient in their care.

1. *Reframe by soliciting corroborating experience with death beyond the professional setting.*

> "Jean just shared her close contact with death and its impact on her. I'm wondering what experiences each of you have had with someone dying."

My reframe shifts the response possibility to a broader spectrum of death experiences (or lack thereof) so that members who may not have had a professional experience to relate can respond. (Even if a member lacks any experience, in this framework, sharing that does not implicate their professional competence.) My statement opens the door for corroborative disclosures that are supportive of Jean and provide possible common ground regarding the issue of death that is being discussed in this group.

2. *Reframe as a family issue.*

> "Every family celebrates in idiosyncratic ways, depending on their values, beliefs, culture, religion, or ethnicity. Death is one of those family events that every family celebrates. Jean mentioned having to be present when the news of her patient's death is relayed to his parents. They will now have to celebrate their son's death. I'm wondering how your family deals with and celebrates death? And how does that experience relate to how you respond here on the job?"

My systemic springboard in this case is identification with the boy's family and the anxiety Jean expressed in having to present when the death is reported to them. By raising death in each member's family context, all members are empowered as experts in the context of their own families. This feeling of competence is in stark contrast to their feelings of helplessness and lack of expertise, which led to the avoidance and denial. Again, the response base is broadened and empowerment dynamics are mobilized.

3. *Reframe as a personal–professional issue with which each member must grapple.* To help the group address the here-and-now dilemma and the dilemma's overall purpose, my response in this case reflects the personal and professional dimensions of Jean's disclosure.

> "It appears that everyone is deeply touched by Jean's experience. I know I am. Sometimes it's very difficult to know where the line is between the personal and the professional, and experiences like Jean's really point that out. Maybe we could share our thoughts and feelings about that dilemma. That way Jean wouldn't be so alone in it, and we could all profit from the discussion."

My response reframes the highly volatile emotional material into a cognitive framework that opens the door for responses. It also raises the systemic reality that more than one system is involved. Group members are nurses (professional role), but they are also persons and members of families, just like their patients are human beings and members of families while in the role of receiving nursing care.

Note: I believe group leaders always have more than one response option at any particular juncture in the group interaction. Any or all can be effective or ineffective, appropriate or inappropriate. The point is to learn from both what does and doesn't work. That is the systemic way. In this case my inclination is to use response 1 because the following structured activity will raise issues related to responses 2 and 3.

I would also use this incident as an opportunity to introduce a timely structured exercise that provides direction, understanding, and insight into the systemic dynamics of death and relates to the group's purpose. The title of the activity is "Draw Your Childhood Table." I would introduce the activity as a homework assignment at the end of this session. After processing Jean's disclosure via one of the above reframes, I would ask the group members to draw the shapes of their family's dining table when they were between 12 and 16 years old. They are to place each family member around the table and supply descriptive phrases for each person including themselves. In addition, descriptive comments about family dynamics are to be written on the table top. At the next session I would ask members to describe their families, using their tables. At the end of the sharing, I would ask members to pass their tables to the person on their right. I would instruct that person to arbitrarily place an *X* on one person at the table and return it to the owner. The *X* represents death. I would then pose the following questions to the group: If that person had died at that time in your life, how would you be different today? How would your family be different?

This activity raises the personal and systemic implications of death for the group members and sets in motion discussion that relates to their professional roles, thus facilitating movement into the work stage of the group process.

Gestalt Therapy
Implemented by Mirriam F. Polster

This situation dramatizes one of the functions of a group leader. Here is the first statement in 4 weeks of a concern that I know all group members share. And yet, when one of them begins to address this problem directly, the others deflect and miss making contact either with Jean or with each other by confronting their own difficulties about the death of a patient.

The ability to confront pain either in oneself or in another often rests on a sense of self-support. When I feel extended beyond my customary boundaries, I am experiencing a loss of the support systems that usually provide me with orientation, vitality, and the belief that I am in control of my own actions and competent to meet the requirements of the circumstances in which I find myself. These I-boundaries (Polster & Polster, 1973) are the flexible, permeable demarcations between what I have been thus far in my life and what I am willing to become, what risks I am willing to take, what new and intense experience I am ready to move into, and my willingness to assimilate the unfamiliar excitement this experience may generate.

These student nurses are moving into uncharted territory. They may have confronted death before, but they were not then professionals. Their sense of participation in those deaths must have been more marginal. Surely they had little or no sense of responsibility or participation in the decisions about the actual care and treatment of the person who died.

Jean has been the initiator in previous sessions, and she is again this time. Perhaps she is more open to her feelings and therefore is often the first one to venture into new developmental areas. Her sense of self-support has enabled her to move into her experience many times before and has served her well previously. But now she confronts a situation where her self-support system is temporarily insufficient. She takes the logical and appropriate next step—she looks for what support she can get from her environment, her fellow students.

But her colleagues seem unavailable. Diane continues as if nothing had happened. She changes the subject—to a brighter topic—as if Jean had not spoken or as if Jean had committed a social error that she was politely ignoring. Tom and Julie are happy to collude in the deflection (Polster & Polster, 1973). Their self-support systems may well be more primitive than Jean's. Unwilling to confront the pain she has expressed, they try to deny it altogether, to make it go away. This is not only a more primitive stance but also more precarious (demanding more denial and deflection to sustain) and more self-limiting. Jean moves with intensity and feeling into her evolution as a professional. They hope to become professionals but may be less willing than she to accept the personal changes that are inevitable.

I would return to Jean at this moment and ask how she feels about the lack of response to her expression of sadness. I might tell her what feelings she has aroused in me and ask if anyone else was also moved. I am interested in Jean obtaining the support she seeks now from the community and in mobilizing her own self-support as she continues to explore the sadness she is feeling. She has said that she believes this occurs often in nursing—and she is right. It is important, too, for her fellow students not to pass over this moment and treat it antiseptically. They may learn from Jean's courage and find ways to face up to the sadness that will (if it has not yet) rise before them, too.

I might ask Jean to visualize the young boy and to speak to him in fantasy, to tell him about what she might have liked to say to him while he was alive and that she left unsaid. I would ask her to imagine his response. How might he reply? Speaking through Jean, he might respond with blame or understanding or confusion or gratitude or a whole range of feelings, all of which might be what Jean herself is struggling with and is dreading that the boy's parents, too, might think or feel.

As she does this, I would watch to see how Jean supports herself, whether she sits in a way that is upright, flexible, and supported or whether she slouches down and slumps defeatedly in her chair; whether her breathing is adequate to the words she is saying or if she is breathing shallowly and runs out of her vital supply of air just when she is confronting sorrow and needs more of it. I would want the dialogue to continue until there is a sense of meeting between Jean and the fantasized dead boy and then perhaps ask Jean what she might like to say to the boy's parents, encouraging here, too, the establishment of dialogue that could lead to an eventual sense of completion and rest. Sadness cannot be avoided in Jean's profession. She knows this. But missed communication can add more pain to already existing pain.

By fully going with Jean in this deep experience and seeing it through to a fruitful sense of closure, the stage is set for other nurses to explore their own feelings in depth. It adds momentum and support and gives form to what may have been, up to now, feelings that the other student nurses believed they had no way into. To see someone come through a painful experience is inspirational.

Individual Psychology
Implemented by Guy J. Manaster

Among Adler's early recollections (used as a projective device by individual psychologists) was one about death. He believed that concern about death was a primary motivation in his and others' decision to become doctors. Stories are told about Adler lecturing to medical students and asking them to think of the earliest incident or scene they could remember. Usually, more than 60% of the students' earliest memories dealt with death. This only points out that Adlerian psychology has long been aware of death as an issue that must be faced intellectually and emotionally by members of the medical profession.

In this situation I am aware of the importance of the issue of death for the group. The group is equally aware of the need to face the issue. Jean raised it and is distraught, and the group has rushed on. Adlerian therapy is noted as one of the earliest directive therapies and users of the paradox. I think this an appropriate moment for a paradoxical intervention into the group process.

I would say something like, "Excuse me, but the discussion so far today seems to be moving in a definite direction that illuminates our task. The death of a young patient today has really upset Jean. Diane, Tom, and Julie seem very positive about working with new successful treatments and usual childhood diseases. Why don't we get to work figuring out how we can be nurses who work only with well people."

Should the group somehow not pick up on this idea, I would continue with it until someone noted the paradox and its absurdity. I doubt it would take long. Probably someone would reply immediately to my statement with something like, "How can one be a nurse and work only with well people? That isn't nursing."

I might answer with a variation on the old story about the mother who wanted her son to be a dermatologist. "Maybe you could be dermatological nurses. It's a good business. Your patients never die and never get better."

Pause. Silence. Wait.

"I mean no one wants their patients to die. And no one here wants to talk about death or dying, or even talk to Jean who tried to get us to talk about it and went through a lot to bring it up."

Pause. Silence. Wait.

It is inconceivable to me that by this point the group would not have faced the issue, begun to discuss it, and particularly come back to Jean. Yet, it is possible. For the sake of illustrating how directive an Adlerian therapist can be, I would continue as if this last silence was not broken. After a prolonged and, I assume, uncomfortable period of silence, I would go on: "If you are to be nurses, you are going to treat the critically ill. Some of them will die. It will be rough. It will be less rough if you understand how you think and feel about death, dealing with dying people and their families. But this will be something you will have to work on now and periodically throughout your career—if you intend to be a nurse. And if you now choose not to become nurses, *you* will still die—maybe you can put off thinking about it longer if you are not in a health profession, but you will die and will in all likelihood have to consider it later if not sooner.

"If we cannot talk about death and dying, here, now, I suggest we break and meet next week to talk about new careers." I would ask Jean to stay and talk with me about her concerns.

Even after this terminating statement, I would be more than willing to begin the pertinent discussion if the group wanted to do so. However, if there was no dissent, I would get up and take Jean to another office to talk.

This may seem harsh and heavy, but Adlerian theory credits people with great strength and resiliency. It also clearly implies that all decisions are individual decisions, that individuals bear the burden and responsibility for their decisions and lives. I believe that I am merely throwing the burden where it belongs—on each group member.

During the week, all members may struggle with the issue. Although I would hope to speak individually with any who decide they would rather not confront the death-and-dying issue and want to change careers, it seems a good time to make the decision—and it is their own decision to make individually. Reality may be harsh, and they are facing the reality of their chosen career. Most will be back, probably all, and we could then discuss the issue in the face of reality and their resolve.

Throughout my elaboration of these critical incidents from my Adlerian, not *the* Adlerian, perspective, I have had to make guesses and intuit persons from very limited material. Adlerians generally make guesses from little information within the framework of the theory, but with the client there to verify or disregard the therapist's interpretation. Therefore, as a bit of a hedge, I will end with Adler's line: "Everything can be different."

Interpersonal Psychotherapy

Implemented by Victor Yalom and Mary Jean Paris

It is important to recognize the premise for which this group has been formed and how it conflicts with some of the basic tenets of the interpersonal approach to group therapy. Usually, members of the therapy group have no or limited contact with each other outside the group. This tenet regarding member contact contributes to the ability of members to give each other honest feedback, because no real-world immediate consequences to events will occur within the life of the therapy group. It is obviously not the case in the real world when one chooses to give honest feedback to one's boss, partner, or relative.

The purpose of this group is primarily supportive in nature, aimed at helping student nurses deal with concerns about their patients. Given that these are student nurses who work together and they are in this group to specifically deal with work-related issues, the leaders will be very cautious about encouraging members to give each other feedback that might make their relationships uncomfortable for them when they are back on the hospital ward. Thus, interventions that promote interpersonal learning will be appropriately de-emphasized, although not eliminated, from the therapists' repertoire.

Given this setting, Jean is in a potentially vulnerable position by expressing feelings that are quite painful for her. The primary concern at this point would be for Jean not to be left feeling exposed or unsupported, which might indeed be the case if she does not get any response. We would most likely deal with the denial directly by interrupting it and encouraging or pushing for a more constructive response. For example, one of us might say, "I noticed that we all quickly moved away from the intense issues and feelings that Jean brought up. It is pretty scary stuff, yet I'm sure the rest of us have some reactions. Would anyone be willing to say what their reactions were?" Jean has taken a risk speaking honestly about her personal concerns; our goal is to support and validate Jean's courageous attempt, and we would invite other members to do so as well. This would also be an opportunity to talk about feelings of shared vulnerabilities in the therapy group. We would encourage and give permission to the other members to talk about their own difficulties in dealing with terminally ill patients—the intent of the group's formation. We might also draw a link between the way they backed away from Jean's emotional expression and how they use denial in their daily work—and help them explore when denial serves as a healthy coping mechanism and when it is potentially problematic.

The differences between this group and a general psychotherapy group is that in the latter we might ask Jean how it felt when the other members seemingly ignored her display of emotions. This is an example of a more interactive approach of the interpersonal model. We might also ask the other members what was going on inside them that prevented them from responding to Jean's pain more directly or how they felt when Jean said that she does not think the group is "truly aware of what nursing is really about." These kinds of interventions push members to go beyond dealing with intense emotions in relationships with themselves and with others.

Over time, it is possible that a collegial support group might evolve to allow for such intimacy an authentic participation, although this is less likely with students who have heightened concerns about appearing professionally competent and thus may be even more guarded about revealing vulnerabilities. However, such a development would have to be led by the group members and explicitly agreed to, and not pushed through by the desires of the therapists.

Psychodynamic Therapy
Implemented by J. Scott Rutan

Perhaps the most important text on interpretation is the fairy tale "The Emperor's New Clothes." In group therapy we are often keenly aware that there is "an elephant in the room," a supremely important topic that is not being addressed *directly*. The key notion is that the issue is not being addressed directly. The psychodynamic assumption is that it *is* being addressed as best as the group can address it. It should not surprise us that this group does not immediately begin to confront the horror of dealing with dying patients directly. Rather, they questioned why they chose nursing (presumably implying that they had not done so in order to help people *die*). They also spoke of their training schedule (implying they were not being trained properly to deal with what faced them?). They spoke of the insensitivity of some staff (who did not comprehend how much personal pain they were suffering?). They spoke of loving their work in maternity (where *life*, not *death*, is the order of the day).

Jean dared to speak the unspeakable. She mentioned the despair and anguish that brought them together. Perhaps in terms of group development the group is not yet ready to join her at that level. So others point out that there *is* some hope. This does not have to be understood as group avoidance but as group coping. It is important to point out that under the psychodynamic umbrella fall many specific theories. Classical Freudian theory would understand the group's behavior as avoidance of the feelings raised by Jean. Object relations theory, on the other hand, would focus on the group's attempt to *connect* at the best level they can manage at the moment.

I would have likely intervened by saying, "Each of you has come to this group because you find your role as a nurse has led you into an aspect of nursing for which you feel somewhat unprepared. You have spoken of why you chose nursing, the inadequacy of your training, and the insensitivity of some staff. You also mentioned that maternity work is much more rewarding. Today, for the first time, it was mentioned that in fact you work with dying patients. And that is likely not what you expected. It is grueling work. It should not surprise us that the immediate responses to Jean's reminding us why we are here are associations to some positive experiences." What guides the psychodynamic therapist here is the assumption that what followed Jean's comments was not a change of subject but an elaboration of the very same subject. By making the preceding comment, it would be hoped that Jean would feel less excluded and the group as a whole would be more ready to move to the painful and unacceptable feelings.

Rational–Emotive–Behavioral Therapy

Implemented by Albert Ellis

I would assume, on the basis of rational–emotive–behavioral therapy (REBT) theory and group therapy in general, that the members of this group are unwilling to deal with the serious issue raised by Jean, but that it probably would be better for them to face it and thereby help themselves and each other come to some kind of resolution about it. The main REBT assumption I would have is that people shy away from discussions of death, their own and others, largely because they have low frustration tolerance. Individuals do not want to accept (1) the fact that, to be afforded the boon of living, we also have to die; and (2) that death is sad and deplorable but not "horrible," "awful," or "depressing."

Humans naturally and easily tend to believe that it is because (1) we are born with a tendency to whine about and refuse to accept some of the grimmest realities of our lives; and (2) we are reinforced in these irrational beliefs and reactions by cultural phenomena, such as the teachings of our family, church, mass media, teachers, and the like.

The assumption of REBT, on the contrary, is that humans are almost all capable of accepting what they do not like: of facing the harshness and hassles of their existence and gracefully lumping them. We are "existentially anxious" in the face of dying and death, in the sense that we are virtually all seriously *concerned* about these phenomena and want to do our best to ward them off as long as we can. We have self-preservation drives, partly of a biological nature and partly taught, that motivate us to take death quite seriously and to take precautions against its early occurrence. But our "anxiety" about it is only existential in the sense that we virtually all feel it. It is not self-preserving, as it is deep concern, and it can largely be reduced. "Anxiety," in REBT terms, is *over*concern or *needless* concern: namely, the idea that any unusual hassle or death *should* not, *must* not exist; that it is *awful* when it does; that people *cannot stand* the thought of it; and that the world is a *horrible place* when it inevitably presents obstacles and difficulties of this sort to people.

Although REBT, does not therefore try to interfere with concern, cautiousness, or vigilance, it does try to separate these feelings and actions from those of anxiety, obsessiveness with life and safety, and panic. In the group in question, my assumption would be that the members are largely panicked about the thought of (1) dying themselves and (2) the death of their loved ones or their patients. They therefore submerge or squelch this state of panic by refusing to look at the problems that Jean is presenting, and they go back to the same kinds of relatively trivial issues being discussed before Jean "uncomfortably" raised the topic of death. Although they are quite entitled to do this and to avoid thinking about death if that is what they really want to do, a healthier reaction would be for them to face this issue, deal with Jean's concerns and their own problems regarding it, and then "drop" it largely *because* they have dealt with it and not because they have swept it under the rug.

In an instance like this, where some would say that the group members have "unconsciously" copped out and avoided the issue of dying, the REBT therapist would agree that this is probably true but would not see their "unconscious" reaction as one that is exceptionally deep seated or unavailable to consciousness. Instead, REBT would assume (as I would) that they have semiconsciously (or what Freud originally called "preconsciously") squelched this issue and that they could fairly easily look at it again and bring it to their consciousness. So, I would make an attempt to get them to do this: to bring the issue of death to their consciousness again and deal with it, experientially and philosophically, until they overcome their irrational beliefs about it.

I would open up discussion of this problem by saying something like this to the group: "I find it very interesting that you are pretty much ignoring the problem of death that Jean has raised and that you are going back to discussing what would seem to be less important and less emotion-filled issues. I am wondering whether there is something you consider 'too uncomfortable' about this problem to deal with. Of course, some or all of you may really have faced it squarely in your own life and resolved it. But I wonder whether you, like Jean, have some real problems when one of your patients dies and whether you are not avoiding dealing with these problems."

I would assume that, having directly raised this issue, some or all group members would admit to having some problems dealing with issues of dying and that some of them would recognize that they had deliberately avoided the topic that Jean raised, going back to discussing less important things. If so, I would then say, "Why do you think that you have so much trouble in dealing with the issue of death? What are you telling yourself when you think about it—as you momentarily did before when Jean raised the issue—and then sweep it under the rug?" By this kind of questioning, I would expect some of the group members to admit that they were horrified about death, that they did think it must not exist, and that they could not bear to discuss it openly. I would expect members to say it was very unfair that they and their loved ones had to die some day and that the world was a pretty awful place for having this kind of unfairness in it.

As they brought out these ideas, I would actively dispute and challenge them, and I would try to get them to question each other's irrationalities in this respect. I would ask, "Where is the evidence that death *must* not exist?"; and I would try to get them to see that it is really inevitable and *has to* exist, if it does. I would ask, "What makes it *awful* or *terrible* if you or one of your loved ones dies?"; and I would try to show them that it is only highly inconvenient, only very sad—but not "awful," meaning *more than* inconvenient or sad and more unfortunate than it *should* be. I would ask them to prove that they *can't stand, can't bear* the thought of dying or having one of their loved ones die and attempt to demonstrate that, no matter how much they dislike or feel greatly displeased about it, they definitely can stand it and can even experience a great deal of happiness while they still live on after their loved one has died. Finally, I would ask, "Why is the world a *terrible place* and life hardly *worth living at all* in view of the fact that we all die and cannot avoid this possibility?" I would attempt to help them see that this is not true: The world is a place where bad things exist—but is not itself, or in its entirety, *terrible*—and that as long as they live, they almost certainly *can* enjoy themselves to some considerable degree, even after suffering the loss of loved ones.

I would, in other words, actively try to help almost all the members of the group see that they are not merely concerned or sad about death and dying but that they are distinctly *over*concerned and exceptionally anxious. I would show them exactly which irrational beliefs are giving them this overconcern and show them how to learn the REBT methods of logically and empirically disputing, questioning, challenging, and surrendering these beliefs. I would hope, in the process of my dialogue with the group members (and I would expect to be actively and directively engaging in a Socratic-type dialogue with the group as a whole, or at least with several of them), that I would jolt some of their current ideas about dying and death and help them get on the road of a more rational, self-helping philosophy of death. In the course of my talking with the group members, I would assume that many of their "hidden" or "unexpressed" concerns would surface (especially as they backed each other with irrational ideas) and that some of these would begin, at least, to be worked through.

To get back to Jean's problem and to show the members of the group that their fear of death was not the only issue involved, I would at some point take the conversation back to Jean by saying, "You seem very sad about the death of the 10-year-old boy who was your patient. I can well understand that since I am sure that you became rather attached to him during the past several weeks and that you also feel exceptionally sorry about the death of any 10-year-old boy, especially from a disease like leukemia. But I would like you to get in touch with your sadness for a short while and tell me what it really feels like, and particularly tell me if it is only sadness or sorrow about the boy."

Jean, in getting in touch with her actual feelings, would probably reveal other feelings, such as depression, guilt, and anger. If this were so, I would say something like, "Well, I can easily see how you would feel depressed. Most people, having gone through what you have just gone through, would feel about the same. But, perhaps very peculiarly, I would say that they were self-defeating and that you are feeling depressed. I would contend that you—and they—are healthily sad or sorrowful, but that you are unhealthily depressed. Do you know why I would say this?"

The group up to this point has apparently not been taught REBT principles, so Jean is not likely to know why I consider sorrow and sadness healthy but depression unhealthy. If she acknowledged confusion, I would say, "Your sadness springs from your belief that it is more unfortunate, very bad that this 10-year-old boy has died of leukemia; that it is unfortunate for him, his parents, and you. And that is correct; we could rightly and empirically say that it *is* unfortunate. The boy wanted to live, his parents wanted him to live, and you certainly wanted him to live. And you are all not getting what you wanted—and are getting just about the opposite. It is therefore most unfortunate, sad, or regretful that this frustrating set of conditions exists; and you and his parents would definitely be foolish if you concluded that it was good or even unimportant. But depression—yours or theirs—comes from an extra, irrational idea that this unfortunate, sorry state of affairs *should not, must not* exist, that it is *awful* that it does exist, and that human life is pretty *horrible* and *useless* when such unfortunate events exist. Isn't that what you're really telling yourself—that the death of the boy *should not* have occurred and that it is *awful* that it did?"

Assuming that Jean admitted that she was telling herself something like this, I would show her that it is not the activating experience (A) of the boy's death that is creating her emotional consequence (C) of depression; rather, it is her irrational beliefs (B) *about* this experience that are making her depressed. And I would show her how she could change these beliefs to rational or coping beliefs, such as I wish that boy had not died, but he inevitably did. "Too bad! But I can definitely *stand* his cruel death even though I'll never like it nor similar deaths of young children" and "The world is a place in which bad things like this will always to some extent exist, but it is not *totally* bad; it still has a lot of good, enjoyable things in it. And as long as I still live, I can definitely lead a good, enjoyable existence."

I would try to get the other group members to join in with me, as we all tried to talk Jean out of, not her feelings of sorrow and sadness, but those of depression. Also, if she were guilty or angry, I would show her how she was needlessly creating these feelings—and how the happenings of her life, or what she had done or not done about them, were not the real issue. In getting the group members to help me show Jean that she was healthily sad and unhealthily depressed, guilty, or angry about the boy's death, I would be helping them face the problem that they have so far avoided—dealing with death. I would presumably also help some of them with their own expressed or unexpressed feelings of depression, guilt, or anger about death.

As this was going on, or after much of it had been completed, I would go back to the group's problem of ignoring the issue of death. I would try to show them that such defensive behavior covers up their underlying anxieties and that, if they faced these anxieties by finding their philosophic source and changing their philosophies so as not to make themselves anxious any longer, they could deal much better with their emotional and practical problems.

In several ways then, I would take the current group situation, make a dramatic issue of it, and almost force the group members to expose, confront, and start to change their disturbed feelings. I would also give them some desensitizing homework assignments such as recording all their thoughts about death, visiting a morgue, or discussing death openly with a friend or with relatives of dying or dead patients. I might also give them the emotive exercise of rational–emotive imagery. I would ask them to think about a close friend or relative's death, let themselves feel disturbed (depressed or anxious) about this intensely imagined fantasy; change their feeling to one of keen disappointment, sorrow, or regret but not depression or anxiety; see what went on in their heads to effect this change in feeling; and then practice doing this same exercise for, say, 30 consecutive days until they could automatically think about death and *only* or *mainly* feel sorry and regretful but not severely upset.

In various cognitive, emotive, and behavioral ways, therefore, I would work with this group on facing the problem of their own and others' death and of feeling appropriately about this. REBT group therapy is one of the few forms of therapy that specifically tries to show group members the difference between healthy negative emotions of sorrow, regret, frustration, and annoyance and the unhealthy negative emotions of depression, anxiety, despair, hostility, and worthlessness. The group sessions and experiences would be employed largely as an educational device to dramatically help the members think about, feel about, and work on their disturbed reactions to death and dying.

Reality Therapy

Implemented by Thomas E. Bratter

I would agree to provide a learning experience for the student nurses regarding their work with the terminally ill. Before accepting this challenging assignment, however, I would find it most important to revisit my mother's death to discover if there were any unresolved issues and whether I had come to peace with the insensitive and at times unprofessional treatment of various hospital personnel.

This experience, though intensely painful to recall, is most important when considering running a group such as this. Truthfully, the targets of my rage were the nurses who appeared so insensitive and incompetent. In addition, with the exception of a neurologist, all the physicians and medical consultants connected with the hospital remain objects of my contempt and hatred, not because my mother died but because they did not render competent or caring treatment.

I would conduct the group because, at the appropriate time, I could provide a personal reaction of how a family member of the terminally ill viewed the nursing and medical profession. For reasons that will become apparent later for this specific group, I would apply a humanistic approach because the experience is more a learning one than a therapeutic one. But becoming vulnerable would in no way affect my credibility as the group leader while working with student nurses.

The group leader is more than just a member of the group. The leader retains the responsibility for determining the agenda so that both the individual who wants to work through a problem and the group can benefit. Generally, this benefit can be achieved by restating the issue so that all either can relate to or identify with the person who is speaking. This intervention, in brief, can be considered the art of being a group psychotherapist—that is, the ability to involve everyone while trying to achieve a solution. At times, a group leader may need to assume the role of catalyst when the group either becomes immobilized or begins to discuss topics other than therapeutic ones.

The student nurses who want to discuss "their personal difficulty with dealing with terminally ill patients and their families" present many interesting and somewhat unique challenges for the group therapist.

1. The original contract, which concerns the need to discuss difficulty with dealing with the terminally ill, has been negotiated by someone other than the group with me. It is indeed significant that the head nurse contacted me rather than providing the group experience herself. My guess is that the student nurses would come to the initial group with varying expectations, with some confusion, and with some resentment about being told by a person in authority that "each needed to attend a group." The leader cannot assume there is any consensus among the potential group members and any motivation to form a group.

2. It is important to recognize that the members already know each other and have many opportunities to interact both in competitive (academic) and cooperative (work) environments. Each person has an image and an identity that obviously affects the eventual cohesion and intimacy of the group. Each member already likes and dislikes, respects and disrespects, trusts and mistrusts someone in the group, which will complicate the formation of the group. Confidentiality would become a crucial issue because, during inevitable daily interaction and power struggles, some data gained in the group can be used opportunistically and manipulatively.

3. A natural we–you dichotomy has been established prior to the formation of the group. Though members may have had some conflicts with each other,

they do share a common experience of being student nurses. They will have some incentive to discuss occurrences that they have experienced during the day. The group leader will be identified as the "outsider," which means that there is more reason why I will need to prove myself as a credible and trustworthy resource person. Having been selected, without any student nurse input, by the head nurse also will need to be discussed prior to the group trusting me.

4. Before starting this group, I would know there would be some confusion and conflict regarding the format. One of the first demanding clarification would be the nature of the group—that is, would it be therapeutic, didactic, sensitivity, problem oriented, and so on.

I would be sensitive to permitting the student nurses to progress at their own pace. I would play a waiting game until one member would begin to relate to a relevant issue before attempting to focus attention. I would respect the members' right in this unique situation to determine when they felt sufficiently comfortable to disclose an intimate personal or professional concern regarding death. In an effort to stimulate this discussion, however, in all probability I would suggest that the group read some of LeShan's works (1959; 1966; 1969). If I knew of a television program about death, I would suggest that the group watch it.

Jean showed both initiative and courage to confront her remorse about a 10-year-old boy's death. I would intervene on her behalf and attempt to redirect group attention and concern to help her with her grief. I would say, "I can appreciate your reluctance to want to focus on what Jean said because it is painful for us to accept the awesome realization that someday each of us will die and that sometimes we cannot help someone live longer. What I am wondering is, What we can do to help Jean deal with her grief?"

Perhaps my most important contribution would be to serve as the architect or catalyst for the student nurses to form a supportive self-help group. Since the student nurses work daily with the terminally ill, they could rely on each other for consolation, guidance, and understanding. All personnel who are exposed to working with perpetual illness and dying should be provided with this kind of support system to help resolve the feelings of frustration and failure. If this model would be effective, I would think it could be implemented for all medical and nursing personnel and those who work with the aging and other subpopulations that tend to drain the psychotherapist. I believe, as does Glasser (1965), that there clearly is a need for this type of self-help support system.

Solution-Focused Therapy

Implemented by Rebecca LaFountain

In solution-focused groups I encourage counselors to form their groups with clients who present concerns that are heterogeneous rather than homogeneous. The practice of establishing multi-issue groups increases the likelihood that clients will present a wide range of experiences and abilities on any one characteristic. For example, in this scenario all ten of the group members are experiencing difficulties in dealing with terminally ill patients and their families. Their discomfort contributes to their avoidance of the subject. They have no one in the group to model appropriate ways for them to disclose their feelings or to suggest possible solutions.

If the group was composed of ten student nurses with a variety of concerns, at least a few of them would have likely developed some coping strategies for dealing with death, either on a personal or professional level. Those members would be the ones that I would rely on to lead and promote a discussion on the topic. A premise of solution-focused theory (SFT) is that individuals create successful solutions based on the strengths that they already possess. Therefore, in multi-issue groups, clients contribute a variety of strengths. Those student nurses who are appropriately handling their interactions with terminally ill patients and their families may likely be experiencing other difficulties. They will in turn look to others in the group to model behaviors and solutions. Perhaps one such student nurse may be having difficulty working in the maternity wing after learning she cannot have children. Just as she may be able to help another participant in the group, a heterogeneous group will offer her the opportunity to discuss her concerns because others in the group may have encountered infertility. It is interesting that these two different presenting concerns both deal with loss. If none of the group members discover this similarity, as the group leader, I will definitely point out the commonality.

If no one readily responds to Jean's disclosure about having to report a young boy's death and accompany the physician in informing the parents, I would acknowledge to Jean how painful the experience must be and show appreciation for her sharing it with the group. I would ask group members if they had any similar experiences and to share how they handled the situation. My question addresses their actions more than their feelings. SFT counselors do not discount feelings, but they believe that "it is much easier to *act* your way to a feeling than to feel your way to a new action" (Walter & Peller, 1992, p. 78).

If no one responds to my direct question (whether anyone else has experienced dealing with terminally ill patients and their families), I would be even more direct in my questioning. I would draw on what I know about each person's presenting concern from the prescreening and session 1 and attempt to make linkages. I may say, "Karen, Jean is struggling with loss in her situation; do you see any connection to your presenting concern of having difficulty working in the maternity ward?" SFT groups are intended to be brief. The average length of the groups I facilitate is six sessions. For this reason I cannot wait for members to respond; I need to use interventions that encourage movement and energy. Emphasizing group members' strengths as a means to solutions can encourage group involvement. To illustrate this concept, let's assume that Lynn, a group member, does respond to my question following Jean's disclosure. She says, "I used to get really upset about all the death around me. But I began to realize that the only control I really have is to treat my patients and their families with the utmost respect and dignity. Even if I can't save lives, I know that I do my absolute best in their final days. Every day I ask myself, 'What can I do today to positively touch the lives of my patients?' And you know, in a way it is rewarding." I would point out to the group members that by examining her beliefs Lynn found a solution—to emphasize what she has control over as opposed to that which she has no control. This may serve as a catalyst for others in examining their beliefs and finding solutions. I would also point out that she is using a form of a process goal when she asks herself, "What can I do today to positively touch the lives of my patients?" I would encourage her to restate it to herself as, "Each day I will positively touch the lives of my patients by treating them with respect and dignity."

I would choose my interventions, taking into consideration that it is probably fear that immobilizes the group members. One intervention that helps clients address their fears indirectly is a variation of De Shazer's (1985) miracle question: "Suppose that tonight while you are asleep there is a miracle, and you feel free to talk about your major concerns in the group. What will you be doing differently? What will you be talking about?" As the group members share their responses, they would essentially express those things they fear and wish to avoid. I would recognize and acknowledge their fears and help them move toward establishing process goals.

In SFT groups there are a variety of strategies to "break the denial." Most important, however, is the formation of the group so that it optimizes the group process. This involves appropriate prescreening and the selection of a heterogeneous group so that group participants can serve as models to each other on a number of issues.

Systems-Centered Therapy

Implemented by Yvonne Agazarian

> *Each of you in this group are working every day with the process of life and death. You go through anguish or resignation when your patients die—you experience relief when they go into remission—you feel hope when there is the promise of a new drug. Do you see that, today, as individuals you may have come down on one side or the other of this emotional roller coaster without recognizing that there are always two sides to everything? However, do you notice that the group as a whole has been able to contain both sides at once? Today, for example, Jean is the group voice of despair and anguish, and Diane, Tom, and Julie are voicing the group hope.*
>
> *It might help us to remember the goals of this group. We have formed this group because dealing with dying patients and their families is truly very difficult, and managing the impact of your work is what this group is for. Now that— in this, our fourth session—we have raised some of the issues that are important to us as nurses, I am going to introduce you to some methods that will make it a little easier for you to work with them. First, we must make sure that no one of us works alone. It is not good for any of us to think that we are the only one hopeful in a despairing group or the only one despairing in a hopeful group. The truth is, of course, that we always have both experiences, although when we go too far down one side or the other we think that this is all there is. Let's start by seeing who will join Jean in exploring how it is for us when we are sad and who will join Diane, Tom, and Julie in exploring how we can remember hope in the face of despair.*

Every group has a good and bad split—development depends on being able to hold both good and bad together in all phases of development. In this group the members have split, and the group as a whole is containing both the good and the bad in different subgroups. The larger subgroup (all members except one!) is acting out flight from emotion, and one small subgroup (Jean) contains the group emotion that is expressed in the despair around the 10-year-old boy's death, in the anguish of the nurse who must be present when his parents are informed, and in the hope in new treatments. The systems-central therapy (SCT) approach to life, however difficult, is to recognize (through experience) that if one denies the reality of tragedy, then one is doomed to experience either blind optimism (which leads to a superficial enchantment with life) or blind pessimism (which leads to denial of the joy in life and condemns us to a remorseless experience of pain and despair). When the boundary between "good" and "bad" is crossed, however tragic the reality, experience contains pleasure as well as pain, curiosity about what comes next, and the ability to hope.

The process that guides this particular intervention is the fact that the group members are working in a context where the process of dying can preempt the life that is also present in the process. The group's goal is to increase the ability of the members to integrate realities that they, as nurses, work with every day. Thus, their work is to confront a reality that contains living as well as dying. By moving toward this goal, members will learn some important things for themselves, which they will then be able to take into their role as nurses; their patients, too, will do better if they are helped, by their nurses, to contain both sides of living and dying in the process.

This functional intervention will only have meaning to the group as a whole when there is an understanding of the defense of splitting. So, the first step is to acknowledge the group communication as a group-as-a-whole communication and to inhibit the group impulse to make Jean an identified patient or a scapegoat. The reframing of the group process that has occurred in this session introduces to the members their use of the defense of splitting. Framing splitting as the "voice of the group" directs attention to the subgroup rather than to the individual member, who might take it personally. The intervention continues by reminding the group that the criteria of membership also relate to the goals of the group. The proposal to introduce a method for working presents the group with a structure that vectors the group toward processing their experience in functional subgroups.

The desired outcomes are (1) to have the feelings of both pain and hope legitimized in the group, (2) to have the exploration of all sides of nursing available, and (3) to have the process of modifying defensive communications managed by the leader while the content of the intervention is kept relevant to the group goals.

The most outstanding condition of the incident is the level of denial manifested in the group behavior. This level of denial is unusual in an SCT group, and when it does occur, it is relatively easy to bring to the group's attention. For example, it would have been easy, in an SCT group, to say, "Hey—what happened to Jean's communication?" Members could be expected to stop and explore their individual reactions to what had just occurred. (Certainly by session

4, SCT members would already know about the universal human impulse to scapegoat differences and to be aware that groups tend to deny the scape-goating impulse by creating the role of victim or identified patient.)

Transactional Analysis
Implemented by Herbert Hampshire

This situation points up the danger of the therapist colluding with patients in avoiding anxiety-laden issues. It would be unlikely that session 1 would go by without my commenting on an automatic avoidance tendency, and I would early on provide a context in which the feelings involved in avoidance would be talked about and related to directly. Typically, I would, within the first 15 or 30 minutes of a group initiated for a specific purpose, comment that I under-stood the purpose of the group was to deal with the difficult issues of treating the terminally ill, that I appreciated that it was tempting to avoid them, and that the members might begin by talking about how they experienced being in a group set up for this purpose.

The same therapeutic dilemma created in session 1 is again set up in session 4, with group members automatically responding to Jean's emotion by moving to "safer" topics. It is important, at the point that Jean moves the group to the difficult issues, for the therapist to side with that openness and not to side im-plicitly with the defense against it. Thus, Diane's comment must be responded to immediately. A simple statement, such as "It is uncomfortable to respond di-rectly to Jean's emotions," would be sufficient to direct Diane and the rest of the group back toward her feelings.

Since the series of avoidant comments have taken the focus away from Jean's reactions, the problem for the therapist is to bring the group back without being Parental or critical, which would only serve to increase defensiveness and to produce a protective veneer of anger at the therapist. It is more effective to stroke what is wanted than to respond negatively to the avoidance. I would be likely in that context to ostensibly ignore other comments and address Jean di-rectly. I might say something like, "Jean, I understand your anger and sadness. And you're right that it's natural for the group to want to avoid the difficult is-sues of death. But it's important to talk about it. Talk about your experience of being with the boy's parents when they were informed."

Although Jean would start out talking directly to the therapist and other members would avoid eye contact and direct involvement, it would very rap-idly be possible to focus on the others' reactions and, by inviting them to ver-balize them, to produce interaction among the group members themselves. Be-fore long, it would be essential for other members to talk specifically about their experiences with death—either within nursing or in other situations. Part of the purpose would be to lead them to a realization that many personal connections, both through feelings and circumstances, are automatically being suppressed. The additional aspect of purpose here is directed at dealing with not only the specific "forbidden" topic but also all the mechanisms of taboos in general.

Even groups that are not organized around a particular issue encounter this phenomenon at some point in their development. As one person attempts to deal with more intimate aspects of a sexual problem, or someone brings up sexual feelings toward the therapist, or a group member reveals a possible fatal illness such as cancer, all the prohibitions about openly discussing "taboo topics" become engaged.

In most instances, the primary task of therapy is merely to create an environment that supports open communication. It is not so much that conflicts are in the area as it is that reactions to the issue are not verbalized within the context of the programming. Just being able to "say it" is frequently sufficient to defuse it as a problem.

Another issue to be addressed in this group is how the members related to death as an aspect of nursing *before* they entered the profession. By dictating avoidance of areas, programming often keeps people relating to reality in a very ineffective and childish manner. What is often revealed in situations like this is that people both (1) know what problems are likely to occur and (2) have the personal resources to cope with them. The problems lie in the sanctions against focusing on exactly what difficulties are likely to emerge. Unless the nurses accept this point, they can unwittingly believe that they did not have the perceptiveness or sufficient grasp of reality to know that confronting death was likely to be an aspect of nursing.

Theoretical Practitioners' Congruence With Their Theory

CLIENT-CENTERED THERAPY

Recall that we discussed that client-centered therapy can be viewed through three variables: (1) external, (2) group member, and (3) group therapist; refer to them if you need. In the meantime, let us see if our TP is guided by these variables.

He tells us what thoughts are traveling through his mind. Normally, as a client-centered therapist, he does not interpret, but here he is letting us know how he perceives the individuals, what they need, and what motivates their behavior. Considering therapist variables, he conveys his trust in the group to move the process. He offers empathy to Jean. By allowing us to be privy to how he is thinking and feeling, we witness how he brings his *whole person* to the group, including giving himself permission to cry. He accepts the group where it is at and does not enter with any preconceived notions about where it should be going. When he helps members feel free to experience their feelings as being real and not artificial, he facilitates the process through modeling empathy and positive regard.

Our TP also attends to a number of group member variables such as the need for safety, psychological and emotional intimacy (expressing empathy, modeling self-disclosure), mutual trust (believing that members will eventually reach deep levels of emotional intimacy), and psychological openness (reinforcing Jean's emotional disclosure and offering his own).

Finally, he allows the group to choose its own direction. He offers facilitative actions to help members express their feelings and thoughts, and he helps group members remain in the present with regard to the way they were experiencing the moment. In essence, he uses the immediacy of the incident to facilitate group process. This use of immediacy is reflective of his employing external variables.

COGNITIVE–BEHAVIORAL THERAPY

In Critical Incident 2, our cognitive–behavioral therapy (CBT) TP introduces ethics; here he does it again, but he is much more vociferous about it. We can understand this reaction because CBT therapists are concerned about building group cohesion, contracting (group orientation), and self-efficacy. Also, we are apprised once again about the pretraining process and its significance. Finally, we see the importance of members experiencing the feeling of voluntary membership.

By informing us from the outset that the group may not have been composed of volunteer members and that the actual contract was made with the missing member, the head nurse, he thus views the situation as being one about ethics. We are introduced immediately to the importance of voluntary membership and the pretraining of members in order to have them to identify their goals—that is, *what* they wish to change. Pretraining may include *assessment* of what they will do on an ongoing basis. For instance, our TP asks the members if they wish to continue in the group. He asks them to write on their cards the possible ways they might address the issue. Assessing the members' readiness to address the issue, he claims, will probably reveal avoidance behavior, which he sees as being the "bread and butter" of CBT. Concerned with safety, he adds that the depth to which the issue is addressed will be determined by him and his cotherapist. He also strikes out in a direction to gain member-to-member interaction by turning to Jean and requesting her to share how she feels regarding the group's avoidance and urging the members to share how they feel about her disclosure.

FAMILY-CENTERED THERAPY

We are struck immediately by the degree to which our family-centered therapy TP demonstrates the integratedness of his approach to this incident. He infuses existential factors, group dynamics, family therapy constructs, and psychodynamic thinking in the formulation of his intervention, which includes a structured exercise.

Death is immediately perceived as posing an existential concern for all members, not just Jean. However, from a psychodynamic perspective, the group's pain is so great that it is using denial as a means for managing it. Our TP is therefore intent on helping the members get past their fear. To achieve this goal, he turns to family theory and technique. He employs the technique of reframing, which is intended to diffuse the toxicity of the boy's death. Reframing is followed by introducing a structured exercise designed to draw members' attention to their family of origin from which our TP intends to have the group as a whole address their experience with the imagined death of their own family member. He employs empathic listening to Jean and the group as a whole (e.g., "the silence is so loud") and emphasizes retaining a here-and-now focus. Finally, he is conscious of the stage in which the group is in currently, while preparing it to enter the work stage. These are certainly strong pieces of evidence of his being aware of group dynamic theory.

GESTALT THERAPY

This incident provides us with a window to witness how a Gestalt therapist employs a number of processes that are distinctive of this modality and for which it is most noted. We are immediately exposed to responsibility through the I-boundaries. Risk taking is encouraged and rewarded. One task is to help members become more emotionally available to themselves as well as to each other (supportive). Member behavior becomes a focus of the leader's attention. We also observe how a game of dialogue (the experiment) is employed and learn why. Our attention is also drawn to how Gestalt therapy trusts that, by witnessing another member work, others gain self-knowledge through vicariously experiencing the process.

Once again we are exposed to how spontaneous, self-aware, and creative our TP is. She demonstrates how integrated she is as she quickly notes the need to establish the I-boundaries and when she discloses the affect Jean has upon her. She is concerned about the lack of availability that Jean has for support from the others and perhaps even for herself. From this concern, it seems, evolved (spontaneously) the offer to have her experiment in a game of dialogue with the dead boy. By engaging in this fantasy, she helps Jean deal with her internal splits. While Jean engages in her dialoguing, our TP attends to how she is presenting herself behaviorally. Is she communicating self-defeat or flexibility? Accordingly, our TP learns whether Jean is self-supporting or not (i.e., How congruent is she?). Simultaneously, our TP also expects the other members to be vicariously joining with Jean as she works. The hope is that they, too, will take courage from the experience to risk as Jean has to face their unfinished business regarding death.

INDIVIDUAL PSYCHOLOGY

According to what you were presented with earlier, Adlerians believe in the strength and creative powers of individuals to determine their own destiny. Our TP tests these beliefs in this incident. We also learn that Adlerians need to be spontaneous, listen for themes, and interpret behavior, as well as be able to confront emphatically. This can mean that emphasis is on the outcome of a therapeutic intervention and stresses cognitive understanding. Thus, less emphasis is placed on the significance of emotions themselves.

Our TP quickly informs us that the issue of death is to be expected and that he recognizes it to be an emotionally toxic one. However, his means for dealing with the incident do not acknowledge feelings of either Jean or the other members. Instead, he introduces a paradoxical intervention, a rather emphatic way of confronting the group. He acknowledges that "this may seem harsh and heavy." However, he cites the Adlerian principle that individuals have strength and are resilient (creative), and he rationalizes that it is the way to hold members responsible for how they conduct their lives. This deliberate and obvious use of the paradox also elevates the central position the leader can take. Our TP even tells us how directive he is as an Adlerian therapist. Instruction takes a very didactic form and increases the pressure for individual action and decision making. We can conclude from this action how Adlerian therapy came to be known as individual psychology.

INTERPERSONAL PSYCHOTHERAPY

This incident drew an important first declaration from our TPs regarding the fundamental tenets of interpersonal psychotherapy: the selection of group members (i.e., the population they should be drawn from), the importance of honest feedback in influencing interpersonal learning, the group as a social microcosm (here as a work group), culture building (i.e., what will be tolerated, supported, etc.), and attending to process.

Our TPs waste no time determining that the group is formed from a population that places major restrictions on the conduct of interpersonal therapy. We are told that, since the members work with each other, honest feedback will be hard to give because it might make their work relationships difficult. However, our TPs do not hesitate to begin building the culture of the group by offering support for Jean and encouraging member interaction that would address their reactions to her disclosure. It is important to underscore how our TPs solicited responses from the others. They frame the issue of death as "pretty scary stuff," thereby softly and empathetically acknowledging that there may be reason to hide from the pain. By so doing, our TPs set in motion that talking about such "scary stuff" can be tolerated, at least by them (i.e., they would not abandon the members if they chose to talk about it), and that death had a place in the group—that it was okay. Curative factors that exist in the group—such as existential factors, safety, universality, and altruism, which were being activated by the intervention—are also implied.

PSYCHODYNAMIC THERAPY

What we might expect from our psychodynamic therapy TP is that he would invoke some of the classical constructs such as resistance and regression. We also anticipate how he will deal with "the ignorant client," who unconsciously employs defense mechanisms. We refer to the leadership dimensions (see Chapter 7, Figure 1) of the group therapist. His role is to address the gratification–frustration dimension and his focus is on the here and now, the group as a whole and the individual, and the process–content dimension. Finally, our TP addresses the interconnectedness of thoughts and feelings from a group-as-a-whole position.

Our TP quickly assesses the incident and determines that the members are not in avoidance but in fact are dealing with the pain as best they know how. This focus determines how he will work from that moment on. He simultaneously considers Jean's level of development and determines that the others are not as far along as she is. This group-as-a-whole to individual-member focus also helps frame the intervention he will make, which takes a here-and-now orientation. He considers the safety needs of the members as he offers an empathic understanding of that current emotional position. The intervention is also designed to connect all members together through their thoughts and feelings. He can achieve this objective because he does not change the subject regarding death. His intention is to help them face their pain—that is, bring it to their conscious awareness.

Rational–Emotive–Behavioral Therapy

As we consider how our rational–emotive–behavioral therapy (REBT) TP maintains congruence with his theory, let us focus on group process. Will he encourage interaction? Structuring the group in order to utilize REBT principles needs to be addressed. The three "musts" need to be addressed in some way. Will he once again assign homework?

We first learn of our TP's position as he permits us to listen in on his thoughts about how he views the way such incidents occur in the first place. It is as though he is preparing himself for how he is about to structure the group. In fact, his opening remarks as he makes his intervention do precisely that, because he tells us he "directly raised the issue." He then challenges the three "musts" as he deals with each idea the members brought forth. He is clearly central to the interaction he is encouraging. He not only uses REBT principles but also concludes that the group has not been grounded in them, and through Jean he teaches them. Again, he intentionally engages the group because it is through member interaction that help is most potent. He does not disappoint us when he assigns homework that is designed to desensitize group members by asking them to record all their thoughts related to death, visit a morgue, and so forth. We also learn that he would employ an exercise that would have the members fantasize the death of a friend or relative and to do so over 30 consecutive days. Once more, this exercise is used as a means to desensitize the thought of death so that they would not become severely upset.

Reality Therapy

Let us once again focus on group processes. Reality therapy, as you recall, has seven processes: therapist involvement; present-behavior focus; behavior evaluation; developing positive, responsible behavior; commitment; no excuses; and avoiding punishment.

Our TP, we soon discover, becomes involved by virtue of his own disclosure to us regarding the personal experience he had with his mother's medical treatment and subsequent death. He informs us that he expects this to play a part in his work with the nursing students. However, he raises a number of concerns beginning with whom the contract was made (i.e., the head nurse, not students). He acknowledges that members have a history with each other, which can affect cohesion and intimacy and raises the matter of confidentiality. He is sensitive about his relationship with them (i.e., he is the outsider) because they did not participate in selecting him. Finally, he questions the purpose for forming the group: Educational? Therapeutic? Others? All these concerns address matters of involvement, responsible behavior, and commitment. He is concerned to let the group develop naturally until members feel safe to discuss death. He considers homework that would help ease them into discussing it. In response to Jean's disclosure and the group members' ways of managing death, he develops positive, responsible behavior by redirecting their focus to her. However, notice how he makes this intervention. He makes an effort to avoid punishment by behaving empathetically and solicits from them behavior that would be helpful (i.e., responsible). Eventually, this form of supportive behavior can have its own reward and lead to the group members' forming to support one another.

SOLUTION-FOCUSED THERAPY

Solution–focused therapy (SFT) is also at times referred to as brief therapy. We learn from our TP that she has no plans in keeping this group together for more than six sessions. This influences the process of therapy and how our TP works as a therapist. However, a number of familiar SFT principles are evident as we witness her work. Among them are the here and now, trusting individuals to determine their own solutions, the evolution of support and solutions through member interaction, and the importance of prescreening to ensure diverse member issues.

After informing us that prescreening would have ensured a heterogeneous set of member issues in order to draw diverse solutions from the members, our TP offers empathy to Jean and immediately moves to activate group member interaction. Turning to members for solutions underscores using the group as a resource and supports the potency of members. Our TP also seeks solutions from specific members, knowing that she is working on a brief timeline. Using *how* individual members may have found their own way of managing death-and-dying issues can lead to encouraging others to find their own solutions. Of particular interest to us is the well-known miracle question that is very much a part of SFT therapists' repertoire. By invoking it, our TP focuses on (and reinforces) how the members can establish process goals.

SYSTEMS-CENTERED THERAPY

We can expect our systems-centered therapist (SCT) TP to move quickly to have the members form subgroups, to redirect the forces or energy given for denial toward more productive areas (vectoring), and to address boundarying (or containing) the issue.

Our SCT TP reframes the moment. Its affect lessens the heightened anxiety of the incident while helping members focus on their splits. The act of denial is not stated as such. Thus, we can see how our TP moves first to contain the issue of life and death within the group as a whole, before moving members to subgroups. Subgrouping blocks the group from scapegoating Jean. Our TP also moves the members to choose their subgroup—that is, on which side of their split they wish to work. She refers to this as vectoring them towards processing their experience in functional subgroups. She quickly has the members take responsibility, even though she initially took a central and active role or position in the group.

Transactional Analysis

Here again, we are told that in transactional analysis (TA) groups this incident would not likely have occurred. Yet we are in a position to anticipate certain TA concepts and processes to show themselves as our TP restructures the moment. We can expect some reference to member ego-states; perhaps the exclusion or contamination dimension might be addressed and analysis of member transactions might be given. What may be of further interest is how our TP uses his person—that is, how he demonstrates his authenticity, equality, and openness. We can also expect he will he attend to group structure and offer analysis.

Our TP does not collude with the group members in avoiding their anxiety-laden issues; that is, he acts more authentically and openly. Therefore, he sides openly with Jean by ignoring the statements others were making, empathizing with her, and encouraging her to talk about her experience. By encouraging and supporting her Adult ego-state, he intentionally attempts to draw the others into the moment. Interaction is an important part of the process and helps members learn how such toxic topics as death and dying can be successfully faced.

He helps us see that he is deprogramming members' earlier childhood/childish means for managing such taboo areas and teaching them to learn to rely more on their Adult side to manage these concerns.

Theory Evaluation Form

1. Which theoretical practitioner do you most resemble? Why?

2. Which theoretical practitioner do you least resemble? Why?

3. What does your response to Question 1 tell you about yourself and your leadership style as a potential or present group therapist?

4. What does your response to Question 2 tell you about yourself and your leadership style as a potential or present group therapist?

5. After rereading how the theoretical practitioner of your choice responded to the incident, how would you modify your response?

CHAPTER SIXTEEN

A Member Chooses to Leave

How is a therapist affected when a member of a group suddenly discloses that this is the last session for him or her? Our theoretical practitioners are faced with this dilemma in Critical Incident 4.

Critical Incident 4

This group is composed of four men and four women. Initially, members of this group had come to you individually because they felt unhappy with their lot in life. They felt fate had dealt them a poor hand. They presented themselves to you in ways that expressed a low sense of personal worth. Recognizing that they all seemed to have symptoms of low self-esteem, you invited them to join together in a group to deal with what appeared to be a common area of concern.

Briefly, the members are described as follows:

Deborah is 22 years old. She is single, holds an associate degree from the local community college, and is employed as a legal secretary.

Peggy is 23 years old. She has been married for 6 years and has three children ranging in ages from 2 to 6 years old. She listed her occupation as homemaker.

Jean, short and heavy in stature, is 34 years old and married. She had dropped out of school after tenth grade. She drives a school bus.

Andrea is 28 years old and recently divorced. She had interrupted her college education 8 years ago in order to help her then-husband pursue his doctorate degree. She presently feels at a loss as to where to pick up her life.

> **Jim** is 25 years old. He is single and was recently discharged from the army. He works as an automobile salesman until he can decide what he wants to do with his life.
>
> **Bob** is 35 years old and married. He was referred to you by his family physician, who was concerned with the disclosures Bob had made about feeling "trapped and not going anywhere."
>
> **Ron** is 32 years old. Recently divorced, he feels his marriage was a disaster. He feels worthless because most everything in his life seems to go the same way as his marriage.
>
> **John** is 30 years old and is in his second marriage. He was unable to bring his wife with him when he first visited you. He explained that he feels lost in his marriage and is afraid it is going to end as the first one had.

This is session 5. The first three meetings saw the group move through the initial stages of development, which included orientation, resistance, conflict (questions about trust), and a struggle for power and confrontation. Toward the end of session 4, there seemed to be signs of group cohesiveness and a readiness for self-disclosure. Peggy, for example, expressed her disillusionment with her present roles of mother and wife. She said she was unhappy with herself and felt powerless to do anything about it. The group seemed ready to listen to her and willing to offer its thoughts on how she might be able to work out her problem. Andrea disclosed some deep-seated feelings of resentment toward her ex-husband, especially over the way he ignored the sacrifice she made on his behalf. In a similar way, the group appeared receptive to Andrea and demonstrated a willingness to offer assistance to work through her difficulty. This activity had the effect of encouraging other group members, including Bob and Ron, to risk disclosure as well.

Much of what had begun in session 4 carried over into this session. Early in the meeting, Ron begins by stating how much he values the group's willingness to hear him out and that he has given much consideration to their suggestions. He no sooner completes his remarks, when John, taking advantage of the very brief silence, announces to the group that he is making this his last session. He says he plans not to return after tonight's meeting. You quickly note the effect his words has upon the group members and that they appear quite stunned.

Client-Centered Therapy

Implemented by William R. Coulson

If anything could both stir my fears about being left alone and reinforce the suspicion that I am not a good therapist, this incident would be it. Why would John want to leave so soon? It is only session 5 and he has hardly begun. If I were a better therapist, he would have been hooked before now.

Maybe I exhausted the need to be self-critical in responding to Critical Incident 1 because my final notes for comments on this situation neglect such personal thoughts. I am prepared instead to write about the purpose of group therapy, about the importance of involving members of the group with John, and the key role of community in group work and life.

The bind I feel right now is similar to the one I sometimes feel in a group (and I suspect members often feel it about themselves, too): "Shall I be personal or not? It's embarrassing to be personal. I must sound like a baby." Yet, I want to be personal. I want you to know that I have my reasons for what I do, reasons having to do with my personality, my upbringing, and my likes and dislikes. I do not want to impart to group members all the reasons for my actions in leading the group.

With regard to John's announced departure, the therapist has to face the possibility that John is right; he should resign from the group. It is doubtful this is the proper moment because the group, including John, seems hardly to have gotten started. But *some* time will be a good time for him to go, and we will have to anticipate that (1) because it is his life, John will know that time better than we and (2) even at the right moment for him to leave, we are likely to want to keep him. He will by that time have become a friend.

Even when there is a specified end to the group, some people will decide to leave before it is over. Sometimes they will come to you privately and announce their intention. This is a problem. If you support their departure, you deny what you may have been working for in the group: a community in which members care about what happens to one another. But John did not approach you in private. He brought it up in the group and, to his credit, did not wait until the last few minutes of the session. There is time to talk it over, time for the members to sort out how they feel about his announcement and discuss their feelings with him—which is precisely what I hope would now happen.

If people in John's group were not yet friends, they could use his announcement as the occasion to begin. I hope they would discuss with him his decision to leave, encourage him to talk, give him understanding and respect. It would be hard for them not to mix up their wishes and his, but the therapist could help by remaining relatively objective. If the therapist could not be objective because of his or her own interest in John remaining in the group, the therapist should disclose this.

In any case, I would not want to rush in or deal with John's announcement as an expression of his psychological problems. I would hope for the members of the group to speak to him, thus, I might remain silent at first.

John might yet leave the group. But in the end I cannot think of anything better than to trust his judgment.

Cognitive–Behavioral Therapy

Implemented by John V. Flowers

Behavioral group therapy involves the member expectations that are quickly generated in the pretraining and early group sessions. Obviously, a member leaving unexpectedly happens as often, perhaps more often, in a behavioral group as in any other form. The assumption in this incident is that member transition is traumatic. This assumption seems very germane to long-term, closed-entrance groups. Behavioral groups are short-term, most frequently between 6 and 12 sessions in length and often open. Except for very structured psychoeducational groups and very short groups of 4 sessions or less, members can often be added during the life of the behavioral group. This group norm difference generates a much more fluid expectation of member entrance and termination.

In behavioral groups the other group members are almost never stunned by a member's leaving. Part of this difference in what happens in group reflects a much deeper difference in the conception of therapy itself. Behavioral therapy is neither long-term nor a single-unit process. Although a client comes to therapy and leaves, the presumption is not that this event is singular and that this is necessarily the client's last visit for emotional, skill, or cognitive learning. The therapy process is more like a medical process (not a medical model) in which clients go for what they need, or for as long as they can, then leave, often to return for other needs or when they are more able to productively use the group's input. Clients leave the group for all kinds of reasons, good and bad. The client's leaving is not a seminal event and not necessarily a trauma.

Having said this, there is still the question of what to do in this session. The first task is a gentle probe: Is the member willing to share why he or she is leaving? Therapists must assess whether the client wishes to inspect the decision and disclose the elements or not. If the client does not wish to disclose and inspect the reasons for leaving or if the reason is nonsolvable (moving away, etc.), the leaving ritual in my behavioral groups involves asking the remaining members to address the following issues (less formally than the list indicates):

1. What did you appreciate about John?
2. What more would you like to have gotten from John?
3. What do you hope John got from group?
4. What do you wish for John in the future?

If any member tries to convince John to stay in group, leaders gently remind the member and John that comings and goings are common and that John is free to do what he thinks is best or necessary. Therapists always reinforce the idea of coming back to therapy when it is appropriate. Occasionally, this discussion with the leaving member prepares the way for further discussion with the group about leavings and loss, if that discussion is germane to the group's purpose. Such a discussion might be more germane in a bereavement group and less so in the assertion-training group. Therapists must weigh time use versus effect. In other words, the question is not "Is this a worthwhile theme to pursue?" The question is "Should we pursue this theme given the group agenda and time we have left?"

There is of course the troubling therapist's thought, "What did I do wrong?" Once again, this becomes a far more productive question when there are two therapists in the group. Two therapists can discuss this to determine if they can learn from the early termination. If there is something to learn, learning it will produce better therapists. If there is nothing to learn, it is easier to accept this in a two-party discussion than in a one-party self-reflection.

Family-Centered Therapy
Implemented by James P. Trotzer

Four constructs drawn from four systemic perspectives come to mind as I consider my response to this critical incident. The first two constructs frame the nature of the group and formulate the therapeutic dynamics that I believe are most relevant to it members. The third illuminates the dynamics of the incident as they relate both to the member who precipitated it and to the group. The fourth presents my response.

I derive the first construct from the family life-cycle developmental perspective. My view of this group is that it is composed of young adults who are grappling with the struggles endemic to the "Trying Twenties," even though several members are in their thirties. They are all young adults who are "launched and lost" in some respect. They have all experienced starts, stops, setbacks, detours, and disappointments in their efforts to find their way in life and establish themselves as successful persons individually and in relationships. Their experiences have left them with residual self-doubts, lack of purpose and direction, and a sense of powerlessness. Consequently, my first objective as group leader would be to "normalize" their experiences rather than "pathologize" them. This perspective instills a hopeful, energizing dynamic into the group and promotes an attitude that things will work out rather than a sense that "fate dealt them a poor hand."

Bowen's (1977) theory emphasizes the individuation–differentiation process as the foundation to human functionality. It provides me with the second construct relevant to this group. In this case, I see each group member presenting symptoms of poor self-esteem and low personal worth. As such, the therapeutic thrust of the group must provide resources to facilitate the development of autonomy (i.e., build ego-strength) by first revisiting the identity question ("Who am I?") and then assisting each group member in individuating and differentiating that identity in the group as a stepping stone in doing so outside the group. My job would be to facilitate that process.

These two constructs form the basis of my systemic assumptions as I work with this group. My objectives would be to normalize members' life experiences and empower them by encouraging them to risk self-exploration and build ego-strength, which lead to autonomy. The group provides a temporary arena that extends a "just like a family" umbrella for members to function under until they get a sense of confidence and direction established.

The third construct, which I consider relevant to this incident, is enactment, which is drawn from the structural approach to family therapy (Rosenberg, 1983). My view is that enactment accurately explains the behavior of John and the plausibility of his behavior occurring in this group. John's disclosure that this is his "last session" is an enactment that prompts a two-pronged response on my part—one directed toward John and one toward the group.

Enactment refers to the recapitulation in therapy of specific behaviors or patterns that persons, couples, or families engage in outside therapy. In this case John is enacting in the group the same pattern that he carried out in his first marriage and is currently enacting in his second marriage. His fear that his second marriage will end like the first is thus realistic. The generic descriptor of note is that he "feels lost." It is likely that John feels lost in this group just as he did in his first marriage and does in his second. I would ask myself, "Where was he in the previous session when other members were disclosing themselves?" Most likely he was "feeling lost." Thus, the "only" option that appears available to him is to leave. At least that way he has some direction and some impact. Naturally, when John announces his intention to leave the group, members respond in a predictable manner—they are stunned. This reaction affirms that John is no longer "lost" in the group. He now has a clear identity, a direction for himself, and an affirmation that he is someone because he has influenced the group.

I see this incident producing a systemic reality of critical importance. This group may be "just like a family," but it is not a family. There are no family ties that can be mobilized to hold on to John or influence him to stay or prevent him from going. As such, this is a crucial incident because, whether John goes or stays, the group norming process will be affected. A family is a group of individuals with a history, but a counseling group is a group of individuals that form a history. I know that this event will be an important one in the group's history making. Thus, I see the need for a two-pronged leadership approach, which brings me to my response and the fourth systemic construct.

The fact that John has stipulated this as his last session suggests an immediate connection to a brief therapy or solution-focused posture (De Shazer, 1985), given the reality of the precipitous ending. My summation of the challenge inherent in this event is, "Since John has dropped the bomb, how can the group help him go out with a bang?" In other words, how can this enactment become therapeutic for John and the group whether he makes good on his assertion to leave or not? The precipitated group crisis indicates that both John and the group are on the brink of a breakthrough or a breakdown—John in regard to his pattern of getting lost and leaving and the group in regard to moving into purposeful work or losing its sense of purpose and direction (like each of the group members).

The fourth construct emanating from the brief therapy perspective prompts me to become solution focused and apply an adaptation of the miracle question. Instead of confronting John or mobilizing group pressure to influence him, I would pose the following experiment as a means of dealing with his intention to leave: "John, given your inclination to make this your last group session, would you be willing to engage in an experiment with the help of the group?" It is called the 'miracle experiment.'"

Assuming John agrees, I would then present the following scenario. (In the event that he is hesitant or resistant, I would then raise accountability, mobilize peer pressure, or do both, regarding his response to the experiment rather than his intention to leave the group. The same dynamics will occur because once again we have an enactment.) "John, let's say you go home after group and go to bed at your usual time. During the night an unexplainable phenomenon occurs and you are zapped with some unknown rays from outer space (a kind of ozone intrusion). When you wake in the morning, the feelings you currently have about your self, your life, your marriage, and all your fears are gone. No matter how hard you try, you can't remember them. What would your life be like? What would you feel? What would you do? What would you think?"

I would use all my attending skills to encourage and elicit John's responses in a brainstorming motif and then broaden the involvement to the group members by inviting them to provide input and feedback. After a brainstorming period, I would then facilitate a shift from divergent thinking to convergent thinking for the purpose of concretizing and specifying "doable" aspects of the ideas expressed. As a means of closure, I would offer the "doable" behaviors or patterns to John as a parting gift from the group, with an invitation to him to make a commitment to implement them. Depending on his response—that is, whether he accepts, rejects, or is noncommittal and whether he opts to leave or expresses interest in continuation as a group member—I would bring the group session to a close on a positive note accentuating what John is taking with him and how the group has assisted him. In any event, the door is left open for John to continue. On the other hand, I would inform the group that time will be designated next session for processing the experiment and John's exodus. The "ripple effect" of this solution-focused, brief-therapy intervention will likely move the group into the work stage of the group process with a norm of helping members individuate. Thus, John's initiative will serve a beneficial purpose to him, the other members, and the group as a whole while preserving his free agency as an autonomous (individuated) group member.

Gestalt Therapy
Implemented by Mirriam F. Polster

So far, John has been able to make it through the group sessions by listening and apparently not revealing much about himself. But the group appears to be moving into fuller levels of trust, responsiveness, and intimacy, and his silence may become more and more noticeable. He wants out—abruptly and with no explanations given.

In the face of his terseness, we can only speculate about what lies behind his bare-bones statement. Of course, he has every right to leave the group. Nevertheless, I want to know why. I also want to be sure that he is saying what he actually wants to say. Possibly John does not know how to express his despair without delivering an ultimatum, desperate as it may be, and then he has to stonewall it out and gets stuck with it. Perhaps he is discouraged and feels his problems are worse than anyone else's, and that even *if* he could talk about them, there are no solutions. His wife does not seem available to work with him on their troubles—why should strangers be any more sympathetic or helpful?

I might ask him to expand on his announcement by saying to the group, "Since I can't such and such in this group, I feel like leaving." This statement is not only more *specific* but also brings him into relationship with the group. He is not alone and toughing it out all by himself, he is speaking *to them*. In a roundabout way, he may be telling them what hopes or expectations he had in joining the group in the first place and how he is not getting what he wanted. Maybe he feels that he has been wasting his time, sitting around with a bunch or losers who could not possibly help him. Maybe he feels that since he has not come up with any solutions or helpful suggestions for anyone else, he has no right to ask for their time and attention in his difficulties. The time has come to put up or shut up, and he does not feel up to it. He has one failure behind him, another in the making, and his experience in the group is going to be still another one. But if his announcement causes another member to ask him why he wants to leave, John could begin a different way of dealing with his despair instead of acting like a desperate animal, who, when caught in a trap, gnaws off his own leg to gain release.

John is only one of eight individuals who are affected by his announcement. The other seven, as we already know, have a "low sense of personal worth," and their reactions to his statement probably tap into some of their own fears and self-doubts. They may even suspect that their disclosures are partly responsible for John's decision to leave.

There is a remarkable element of omnipotence in the way their low opinion of themselves provides them with a perverse sense of power. They consider themselves to be poor souls of little value, *but* here they are speculating that their words and their presence are so powerfully unattractive that they could drive John away. This indeed is power even if it is backward. They are juggling a paradox between their grandiosity (I am so powerfully unattractive I can make John want to leave) and their sense of low worth (John doesn't want to be in a group with me). So, they shuttle between feeling that they have no effect or that they have too much effect. John is surely not the only person in their lives with whom they oscillate between these two possibilities. Obviously, the need for a specific statement from John about why he chooses to leave the group is important to them, too.

If John responds to my request to explain his desire to leave the group by saying, "Since I can't talk about my trouble in this group, I feel like leaving," I would want to know why John feels he cannot talk. Do other people begin quickly to talk about their own concerns, making it difficult for him to get a word in edgewise? Are his problems so much worse than theirs that they seem unapproachable? Is it unacceptable for him to ask for and to accept advice? Is he supposed to be able to handle his own difficulties by himself, "like a man"? Is it hard for him to talk about his fears in front of women?

Answers to these questions will provide links to parts of John that he has shoved in the background and kept unspoken. They are things he tells himself that keep him feeling inadequate and worthless and prevent him from talking about what troubles him. He does it here in the group; at home he may do much the same with his wife.

The act of regulating an individual's own experience with admonitions, slogans, and rules (or any of the other forms that "shoulds" can take) is called *introjection* (Perls, Hefferline, & Goodman, 1951; Polster & Polster, 1973). By introjecting, John has given up the rights to the primacy of his own experience and tries instead to make a life out of secondhand, hand-me-down opinions, dictums, and beliefs. The energy that could go into using his personal perspective as a basis for interaction with other people is devoted to a silent struggle to keep down his protest against these alien standards. He has learned to swallow down the aggression he needs both to move out forcefully into the world and to restructure what is offered by the external authorities there. He has absorbed uncritically what others have told him he *should* think, feel, or do.

In working with John's introjections, reawakening his criticism of and disagreement with these rules is important. He has suppressed his own bewilderment and confusion, and he has muted his ability to question to the point where he remains silent until he becomes scared or desperate and then feels compelled to bolt. These tactics may have served him well at some time when he was more dependent on remaining on peaceful terms with the important people in his life. Currently, they are not working well for him. This may also be true for others in the group.

I could bring John's internal struggle into the open by asking him to begin a dialogue between the part of him that habitually tells him what he "should" do and the part of him that wants to behave differently. Up until now, this has been a silent debate, debilitating and underground. Articulating it loosens the energy that John is presently using up in suppression.

If I choose to work with this as a group issue, instead of individually with John, I would ask if any of John's prohibitions sound familiar to others in the group. Is there a voice within them that scolds or dictates? The same kind of dialogue could be introduced between the warring factions within one of the people in the group, or one person could play the introjected dictator while someone else speaks for the rebellious underdog. This kind of dialogue could lead to a shared experience of members' feeling helplessness, sadness, rage, disgust, and, eventually, healthy protest. Their grandiose fear of the power of their unattractiveness would become apparent, and we could begin to invent ways of feeling powerful without feeling worthless.

John may be in for some surprises when he hears the reaction to his announced departure. Depending on his response, he might want to reconsider his decision. It may have been his clumsy way of saying that he wanted to begin working in the group.

I would have responded in two other important, and different, ways to this group situation. First, I disagree with the basis on which this group was formed. All these people have a low sense of self-worth. I look for more heterogeneity in forming a group. One of the most valuable elements in a group is diversity, the spread of opinion and reaction. Choosing a group because of commonality of self-opinion minimizes this. I know there are many ways to be depressed, but this is still an impoverished form of variety.

Second, I would have made a contract with the group when we began, agreeing that each individual may of course choose to leave the group, but they must inform the group 1 week (if it is a weekly group) before they actually do leave. This allows time and opportunity for the group to respond more directly and fully to their reactions about the member's departure.

Individual Psychology
Implemented by Guy J. Manaster

Individual psychology views each individual's development of personal and unique goal(s) as being within the individual's own framework of values of self and the world. Stress on the whole, indivisible person does not prohibit Adlerians from seeing similarities between people's goals, styles, and values, but it does demand that the practitioner emphasize the unique perspectives of each individual. In this situation, where the similarities seem dominant, the non-Adlerian therapist may tend to proceed as if all members have the same problem and therefore a single answer or response would hold for all.

Individuals in this group appear, in some way, to have come to the conclusion that life is too much to handle. Their views may be that they are not intellectually up to the challenge (Deborah, Peggy, or Jim may feel this way), are physically deficient (possibly Jean), or generally of little worth (Andrea and Ron). They may feel that life and people "use" others (Andrea may see life this way), that life "controls" individuals (Bob seems to feel controlled), or that life is too confusing (Ron and John seem overwhelmed and confused). Through analysis of each group member's goal, views, and lifestyles, members would have some notion of their own views and goals. Moreover, all members, in the process of the group to date, would have explored—alone, with the group leader in a private session and within the group—their lifestyles as lived: the patterned pursuit of their unique goals in daily life with all its problems. In the group we would have discussed the particulars for each person and the commonalities and similarities of perspectives and behaviors.

I would also have begun exploring and exposing members' expectations of life and of the group. During the initial three meetings, when questions about trust and conflict came up, I most probably would have begun this process. The question posed might have been, "How can we as a group trust anyone, especially a bunch of people as messed up as we are?"

The discussion that followed should have brought some affirmative statements about trusting: "I trust Ron" or "I sort of trust Jean pretty much." I would also be hoping for and encouraging statements of worth from group members. So if, for instance, Peggy had said, "We may be messed up, but we're not all doing that badly, and we're here to work on our problems," I would have responded with something like, "You're the ones saying how messed up you are. I think you all have points of view that lead you to expect the worst, and you often see to it that the worst happens. I think you are worthwhile and can make it. Peggy, it seems to me you're saying, 'We're not so bad, we're just not good enough.' I'd say, you're not so bad at all, you're just not perfect. No one is. What we need is what Adlerians call 'the courage to be imperfect,' the courage to take a risk and know that things don't always turn out right, but if we take a chance, participate by doing our best, things won't always turn wrong—but they will sometimes."

Again, I would be trying to show the group the Adlerian view of personality, social psychology, and mental health. If this view had begun to sink in when John makes his stunning announcement, then what would happen? The group would ask John why, and obviously his reason for leaving the group would determine to some extent the group's response to his leaving. The questions I would want answered are (1) How are John's reasons for leaving (or saying he is going to leave) the manifestations of his lifestyle? (2) How does the group react, analyze, and proceed with John's announcements?

From an Adlerian position, all behaviors illustrate lifestyle—but this position, like any rule without exceptions, has its limits and pitfalls for its proponents in the extreme. If John says he cannot return to the group because he is being transferred to another city by his employer and both he and his wife are pleased with the move, it would seem to be a good break for him, encouraging, and we should wish him well. This reason for leaving would not illustrate his lifestyle, although the manner of his announcement well might. If on the other hand, he says he cannot return for reasons such as his wife does not like him out at night or does not want him talking about their relationship to others or, more likely from the brief description we have of John, he does not feel things will work out in the group and he does not know how to act in the group (which may take some probing to find out), we have a good example of a person living his lifestyle in the group. The group, including me, must show John what he is doing and how this continues a behavior pattern rather than allowing the group experience to serve to break the pattern.

Within the give-and-take of the group's exchange, its interest in, affection for, and some dependence on John should emerge. Should this not occur early on, I would ask, "Does anyone here like John, want him in the group? How did you see him helping the group, helping you?" A general support for John would come, along with disappointment in and anger about his leaving. John could identify how he elicits negative as well as positive feelings. At the same time, the other group members could see how their reactions are, in essence, automatically programmed within their lifestyles by simultaneously responding to the intentions of John's behavior.

There is a good bit of time left in the session for the discussion needed to reach John and the other group members. For John, we need to end the session so that, if he persists in his decision to leave, he would know his decision is reasonable (if it is) or know why he is leaving, if it is part of his lifestyle pattern. In either event, John would know that from the "group's mind" he has not been rejected and remains accepted and acceptable. If he decides to change his mind and stay, he should also know why, and we should help him discriminate between feeling coerced into staying and making his own decision.

Each group member should have the opportunity to state and investigate his or her own feelings and the reason for those feelings about John's leaving. My task for each person would be to make the reasons as clear as possible within their own lifestyle framework.

However, the *overall* task for me is to convey a commonsense lesson that, it appears, everyone in the group needs to learn: Living in society, like being in a group, includes disappointments and failures that are to be met, learned from, and left behind. John's announcement and decision is not fate again striking us. His decision, whether we like it or not, is an individual decision that we ultimately must respect even if we quarrel with his rationale. Our responsibility is both to our self and to others. The joy is in the task, in the doing, for we cannot expect to perfectly answer, to perfectly struggle over the elements of the age-old dilemma posed by Rabbi Hillel:

> If I am not for myself, who will be?
> If I am only for myself, what am I?
> And if not now, when?

Interpersonal Psychotherapy
Implemented by Victor Yalom and Mary Jean Paris

As previously mentioned, the prescreening process of potential group members is an absolutely essential part of the formation of a successful therapy group. Besides acquiring routine intake information, we attempt to predict how a new member will behave in the group. We warn them of potential stumbling blocks, strong reactions, and feelings of discouragement they may encounter in the early meetings. It is difficult for members to predict the effectiveness of the group during the first few meetings, and we therefore ask members to suspend judgment and to make a commitment of at least 3 months, to evaluate whether the group is the proper vehicle to help them achieve their therapeutic goals. Although having some dropouts in the beginning of a therapy group is often unavoidable, we usually encourage members to stick it out, unless it becomes clear that we have erred in the selection process and the group member is likely to remain a deviant. Premature dropout is not therapeutic for the individual and has an adverse effect on group cohesion. In this case, we would certainly make a concerted effort to have John fully explore his decision to leave rather than passively accepting his "decision."

The vignette tells us little about the nature of John's interpersonal difficulties, except for the stated problems in his marriage. Information regarding John's interpersonal and group relationships (e.g., history of friendships, work relationships, degree of intimacy with members of both sexes), which we would have acquired during the prescreening process, would be useful to know in deciding how best to intervene here. However, we can certainly make a general statement that when a group member, with no forewarning, announces he is leaving the group, we would focus our attention on the important issue at hand: why he has decided to leave, what he hoped to get from the group that he was not getting, and whether he has any understanding of what has contributed to his disappointing experience. We would assume that somehow his behavior in the group so far is a representative indicator of his presenting interpersonal difficulties, and thus we would listen to his responses for any data that might support this hypothesis and reflect this back to him.

As an example, if John is passive or emotionally unavailable in his marriage and he has also been relatively inactive or unengaged in the group, we would highlight to him the consequences of this stance. One consequence is that he is almost guaranteeing that the group will not be a rewarding experience. We also would ask for feedback from the group—for example, how have they felt about John's level of participation or emotional availability? For instance, if John felt he did not fit in, we would ask other members how they feel about John and if they agreed with his perception of himself in relationship to the group. We would also probe from other members how his passive stance affects their desire or ability to engage with him, and let John know that their reactions to him may shed some light on how his wife experiences him and thus be extremely useful to him in understanding what is awry in his marriage.

Thus, we would use the situation with John to highlight and reinforce our working model. In essence, we are teaching the group how to work in the here and now, thus shaping explicit norms that will assist the group in functioning more productively. This focus is especially important at the early stages of group development, so members have at least some cognitive understanding of how the group works. This helps decrease the overall level of anxiety in what can be an ambiguous and overstimulating experience and helps teach them how to use the group in the most helpful way.

We would hope that John will stay long enough in the group to understand what causes him to withdraw, as well as to discover what interactions that would make it easier for him to open up and engage more. Then he could use the group as a place to practice learning how to be more emotionally engaged with others and ultimately use these new-found abilities to be more intimate in his marriage and in other relationships.

We should also note that if John had indeed remained relatively silent, we would have hopefully intervened earlier than session 4 to try to draw him into the group. One of the ways—aside from simply encouraging him to share any thought, feeling, or reactions—would be to explore what his resistance or fears are regarding participating in the group. This explanation may reveal, for example, that John believes that his concerns are silly or not as important as the issues of others, thus leading him to hold back. Obviously, such an impediment to fuller participation would in and of itself be an issue, possibly even a central theme for John, that could be fruitfully explored over the course of the group.

Psychodynamic Therapy
Implemented by J. Scott Rutan

This group is composed of people who felt "fate had dealt them a poor hand." I am struck by the passivity implied in this statement. It would appear that each member uses projection as a primary defense. There seems to be little curiosity about what the members themselves have contributed to their plight! This attitude not surprisingly results in low self-esteem. Though painful to recognize that we contribute to our woes, it at least gives a sense of agency and power. Thus, for me, a primary goal of the therapy would be to instill a sense of curiosity about what all members contribute to their present state of unhappiness. The goal of psychodynamic therapy is insight, or self-education. Dynamic therapy belongs to the philosophical tradition of "The truth shall set you free." Thus, for the group members to come to some self-understanding about how they contribute to the situations in which they find themselves offers a powerful opportunity to do things differently in the future.

John comes with a specific presenting problem—he fears his committed love relationships will not last. Should we be surprised that *he* is the one who first feels the need to flee *this* set of committed relationships?

John's stated decision to leave the group presents a major problem. The character style of the members is to feel passive and powerless. Thus, they would probably feel incapable of effecting his decision. Furthermore, his decision confirms their conviction that bad things *happen* to them and that they are powerless to counter them.

From a psychodynamic perspective, we assume that everyone who has entered a therapy group is *at least* ambivalent about remaining. If we come down on the side of the ambivalence that suggests John should remain, then he is only responsible for the side of the ambivalence that wants to flee. My job as group therapist is to help John understand how his wish to leave the group he has agreed to join fits into his characteristic style of coping.

I would not speak immediately, preferring to hear how the group deals with their feelings about John's announcement. When I did speak, I would say, "So, John, you come to us worrying that your marriage will not last. Yet it is *you* who decides to end this marriage. How are we to understand this?" "Again, the dynamic principle here is that overt behavior is just the tip of the iceberg. The goal of treatment is to help John and the others become curious about what lay beneath behaviors and feelings.

There are other equally viable ways of attending to this situation from a psychodynamic perspective. One would be to explore with John the feelings he is having that lead to the decision to leave. ("What are the feelings that drive this decision, John?") Another would be to be curious about the manner of his decision—that is, not involving the group in the decision but presenting as an "Executive Decision." ("John, I am struck by the unilateral nature of your decision. What do you feel would have happened had you raised, with the group, your dissatisfactions?")

Rational–Emotive–Behavioral Therapy
Implemented by Albert Ellis

I would assume that most of the members feel stunned by their sense of being rejected or deserted by John's withdrawal from the group, for two reasons: (1) These group members are all humans, and virtually all humans are exceptionally prone to feelings of inadequacy and self-downing; and (2) these particular individuals have been placed in this group because they all seem to have "what was symptomatic of low self-esteem."

They are probably putting themselves down for not having been more effective in the course of the group process, thereby not helping John enough to keep him as a group member. They are perhaps angry at John for not giving them more of a chance and perhaps also angry at the group leader for not getting things more organized sooner so that John would not quit the group. Because John is also human, and perhaps a typical member of this self-flagellating group of individuals, I would assume that his quitting has something to do with his own feelings of inadequacy and hopelessness. Just as he feels lost in his second marriage and concluded that it is going to end as the first one had, he also feels lost in this group process and has concluded that he is going nowhere in it and is wasting his time by staying.

I might first check out my assumptions by asking John his reasons for leaving the group. If he had "legitimate" reasons, I would mainly acknowledge these, tell him that the group will probably continue without him, and invite him to rejoin if and when he feels inclined to do so. Even more important, however, because I know that the group members appear "stunned," I would probably work first with them and their emotional problems. I would assume that "stunned" mainly means panicked and self-flagellating; I would spend time checking to see if there is evidence behind my assumption.

If it proves that the members are indeed panicked and self-downing, I would take it that this is *not* directly caused by John's proposed desertion of the group but by their overinvolved, personalized, and irrational reaction to that desertion. In accordance with rational–emotive–behavioral therapy (REBT) theory, I would assume that the activating experience (*A*) of the group members, John's desertion, contributes to but by no means "causes" *C*, their emotional consequences of shock, horror, and worthlessness. Rather, *B* (their irrational beliefs) about *A* are mainly "causative" of *C*.

I would more precisely tell myself, "The group members are probably assuming that they have done something wrong to merit John's desertion; that they *should* not, *must* not have done this wrong thing; that it is awful that they did; and that they are *pretty rotten* persons for having done it. These nutty evaluations or conclusions are driving them to a state of panic." I would find methods to get them to see this and to give up their absolutistic *musts* and consequent self-damnation in order for them to accept themselves with their wrong doings, assuming that these have actually occurred.

I would also assume that, if the group members are indeed angry toward John or the group leader, they are foolishly *making themselves* irate about these people's "inequities" and that they can be taught, through the use of REBT, not to anger themselves about this or about virtually anything else. I would be determined to show them what they are needlessly doing in this respect and how to make themselves unangry and, instead, only sorry and annoyed about John's or the leader's behavior.

I would ask myself where my interventions were likely to do the most good and what specifically these interventions should be. I would probably choose the group itself, rather than John, as the focal point of these interventions. I would do this for several reasons: (1) The purpose of REBT is to help as many people as possible in the most efficient manner, and helping seven group members seems more important to me than only or mainly helping John; (2) in focusing on the group members rather than on John, he might feel relatively unthreatened and therefore listen better to the REBT problem-solving process and be as much or even more helped than some of the other members; (3) John may well have made up his mind to quit already, and trying to help him at this stage might prove useless; and (4) if time permitted, the first focus on helping the other group members might be shifted back to John so that he might be focused on, too.

Although the group members might be both angry and self-downing about John's proposed desertion, I would probably choose to focus on the latter rather than the former emotional difficulty. For one thing, it seems more important because it is related to the basic problems of virtually all group members. For another, it is less dramatic (though perhaps deeper) and less likely to get the group members off on a melodramatic tangent, which would stir up their feelings, all right, but quite possibly sidetrack them from understanding what is going on in their heads and hearts and from doing anything definite about it.

Shuttling back between dealing with, first, the emotional disturbance of panic and, second, that of anger is not considered de rigueur in REBT. Because we have a kind of quadratic equation with two unknowns, anger and panic, understanding and resolving either of these disturbances are likely to be impeded by dealing simultaneously with both. I would therefore concentrate on only one of these emotions first and would probably choose self-downing behavior as a place to start.

This group has apparently been given no behavioral homework assignments as yet (because who knows what muddled theory of group therapy its present leader is following!), so I would think in terms of in vivo desensitization assignments, both within the group itself and with outside assignments between sessions. On this particular occasion, I would begin this desensitization process by trying to incorporate some of it in this very session in which I am about to intervene.

I would start by addressing the group members along the following lines: "You seem positively stunned by John's announcement that he is about to leave the group. Am I right about this? How, exactly, do you feel about the fact that this is going to be his last session?" I would then get more details of their feelings, including, probably, rage, depression, hopelessness, inadequacy, and panic. If so, I would first zero in on those involving self-recrimination and self-downing: "It looks like several of you are blaming yourselves for not having managed to build an effective group and therefore not helping John enough. Now, we could argue this point: No matter what kind of a group you build and how effective it generally is, John might not accept help or might not allow himself to benefit from it. But let's suppose the worst: You really haven't worked hard enough to weld yourself into an efficient and helpful group, and John is rightfully quitting because he has got little help from you. If so, why *must* you have been more efficient? Where is the evidence that it is *awful* that you haven't been? In what way can't you *stand* being so inept? How does your poor group behavior prove that you are basically rotten people?"

In other words, I would show these group members that they were needlessly upsetting themselves about John's desertion of the group and indicate how they irrationally—at point B (belief system)—*muster*bated, awfulized, and put themselves down as humans for their (assumedly) poor and nontherapeutic behavior. I would try to convince them that, no matter how legitimately they were assessing their *deeds* and *performances*, they were illegitimately rating *themselves* for these poor performances. And I would teach them, through individual and collective dialogue, to actively challenge and dispute each others' faulty thinking. I would attempt to get all of them—or at least as many as will dare to change their fundamental philosophies of life—to give up ego- and self-evaluation and to keep their identity or the power to choose more of what they want and less of what they do not want. Otherwise stated, I would attempt to help them enjoy rather than "prove" themselves.

In attempting this (almost Herculean!) task, I would specify emotive and behavioral exercises for the group members. For an emotive exercise, for example, I might deliberately have John vent his spleen on them and tell them how much he despised them for not being very helpful to him or to themselves. As the group members made themselves enraged or ashamed in the face of his tirade, I would try to help them change their feelings of rage to annoyance and from shame to disappointment and help them see that they could probably only do this by radically changing their cognitions. Thus, if one of them first felt enraged at *John* and later only frustrated by John's *behavior*, he or she would probably be internally saying, "It really is too bad that John doesn't appreciate the help we've been trying to give him and that he is copping out by quitting the group before he gives us more of a chance to reach him. But that's his prerogative; and there is no reason why he *has* to give us a full hearing." And if another member first felt ashamed at John's tirade and then only disappointed by it, he or she might later think, "Maybe John is right, and I did not do everything I could to understand and help him. That's poor behavior on my part, and I'd better do something about it. But I am entitled to my errors, fallible human that I am, and there is no necessity for me to be less fallible and to help John." Seeing and practicing these new cognitions, after they had temporarily changed their unhealthy feelings (rage and shame) to healthy ones (frustration and disappointment), would then help these group members to feel less enraged and less shameful when new difficulties arose in their lives.

In terms of behavioral assignments, if Andrea (let us say) was very angry at John for not speaking up sooner and letting the group know how he felt about its ineffectiveness, I (with the collaboration of the group) might suggest the assignment of her deliberately keeping in close touch with her ex-husband, at whom she might also be angry, and working on her feelings until she only disliked his behavior and refused to condemn him totally for his behavior. And if Ron was notably self-downing because he felt that he and the group had not helped John sufficiently, I and the group might suggest the homework assignment of disclosing to his friends some particularly foolish acts he had recently done and working on not putting himself down in case they laughed at and denigrated him for these activities.

After dealing with group members individually and collectively, and after trying to see that they really understood that John was not upsetting them and that they had the choice of reacting in healthy or unhealthy ways to his leaving the group, I would try to spend some time helping John with his problem of wanting to quit the group. Assuming, again, that he did not have very good reasons for doing so and that he was falsely concluding that he could not possibly be helped by the group, I would first try to show him that this was a dubious assumption. He certainly might not be helped because of his own and the group's inadequacies, but there was no evidence that getting help was impossible and that under no conditions would he be able to receive it or use it.

In the process of doing so, I would try to show John that—something like the reaction of the other members of the group—he was putting himself down and concluding that, because he had failed in the past, he would *always* and *only* fail; that he was essentially a *rotten person;* and that, as such, he really deserved to keep failing and had no possibility of succeeding at therapy or almost anything else in the future. I would actively dispute (point *D*) these irrational beliefs (at point *B*) and would try to show him how to dispute them himself, outside of the therapy. As in the case of the other group members, I would try to devise (with John's help) some emotive and behavioral exercises that would also motivate and encourage him to make a basic philosophic change in his attitudes toward himself.

Thus, I might use rational–emotive imagery, in the course of which John would imagine himself seriously failing at some important task and being rejected by others for failing. After he imagined this, and probably felt severely depressed, and after he was in solid touch with these feelings, I would get him to change them to feelings of keen sorrow and regret but not depression. When he had achieved this, he would practice, perhaps every day for 30 or more days, this process of rational–emotive imagery to reinforce these more healthy feelings whenever he thought about failing or actually did fail at some project that he considered important.

If time permitted (or in subsequent group sessions), I would work with group members (and with John, if he decided to stay in the group) on their feelings of anger at John, at the group leader, and at the others. REBT clearly distinguishes between people's healthy feeling of being highly annoyed and irritated at the displeasing acts of others and their unhealthy total condemnation of these others as humans. It helps clients make this kind of distinction and feel and express intense displeasure or annoyance without being globally intolerant of the *people* who exhibit annoying *qualities.*

Would I, in the course of leading this session, neglect some important elements of the group process? Yes, I probably would, for I am not interested—except from a research or general psychological point of view—in group process half so much as I am interested in helping group members. Humans normally live in groups and are healthily and unhealthily affected by group processes. My job, as a psychotherapist, is to help them live more happily; incidental to this goal is understanding what is going on in the group process. More important, I want to understand the group *members* and how to intervene to teach these members to overcome their emotional disturbances.

Reality Therapy
Implemented by Thomas E. Bratter

The conglomeration of people and their presenting problems of being passive, feeling unfulfilled and worthless, would constitute an ideal group for reality therapy. By virtue of their common problems, this group can offer participants an opportunity to identify with each other and form a support network to reinforce newly acquired behavior.

John is illustrating a central group concern. He is verbalizing a combination of resignation and impotence while feeling sorry for himself. Because no one apparently wants to respond to him, I would assume the initiative: "I feel sad to hear you are considering leaving the group because I both like you and think you can contribute something important. I do respect your right to choose whether or not you wish to continue. I believe you are confusing a crucial point. You may not be able to control the conditions that challenge you, but you certainly can control what you do. You mention you have been hurt in your first marriage and that your second one seems doomed. You may be right. Some relationships probably are best to end, though we do not know if this is the case with you. It is more than likely, although there are no guarantees, that we might be able to give you some suggestions that will help you revitalize your relationship with your wife. Your announcement surprises me, so I would appreciate it if you could give me the opportunity to think about your situation during the week, and then we can discuss your decision next week. I am interested to learn some of the reasons for you wanting to leave us. Hopefully, then, other members will relate to what you have said."

In all probability, John would discuss how he feels. "I feel depressed, drained, discouraged, and defeated about everything. What is the use to continue?" While other schools of psychotherapy would consider these revelations to be significant examples of insight and "being in touch" with one's feelings, I would be unimpressed. I would prefer for John to describe what he does so that I could try to help him understand the correlation between action (behavior) and feelings. If, for example, John currently is not engaging in any responsible, productive, and gratifying behavior, there is no reason for him to feel particularly happy.

My guess is that John neither feels loved or loves, which probably is creating his unhappiness. John's decision to terminate creates a crisis that will jeopardize the continuation of the group. If John can be persuaded to remain and begin to work on his areas of concern, the group can coalesce and become a nurturing unit, which will provide the incentive and support that John needs. Though I would respond to John's comment seriously, I do not believe he really is committed to leaving. Instead, he may be testing whether or not we sincerely care about him. He knows he has few options. I nevertheless would be prepared to verbalize my concern without feeling I have been manipulated.

Solution-Focused Therapy

Implemented by Rebecca LaFountain

As a group leader I attempt to understand members' beliefs in order to help them find solutions; likewise, as a group leader I need to understand my *own* beliefs that contribute to the way I respond to members' behaviors, such as John's announcement that he is leaving the group. If I believe that it is totally my responsibility to make the members happy, to ensure that everyone meets their goals, and so on, then I am going to feel like a failure when John announces his intentions to leave. Because, as a solution-focused therapy (SFT) group leader, I work cooperatively with members to cocreate solutions to their difficulties, I also *share* the responsibility when they make little progress in the group. To be specific, I believe that it is my job to help facilitate change in members, whereas it is their responsibility to "make it happen." As a group leader from this perspective, I want to examine what worked to help members make gains so that I can repeat those interventions more often. Likewise, I want to figure out what did not work, so in its place I can do something differently.

The first aspect I would consider is group format, specifically whether or not to make the group time limited or ongoing. I believe that members are ready to leave the group when (1) they report at least a small but significant change has occurred related to their initial difficulty, (2) the change appears to be long lasting, and (3) they indicate that they can manage things on their own. Because some members are ready to terminate from the group earlier than others, I take this into consideration when establishing the group. In this scenario the group definitely seems to be time limited, a group where everyone begins and ends on the same dates. The other alternative, an ongoing group, has an open-ended format where members come and go as they meet their goals. The heterogeneous nature of SFT groups makes them suitable as open-ended groups because, as new members join, participants who have been in the group can serve as models for the new members. The most recent participants will easily learn the language (e.g., solutions, process goals, obstacles) and become integrated in the group. The coming and going of group members allows participants to experience change and loss in the here and now. The solutions that participants use to handle the loss of group members can be generalized to other losses in their lives outside the group. Compared to groups from other theoretical orientations, the development of relationships plays a minimal role in SFT groups.

Although this particular group is homogeneous (a practice I would probably not follow) in that they all present with issues of low self-worth, it appears that their degree of unhappiness is at varying levels of the continuum. For this reason I would probably establish the group as an ongoing one because members will very likely reach their goals at different rates. When the expectation is that group membership will change as participants attain their goals, an announcement by group members that they are going to leave will not be as shocking to participants as it is in this scenario when John states that it is his last meeting. Hopefully, group members will not choose to leave until they meet the appropriate criteria for termination; however, in situations where termination is premature, such as in John's case, it gives the person leaving an "out."

As the group leader, when establishing the group I may want to set the expectation that group members will not leave until they meet their goal; or better yet, I will ask participants to decide what the group norm will be in regard to termination. Some groups may decide that termination is acceptable at anytime, whereas others may require group consensus prior to a member's leaving. Of course, I would have to inform the participants that ethically I cannot make people continue in a group when they choose not to but that their establishment of informal group norms is permissible. This type of arrangement certainly establishes the tone for much interchange and feedback and makes the group members accountable to each other.

Because it is apparent that John's termination is a premature one, I need to learn from it and understand if I would have made a different decision regarding his inclusion in the group, following the prescreening. The purpose of the prescreening is twofold: (1) to allow clients to make an informed decision regarding participation in the group and (2) to afford counselors the opportunity to select participants who are amenable to changing themselves (rather than others) and who articulate an attainable goal. In retrospect, as I reread John's presenting problem, I get a clearer understanding of his beliefs. I read from my notes that "He is in his second marriage. He was *unable* to bring his wife with him when he first visited me. He explained that he *feels lost in his marriage* and *is afraid it is going to end as the first one had*." I realize that, because he could not articulate a goal (he spoke only of his pain), perhaps I did not do a good job of prescreening him for the group. His belief was that he was helpless; that should have been a clue to me that he felt powerless to change at that point.

I feel a responsibility to help facilitate change in clients, so I want to assess those interventions that promote change and those that I need to do differently. I realize that, with the majority of the group members, I have helped to facilitate change by "asking the right questions." For example, by asking in the prescreening and session 1, "What is it you would like to change or do differently?" and from a series of subsequent questions, which involve some hypothetical ones, members come up with process goals. Ultimately, we cocreate solutions in a collaborative process that involves the group members and me. Unfortunately, John was not able to voice a process goal. Although I attempted to restate his use of absolutes "I feel lost in my marriage" with "at times you don't know where you are headed in your marriage," I realize that I failed to help him reframe his goal into a concrete and observable goal. This is the first of three major obstacles that counselors encounter according to O'Hanlon and Weiner-Davis (1989).

A second counselor obstacle occurs when counselors mistakenly encourage members to repeat unsuccessful solutions. I realize that when John shared with the group that he "is afraid his marriage is going to end as the first one had," I allowed the group to discuss with John what had not worked in his first marriage, instead of encouraging the group to help him discover what is working in his current marriage. In so doing, I am "guilty" of the third counselor obstacle, focusing on members' complaints instead of their strengths, exception times (those instances when the difficulty isn't occurring), and successful solutions.

When John announced his intentions to leave the group, I would have allowed the group members to react and respond in ways that they choose. It is possible that John's announcement came at a time when he is feeling particularly vulnerable and fearful of the imminent change. In the event that he perceived their feedback as accepting and encouraging, it is likely that he may have chosen to stay in the group. In that case, I would share appreciation for his willingness to bring up his concerns in the group, and I would make it a priority to help him establish a goal, to focus on what is working for him in his life, and to emphasize his strengths, exception times, and solutions.

If John stayed firm with his decision to leave the group I would share appreciation to John for his involvement up to this point. I would help him recognize any gains that he had made in the group by pointing out those that I had noticed (his willingness to share, his efforts to try out new behaviors, etc.), and I would encourage other group members to share what they noticed as well. I would try my best to help John and the group members realize that John's leaving the group is not a failure but an interval of time where he can try out some of the solutions discussed in the group. I would leave the door open to John to return to a future group I may run or to be part of an ongoing group. Because John has learned the language of change associated with SFT theory, it should not be difficult for him to jump back in. At the time he returns, however, I would emphasize the need for him to define a concrete process goal. I would help him discover those aspects of his life that are working well for him and what he is doing to make those things happen. In addition, I would help him focus on his strengths, the exception times, and the successful solutions he is using.

When a group member prematurely decides to leave a group, it is a reminder that people change at different rates and need different levels of support. It causes me to review possible counselor obstacles and whether I need to modify my interventions.

Systems-Centered Therapy

Implemented by Yvonne Agazarian

> *Well, group, we have noticed before that there are two sides to every question and that we come to recognize both sides when we explore first one side and then the other in subgroups.*
>
> *If I am substituting for another leader and the group does not know about subgrouping, then I would introduce the method of subgrouping (see Critical Incident 3) as a way of resolving group conflict first, as a frame for the intervention.*
>
> *In the group today, Ron has been continuing the subgroup that worked so hard in the last session. He is speaking for the members who feel they <u>are</u> getting what they want from the group when they bring in their issues. Then John comes in and begins the other subgroup, speaking for members who want to take issues out of the group rather than bringing them in.*
>
> *Both sides of every issue are always important, as we know. So, John, would you talk some more about what is going on for you that makes you want to take yourself out of the group so that other members can explore this with you?*

This intervention relies on the method of subgrouping as a conflict resolution technique to contain the group dynamics that unexpected deviance arouses in a group. These dynamics predictably manifest in the communication pattern to deviant, in which the group (or the therapist, or both) asks all the questions, the deviant gives all the answers, and the group (or the therapist, or both) will first try to convert John-the-identified-patient or, if that fails, will attack John-the-scapegoat.

Functional subgrouping provides an alternative: Members are encouraged to explore, with John, the impulse to "leave" issues out of the group, and John gains an opportunity to talk about his dissatisfactions without painting himself into a corner and having to honor his threat to leave, and to leave only if it turns out to be a commonsense next step for him.

Two interventions would be appropriate to this event. This first is subgrouping, and it depends on the group understanding the purpose of subgrouping (to contain the conflict in the group as a whole, rather than in individual members, so that both sides of the conflict can be recognized, explored, and integrated into the group). The second intervention would be to remind the group that the contract on entering the group is to allow time to evaluate, with the group, where the member is in relationship to his or her personal goals, to recognize unfinished business, and to do the work of separation from the group so that the member does not leave containing the group projections and the group is not left with the member's projections.

In this context, reminding John of his contract would be to encourage him to take the issue "just" personally (which everyone does, all too easily). Personalizing encourages the barrier experience, in which both the full personal implications of the issue and the outside context is excluded from consciousness. Personalizing fuels both the repetition compulsion and personal anguish and is the core difficulty both in therapy and in living. Reminding John and the group about the "contract" would be likely to provoke a barrier experience of either guilty compliance or stubborn defiance. On the other hand, subgrouping has the potential of introducing three other contexts (member, subgroup, and group-as-a-whole perspectives) to the personal context that John is acting out.

The best consequences would be for the group to subgroup around issues that are not being addressed in the group, within the norms of self-disclosure that the group is in the processing of establishing.

The wished-for outcome may be compromised, however, in that John may actually be an inappropriate disposition to this group. It is possible that his personal goal was to get couples' therapy rather than group therapy and that he does not yet see how group will help him with his fear that he is on the brink of another marital failure. Should this be the case, subgrouping will give him an opportunity to explore this as an issue, and it may turn out that in the process both the group and therapist will encourage him to make further proactive attempts to get couples' counseling with his wife and then to see if group would be an appropriate adjunct or alternative to counseling.

The outstanding condition of the incident is that John's threat to leave is deviant to the developing group norms. The group is surprised and startled, and members are neither resonant nor attuned to John's position. Predictably, the impulse will be to act out against the person who startled them, rather than contain their surprise, become curious, and explore it.

A theory of living human systems, from which systems-centered therapy is derived, proposes that all living human systems survive, develop, and transform through the process of discriminating and integrating differences (Agazarian, 1997a). Functional subgrouping operationalizes this proposition and is expected to contain the dynamics while the conflict is explored, instead of acting out the dynamics in predictable and stereotypic ways. John's announced intention to leave compromises group survival and development and threatens a regressive transformation.

Transactional Analysis
Implemented by Herbert Hampshire

Some aspects of this situation would not be likely to develop in a transactional analysis (TA) group. The most glaring one is the announcement that this is John's last session. Everyone, before joining one of my groups, is informed of the "operating procedures," which form the basis of the only "group contract" asked of members. One of its primary elements is the proviso that any member who terminates will discuss that intention early in one session and then in two subsequent meetings. One purpose of this procedure is to avoid exactly the situation presented in the incident. The agreement provides protection both for the individual who is terminating and for the other group members. Without it, it is likely that a rise in uncomfortable emotion or a confrontation that seriously undermines a member's defense structure will lead to impulsive acting-out, which is destructive because of its relative nonreversibility. Patients frequently consider termination and see, through the process that ensues, how they are programmed to run away from intense feelings. The structure provides them an opportunity to look at their impulse and see what is behind it, and the "decision" to leave thus becomes an authentic and productive demonstration of their reaction. Without that structure, members are often out of the group before realizing they did not want to leave, even though they were reluctant to express their hurt, anger, or fear.

The structure also protects the group from a form of emotional blackmail. Precipitously announcing one's termination from the group is tantamount within the group culture to threatening suicide. In this example, John has threatened the group with his disappearance, giving them one last opportunity to express any feelings they have toward him. No matter how pressing any other issue may personally be for another member, the situation creates a powerful pull toward dropping everything and relating to the imminent threat to the group.

The composition of this group provides an opportunity to note the value of individual contracts. Eric Berne (1964) advised against homogeneous groups because he saw them as supportive of each other's game-and-racket patterns on the unconscious premise that "if you don't call me on mine, I won't call you on yours." Contracts provide a potential antidote because they highlight the individuality that exists beneath ostensible similarity.

The common element in the experiences of these patients is that they are "unhappy with their lot in life," and it underscores shared resistance to assuming responsibility. From that statement alone, one would expect the individuals in the group to perceive the group, and to see things generally, as *happening* to them. Allowing them to begin without specific sets of purposes and goals supports the passivity of their patterns and enhances the probability of an outcome in which they are "unhappy with their lot in groups."

Because all group members share issues of responsibility, I would be cautious about doing something to "handle the situation." There is the danger in a "critical situation" that the therapist will implicitly agree with patients that they are powerless or incompetent and that intervention by the therapist is now needed. Highly charged encounters that have no simple or obvious resolution are in fact optimal for members both to discover how people actually function and to allow them to generate new response options. It is precisely these kinds of situations that cause problems in everyday living. A therapist who allows patients to sit around discussing problems in living in a relatively subdued fashion and then, when something upsetting happens within the group itself, rushes to the rescue is doing what Berne (1966) called "making progress rather than producing cure."

In this instance, I notice immediately that two elements of the session have been group directed. Ron has talked directly to the group members about perceptions of their responses and about reactions to their input. John's threat to leave is even more direct evidence that group members are beginning to connect emotionally to the group. This connection to one another is a precondition to beginning to play out programmatic issues in observable form, rather than merely talking around them.

The first order of business for me when "something happens" is to notice quickly what each person's ego-state is and what they reveal about their programming. Some will be afraid, some angry, some hurt, and some aloof. Some may feel secretly pleased, relieved, or victorious. The intensity of each person's response reveals the degree to which the incident relates to their programming. A particularly strong response often provides evidence about large segments of the script mechanism. For example, I might in this instance notice that Andrea responds to John's announcement with the immediate fear response of a 4-year-old child, followed rapidly by a reaction of controlled grief and resignation. I might speculate that an important figure, such as her father, had died if not committed suicide when she was 4 years old. That would relate directly to a script focused on Andrea working to please men only to have them desert her. When I see the response of this intensity, significance, and clarity, I frequently focus on it directly, ostensibly ignoring "the crisis at hand." This serves several purposes, one of which is to shift the context away from "crisis" to recognizing an event as simply an event. Also, it allows, by virtue of capturing the momentary reexperiencing of pivotal script situations, highly "efficient" therapy. In addition, this strategy consciously interrupts the flow of any game or script payoff that John is setting up. By the time we get back to John, his affect is likely to be more authentic and more genuinely related to the reaction he did or did not perceive himself getting.

Even when there is nothing as dramatic, there are always subtleties of reactions that reveal elements of programming. I particularly focus on identifying "intersections" and overlaps in individuals I-patterns. Andrea is an obvious person to focus on because she has experienced separation from a man before. Jean's reaction would be important because she has "dropped out" herself. Bob would "intersect" with John because his pattern is to remain "trapped and not go anywhere" rather than to take action such as John has. Ron's response is important to notice because he is the person who is being at least implicitly transacted with. At a Child-to-Child or Parent-to-Child level, John is communicating, "My problems are more important than what you are talking about now." Ron's work in the group has suddenly "turned into a disaster." I would want to know if he has a pattern of getting "overruled" by people whose feelings are more intense or whose problems are greater than his. Is the dissolution of his marriage related in any way to this? It is inevitable that he will have anger at having the rug pulled out from underneath him, and his response will clearly indicate the way he relates to competitiveness in relation to feelings. It is quite likely that Ron will reveal in this circumstance any problem he has derived from sibling rivalry.

It is significant that the pacing of sessions had moved toward self-disclosure and that women appeared to be "going first." Peggy and then Andrea had opened up, leading to Ron and Bob talking. Because there is a specific theme among the women of being victimized in relation to men, and among the men of not relating well to women, this pattern may be a powerful theme underlying the group process. Shared issues produce group process and must be individualized and related to directly to interrupt patterns. John may be feeling not only the increasing intimacy of the group but also some perceived pressure to "take his turn." His reaction may be related to coercion he feels from women, as well as competitiveness he experiences with me. This area of speculation is rendered more viable by the recognition that John was "unable to bring his wife with him. . . ."

Because some element of transference exists in all responses in a group, I would particularly focus on what reaction John is "pulling for" from me. I would want to notice, for example, whether he makes his announcement directly to me or whether he pointedly did not look at me when he spoke. He may be inviting me to control him and "not let him go," or he may be challenging me to prove that I care about him. It is essential to know how John perceives me relating both to him and to other group members. It is likely that he is, after session 4, seeing that others in the group are beginning to "get to work" while he continues to feel "lost" and under pressure, as he has been in both of his marriages. If he had a pattern of parenting in which he concluded that he could never ask for assistance or rely on someone, I might ask John to focus on how isolated and unsupported he is feeling. If he had a parent who always rescued him, I might point out that it is all right for him to be in an uncomfortable struggle and to stay and work it out.

It is important to point out that most of the analysis in TA terms is going on in my head and not in the group. "Why" someone is behaving in a particular way is important for me to understand as a therapist but not for the individual to spend his or her time discussing. What is central for members is *how* their functioning blocks their satisfactions and *how* they can function beyond their programming and out of their script. I frequently share with new members Berne's (1964) dictum: "Change today; tomorrow we can figure out why it was so difficult to change the day before."

Concretely, in this instance, I would invite any group member to tell John how he or she was reacting, or I might ask John to tell group members how he wanted them to respond. Because the underlying issue of passivity and responsibility exists in the group and because John has not opened up before, I would be more likely to go to John. I would do this, however, only if the "stunned" silence continued until it became unproductive and it was clear that none could get themselves out of their paralysis.

John would probably require some encouragement to verbalize how he wanted people to react to him and how his perception of himself in the group led him to view leaving as his only option. As I moved him to a point of communicating clearly, I would invite him to speak directly to one or more group members. If the dynamics within the group were especially powerful, I would suggest John talk to a specific person whose programming would "automatically" interact with his and therefore shift the context. Andrea would be a possibility because she has demonstrated a capacity to verbalize her resentment, as distinct from John's wife who simply pulls away. If John were more focused on his own dynamics at that point, I would simply allow him to select any person to talk to.

Whatever specific set of transactions were produced, the feelings related to and from John would be made apparent, and the group would individually and collectively move toward reacting to them in new ways.

Notice that it is not, in the final analysis, critical whether John actually leaves. What is important is that the issue be dealt with in a way ensuring that (1) everyone derives value from its having come up and (2) John is not left in a position of avoiding therapy because of his programming. If his decision to leave is made from the Adult ego-state, it ceases to be an appropriate focus for therapy.

Theoretical Practitioners Congruence With Theory

CLIENT-CENTERED THERAPY

Once again, we refer to the key group member variables and group therapist variables of client-centered therapy. We need to see if our TP adheres to them. Also, we want to see how our TP implements his role by the functions he performs, such as accepting the group, accepting the individual, using feelings or self-disclosure, and avoiding interpretive or process comments.

Our TP lets us know that he is feeling existential concerns (e.g., aloneness) and believes others may be feeling them as well. He also is sensitive to his feelings of adequacy and (im)potency as a therapist. As for therapist variables, he conveys very clearly that he has trust in the group to address John's leaving: "I would hope for the members of the group to speak to him; thus, I might remain silent at first." Thus, trust also is reflected here, for he decides to maintain a low profile as a therapist. By doing so, he expects the group will take responsibility for dealing with this critical moment, thereby relying more on themselves and less on him as a force for change. What else is in evidence is his belief in the individual—that John will do what is right for himself even though it means leaving the group before he hardly got a chance to become part of it?

Our TP is also on the verge of making a self-disclosure regarding how he is affected by John's announcement. He will do this provided he can remain objective and not try to dissuade John from taking responsibility for his decision. We are told that any form of interpretation of John's behavior is out of the question.

The other key variables, external and group member, are represented. For instance, focus is on the immediacy (external variable) of the moment. Attention is not diverted from the affect of John's announcement. Structure is very limited at the most: that is, allowance is made for the group and individual(s) to choose the direction to be taken at the moment of the disclosure. Finally, the member variable of psychological openness for individual differences is evidenced by the way our TP chooses to manage John and its affect on individual members of the group.

Cognitive–Behavioral Therapy

This incident addresses a number of CBT concepts. For example, key concepts of the use of *here* and *now* and *learning* show themselves. As for therapist roles and techniques, we want to find the building of group cohesion, encouragement of interaction, some element of the transfer of learning, the concept of reinforcement, encouragement of feedback, and group problem solving.

Our TP begins by informing us how he is not surprised that a member might leave; in fact, he even appears to have anticipated it. Immediately we see how he is attuned to group process. He helps the process along when he later moves the group to engage in addressing John's leaving. His structured exercise, we note, addresses cognitive objectives and focuses less on how members feel about John's announcement. There is also an effort made to address learning— in the sense that our TP wants to learn the events that preceded and followed John's behavior. This attempt to learn about the member may be considered as conducting a functional analysis of a member's behavior. We cannot ignore the significant role feedback plays and the deliberate use of the group as a whole in this regard. Lest we believe that CBT is a cold and emotionless modality, we are made privy to our TP's feelings regarding the "troubling therapist's thought 'what did I do wrong?'" There is a strong implication that our CBT TP has not lost touch of his humanness. Moreover, humanness is evidenced further by discussing this troubling thought with his cotherapist, regarding what can be learned from the experience of early termination. One final point: We are told how important time management is. Our TP realizes the reason for the group's formation, but he is willing to turn to the group to solve the problem of whether he should "pursue this theme given the group agenda and time we have left." What catches our attention and has appeal is a willingness to renegotiate the contract; the here and now seems to take precedence. Consequently, members are given an opportunity to determine how they wish to address this inter-actional problem. What better way to encourage active, present, voluntary, and collaborative participation of group members?

FAMILY-CENTERED THERAPY

Among the first things we stated when we introduced FCT is that integrates family theory; psychodynamic, individual, and developmental psychology; and group therapy. It is from these modalities, when taken together, that FCT techniques evolve. In this incident, we have witnessed how our TP draws heavily from his knowledge of family therapy and group therapy.

Our TP's first words leave us no room to speculate if he relies on family theory and group therapy. His early analysis of the members lets us know they are struggling with individuation issues and self-esteem. These are develop-mental concerns that he is prepared to "normalize." He refers to family thera-pists such as Bowen who addressed the process of individuation and differen-tiation and to Minuchen's structured therapy and the concept of family reenactment. Our TP decides to turn to De Shazer for the technique he will in-voke (the miracle question). Though drawing on family therapy, he simulta-neously is thinking group therapy. He is conscious of the group in many re-spects being like a family (Yalom) and yet not. He is aware that the group members collectively develop their own history and that the impact of John's disclosure upon the group in its early history can have a decided affect later. Realizing this, our TP is prepared to deal with it. There is an element of the here and now. Although much of the intervention focuses on John, our TP does consider the ripple affect of his intervention upon the group and antici-pates it will move the group to a work stage.

GESTALT THERAPY

The creative side of our Gestalt therapy TP rises again. However, we find that as she ponders this incident she asks a number of questions, including the "why" question. Remember, according to Gestalt therapy, there are few real questions. Our TP is very much in the here and now and tries to use it with John and the members. Remember the technique of dialoguing? Its use here is to address the concept of integration. We also watch how she asks John and other members to risk through experimenting. Focusing also is in evidence here. How and where she does it is what gets our attention.

Our TP asks the "why" questions to herself a number of times regarding the reasons behind John's pronouncement. They are real questions because there are no statements behind them. They also help her formulate hypotheses that generate the intervention(s) she will employ. Notice she is trying to understand

John. She is also conscious of the vicarious experience group members may be having because his announcement may be tapping into "their own fears and self-doubts." Responsibility also receives her attention. The existential issues of omnipotence in this regard are addressed. She sees it as a paradox that people with such low self-esteems can believe they may be responsible for John's exodus and that John may be dealing with his own splits related to power—that is, what he should, could, or ought be doing with regard to his troubles. Believing that John has arrived at this place in his relationships through such introjecting, our TP chooses to engage him in the experiment of dialoguing with his top dog and underdog, the outcome of which is to move him to being integrated. She also plans to invite other group members to engage in the same experiment, either in the same form or through role play. By universalizing (sharing) the experience, the desire is to have members learn how to become powerful as integrated persons.

INDIVIDUAL PSYCHOLOGY

Our point of view, as we witness our TP at work, needs to consider what concepts, techniques, and processes are being employed that most represent individual psychology. Consider the following being demonstrated: individual member's lifestyles, social interest, harmonious social living, self-determination, building of positive relationship between therapist and group members, developing group cohesiveness, focus on group assets, urging members to investigate the meanings of their behaviors, and focus on cognition. These are quite a few matters for us to have kept in mind, but our TP did manage to touch them all.

We first hear him address the matter of individuality. Its importance is stressed even though the members appear to have the same problem. John's lifestyle and those of the members are to be investigated by each of them. However, our TP first affirms the members by stating he believes in them. He also activates the group by using them to impress on John how his lifestyle pattern continues in the group and that he needs to break it. Of course, this cannot take place until social interest is developed. The focus is not only on John but also group members who are asked to explore their reactions to John in the context of their lifestyle program. He closes by hoping to elevate members to a place where they can use their common sense. Throughout our TP's work, we constantly are reminded of the emphasis placed on cognitive as opposed to emotional understanding.

INTERPERSONAL PSYCHOTHERAPY

When we witnessed our TPs address this incident, what we looked for was evidence of dealing in the here and now, attending to process, making effort to understand the metacommunication, seeing if attention is paid to curative factors that may be operating, using feedback, and focusing on interpersonal learning.

Once again, our TPs emphasize that prescreening plays a significant part in member selection. Furthermore, we are informed that every effort is made to try to avoid dropouts, especially because of the effect it has on the group cohesiveness. We understand that attending to the here and now can lead to uncovering how current behaviors are a reflection of a member's social microcosm. Thus, by attending to John's behavior in the here and now, our TPs and the group can make estimates about how it represents his presenting style elsewhere, including in his marriage. The TPs also use the power of consensual validation by engaging group members to give feedback to John, related to the affect his lack of emotional availability has had upon them. By encouraging group interaction and participation, members experience the value of interpersonal learning. Finally, we learn that our TPs would have responded sooner to John's form of nonverbal communication (i.e., metacommunication); that is, they would have heard him trying to communicate something. For them, his silence and virtual withdrawal from the group spoke too loudly to be ignored.

PSYCHODYNAMIC THERAPY

One of the first things we learned about psychodynamic therapy was that therapists do not expect members to be passive or dependent. This expectation poses an interesting challenge for our TP, especially if interaction is expected. It is through interaction that analysis can be made and insight achieved. We want to see how our TP addresses defense mechanisms and to see how he empowers the members. Another interest is to determine what therapist-role dimension he employs and his group focus.

Analysis was quickly made: The group members employ projection as a defense mechanism. They avoid taking responsibility for their "plight" by not being curious. Our TP informs us that his goal is to empower through insight. Members, as well as John, receive his focus. Attention to process is significant to psychodynamic therapy. Our TP gives that attention when he wants to help John understand the motives behind his leaving ("to get beneath the behaviors to the feelings"). He appeals to the group indirectly when he asks John what he feels would have happened had he raised his dissatisfactions with the group. Implied in this intervention is to have the members also wonder about how they might feel in response to John's expressed dissatisfactions. Notice that throughout our TP has drawn his interventions from first maintaining a low profile, the *group therapist dimension of no activity*. This position is intended to allow members to take the initiative, while he listens, experiences, and draws hypothesis—all of which will eventually feed into the formulation of interventions he will use.

RATIONAL–EMOTIVE–BEHAVIORAL THERAPY

If you recall, REBT has four objectives, which are a healthy outlook toward oneself, others, reality, and the future. In this incident it would be helpful to keep these objectives in mind as we consider our TP's way of managing it. We want look to see which cognitive methodology he employs and group processes that are activated.

Our REBT TP initially appeals to our intellectual side. He explains the nature of most human beings. What he is allowing us to know is the early hypotheses he has made regarding the nature of the members of this group. He informs us that they do not have a healthy outlook of themselves—that is, they are putting themselves down—nor of others (e.g., they are angry toward John). He also considers behavioral homework, both within and outside the group, that is designed to desensitize the group member. During the in-group work, he invokes the A-B-C-D-E construct with the members individually and together (group as a whole). Much of his efforts in the group address here-and-now (the present) experiences in an effort to develop a healthy perspective on reality. No clear specific evidence shows his focusing on a healthy outlook of the future, although we may say it is implied through the way he is working. Underscoring our TP's closing remarks regarding group process is important because they emphasize concern for the individuation process. In effect, he says that the means for the way he works are justified by the ends. He informs us that group process would not receive his focus of attention because his greater concern is to help group members live happier lives.

REALITY THERAPY

As you recall, reality therapy views those who struggle with personal psychological and irrational problems have not met the basic needs of being loved or giving love. Reality therapy holds the belief that such individuals have chosen inadequate ways to satisfy them. Our focus this time is to see how our reality therapy TP addresses these needs. For instance, the group processes of therapist involvement, focusing on present (member) behavior, evaluating (member) behaviors, developing responsible (member) behavior, commitment, and avoiding punishment are what can be used to meet those needs. Let us see.

Our TP ascertains that the reasons for members being in the group are ideal for reality therapy. Their presenting areas of concern certainly indicate that by reality therapy standards their basic needs have not been met. He tells us that in John's behavior we find the embodiment of the group concern (i.e., John neither loves or feels loved). Therefore, he focuses on John by means of his own disclosure (i.e., therapist involvement). He also speaks in positive tones. For example, he says he wants to revitalize John's relationship with his wife. He addresses John's current behavior—that is, what he currently does to address his present personal condition. He also conveys his intention to help John develop positive, responsible behaviors. In other words, the TP will first identify the behaviors that may be contributing to John's current emotional status and then help John identify those that are more positive. Our TP also offers care and concern for John; that is, he offers him love, which is further underscored by conveying his commitment to John. Our TP communicates the latter by asking John to give him a week to think about his situation in order to help him. Finally, all of our TP's efforts are free from punishment.

SOLUTION-FOCUSED THERAPY

Before a group is assembled, we learn that prescreening of members is a significant dimension of SFT. It is during this period that therapists attend to potential members' language and their beliefs. In addition, therapists are better able to determine who will most benefit from group therapy. During therapy, group process receives a strong emphasis, and attention is paid to the here and now of members' behaviors. Reframing the way members perceive their problems (themselves) is a process goal. We want to see if reframing members' language occurs so that members' beliefs are presented in a positive and realistic way. We also want to see to what extent our TP uses encouragement, the therapeutic factors, feedback, other members, and perhaps a way of doing something different.

Our TP's self-talk allows us to be privy to how she employs solution-focused thinking and language on herself as a means for addressing this incident. Not only does she want to know each member's belief, but she also feels the need to revisit her own, including determining how much responsibility she has for this incident's occurrence. We learn that the homogeneous composition of the group disturbs her, because it does not represent that principle of SFT. She does, however, even with this limitation, plan to use the key concept of scheduling, which includes (1) time-limited and open groups and (2) member termination. She chooses to solve for the latter concern by involving the members. Not only will they have a say when member termination can occur, but the employment of this principle will also encourage interaction, feedback, and reinforcement of members being accountable to each other. Responsibility receives our TP's attention from another perspective. She holds herself largely accountable for John's presence in the group. Claiming she failed to determine his readiness for membership during prescreening, she reviews his language and lack of articulating a process goal and cites that enough evidence was known then and there to have excluded him. She continues to tell us how else she failed: by allowing the group to focus on what failed in John's marriage rather than what is working. Having not sought those exceptions when problems were not occurring, successful solutions were not identified.

With our TP's ownership of the circumstances that lead to the critical incident, she then reframes the moment. Rather adroitly, she takes aim at the group as a whole first and tells us she would allow members to react as they choose; as the therapist, her voice would offer support and encouragement to John for his disclosure and move his attention to focus on what is working for him, emphasizing his strengths, exception times, and solutions. We also learn that if, after his response to our TP's intervention, John still chooses to leave, she would have him focus again on the gains he has made and encourage group-as-a-whole feedback (i.e., consensual validation, which is a curative factor). She would also reframe his leaving not as a failure but as an interval in time to try some of the solutions he has learned. Once again, through such reframing a positive and encouraging spin has been placed on John's and the group's problem. We can conclude that our TP not only looked at this incident from a different point of view but also did something different.

Systems-Centered Therapy

This incident probably will not pose as a reason for our SCT TP to deviate from her theory. Therefore, we are prepared to observe the forming of subgroups in order to contain the problem within the group, avoiding scapegoating, therapist structuring of the group, and allowing for members to take responsibility for which subgroup they will join. We may expect to see reference to phase of group development, including member behaviors and therapist intervention.

Our SCT TP immediately helps the group members feel less anxious when she reframes the moment as being a familiar experience (i.e., she normalizes the incident). She reminds them that they have learned to face problems by acknowledging problems have two sides; thus, just that quickly, she has John and the others forming into subgroups around his presenting area of concern. By now we also have come to learn this action avoids the group scapegoating John. Our TP's intervention also referenced that Ron was continuing the group's work from the previous session (and John's intention to leave). The implication is that the group is possibly in the first phase of group development but transitioning from phase one to phase two. With the exception of John, Ron is giving voice to the intimacy the members seem to be sharing; and John's decision to leave has the potential to do harm to both himself and the group.

Transactional Analysis

Recall that according to Berne, the fourth life view, "I'm Not Okay—You're Okay," meant that most people are striving for worthiness in comparison with others and will often engage in behaviors to gain strokes. This group was composed of persons who basically saw themselves as "Not Okay." Therefore, for us, this incident begs the question of how much attention our TP will pay to the games members play to gain strokes and how John's behavior will be interpreted because he too saw himself as "Not Okay." Some of the means used to seek strokes include withdrawing, pastiming, engaging in rituals, certain activities such as work, games, and real intimacy. We also want to see if our TP presents himself as authentic while skillfully diagnosing and analyzing member's, the group's, and John's behaviors. Also, John's early leaving raises for us the concern of whether this would happen in a TA group. The behavior of the group leader, if you remember, is a group process. It holds therapists responsible for screening and preparing members to be productive in the group. It is during the screening that structure is presented, commitment is discussed, and procedures are addressed. Contracted agreements are also made at this time. How carefully our TP listens for and observes the games being played and the payoffs received, as well as exposing them, receives the focus of our attention.

What we learn first from our TP is how and why this incident would not likely have occurred in a group he would lead. He informs us that a homogeneous group, vis-à-vis members having similar problems, sets them up for game playing, especially when the members' life view is "I'm Not Okay." He also speaks to the group contract that would have been in place in session 1 and that would disallow John to leave as abruptly as he planned. Notice our TP is concerned to protect both John and the members through such a contract. He identifies how the potential game of emotional blackmail would be avoided if the group were structured according to his TA model. We also take note of how he reframes John's announcement as akin to threatening suicide and the powerful affect this has on the group. Our TP almost sounds intolerant of the leader who formed the group and allowed the members to interact as they did. He refers to such leaders as "making progress rather than producing cure."

So, with his criticism of the group being stated, our TP allows us to see that he would first assess each member's ego-state in order to learn about his or her personal program. He might, he says, "ignore the crisis at hand" and immediately address a member's ego-state and script. He explains why he would opt to do this and includes disrupting "the flow of any game or script payoff that John is setting up," which may ultimately lead to his becoming more authentic. We take notice of the way he assesses member-to-member transactions and ego-states, such as John's "Child-to-Child or Parent-to-Child" interaction with Ron. Our TP quickly picks up on the theme of "victim" put forth by the women and the men and the effect it has on group process.

Our TP is also being authentic. He is aware of transference issues and tries to analyze the reaction John is trying to "pull" from him. Accordingly, he then considers the type of intervention he would employ. His choice to work with John, we learn at the end, is to help him not be left in a position of avoiding therapy because of his programming. Therefore, our TP would try to have John's decision to leave be made from an Adult ego-state. He would then see the group members reacting and dealing with the feelings they had toward John in new ways.

We can conclude that our TP would have striven to help the members and John to begin a life view of "I'm Okay—You're Okay."

Theory Evaluation Form

1. Which theoretical practitioner do you most resemble? Why?

2. Which theoretical practitioner do you least resemble? Why?

3. What does your response to Question 1 tell you about yourself and your leadership style as a potential or present group therapist?

4. What does your response to Question 2 tell you about yourself and your leadership style as a potential or present group therapist?

5. After rereading how the theoretical practitioner of your choice responded to the incident, how would you modify your response?

CHAPTER SEVENTEEN

A Deep Disclosure Near Session Termination

In this incident we find how our theoretical practitioners deal with the group when a relatively nonverbal group member suddenly discloses deep-seated emotional feelings near the end of the session.

Critical Incident 5

The group is heterogeneous in composition. During the preinterview sessions, the presenting areas of concern were somewhat similar. The group members appear to be having difficulty dealing with the significant others in their lives. Their relationships seem to be shallow and have very little meaning. The reason they sought you out was to find some way of bringing significance and value back into their personal lives. They all seem tired of bobbing like corks aimlessly on the sea of life.

The membership of the group is composed of five women and three men, ranging in ages from 28 to 45 years old. Briefly, they are described as follows:

Sally is 28 years old, single, and holds a bachelor's degree in biology. She is a laboratory technician and is engaged to be married.

Francine is 34 years old, divorced, and has custody of her two children. She is employed as a cocktail waitress.

Janet is 39 years old, married, and childless. She is employed as an elementary school teacher.

Sarah is 43 years old. Her husband is a pediatrician, and they have three children; two of them are in college. Sarah has returned to college to get her master's degree in psychology.

Sandra is 45 years old. Her four children have completed college and are on their own. She appears uncertain about the direction her life is going to take. Her husband has three more years before he retires on a very substantial income at age 65.

Samuel is 29 years old. He is married but is living separately from his wife. He is a successful sales representative for an international brokerage house.

Jonathan is 32 years old. He owns a very successful insurance agency in town. He has completed four years of college at the local university.

Franklin is 28 years old. He married his high school sweetheart 11 years ago. He has three profitable gas stations throughout the area and is president of the Chamber of Commerce.

During the first six sessions, which last for an hour each, much time was spent exploring each other's values, motives for joining the group, and the like. Before any of the members joined the group, you had told them that there were five or six other persons who seemed to be expressing similar concerns, and if they wanted, they could volunteer to join the group. The expressed goal, or purpose, was to share and perhaps work out what appeared to be barriers to enjoying more effective and meaningful personal lives. All members appeared quite agreeable to cooperate and join. Their general attitude was that they would like to do "anything" to get themselves out of the holes they felt they had dug for themselves and thus bring them closer to the people they felt they have a deep love for.

Through sessions 1–6, the group had been relatively open. The members tended toward establishing acquaintanceships (orientation) during the first three meetings. Francine seemed ready and willing to move into personal disclosures. This proved threatening to the majority of the members. You observed their uneasiness in their rapid movement away from Francine to topics that seemed away from and outside the group. Jonathan, for example, preferred to talk about the difficult time he has had building up his insurance business—the amount of hours spent on identifying new clients, advertising, and public relations. Franklin discussed the difficulty he has contending with the major oil corporation (his supplier) in order to sustain his business. Samuel expressed more personal feelings early in session 4 when he disclosed his discomfort and sense of personal failure for not making a "proper go" of his marriage. His confusion is further pronounced because none of the members have appeared to have heard him.

Sarah seems to have demonstrated an ability to keep her involvement at an intellectual level and maintain her wits about her. Her disclosures have been very carefully articulated throughout the first six sessions. She has stated on numerous occasions that she believes she and her husband have an "understanding." She has her life to live and whatever she chooses to do is all right with him, as long as it does not interfere with or disrupt the medical practice he has so diligently developed.

It is now the seventh session (week) and Sandra, who has remained rather silent over the past 6 weeks, has been fidgeting and looking extremely restless throughout the first 45 minutes. You are about to make movements to bring the group from an effectively oriented process to prepare them for the session's termination. Sandra has been a very quiet and inactive member of the group. You have attended to this form of nonverbal involvement on her part and felt it would be just a matter of time before she would choose the appropriate moment for herself to actively (vocally) participate. Of course, tonight's session was not very different from previous sessions in which the group had moved rapidly from socializing to confronting. Members appeared to be establishing some overall cohesiveness when suddenly, without any warning, Sandra burst forth. Her exclamation is mixed with blame, bitterness, anger, and hostility for her lot in life. On the face of it, it appears she is directing all of her feelings toward the group. She claims no one seems to care about her anymore. They all just seem to be "takers" who never give anything back. She is tired of giving herself for nothing and not being appreciated. After all, she has her own life to live, too. She speaks directly to Jonathan when she says that all he seems to care about is his business and it appears that no one else in his life seems to matter. As she continues to ventilate, her disclosure subsides into deep sobs, and tears roll down her cheeks. She is visibly shaken by all that she had just experienced and said, and she is trembling. As your eyes scan the members, you (the leader) recognize how immobilized the group has become. They have sunk into complete silence. All of them turn their eyes from Sandra and are looking at the floor, fidgeting with their fingers, at a loss for what to do or say.

Client-Centered Therapy

Implemented by William R. Coulson

My first reaction upon reading this incident was to imagine, like the rest of the group, that I would be paralyzed by Sandra's outburst. I might feel, "Good Lord, the group is falling apart." In other words, my first thought might be for myself.

I would not be proud of such a feeling. I doubt I would say it, at least at the time. (Later, when we were recapitulating the incident in the group, after the crisis had passed, and members might be reflecting on the moment of panic Sandra had given them, I might confess to my own.) It is possible that if I were really in the group, I would not have felt panic at that point. I might have had a more sophisticated or experienced reaction. But my first thought was that if Sandra scared other members of the group, she might have scared me, too.

I am often looking for a response in myself with which group members can identify. If I do this too often, it becomes a manipulation: I am drawing them out by guessing their feeling and claiming it for my own. I think when I have a reaction like "Good Lord, the group is falling apart," it is because (1) I really am not better than other people—if some group event is traumatic enough to scare them, it could well scare me, too—and (2) deep down, I am afraid that the group will fall apart—other people will have better groups than I, their groups will go on and on, and clients unfortunate enough to have secured me for a therapist will wish they had someone else.

I feel justified in letting you in on my thought processes because it can illustrate the common fear that beginning group therapists have: Groups will run out of things to say. This fear is relatively unfounded. When I start thinking about what I feel, I find a bottomless well. If the immediate purpose of group therapy is for people to talk about themselves and because I assume they also have this bottomless well of reactions to group events, then I do not think we need worry about having enough to talk about.

Carl Rogers and his colleagues studied the effect of client-centered therapy on a hospitalized schizophrenic population. There they made the discovery that when clients' reactions are not available (some of the research subjects in that study simply would not talk), the therapist can talk about his or her reactions. If feelings are the subject matter of psychotherapy, maybe the therapist's feelings are eligible for examination, too.

A basic learning of the "Schizophrenic Project" was that the therapist's internal reactions provide a wealth of data, which can potentially enrich the relationship with the client. Client-centered therapists began to believe that it was as legitimate to listen to their feelings as to listen to the client's.

I think we overlearned the lesson. I know I did. When I read through the list of incidents in this book, my first thought was always for myself, such as "That scares me" or "Now what do I do?" I can defend myself by saying the cues to which I would respond in actual practice would be far richer than I can see on paper. My behavior would probably be an integration of my present feelings, memories of group members' disclosures in previous sessions, and learnings from my teachers regarding how clients look, carry themselves, sit, and so on.

There are technical reasons for listening and fostering the expression of feelings. Expressing feelings helps people become vulnerable to one another and ultimately helps the group cohere and removes barriers to growth in individuals. Sandra, in our situation, is in pain; if I am thinking of myself at such a moment or laying back and scanning the group for their reactions, then I might have become more selfish (or more the technician) than I want.

Feelings are the very stuff of therapy. When deep feeling is emerging, client-centered therapists will concentrate on facilitating the flow. If the group needs maintenance or if the therapists want to assess their own personal reaction, they can take care of those tasks later.

For me, group therapy at its best is a laboratory in which our common moral commitments are tested and strengthened. The power lies in stimulating the sense of community, in which there are multiple and crossing lines of influence, in which members share perspectives directly with one another, and in which leadership passes from member to member (even in crises), rather than resting always with the therapist. If I find myself using the group in order to do individual therapy, I hope somebody will inform me. In general, I do not think it is the best use of group time.

What consequence would I anticipate following my response? I hope my encouragement would move Sandra toward a deeper understanding of her feelings, eventually ridding her of those that present barriers to personal development and, perhaps more immediately, teaching how her own reactions to people in a group will illuminate her life situation. I would not point out such connections to her. I would assume that drawing connections would be more effective if she did it herself. However, I do believe that by listening closely and reflecting my understanding of her message, I would be able to help clear away the clutter of her feelings—for example, the evident confusion over Jonathan and her husband. Finally, I would be glad for her outburst. Had she kept her feelings to herself, it would have prolonged the confusion. I have found when feelings are openly expressed, they more nearly become self-correcting.

I would hope that the other group members learned from the incident and that in future sessions, when a group member is in trouble, they might respond rather than stare at the floor. If they can learn a bit of self-mastery and courage in the face of group trauma, they will respond similarly outside of group therapy.

I would want to be sensitive to not intervene too quickly. Though I turned toward Sandra this time (rather than joining the group in turning to the floor), I would hope the positive effect of this move would be taken to heart—and that the next time, I would find one of the other members attending to the distressed person before I did. (I don't mean pushing a tissue at her, clucking over her, and shutting down her feelings, but I mean *being with her* in her distress, being a companion as she moved through it. If I were in trouble myself, I believe I would appreciate such help. It could come from anywhere. It would not have to be a therapist who gave it.)

Now and then, I view all functions in group therapy as those of bridge building. In early sessions I listen for connections between what individuals say now and what they said before and between what this one says and what that one said. I sometimes focus on and point to such connections: "That sounds a little like what Janet said earlier, too." I am hoping to build bridges between people.

Once these bridges become firm enough to walk on (I am not the only one building them, of course; the participants are doing it, too), I like to get out of the way. I do not want to be standing in the middle, at the highest point of the arch, blocking traffic while members are trying to get through to one another. I used to be so pleased when members made disclosures to the group, and particularly when I helped them get started, I would "hog" the conversation. I would forget that my goal was to facilitate group development rather than focus on myself. So the second step in my bridge-building program is to get out of the way—to participate, yes, but not take over.

The third step comes when no more special leadership behavior is necessary, when members are crossing bridges to one another readily and when they are passing leadership. Then I might cross a bridge myself, for I believe it is a more adequate reflection of reality when everyone is interested in giving and receiving help rather than in isolating the therapist as a function of his or her training and title. I find what I share with group members—our common human inheritance—far more powerful in determining our happiness than my special training. Group therapy is a premiere opportunity for the tacit acknowledgment of that inheritance.

Cognitive–Behavioral Therapy

Implemented by John V. Flowers

Although negative disclosures about the group certainly occur in behavioral group therapy, the silence of Sandra would not be as likely in behavioral groups as in some other group therapy forms. My response to Critical Incident 1 demonstrates how this democracy of disclosure is accomplished behaviorally. Assigned problem cards focus on disclosures as a criteria and a choice in the therapy group. Sandra would have already been asked to read her card and then been encouraged to talk about either problem long before session 7.

Many group therapists disapprove of prompted and reinforced disclosure, and many members of a group (and group therapists as well) defend nonparticipation on the basis of learning by observation. However, our research has demonstrated consistently that modeling occurs only when there is also participation with the modeler. The member who says he or she is being helped by watching is self-delusional, and the therapist who believes passive observation leads to learning is sadly misguided about basic learning theory and the process of change.

Explosions such as Sandra's are more likely in less structured groups and less frequent in more structured groups. In more structured groups, especially those that encourage balanced disclosure, the pent-up nature of this disclosure would have been considerably lessened simply because Sandra would have disclosed previously. Had Sandra talked more in any previous session, the sheer contrast effect paralyzing the group would be decreased.

This does not mean that structure is always better. Structure gives power and focus but does not easily yield breadth. Structure does seem more efficient and more effective with homogeneous group membership, producing more outcome in a limited time frame. Structure also seems best for those severely disturbed clients whose problem reflects a large element of chaos in their psyche.

Despite the fact that the incident as posed would not have occurred in a behavioral group, disapproval of the group could and does occur in behavioral groups. From the behavioral perspective, Sandra's comments, which seem appropriate given the context, acknowledge the therapists' failure. Behavioral group therapists know that one sign of being heard and taken seriously is the listeners' eye contact with the speaker. The incident of the group not listening to Samuel should have been an immediate focus of attention. Prior to Sandra's disclosure, one therapist should have called the group's attention to the fact that Samuel didn't seem to be heard or responded to in a concerned manner.

Given that the group actually reached the point of the incident, one therapist would move to support Sandra, and the other would agree that the group needed to reorient, listen and attend more fully, and give and take. Sandra would be thanked for her courage.

So that the reader is clear, this intervention would never be done with a group member who regularly confronts the group. If a behavior is rare, difficult, and potentially profitable, it should be reinforced. If a behavior is common, easy, and disrupts the group for no good reason, it should be ignored, confronted, and, in the worst case, excluded. Although exclusion is uncommon, a member can be so disruptive that finding another therapy outlet for that group member is sometimes the only way to avoid doing harm.

The crucial issue in this incident for behavioral group therapy is the silence that led to the intensity of the explosion and its effect on the other group members. If it got to the point where group members were not looking at Sandra, this would be an immediate focus of the leader(s), and discussion about this avoidance behavior would ensue. This strategy is usually enough to break the avoidance cycle. If not, one by one the members would be instructed to look at Sandra and monitor themselves, then encouraged to talk about their response in terms of what Sandra had said.

Incidents of this type are yet another reason to have two therapists and some flexibility about the ending time; for example, the group ends 30 minutes before the therapist(s) have their next scheduled appointment. Group therapy, even more than individual sessions, poses immediate problems that do not always fit the therapist's preset schedule. As the group casualty literature consistently points out, unresolved unexpected attacks are dangerous to all group members.

Family-Centered Therapy
Implemented by James P. Trotzer

Given the narrative of this critical incident and the defined parameters of this group, my first impression is that this event would not occur as it did in a group that I would be leading. Therefore, my response will explain from a process-oriented, systemic perspective why it is highly unlikely that the incident would occur as described.

First, the group is poorly conceived and designed regarding parameters, purpose, and procedures. For example, the group meets for only 1 hour per week. That is highly unusual for an adult, outpatient therapy or counseling group. My adult groups meet for a minimum of 90 minutes. Members can easily maintain their invisibility in group sessions of short duration, whereas a longer group session would likely have exposed Sandra's silence and nonparticipation sooner. Second, the purpose for formulating the group is vague and nonspecific, and the interactive group process through seven sessions has not clarified or concretized its goals or focus. The heterogeneity of the group may somewhat account for this, but I believe the framing of the group is defective. The language describing the group's purpose is general and obscure, and the narrative descriptive of the group members substantiates that inherent vagueness. I quote, "The expressed goal, or purpose [of the group], was to share and perhaps work out what appeared to be barriers to enjoying more effective and meaningful personal lives." Notice how tentative, nonspecific, and obscure the verbiage of this goals statement is. Again, I quote, "They [the members] all seem tired of bobbing like corks aimlessly on the sea of life." The subsequent interaction of the group as described appears to be simply a community of corks now bobbing in unison. Because the direction of the group is unclear, I question the role and procedures of the group leader (me). I have to ask myself, "What am I doing?" and "What have I been doing for the last six sessions?"

As a case in point, the narrative indicates that the leader (me) was aware of Sandra's silence for 6 weeks and that I felt it would be just a matter of time before she would choose the appropriate moment for herself to actively (vocally) participate. This narrative does not reflect my response. I would have been more active. For example, I utilize go-rounds, direct invitations, structured activities, and responses to nonverbal cues to involve nonparticipating members, so it is highly unlikely that Sandra would go 7 weeks without being brought into the interaction or her silence being addressed. (I would also note that it is unlikely that the group would let the silence go unnoticed and unlikely that the member could stand being silent for 7 weeks unless some other dynamic or factor is involved, as I will indicate later on in my response.)

Another problematic feature of this incident reflects on the screening procedure used to form the group and place Sandra in it (despite her voluntary status). From a systemic point of view, the demographic data of each group member, though validating the membership's heterogeneity, also provide data that contraindicate the suitability of Sandra as a member in this group. In other words, I do not believe I would have included Sandra in this group, for the following reasons. The systemic data are more comprehensive for Sandra than for the other members and as such indicate some real questions about her suitability for this group or any other group at this time. She is 45 years old, married to a man 17 years her senior, and has four children—all of whom have completed college. For all that to occur chronologically, she had to be in her mid- to late teens when she married a man who was nearly old enough to be her father and started having babies in very rapid order. The possibility of missed developmental stages in her maturation process and the potential that unstated intrusive experiences or circumstances may have occurred (beyond marrying young and immediately being overwhelmed by motherhood) come to my mind. In the screening interview, I would have explored this background at least tentatively; if any substantiating indications existed, I would have recommended individual counseling or therapy as a prerequisite to group work, or at least I would have referred her to a group with member characteristics more homogeneous to Sandra's.

The style and pattern of Sandra's behavior and affect are also indicative of my reservations about her being appropriate for this group. Given the vagueness of the group's purpose and the apparent laissez-faire (hands-off, passive) leadership approach, the stage is set for a rapid escalation of an intense transference episode once Sandra's psychological tolerance level has been breached. Her disclosures and projections onto the group and its members indicate that she has extensive repressed affect. Furthermore, what is indicated is the fact that her regressed affect is not being managed effectively. The poor management of her affect is due to inappropriate cognitive structures that framed her feelings in such a way that their expression was experienced as a total loss of control. The depth of her affect, its direction (blaming the group and a specific object—Jonathan), and the impact of her affect (she is visibly shaken) all indicate a crisis has been precipitated by ineffective screening and placement and inappropriate group leadership and process.

Consequently, I would now have a major crisis on my hands that requires immediate intervention, first, for the sake of Sandra and, second, for the sake of the other members. My immediate objective would be to calm and support Sandra even if that means I have to extend the group time or continue to work directly with her beyond the closure of the group. My primary concern would be her emotional state and whether or not she can recompose herself and move on to the next events in her life without debilitating repercussions. If other group members indicate a concern for Sandra and express a desire to support her, I would also mobilize their assistance in a recomposing, support process with immediate and continuing dimensions. The immediate aspect would be carried out by staying with Sandra and processing her feelings in a supportive, caring manner with an eye toward responsibility for her physical and emotional well-being and a professional accountability to see she is beyond any clear and present danger point. The ongoing dimension includes a contracting component where I would obtain a commitment from her to contact me via my emergency service if she regresses during the ensuing week. Depending on the state of the client and her openness to support, a temporary support network involving the other group members would be arranged. This support network would be done with clear parameters concerning the nature of the contact and with clear stipulations regarding reportability, first of all to me and also to the group.

However, if any of the potential concerns raised in the earlier part of my response emerge, I would take immediate steps to refer Sandra for individual therapy or a more appropriate group, maintaining my professional role in her life in order to facilitate her transition.

As for the group, the crisis would likely be a jolt that would prompt a more definitive purpose and process and that would certainly engender a shift in my leadership style. However, given my typical style of leadership, Sandra either would have been referred elsewhere or the issues behind the silence would have been forthcoming sooner because of my screening procedures and my role in involving her in the group process. I distinguish this incident from what I consider to be the typical "deep disclosure near session termination," which is not an unusual occurrence in groups I have led. Typically, deep disclosures near the end of a session are reflective of a member who is either at a transition point (not quite ready for prime-time attention) or whose timing of the disclosure can be seen as a form of resistance. If the disclosure is of the first variety, especially if prompted by a surge of pain or other emotions, my primary objective is to calm and recompose the person and the group for the immediate future and, secondarily, to set an agenda for attending to the disclosure in the next session. If the disclosure is of the second variety, I act to maintain the boundaries of the group time limits and hold the person accountable to raise the disclosure in the next group session. In my opinion, this incident involving Sandra broaches a broader ethical and therapeutic issue beyond the current group process. It is reflective of a deeper psychological or personality disorder that requires my attention and, as such, supersedes the dynamics of this particular group process.

Gestalt Therapy
Implemented by Mirriam F. Polster

Sandra's passionate denunciation of the group strikes me as welcome and not at all surprising. It is about time that someone called them on the tacit acceptance of nonlistening and nonresponsiveness that seems to have become a group norm. Because group interaction is a microcosm of how individual group members customarily act, the behavior here is not merely symptomatic; it is a fresh and present demonstration of how these people may act in the relationships that they have already described as troublesome and unsatisfying. They have stated that their outside relationships are shallow and meaningless. In this group interaction, we have all the elements that illustrate how they contribute to their unhappy situations. They do not listen, they look away, they make abstract or impersonal statements, and they become embarrassed when someone else refuses to play by the familiar but juiceless rules.

Contact is the relationship of an organism to its environment and is an essential principle in Gestalt therapy. Laura Perls described contact as "the recognition of, and the coping with the *other*, the different . . . not a state . . . but an activity. . . ." (1978, pp. 31–36). We are all open systems, depending on our exchanges with our environment to nourish, interest, stimulate, and educate us—in other words, to keep us alive and humanly responsive. To make contact, we must have a sense of our own separateness, the individuality that is our contribution to making contact. Contact is a process that requires the ability, rooted in ourselves, to venture into unfamiliar territory and to risk a momentary loss of self because we are willing to engage richly with that which is not us.

Given a moderately benevolent environment, we grow up with increasing confidence in our ability to make contact with the world. We discard, bit by bit, some of our dependency on external support and learn to support ourselves in the risky but exciting game of meeting that which is outside ourselves. But the more we venture, the more likely it is that the world responds unpredictably. So, we are sometimes rebuffed, hurt, or ignored. We begin to develop strategies for these responses. We try to support ourselves as best we can in the face of these disappointments. Often, we begin to distort or cripple the possibilities for contactful engagement. We draw in and constrict the excitement and arousal that might lead us to make overtures to that which is outside ourselves. It is this constricted excitement we experience as anxiety, which results in stilted and unsatisfying interaction with the world around us. This is the root of the difficulty the group was formed to address: their inadequacies in the specifics of contact and their inability to be with other people, to talk to them frankly without hiding, to listen to them without distortion, and to support the excitement and uncertainty of this human engagement.

Before looking at the role of each participant in the present interaction and my actions as group leader, I would like to note that 1-hour sessions are too short for working with a group of eight people. There is simply not enough time for the taciturn or slow group members to jump in. Thus, the pace of the group is skewed in favor of the verbally agile or assertive members. The lively ones talk, and the silent ones feel bullied, robbed, ignored, or out of it. Sandra's complaint therefore has some genesis in the shortage of time.

Even though it is affected by this scarcity of time, her complaint also has its own personal style and content. Some people have taken the time, but she has *given* it. She has remained silent, her gift to the group, and others have taken up the time she might have used, filled it up with empty surface talk, ignored her, and not even felt grateful. So, she bursts forth with an intensity that may be greater than the present situation calls for but that is loaded with a charge of energy from 6 weeks of silence in the group and from her "lot in life" outside it. The way she enters is to accumulate a grievance and then come in with a sense of having been wronged, with accusations and complaints. Nobody seems to care about her.

This is not only a statement to the group, but it also addresses me as group leader. Her complaint has validity. How could I have sat here for 6 weeks without remarking or asking about her silence? How could I have sat for 45 minutes in the present session and be working toward termination of the session without noticing her restlessness? I have colluded in the noncontact atmosphere and, as leader, have contributed a lot toward setting up the apparent group expectation of "hands-off," which is a burlesque of the existential belief in self-determinism.

How have I done this? I have let Sandra stew in her own juice for 6 weeks and done nothing. I have let Sarah palm off sloganistic statements about the "understanding" between herself and her husband and done nothing. I have let Jonathan and Franklin talk about the energy they put into their business activities and not asked them to direct this energy to their interaction with the group. I have heard Francine and Samuel broach their personal concerns, I have seen the unease and avoidance with which these disclosures have been met, and I have done nothing.

I do not believe that these people have come into group therapy knowing how to make contact. They are here to learn, and one way they learn is from me as model. This is an undeniable aspect of group leadership. To ignore it is to ignore one of the most potent influences in any therapy. If I, as a Gestaltist, value the ability to make contact, if I believe in awareness as a mobilizing and enriching attribute, and if I see self-support as a central quality in these actions, then I respond from these beliefs. I cannot become less responsive as a group leader than I am as a human being.

The tricky issue here is how to use my awareness so that it becomes a resource in the group rather than a dictum of how people *should* behave or a judgment of their behavior. I am not in the group to dictate but to explore alternatives, to remark on something that might otherwise go unremarked, to give a sense of the elasticity of our time together that allows for human contact, and to make it more likely that the group members will get better and better at doing this for themselves.

So, I offer two sets of responses to the situation presented in this incident. The first is what I might have done had I been there from session 1 on, and the second is what I might do if I just began work with this group in session 7.

In the first scenario, I would begin the group work with a short statement of my beliefs as a Gestalt therapist and what the people in the group might expect from me by way of observations or suggestions. I would also remind them that they can at any time either differ with me or say *no* to my suggestions. This suggests that reluctance to do something is to be respected and can be at least as informative as compliance.

After allowing some time, perhaps the session 1 and the beginning of session 2, for group members to get the feel of each other, I would begin to attend publicly to the quality of their contact with each other. This might begin with what happens when Francine speaks about herself. I would observe who is listening, whether they are looking at her and she at them, whether they look interested or uncomfortable. When they tried to shift from her discussion to topics that seemed to be away and out of the group, I might ask her how she feels about the change of subject. I would be interested in how Francine has contributed to the lack of interest. Has she spoken lightly as if telling them not to take her seriously? Has her voice been inaudible or her language dull? Does she look at the floor or a wall or the ceiling?

I could explore with the group the reciprocal nature of contact—the person who speaks to support himself or herself with energy, breath, and intention in order to make contact with those who listen. And the listeners, too, are not passive recipients. Their share in making contact is to listen actively, to see how Francine's manner corroborates or contradicts what she is saying, and to tune in to their self-awareness to determine what her personal disclosures evoke in them. Samuel, too, has been confused by the apparent lack of response when he has talked about his sense of failure in his marriage. Again, it is important to assess how Samuel fails to arouse anyone's sympathy, anger, resentment, or identification. How can he continue to speak when nobody appears to hear or be moved?

Jonathan and Franklin do not seem to make the group uncomfortable. They talk about all the energy it takes to make a go of their businesses. But where does all that energy go when they are in the group? I want to discover ways in which that good energy could go into lively interactions here in the group. When they talk to one of the people in the group, do they talk with the same liveliness and concentration? Do they leave space for responses or an interested question, or do they just continue with the recital of their problems as they might to a Chamber of Commerce meeting or to a group of business associates? Can they shift gears? Or are they so rigidly locked into a businesslike form of contact that personal feelings leave them not knowing how to respond? What do they feel, for example, in direct response to Samuel's discomfort?

And Sarah—she who has such a good working "understanding" with her husband—what is her reaction to Samuel? And how does Francine, who might be closest to responding feelingly to Samuel, remain silent and apparently unhearing? There is much interplay here that could lead to contact among the group members if the groundwork for expecting to be heard can be made clear.

By this, I mean the shared responsibility in any communication; the person who is speaking intends to be heard and supports this intention with voice, language, breathing, and body movements—in short, everything he or she has in order to make contact. Those listening are active participants in the two-way process of contact, too. This means they do not change the subject and pretend the uncomfortable word was not spoken. They look and are willing to see and hear clearly what is before them, even if it makes them uncomfortable. They support their own discomfort and can move from that into contact, even with unwelcome news.

But here we are in session 7, and Sandra has burst out in a way that is hard for them to ignore. They become immobilized; they are stunned. Her grievance, as I said, has built up in the time she has spent silent in the group, but it also is loaded with what she feels is her lot in life. She is addressing Jonathan, so we need to sort out specifically what emotion she directs at him and what may be leftover or excess baggage from someone else. She could make specific statements to Jonathan about her complaints. I might also ask if there is anyone else in the group she would like to say something to. Her initial move was spawned by her own distress and desperation. To make it into a contactful interaction, however, she needs to say what she has to say to the very people she would like to confront, instead of remaining silent and waiting, like Sleeping Beauty, for someone to discover her, and resenting them when they do not.

Clearly, this kind of confrontation is hard for Sandra. She is unaccustomed to it, her habitual mode is silent resentment, and she needs experience in supporting her drastic emergence. There are three sources of support that are hers to muster. First, she can call on the support that her body can provide. Is she supporting herself physically? How could her gestures and posture corroborate what she is saying, rather than deserting her and leaving her trembling and shaken? Second, how does her breath support her emotion? Does she take in air adequate to meet her needs for speaking and crying, or is she trying to make do with only a scant supply? Third, she can support herself by what she knows. What is there in particular about Jonathan that has triggered this in her? What does she want that she is not getting? How does she collude in this? What does her silence do for her that allows this to happen and enables her to build up the grudge that she needs to get into the action? Is this the only way she might choose to become more active in the group?

After focusing on Sandra's experience, I would move on to Jonathan and his reaction to her outburst and to the feelings of the other group members as they witnessed it. This is an opportunity to break into a newer and deeper level of feeling than had previously emerged and to look at the fears and doubts of the others. Sandra's expression of emotion is an opening to be explored, not an aberration to look away from and pretend did not happen. The other members do not know how to deal with intensity. They need practice in knowing their response and in being able to articulate it to others. The leader can serve here as a temporary support also, something like a scaffold that allows the work to go on but that will be removed as soon as the structure can support itself.

Individual Psychology
Implemented by Guy J. Manaster

At the critical moment in this situation, with all eyes to the floor and all ears to Sandra's sobs, I would do nothing. I would wait until one of the following events occurred: (1) One of the group members comes to Sandra's rescue, in whatever manner; (2) Jonathan, or whoever else felt implicated by Sandra's accusations, speaks up in defense of himself, the group, and the process to date; or (3) time runs out, and the hour is up. These three options seem most likely, although other things could happen—such as a member beginning a new discussion without regard for the incident.

My hope would be at this point, after more than six sessions, that our combined efforts under the umbrella of Adlerian theory would have resulted in a group feeling, a feeling of and for us as a group, a community, not as an assemblage. I would hope to have conveyed, directly in an educative manner and indirectly by my example of attention to individual group members and their behaviors, that in our group, as in everyday life, we have a responsibility to ourselves *and* to others. This moment in the group is a time for our responsibility for, our feelings for, *an-other* to take precedence. This is a moment when social interest, social–community feelings, is called for and would, I hope, emerge.

Moreover, individual psychology's purposeful, functional view of behavior and emotions should also have been transmitted during the previous sessions. The group members should have developed some inkling of the purpose of Sandra's behavior. They should be able intellectually to discriminate at some beginning level the two messages in her outburst: "I am different, not like, not a part of you, individually, or you the group," and "I feel sad—look how bad I feel, I am crying." Sandra is asking for a response to her verbal and behavioral messages. The question is, What response does she get from the group—not from me, if at all possible, but from the group?

If these most basic and crucial Adlerian concepts had become part of the group mentality, the first possible event would occur: Someone in the group—I expect Francine—would respond to Sandra's call. Inferring more than I should on the limited information I have, I might expect Francine to say something like, "Come on, honey, everyone here likes you. We've just been waiting for you to join in. We all feel crummy about the same things, so come on and feel crummy with us. When we're together, it doesn't feel so bad, and we can get better. It's when you feel you're by yourself that you feel worse. At least that's the way it is for me."

This would probably be greeted by a chorus, not unanimous, of agreement. The discussion would then move, possibly with me posing it, to the questions "How did we come to this juncture, Sandra's part, the group's part?" and "Where do we go from here?"

But what about Jonathan? He might have followed up a positive response, such as Francine's, with his defense, or he might have preceded anyone else's reaction with his defense.

In the context of the group as described—that is, not as an Adlerian group to this moment—Jonathan might well say, "I haven't been doing anything wrong, or against you, Sandra. I've been doing what I thought you were supposed to do in this group." From the description of the first six sessions, I think he might well have presumed that.

But if some of the notions and *values* of individual psychology had been instilled and Jonathan interrupted the silence with "Don't holler at me—I'm telling about my reasons for being here—you tell yours," or something like that, we would have the grounds for exploring two people's reasons for behaving as they have, possibly with sides taken.

But what if Samuel, who apparently has not been heard in the past, starts up things again by going back to his own story. If no one else jumps in to keep us involved with the current important issue, to help and understand Sandra and what is going on, I would. I might say, "Samuel, it seemed that no one has heard you, and now it seems you aren't listening. What just happened? What about Sandra?" If he cannot answer, which seems probable, I would ask the same questions of the group, maybe adding "and what about Samuel?"

If Samuel had taken another tack, or no one had spoken, and it was almost time to break, I would have continued: "We don't know what to do about, to, or for others! We are all here because we want to find some way of bringing significance and value back into our lives or into our lives for the first time. I am not sure 'back' is appropriate for all of us—I think, probably, values and significance, at least in interpersonal relations, have never been very much part of our lives.

"We have, as a group, characterized ourselves as all being 'tired of bobbing like a cork aimlessly on the sea of life.' It looks to me as if we have been doing the same in here, occasionally 'bobbing' or 'bumping' into one another. But it looks to me as if each of us had been primarily fighting to keep afloat. And we each have our own ways of keeping our heads above water. It is usual for people to try to keep themselves above water, above others, in some way because they think if they are not better than others, above others, they will be below them, they will sink. We have been almost pretending to be a group, and not even pretending to be a group of equals. We've been perfecting our own ways of being superior—as Francine has by showing she's the most open, or as Jonathan has by showing how good and hard working he is, or as Samuel has by showing his good intentions despite his confusion, or as Sarah has by controlling, or trying to control, herself and all around her.

"And now what have we come to? Finally, Sandra has added up the time we've been in group, the slights she sees from everyone, and concluded and now affirmed her place—her usual place and her place again here—she's been 'took,' she's been 'had.' Is this true, Sandra? I know you feel very bad right now, but is it the same bad way you have felt often for a long time when you've been taken by your kids who used you and went on to their own lives, by your husband who has had a good career and used your quiet help in the background?"

This abbreviated summary should, as I have said, been a part of the group process from its inception; the specifications of lifestyle goals for each individual should have been inferred in the group and discussed individually and privately with each group member prior to the beginning of the group, along with infrequent but regular one-to-one sessions concurrent with the group.

What if I had summarized in this fashion at the end of the session? There are two thrusts to it. The first is generalized to the group, providing framework for each member to understand his or her own reasons and goals for not assuming some portion of the group responsibility and taking responsibility for another person. The second thrust is directed to Sandra, with the same message as that directed to the group. The purposes of this summary are to illustrate (1) how each person is attempting to elevate himself or herself in their own special way, from their own unique perspective; (2) how this strategy does not serve the articulated purposes of the group but does serve their lifelong lifestyle goals and perpetuates their nonbelonging; (3) how responsibility for and interest in others is essential for group living and individual growth as part of a therapy group; and (4) how this holds true, also, for being part of the human group. I probably would not, nor could not, convey all of that in the summary, but it is the essence of what I would want to impart. And the question remains about what effect would accentuate and applaud the commonality of the problem and the attempts by anyone who attempted to modify their self-glorification for the common good and for Sandra's good.

At the same time, I would have to be watchful of Sandra being too effective and gaining the unreserved sympathy and apology of the group. If she did and everyone responded with something to the effect of "I'm sorry we have overlooked you, that we've only talked about us," I think I would break in with real applause. I might clap my hands and congratulate Sandra as one of the all-time great guilt purveyors, turning the incident into a lesson in purposeful behavior, in people getting what it is they want.

Interpersonal Psychotherapy
Implemented by Victor Yalom and Mary Jean Paris

As leaders, it is quite doubtful that we would ignore a group member who sat silently over the past 6 weeks, especially a member like Sandra who was "fidgeting and looking extremely restless" throughout the greater part of session 7. We would have encouraged her to participate and shifted the attention to her from time to time to help draw her out. We would ask her questions such as "Is this a meeting you want to join?" or "What's the ideal question we could ask you today to help you come into the group?" We would attempt to address any concerns she had about the group process. We would elicit feedback from other group members on how her nonparticipation affected them and then would ask her whether this is the desired impact. In these and other ways, we would attempt to enlist a quiet member as an active collaborator in the campaign against her silence.

Our first instinct is to give much needed support and empathy to a member of the group who is so visibly upset—we don't want her to leave the group this evening feeling raw, overly exposed, or just shaken up. Among other things, this emotional state would leave her at a high risk for dropping out of the group altogether, ending up as a group casualty rather than a group success. We might reflect how difficult it must have been for her to sit through six sessions with all those strong feelings inside and that we are glad that she has finally been able to let some of it out, although we realize how difficult it is to do so. It must be very painful for her to experience such a lack of caring and concern in a group that she has come to for support—and yet it is evident that her feelings are so powerful that they must reflect long, pent-up disappointments. We would try to convey to her that there must be something very important to learn about what just transpired—that although we certainly don't know the meaning of it for her, we are confident that she has so much to gain if she can come to a better understanding of her anger and learn how to garner the type of support she desires.

In this highly emotional state, Sandra may not be able to reflect on or gain insight on the particular meaning of her outburst, especially because it is near the end of the session. But hopefully, our remarks would give her something to hold onto during the intervening week, to moderate her discomfort and encourage her to return to the next session. We would probably phone her the following day to offer her some support and to reinforce our message to her.

Since Sandra's outpouring of emotions immobilized the entire group, we would want to reassure the other members who are now silent and appear uncomfortable. Given the level of discomfort, we would briefly check in with them to see how they are doing. We would explain that in the usual course of group therapy there will be times when very difficult feelings do come up in the group and it is not always neatly wrapped up at the end of the session. Some members might be quite defensive or angry at Sandra, but she is not in an emotional state where anything productive is likely to occur if they express their anger at her. We would like them to do more than simply stare at the floor; however, if they start to vent negative reaction toward Sandra, we would politely but firmly tell them to hold off on expressing their feelings directly to her. If any members appear to be particularly shaken up, we would briefly work with them so that they are sufficiently calm to end the session. So as not to appear arbitrary or overly controlling, we would explain that, although they understandably have strong reactions, there simply isn't time left in the meeting to work through their feelings toward Sandra in a way that will be helpful, but we will make sure we start out with this first thing next week.

Our efforts here—geared towards containment of affect and protection of Sandra—are certainly not general prescriptions for dealing with intense emotions; rather, they are responses to the specific convergence of factors in this vignette. These factors include the early developmental stage of the group, Sandra's prior lack of participation to date, the assumed weak bonds she has developed with individual members or the group as a whole, and the limited time remaining at the end of the session. As in individual therapy, therapeutic relationship, timing, and context are guides for the intervention, although in a group the concept of therapeutic relationship is broadened to include relationships among the members, not just between patient and therapist.

In this case, although the experience may be initially jarring for Sandra and the other members, such emotionally laden exchanges are often pivotal moments in a group's history that are long remembered and frequently referred to. In future meetings, we would want to explore in depth Sandra's stored-up grievances, her sense of having been wronged, and her feeling that nobody, including the group members, seem to care about her. We would try to get her to look at her attitudes and perceptions that contributed to these painful conclusions and have her check out some of her assumptions about other group members. Perhaps some of these assumptions would be validated, but hopefully some of them would be refuted or at least questioned. And as we carefully elicit feedback from the members, she would have the unique opportunity to learn about the impact of her behavior on others in a way that she may be able to digest. Assuming that her experience in the group is indeed a reenactment of disappointing relationships or attempts at relationships, one can only imagine that she has not heretofore received feedback in a supportive manner—others have probably either fled or counterattacked, further reinforcing her belief system about the unfair laws of human relationships.

Other members also have the opportunity to learn much from this encounter, such as how they respond to anger. In the following sessions we would help them to understand their reactions. Were they afraid, paralyzed, or poised to counterattack? What about their response—were they comfortable with it, and what would they like to change? For example, for members afraid of conflict, this incident would provide much grist for the therapeutic mill, and their ability to describe to Sandra their initial fear would be the first step to approaching conflictual situations more directly in the future.

Psychodynamic Therapy
Implemented by J. Scott Rutan

From my perspective, this group has been moving along very nicely. For a group of people who suffer "shallow" relationships, I could expect nothing else than that the first several sessions would be devoted to "safe," "shallow" conversations. That this changes as quickly as session 7 is remarkable. That the emotional event occurs at the end of the hour is not surprising—psychodynamic theory would hold that at an unconscious level Sandra needs the protection of the "end." Otherwise, she and the group would be faced with the very thing they most want and fear—an intense, deep, and authentic encounter.

It is very important that the group therapist not make the error of extending the group time to accommodate this moment. It is not by chance that it occurred at the end. Rather, I would comment, "We seem to have the opportunity for the very type of authentic, 'nonshallow' interactions that each of you came to learn more about. We will continue this next week. In the interval, I suggest that each of you pay careful attention to what you are feeling at this moment." I would make this intervention for several reasons. First, I would want to support the expression of affect because from a dynamic perspective affect is the primary data for learning. Second, by commenting that we will "continue this next week," I am reinforcing the notion that the group process is continual. Finally, by pointing out how present interactions parallel presenting issues, I present the concept that group interactions are highly relevant in addressing the problems for which the members came to therapy.

Rational–Emotive–Behavioral Therapy
Implemented by Albert Ellis

This critical incident is quite predictable in groups that are nondirectively misled in the manner that this one has been up to now. The therapist, who has not only not been trained in typical psychoanalytic, experiential, or client-centered therapy but also has unfortunately gone along with this nondirective method, does not seem to have the foggiest idea about how people often block themselves from enjoying a more effective and meaningful personal life. The therapist also does not appear to have any notion of what an effective group leader can do to help the members unblock themselves in this respect. Consequently, he or she is too *helpful* and so is desperately hoping against hope that the group members will somehow muddle through and magically help themselves. As normally happens under these dismal conditions, these members have nicely wasted virtually all their time in the group and have been beautifully diverted from helping themselves in almost any way. Almost all of them are probably now the worse for needless wear and tear and more confused about their goals in life and how to achieve them than they were when they began this form of "therapy."

Sandra, being older than the rest, and perhaps recognizing that her precious time is being wasted away in this kind of group process, complains bitterly, in her own natural ineffective way, about what has been going on in the group. Rather than blame the group leader (who she thinks might possibly attack her back), she blames the group in general. This may well represent her usual tendency to blame external people and events instead of squarely shouldering the responsibility for her own thoughts, emotions, and actions; or it may represent the fact that she accurately sees that she has been done in to some extent by this inefficient group process. Of course, Sandra has passively and silently consented to this situation for the last several sessions, and now she knows no better way to vent her feelings about this inefficient group process than to whine and scream. Usually, she does this internally, but in this case she feels that enough is enough and atypically lets her inward anger out.

Sandra, moreover, seems to be even more self-hating than hostile to others, and she foolishly believes that she *has to be* approved, loved, and helped by others—particularly by those for whom she has some feelings and who *should* care for her. She (like most "adults") has always been a baby and is fairly determined to be one for the rest of her life—if she can possibly get away with it. She rather envies the "takers"—such as Jonathan—who at least seem to care for themselves and go after (or at least worry about) what *they* want; but she also at times hates them for not recognizing *her* weaknesses and for not making sure that *she* gets taken care of.

As Sandra lets herself go—with feelings of anger, self-loathing, and abysmal self-pity—she recognizes that she is doing the "wrong" thing because no other group member has "broken down" like this. So she does what most people do at this turn of affairs: She takes her primary symptoms (anger and self-pity) and creates a set of severe secondary symptoms about them. Her fundamental irrational beliefs are (1) "I *must* do well and be approved by others! And isn't it *awful* if I am not!"; (2) "You *must* treat me considerately and fairly! And isn't it *terrible* if you do not!"; (3) "Conditions must be easy and give me exactly what I want quickly, without any hassles! And isn't it *horrible* when they are not!" After creating her primary emotional symptoms of self-downing, anger, and self-pity with these foolish absolutistic ideas, she then uses the same basic irrationalities to create her secondary symptoms.

Thus, when she sees that she has an angry outburst, instead of rationally telling herself, "I wish I wouldn't be so angry and break down in this uncalled for manner, how unfortunate!" she irrationally tells herself, "I *must* not break down in this uncalled for manner; how *awful!* What a perfect idiot I am!" She then feels depressed and self-downing about her anger (rather than accepting *herself* with *it*), and she exacerbates her state of emotional dysfunctioning.

If the group leader were efficient, he or she would not have permitted this kind of situation to go this far in the first place. Once it occurred, however, the therapist can recognize that this kind of passive "therapy" will often lead to outbursts of this sort and help exacerbate people's problems. The therapist could then, at least, *do* something about showing Sandra, and the group as a whole, what her real problems are, how she (and not the group process itself) is creating them, and what she can do about overcoming them.

Taking over the leadership of this group, I would immediately say to myself, "What a therapist-caused mess! However, it does have some good points about it because at least I can use this situation to show Sandra and the other group members what they are doing to upset themselves and how they can more assertively, in the future, refuse to go this far with an inefficient leader and try to get themselves some real help. Too bad that I am, as it were, given an already half-drowned person to try to resuscitate. But it is quite a challenge for me to use this near disaster to illustrate some of the main points of human disturbance and perhaps to dramatize them to Sandra and the other group members."

In other words, in consulting in a bad situation like this one, I would first use rational–emotive–behavioral therapy (REBT) principles on myself, to make sure that I did not anger or otherwise unnecessarily upset myself about this needless disaster. If I did feel angry at the inefficient group leader, I would quickly do the A-B-C-D-E construct of REBT on myself: "At point *A*," I would say to myself, "let us assume that this leader has behaved inadequately. At point *C* (emotional and behavioral consequence), I feel angry. What am I telling myself, at *B* (my belief system), to make myself angry. Obviously: 'This therapist should not have acted so incompetently! Any leader like that deserves to be drawn and quartered!' But on to *D* (disputing of irrational beliefs): 'Why *should* not, *must* not he or she behave so incompetently—when that's the way they are! Tough!' And why does he or she deserve to be drawn and quartered for incompetence? Answer: "There is no reason—he or she is only a confused, fallible human who acted incompetently in this situation, not a totally bad human who deserves to suffer for incompetence. Too bad—but not awful!'"

I would show myself that Sandra's outbursts tend to come from her own A-B-C-D-E construct—not from *A*, the activating experiences in the group, that happened to her. I would surmise that she has one or more profound, absolutistic *shoulds, oughts,* or *musts* by which she creates her problems—that she (like most humans) is a strong *must*urbator. And I would guess from her highly disturbed emotional reactions what her *musts* were. I would also look for her "awfulizing," her "I-can't-stand-ititis," and her global labeling of herself and others as rotten people (instead of as people who behave rottenly in this instance). I would ask myself whether she had both primary symptoms (anger and self-downing) and secondary symptoms (self-downing about her own anger) and would conclude that she probably had both.

I would then start determining what cognitive, emotive, and behavioral interventions and homework assignments I would use to help Sandra and the group see how they were disturbing themselves and how they could refuse to do so in the future.

I would recognize the group elements in this situation—but mainly see them as being at point *A* (activating experiences or adversity) in the A-B-Cs of REBT. Sandra, even on her own, probably has a basic philosophy of perfectionism and intolerance of others' imperfections, which will often get her into emotional difficulties. When she is in any kind of a group—even a "therapy" group—she tends to use this philosophy about how she behaves in the group and how the group members behave toward her. Thus, she tends to think that *especially* when she is in front of other people she *must* act as well as they do and impress them with her goodness or competence; and she tends to think that they (especially the group leader) *must* care for her rescue, seeing how helpless she is! So the irrational beliefs and the dysfunctional emotions and behaviors that I would work on in Sandra's case may be even more prevalent and tend to be shown more intensely in the group situation. But, following REBT theory, I would not delude myself that the group *makes* Sandra disturbed or *causes* her outbursts. The group and the group situation contributes significantly to her emotional problems, but they really do not cause them.

As a group consultant or therapist, I would keep in mind that I am primarily an educator—because, whatever I do with one member, such as Sandra, will be seen and heard by other members. In a group educational setting, then, perhaps I could help several members by talking directly and incisively to one of them. I would also want Sandra to understand (1) herself and her own emotional problems and how to cope with them and (2) how other people continually disturb themselves and how she can accept them with their disturbances and perhaps help them overcome their malfunctioning. I would really like all group members to talk each other out of their irrational beliefs—and thereby automatically and "unconsciously" talk themselves out of their own. So if time permitted, I would try to get Sandra to work with the other members in a REBT manner, along similar lines to those I used in working with her.

I would first say to Sandra, "I'm glad you spoke up like that! I think that this group has been run quite badly so far. I think that your outburst shows that you tend to recognize this, too. You are showing your hostility to the group members and especially to Jonathan. But I wonder if you are really quite angry against the group leader for allowing the group to wallow around like this, in a muddled and virtually unled fashion, for so many sessions? Do you think that you are angry about that?"

Assuming that Sandra replied that, yes, she was angry about the group process and the ineptness of the group leader, I would then continue: "Well, let's assume that you and I are right about this: The group leader has been sadly remiss and has helped screw up things and waste your and the group's time. Now, you and I may be wrong about this because maybe the leader really acted well and your very outburst and what it may lead to therapeutically may prove this. But let's assume that the leader has been quite wrong—stupid, incompetent, unhelpful. In REBT, we call that A—your activating experience or adversity. And at point C, the consequence you feel in your gut, you experience real anger. Now you may think that the group leader makes you angry by his [or her] incompetence. But this is quite false! Actually, you *choose* to anger yourself about this; and you do so at B—your belief system *about* the leader's incompetence. Now what are you telling yourself at B, about what has been happening to you, at A, that makes you feel so angry at C?"

For the next few minutes, I would continue this dialogue with Sandra, trying to convince her (and the other members who are presumably listening to the two of us) that no one has ever upset or angered her in all her life—but that she, instead, angers herself about things like people's incompetence. And, as briefly as possible, I would also try to get her to dispute (at point D) her irrational beliefs that create her anger, thereby to surrender these beliefs. If she did not understand what she was telling herself to anger herself and what she could do to make herself unangry, I would also try to get other group members to supply these answers, rather than supplying them myself, so that they, too, would see how to dispute, at point D, their own irrational beliefs and to give them up.

After speaking with Sandra, I would ask Jonathan, "How do you feel about Sandra's attacking you?" Assuming that he said that he felt hurt, depressed, angry, or otherwise upset, I would try to show him that he largely created these feelings and that Sandra, no matter how badly she might attack him verbally, could not make him feel disturbed. I would say to him, "Let's assume that Sandra is wrong about your caring only about your insurance business and that no one else in your life seems to matter. Let's assume that she has accused you unfairly and unjustly. Her accusation merely constitutes an activating experience or adversity—point A—and cannot in itself upset you unless you tell yourself some irrational demand about it. Now, what did you tell yourself, at B, your beliefs about what Sandra did at A, to make yourself angry or hurt at C, your emotional consequence?"

Again, I would help Jonathan, as well as the rest of the members, to see that he upset himself about Sandra's accusation and that she could not make him feel great pain (except physically, of course, in case she actually assaulted him) unless he told himself some strong evaluative sentence *about* what she did.

I would then ask all the members, "Why did you all let this wasteful group process proceed as it did? Why did you not speak up earlier and try to help the group proceed in a manner that would have been more useful to you? What were you telling yourself about the way things were occurring?" I would help them see that they were probably afraid to interrupt the inefficient group process and risk confrontation with the leader and that they were telling themselves that they could not stand her or his criticism or disapproval if they did so. I would show them how to challenge this irrational belief. I would also show them that some of them probably had an abysmally low frustration tolerance to allow things to go on this way and that they had to take the easy way out because they had irrational ideas such as, "If I speak up about what really bothers me, that will be very hard. In fact, it will be *too* hard! I *can't stand* facing hard things like this! I *must* have immediate comfort and ease and must avoid all real unpleasantness, even though it might help me in the long run."

I would show the group, in other words, that some members went along for the leader's ride because of their own irrational fears of disapproval and their natural tendencies to take the easy and less effectual way out of their difficulties. I would help them see, and to help each other see, the precise self-defeating beliefs they told themselves in order to create their evasive and heads-in-the-sand feelings and behaviors; I would indicate how they could question, challenge, dispute, and change these beliefs. I would give them emotive and behavioral homework assignments to help them revise their basic irrational philosophies.

Thus, I might encourage Sandra to take the homework assignment of asserting herself promptly in any group situation she happened to be in during the next week or two, no matter how uncomfortable she felt in the process. If she carried out this assignment, she could reinforce herself with something she found rewarding; if she failed to carry it out, she would penalize herself by engaging in some distasteful activity (such as cleaning her house or burning a $20 bill). Similarly, depending on how the other group members reacted and disturbed themselves, each of them would preferably agree to do a homework assignment that would help them act and work against their self-defeating ideas and feelings.

Group REBT includes a good many emotive–evocative exercises, which may be experienced during the group sessions or outside the group. Because Sandra and most of the other members of this particular group seem to feel ashamed of expressing themselves and acting in a "foolish" or "humiliating" manner, they might perform one of the REBT shame-attacking or risk-taking exercises. In the group itself they might all be asked to do something that they consider risky, such as saying something negative to another group member, confronting the group leader, or acting in some "ridiculous" manner. For outside homework, they might be asked to do something "shameful" during the week, such as telling a stranger that they just got out of the mental hospital, walking a banana on the street, or yelling out the time in a department store. They would then be asked why they considered this task risky or shameful, how they felt about doing it, and how they could get themselves to do it without feeling ashamed, embarrassed, humiliated, or self-downing.

The preceding interventions are suggestive of those that I would make in this group or in one of my own regular REBT groups. The main goal is to show all group members that they do not just get seriously upset but instead mainly *upset themselves.* They do so by strongly believing in absolutistic and unrealistic *shoulds, oughts,* and *musts.* To change their irrational beliefs and the dysfunctional emotions and behaviors that derive from them, they had better persistently and actively (not to mention robustly!) force themselves to think, feel, and behave quite differently. As an REBT group leader, I vigorously question, challenge, teach, direct, intervene, and—in a very real sense of this term—*lead.*

Reality Therapy
Implemented by Thomas E. Bratter

The first task confronting any reality therapist would be to establish a meaningful working relationship among group therapy members and the group leader. After achieving this task, which can take a few sessions, I would help and encourage all group members to evaluate their individual behavior and, in so doing, define their presenting area of concern. If possible and appropriate, I would attempt to reformulate these individual concerns into a few commonly shared group goals for purposes of attaining some kind of consensus about which issues would be discussed. The group participants would have an explicit understanding about what to expect from their shared experience. I would attempt to determine an agreement regarding individual and group priorities. Once this task is negotiated, the reality therapy group leader functions more as a catalyst-resource person who can facilitate group process so that these issues and concerns are addressed and resolved.

I would attempt to establish an agenda with the understanding that members would confine their attention and comments to the here and now. Discussion about persons outside the group, the past, or events not related to the group would be discouraged unless a relationship existed to current group behavior. Generally, a gentle reminder from the group therapist can suffice to redirect the focus to a situation that has dual relevance for the individual and the group. Defining group goals is a shared concern, but the group leader retains the prerogative to confront individuals when the group is not working effectively. It is unlikely that seven sessions would elapse before any member would verbalize a concern because any skilled reality therapist would help the group relate. More specifically, during the first sessions, the group leader apparently decided to remain relatively passive and uninvolved. Because the group had determined "that they would like to do 'anything' to get themselves . . . closer to people they felt a deep love for," in all probability I would have pursued Francine's personal disclosure before session 7. If the group responded as they did in one of the sessions—that is, "their uneasiness in their rapid movement away from Francine to topics that seemed to be away from and outside the group"—I would recognize the reluctance of the group to relate to Francine and remind them of their commitment to help each other become closer to people, as well as to keep the discussion focused on relevant concerns.

Let us assume that no group leader is infallible and, for some inexplicable reason, I missed Francine's earlier disclosure. During session 7, Sandra has provided the group and me another opportunity to discuss the central theme.

I would pursue the issue by saying, "I sense, Sandra, that you have felt unappreciated for some time. I had hoped that you would begin to confront those painful feelings. I'm glad that you trust us to share your hurt. I think, if the group so chooses, that we can proceed in at least two ways with what you have said. First, I think we can help you examine your behavior so that people will appreciate you more. Second, I think if both you and Jonathan consent we can try to help you understand your reaction to him. I think both points are directly related to your sense of being unappreciated. Well, what do you think, Sandra?"

Sandra: "Well . . . okay . . . yes, it is all right with me. I think I would like to."

I would further comment, "I am wondering if there is anyone who would like to tell Sandra how they have experienced her so far in our group." Sarah might comment at this point by saying, "Sandra, you really surprise me. You have not participated as much as some of us. In fact, you could almost be considered a silent member. I really had no idea you wanted our approval, our acceptance, our appreciation, our respect. I have experienced you as being aloof. But I know what you are feeling because, like you, my family now is self-sufficient and independent. They no longer need me the way they did several years ago. Truthfully, this is what motivated me to get my master's degree so that I can do something useful and worthwhile. What I have deemed is that I needed to change or else I would have become as obsolete as the dinosaur. The truth of the matter is that your family has grown up and no longer needs you to do things for them. I guess you have a choice: to stay as you are and feel sorry for yourself or to change and find some activities that will give your life meaning." In turn, Francine might say, "Hey, I appreciate you. I really do. You risked a whole lot by being honest. Maybe now we can begin to discuss some important and intimate issues. I think what you did took a lot of guts."

I would then summarize these comments by stating, "Sandra, maybe we can combine both Francine and Sarah's comments. Sarah, I think, is suggesting that you try to change some of your behavior so that people will begin to need and appreciate you. Francine is suggesting that you risk becoming involved with people."

Sandra needs to renegotiate her relationships with her family and friends and may need to establish new acquaintances. Unwittingly, Sandra may be relating to her four grown "children" as if they were in high school rather than to their current status as college graduates. Perhaps, Sandra now is demanding that her family "repay" her for all the personal sacrifices she made on their behalf.

It is important for the group leader to recognize the tremendous age differential (28 to 45) in the group, which could be countertherapeutic because each age group has different developmental needs and concerns. If the group is approached correctly, however, there are many creative opportunities for interaction, which can benefit everyone. The group can be utilized as a therapeutic tool not only to help Sandra understand her situation but also to devise a constructive plan. Both Franklin and Jonathan, for example, have verbalized concerns, which, in all probability, parallel those of Sandra's college-graduated young adults—that is, adjusting to their chosen occupation or profession. Significantly, Sandra spoke directly to Jonathan in a criticizing and condemning manner. If the leader and the group could help Sandra "appreciate" Jonathan's realistic concerns, Sandra could be viewed as a resource advocate by her family. The group leader could attempt to place Sandra in a position to offer some pragmatic advice about improving his business, which simultaneously could teach her a more relevant, humanistic way to relate and help her to be seen as an asset by her family. The group could assume a consultative role to both Sandra and Jonathan, which the young man would appreciate and which would help the wife-mother be more appreciated by her family.

The exchange for both Sandra and the group has been an emotional one, and an implicit responsibility of the group leader is to provide some kind of closure. The areas of concern for both Sandra and Jonathan will require more than the allocated time; the reality therapist needs to terminate the group and, perhaps, set the agenda for the next. Rather than provide the solution, I would prefer to end the group by saying the following: "We will need to end in a few minutes because all of us have other commitments. Sandra, I think it would be important for you to consider ways you can suggest for Jonathan to expand his business. My guess is that Jonathan's concerns probably are similar to your family's. I would hope that you (the group) also will think about Jonathan and Sandra during the week. In addition [*said with some humor and casualness*], we can help Sally to help her fiancé and, of course, Samuel and Franklin. Perhaps, we can let Sarah assume responsibility for the next session so that she will gain some counseling experience. We finally have discovered a common group concern. I am not sure how Francine and Janet fit into the picture, but by next time, I assure you, I will know. I think it has been a productive, if painful, session. Perhaps it marks the first time we functioned as a group. Does anyone have anything they wish to add? [*Long pause.*] Have a good week, and I am looking forward to seeing you next Wednesday at four-thirty."

My intention is to help the group coordinate its resources and function as a cohesive problem-solving unit. The collective wisdom of the group always exceeds that of the individual reality therapist. In a reality therapy group, members remain people from the beginning to the conclusion. The passive role of patient is totally rejected. It is therefore assumed that individuals have the capacity to discover for themselves creative and constructive solutions for their concerns. The themes mentioned in Critical Incident 5 certainly lend themselves to the concrete problem-solving action approach to reality therapy.

Solution-Focused Therapy

Implemented by Rebecca LaFountain

To state that Sandra "has remained rather silent" means that "she has been more quiet than the norm" to a solution-focused counselor. I say this because solution-focused groups follow a structure to which all group members are expected to respond. To be this far along in the group, Sandra would have shared what it is she wants to change, her progress goal, and weekly updates. It is likely that Sandra has minimally involved herself, as opposed to Francine and Samuel who readily disclose personal feelings.

Sandra's outburst intrigues me, yet it doesn't surprise me. Throughout the first few sessions I would have been making hypotheses about her beliefs, based on her behavior and the language that she uses, and by session 6 I would either verify or disprove my initial perceptions.

In the initial session, as always, I would have conducted an activity that serves as an ice breaker. The exercise allows participants to learn about each other and to see the commonalities they share. It affords me the opportunity to see how they interact with each other. Often times the activity is merely a sharing of their backgrounds, interests, and the like, but other times it is an activity such as "people bingo," which forces the participants to move about and talk with each other. Because these members have in common that they all experience shallow relationships with their significant others, I would likely choose an activity that mobilizes them into some group activity. I would probably choose an activity I call "Find someone who . . ." where participants seek out others with whom they share similarities (enjoy the same kind of music, have the same hobby, etc.) and sign off on each others' lists. I do not have much information about Sandra, so I am going to take the liberty to infer that Sandra remained pretty passive in the activity, which forced other members to go over to her. I would probably make an hypothesis that her belief is that "she must rely on others to make things happen in her life and to meet her needs—and therefore she doesn't have to take responsibility if she isn't happy with the results." I could probably confirm this hypothesis based on what we know about her from the write-up. It says that she is "uncertain about the direction *her life is going to take*" [italics added] (as opposed to what *she is going to do with her life*). Her outburst, which is laden with "blame, bitterness, anger, and hostility for her lot in life," further verifies my hypothesis.

As I listen to her rage, I begin to wonder if she is really angry that the group format has not allowed her to vent her feelings as she had hoped. I begin to question if and how I mislead her in the prescreening to think that this group would offer her that type of forum and how I could have thought that she was appropriate for a solution-focused group! I begin to wonder if her behavior in this group is just another example of her attempt to apply more of a poor solution to the relationships in her life—resulting in shallowness with her significant others. In the early years of her marriage, she very likely got her husband to attend to and take care of her by whining and complaining to him. (Isn't it interesting that she married a man nearly 20 years her senior?) Over the years she probably escalated to anger and rage to get his attention until finally he no longer responded. At age 45 she is relatively a young woman to have all four of her children on their own. I speculate whether her behavior hurried their departure from the home. As a result, it is possible that she joined the group as a place for comfort and nurturing. It appears that she is perpetuating a poor solution (an outburst) in an effort to be listened to.

As I listen to her, I am struck by the number of labels and absolutes that she uses: "She claims *no one* seems to care about her anymore. They *all* just seem to be *takers* who *never* give *anything* back. She was tired of giving herself for *nothing* and *not* being appreciated" [italics added]. She accuses Jonathan of *only* caring for his business and that *no one* in his life mattered.

I would break the silence by reframing her absolutes into qualifiers: "Much of the time you feel that the group members aren't listening to you. When is a time you felt listened to in here?" Sandra is likely to answer in one of three ways: (1) by identifying an appropriate time when she was sharing and the group listened to her, (2) by stating that she can't think of any time that the group listened to her, or 3) identifying *this* particular event as a time she felt listened to.

The most productive response would be for her to identify a time when she was sharing appropriately in the group. The group members and I can help her recognize the specific incident as an exception time, a time when the difficulty isn't present. I will ask members to speak directly to her and share with her what it was about that specific time that facilitated their listening to her. We can encourage her to create a solution based on the exception.

If Sandra states that she can't think of a time that the other participants listened to her, it would be easy for the members to cajole her and give her undue attention in an effort to overcome their own discomfort by saying things such as "I listen to you" or "Remember the time. . . ." I would need to ensure that this doesn't happen because it will only encourage Sandra to continue to use whining (a poor solution) in an attempt to get others to listen to her. If Sandra says she can't think of a time that she was listened to, I would need to formulate my questions in a way that will optimize a helpful response. One question that I am likely to ask is, "When is a time you were listened to *just a little bit?*" Again, my goal is to help her identify an exception, an appropriate time when she shared and was listened to. We would then explore what she did differently and use the exception as a possible solution.

The least helpful response would be for Sandra to identify this particular event (her outburst) as a time she was listened to. If she perceives that the *only* way she can get others to listen to her is by having an outburst, then she will continue to employ this solution. In this case, I would ask the members how her outburst affected them. I would encourage them to speak directly to her, although I realize for many of them it may be difficult to talk to such an angry person. Dealing in the here and now can be very effective. Hopefully, Sandra would learn from the members that they are not interested in listening to her when she has an outburst. Through the members' many viewpoints, polyocularity, Sandra could get suggestions about what she can do to get others to listen to her. From their input she can develop a process goal and possible solutions.

Because Sandra's outburst occurred toward the end of the session, we would not likely have time to accomplish all of these strategies. We would need to continue the intervention into the next session. For homework assignment, I would ask Sandra to notice those times when others listen to her. I would specifically ask her to notice what she is saying and doing to get them to listen to her. In future sessions Sandra can have as her goal to share appropriately in an effort to have others listen. I would encourage the members to provide her feedback on her progress in the group. As Sandra becomes successful at getting group members to listen to her in the group, she can carry these successful solutions outside the group into her everyday life.

Although the response to this critical incident seems to focus on Sandra, the situation allows the other members to use the skills on which they are working. Because all are struggling with unfulfilling relationships, many of them likely have as their goal the ability to deal with others more directly. While dealing with Sandra, the group members could exercise their skills and work toward their goals in a rather protected environment.

Systems-Centered Therapy
Implemented by Yvonne Agazarian

SYSTEMS-CENTERED THERAPY (SCT) INTERVENTION

It looks as if it has been almost too difficult for you to bring this very important material into the group. Will you look at me, please? [Making eye contact with someone in deep distress is the first step in establishing a communication with the outside world.] *Let's first of all make space for you to have your feelings without being overwhelmed by them. It may seem too much for you now, but if you notice it is probably difficult for you to breathe properly when you are hunched over like that in your distress.* [Discourages the "victim" posture.] *Let's make room for your feelings and give space inside you for your sobs. Stay in contact with me, please. Where, right now, are you hurting . . . I mean physically?* Where is the pain that you are suffering? Is it your head? Your heart? Your stomach? Put your hand on the place where it hurts most.*

By session 7 of any group, norms are firmly set, and it takes considerable energy to change them. This group has functioned from the beginning to avoid personal communications that convey emotion or confusion. In the sessions 1–3, the group negatively reinforces Francine's attempts to introduce personal disclosure by diverting the topic to outside the group. In session 4, the group negatively reinforces Samuel by behaving as if he has not spoken when he brings in his personal material. In contrast, throughout all six sessions (we have no information how the group consolidated its norms in the fifth), the group has reinforced the norms introduced by Sarah, whose personal disclosures are carefully articulated, and intellectualized and whose basic message is that all is right with the world as long as one does not rock the boat. Once again, the group is manifesting behavior that is typical of the early flight phase in group, where emotion is discouraged and intellectualizations encouraged.

This is the context into which Sandra (a relatively silent member) erupts with a storm of blame, bitterness, and anger, which she directs toward the group who "take" and "never give back." Then turning to Jonathan (who is probably the group's most active flight leader), she accuses him of caring only about his

---

*These are the sequences that occur in the first module of defense modification, called the triad of symptomatic defenses, that reduce the symptoms (anxiety, somatic symptoms, depression, and acting-out), which are the most common presenting problems in therapy.

business and nothing for the people in his life. She is flooded by emotion, and the group is immobilized.

The issue here, for an SCT leader, is not that there is emotional eruption (the group needs an infusion of emotional energy if the intellectualized norms are to be changed) but that the eruption has occurred when there are only 15 minutes of the group hour left to do the work. Fifteen minutes gives plenty of time for the group to reorient itself toward its goals, *providing* Sandra's emotion can be contained.

The following issues are salient: (1) how to contain the individual member without creating an identified patient and (2) how to communicate to the group that not only is her input a valuable resource to the group but also is as strong as it is because she is containing the *group's* emotion as well as her own. The intervention given, as you see, is contingent on being able to contain the member.

If Sandra can be contained, this intervention makes room for subgrouping. Subgrouping would prevent Sandra from consolidating a "containing" role for the group. (Certainly for the group as a whole, her role "contains" the ignored group emotion. However, her outburst into the group has a well-worn feel to it, and it is very possible that she is acting out what she herself cannot contain.)*

If the member cannot be contained, a different sequence of interventions would be appropriate. Three contingency interventions are discussed next.

Contingency Intervention 1: Sandra Can Cooperate

Do you know that everyone in a group is not only a voice for themselves but also for the group. And you are quite right in your feelings that, so far, members here can only manage their pain by keeping as far from it as possible, covering it up by talking about things that don't matter quite so much to them. And you did not take part in this way of avoiding difficulties. So, in a sense, you have been sitting here, containing all your own pain and also the pain of the group. No wonder it erupted in such a geyser. Our work now is to have the group take up some of the pain that you are holding. Francine, I know that in the first three sessions you tried to bring in some of yours but couldn't find a home for it in here. And, Samuel, when you tried to give voice to yours, it was as if no one heard you! Is anyone else in here remembering times in these seven sessions where you had strong feelings but could not find a way to express them?

Before you answer, let us look at our time boundaries. We have ten minutes left of this group—that is not enough time to start work on this issue, but we can prepare ourselves to work next week. Will you please think about the things that you have wanted to say about your personal lives in this group and what it was that stopped you from saying them? You do not have to say anything now, but if anyone does want to say something now, it will give us a head start for our next group.

---

*Being able to locate the physical aspect of experience requires that individuals use their observing self-system; once the observing system is mobilized, individuals are no longer flooding out their cognitive processes and can make choices.

Contingency Intervention 2: Sandra Is Not Aware of Her Physical Self

If Sandra cannot tell us "where it hurts," which would put her more in touch with herself, then it would be important to see if she can contain herself while the group is involved in the issue. The intervention would then continue something like this:

> *Sandra, I am going to talk to the group for a moment, and then I am going to come back to you. Is that all right?*
>
> *Group, every one of you at one time or another have had the experience of feelings that seemed to be bigger than you. When this happens in a group, it is almost always because they are bigger than you—that you are carrying not only your own feelings but also some of the feelings that the group is not yet able to carry.*
>
> *As you look back on the last six sessions, you will see how we have encouraged rational coping and discouraged emotion in our group. Sandra is bringing some of the groups' emotion back into the group, and it probably feels overwhelming to you, too. Our work now is to have the group take up some of the pain that Sandra is holding. Francine, I know that in the first three sessions. . . .* [Continue as above.]

This intervention will work only if Sandra can agree that it is all right for me to address the group. Given the criteria for membership of this group (which is composed of people who can manage their outside lives but not their interpersonal relationships), Sandra will probably say yes. If she says no, then I would respond to her in line with the third contingency intervention.

Contingency Intervention 3: Sandra Becomes Distressed When the Leader Addresses the Group

> *"Sandra, it seems as if what I have said is making things worse rather than better for you—as if I am yet another person who takes from you but gives nothing back and that the group has become just like all the other times in your life when you've given yourself and not been appreciated. Do you feel that all I care about is the group? That's not true, and I am glad that you have been able to bring yourself in and express how bitterly you feel. It's particularly frustrating to be so disappointed in here when disappointments with relationships is the common experience that have brought all our members to this group. So, Sandra, do you see that what you are saying goes straight to the heart of the matter? I suggest that in the last few minutes we have left we make sure that we don't lose what you have said today—and that we make sure that we bring back again next time the disappointments we experience with the group, with each other, and with me.*

The intervention method here addresses the individual member first, the group as a whole second, and the potential subgroup third. This follows some strict SCT principles. No one can do his or her work if he or she is not in a state to work. Therefore, "bringing a member" across the boundary into the here and now is always the first step in an SCT group.

Sandra has been a relatively silent member for seven sessions of the group. When, in the session 7, the group's defenses change from social behavior to personal confrontation, the group context changes. (Socializing is a stereotypic defense in the early flight stage of group development, which defuses group energy into intellectualizations. Confrontation moves the group toward the transition between flight and fight and infuses the group with emotional and potentially aggressive energy.) This shift in group context unbalances Sandra's defensive silence, and she erupts into an externalizing, hostile defense (appropriate to the fight stage!).

The feelings expressed in hostile externalizing defenses are often mistaken for an emotional outburst but are actually generated by thoughts. Thoughts often substitute a cognitively generated experience for the emotional one. By hostile externalizations, people avoid "feeling" their emotions by attributing their discomfort to the outside world, which automatically puts them into a defensive victim-role position.

In psychodynamic therapy this phenomenon is framed as a transferential repetition compulsion (to the schizoid-paranoid position) and interpreted either intrapersonally or interpersonally. In contrast, the systems-centered approach frames it as a problem of boundary permeability* and works to make the boundary permeable between apprehensive knowledge (the information contained in nonverbal sensory/emotional experience) and comprehensive knowledge (comprehensive organizations of information that results from discriminating and integrating information verbally). Apprehension experiences reality; comprehension explains it.

In Sandra's case, her outburst of bitter, blameful hostility is generated from a paranoid explanation of reality that escalates until she is flooded; her common sense is overwhelmed. At this point the group is also overwhelmed and takes on Sandra's initial role of silence and restless fidgeting.

The preceding interventions are designed to follow a systematic sequence that will relocate Sandra inside herself and bring her into awareness of the context of the group (first to restore her ability to observe her self-centered system and then to restore her perception of her self-centered system in a systems-centered context). This is the SCT method that enables members to learn how not to take group process *just* personally.

The sequence of interventions are intended to have the following results. The first intervention is intended to establish eye contact. Eye contact changes the relationship between self and self and introduces the potential of a relationship both with the self and with the other. The question "Where does it hurt?" is intended to establish a connection with the physical self, the source of primary data. (If a person loses the self in contacting the other, relocating the person physically restores the experience of self.) The step after that is intended to undo the relationship between posture and feeling (slouching and victim). Making space for feeling undoes the painful restriction that is a person's at-

---

*Groups "store" differences that they are not yet ready to integrate by creating a "containing" role, which serves as an encapsulated subsystem in the group system, that is then ignored as if the information it contained did not exist.

tempt to control his or her feelings. As soon as a person "makes space," the tension in the muscles change, and the discomfort that comes from constriction is removed. "Sobbing freely" restores contact with the person's authentic emotional experience.

The step of asking "Where does it hurt?" has another function: It both restores the relationship with the self and increases the potential connection to his or her emotion. If Sandra locates her pain in her head, she may be beginning to somatize as a defense, and this defense will have to be undone before the work continues. If she is not somatizing, she may be "coding" her emotional experience (e.g., if she hurts in her heart, she may be closer to experiencing her "heart-breaking" grief; if she hurts in her abdomen, she may be closer to "a belly full of rage").

These contingency interventions will succeed only if Sandra is able to see herself in relationship to the group as well as to herself. Both the first and second contingency interventions are intended to revector the energy both of Sandra and the group. If the first intervention succeeds, then the group as a whole can be relocated inside reality time boundaries with their energy vectored towards the work goal (thus restoring all system levels—member, subgroup, and group as a whole—to the relationship between role, goal, and context). Shifting the focus from a distressed member to the group always carries the potential for a reescalation of distress. If neither the first nor the second intervention succeeds, then the third contingency intervention makes another attempt to reestablish the relationship with Sandra at the personal level. In truth, when an intervention "misses" the person, the person *is* dropped, and it becomes important to reestablish contact on her or his terms.

Predicted consequences are as follows: (1) Sandra's emotion will be contained, (2) the work of getting her centered will introduce a new technique into the group, (3) the group will not project their emotion into her and require her to contain it in the role of identified patient or scapegoat, (4) the group as a whole will recognize the denied emotional component, and (5) different members will pay attention to the driving and restraining forces in themselves and in the group that makes it difficult for them to cross the boundary with both their intellect and emotion.

The most outstanding condition of the incident was the timing of Sandra's emotional input into the group. In contrast to many psychodynamic groups, where unfinished business is left unfinished with the expectation that it will leaven the dough of therapy, SCT encourages members to make the transition from the role of member back into their social role in the last few minutes of group. Such encouragement gives members practice in one of the more difficult aspects of taking social responsibility: awareness that, as the context shift, the goals of the context also shift and so does the role; and that every shift in role requires a shift in the behavior that is appropriate to the role and goal of the context.*

*In *The Visible and Invisible Group* (Agazarian & Peters, 1981), "role" is framed as a bridge between group and individual dynamics: "containing" for the group the differences that the group cannot yet integrate and a regressive acting-out for the individual the split-off and encapsulated role that could not be integrated at the time it was developed.

In SCT this principle is formalized by taking 5 or 10 minutes at the end of group and asking members to notice if anything has surprised them, satisfied them and dissatisfied them and if they discovered anything or learned anything. Surprises tap into information about their experience that they did not expect. Satisfactions and dissatisfactions are the first step in their ability to identify what were driving and restraining forces in their work in that group session. Discovery is the nonverbal insight (apprehension), and learning is insight translated into comprehension.

In this group the principle is introduced indirectly by bringing the group's attention to the realities of its time boundaries,* and by focusing on what can be learned about this session that can serve as work in the next. Such focusing encourages the observing self to think (puts the ego back in control!).

Transactional Analysis

Implemented by Herbert Hampshire

Some elements of this incident that are unrepresentative of a transactional analysis (TA) group and the way it would be set up. TA is a contractual form of therapy, so each person in the group defines a specific problem and related outcome that they and I agree to work toward. Thus, the purpose of the group would never be construed as "to share and perhaps work out . . . barriers. . . ." The TA emphasis on the personal agenda of each member is important in undercutting the normal tendency at the outset to move toward cohesiveness through the identification of more or less superficial similarities. Therapeutic movement is impeded to the degree to which a group member is blocked in experiencing his or her individuality. If individuality is given priority, then the natural similarities of shared emotions and experiences become supportive. Where the order is reversed, the similarities work to block individuation and depth.

Another basis for focusing on individual and specific contracts is the emphasis on personal responsibility. Each person is led to a recognition that he or she is in a group for his or her own *purpose* and is responsible, with the therapist, for achieving that *purpose*. The only responsibility each has to other group members is to recognize that any interpersonal situation involves some resources (such as time) that are finite and others (such as support, assistance, and love) that *appear* limited. It is essential to structure the group situation to

---

*Boundaries are both intrapersonal and interpersonal. When someone is flooding with emotion, the boundaries between the emotional and cognitive subsystems (or subgroups) are too permeable, and emotion threatens to swamp the system. It is therefore important to restore an appropriate permeability between emotion and cognition. This is done by mobilizing the "observing self-system," which, somewhat like an observing ego, can collect data about the intrapersonal system, as a step toward the person being able to see themselves in context: a sort of bird's-eye view of their self-centered system, first, and of their self-centered system in a systems-centered context, second. SCT engages the observing self-system by encouraging the person to recognize the difference between thinking and emotion. Emotion involves physiology and is not verbal; thinking involves cognition and is verbal. (Feelings are generated by both emotional and cognitive experience, and SCT members learn to discriminate feelings that are related to emotion, feelings that are generated by thoughts, and feelings that are generated by both.)

allow each person to recognize and move beyond his or her programming, which impels them to "be nice," "take turns," or "let others talk when they are dealing with problems that are important or more upsetting." All these programmatic constraints result in people living in unfulfilled ways, experiencing deprivation, and building up feelings of futility and resentment toward an ungiving world. Allowing each person to be responsible for himself or herself enables the development of an orientation toward others that comes out of a mature, autonomous recognition of "the way the world works" (e.g., the realization that not everyone can get assistance simultaneously).

One of the outcomes of this difference in "set" created by TA is that sessions 1–3 of this group would not have been spent "establishing acquaintanceships." My most frequent opening for a group session is, "Who has something they want to work on?" Someone begins to deal with an issue of personal significance, and any attempt to move into idle conversation is identifiable as defensively motivated pastiming and begins to reveal how people relate to important issues in their lives. The group process is thus used rather than fostered.

A difference that is more structural is the use of 1 hour for a group of eight. Eric Berne's rule of thumb was to allow time equivalents(s) of 15 minutes multiplied by the number of members. A group of six would meet for $1\frac{1}{2}$ hours and a group of eight for 2 hours. This ostensibly minor point has broad significance, in the sense that the therapist is literally responsible for the "reality" existing for the group. If structural properties of the therapy situation are in fact productive of negative emotional outcomes, such as deprivation or frustration, it is difficult for individuals to discover and move beyond how they unwittingly set up situations in ways that deprive or frustrate them. A situation that does not work actually reinforces a life script that is based on the conclusion that life and relationships do not work.

By session 7, I would have made a number of interventions to alter the interpersonal gestalt of that session. I would have commented on Francine's pattern of early self-disclosure and on the various patterns of moving away. If I had the sense that Francine was actually "coming on too strong" as an unwitting way of driving people away, I might have explored the possibility that she was revealing her script mechanism and replaying an early childhood circumstance. I would explore, for example, whether she had a remote father who, like Jonathan, escaped emotion by tending to business and whether her mother dealt with personal frustration by pushing Francine toward her father. Mother's behavior would effectively pressure father into distancing behavior, thus reinforcing mother's unconscious decision that getting anything from men is hopeless. It would also implicitly "instruct" Francine in the futility of relating to others, especially men. In addition, it would demonstrate how to keep that kind of decision looking like a "truth" about the world. We would have shifted away from Francine's "content" about herself to a focus on her feelings about the responses she was getting in the here and now from individuals in the group.

It would have been possible to use Francine's revelations or other members' contributions to focus on the ways in which the interpersonal situation of the group re-creates the family dynamics in which their programming was formed and script decisions were made. Sarah might have been led to see how she has always "had" to keep things on an even keel and how intellectualizing and "being reasonable" blocks her from any deep, meaningful contact with others, including her husband. Samuel might have been encouraged to see how he empathizes with Francine when she seems to be working toward opening up and relating, yet with little success. He could use her behavior to see how he also does "what he's supposed to" and ends up feeling victimized by others' lack of responsiveness. Because he is so removed from his own anger at others, he might be able to see its existence by focusing on how Francine must feel.

There is a sense of choreography in group transactions in which the therapist is able to focus people on what they see and react to in others. Through this choreography they are led to relate to each other and the therapist in ways that are inconsistent with their own programming and script. Constantly being sought is a way to shift the context of transacting so that the affective experience underlying relating no longer reinforces the script but produces more authentic and autonomous functioning. Cathecting a different ego-state, identifying an unconscious game setup, or producing an encounter that is contradictory to a script decision is always in the service of effecting this "contextual shift," the mechanism of therapeutic change.

One of the main differences that would occur in the group if conducted as a TA group relates to Sandra, who would not have been supported in remaining inactive for so long. I might, as a matter of fact, have encouraged Francine to speak directly to Sandra. My purpose would have been to draw Sandra out, to increase the probability of Francine being responded to directly, and to allow Sandra to discover how she feels about people who, unlike her, are able to speak up for themselves and go after responses from others more directly. I might also have simply noted that she seems to be having difficulty getting what she came in for.

Given a different time frame, the circumstance described might occur. Sandra might manage, particularly if there were enough happening of therapeutic value, to play out her passivity and to remain silent for the better part of one or two sessions. That would occur, most likely, if these were her initial sessions in an open-ended, ongoing group and she were being given a chance to "ease herself" into working.

One of the first things I am aware of is the time, noting that only 15 minutes remain. Within the therapy situation, time is the equivalent of reality, and my purpose is to make sure that optimal functioning occurs *within* reality and is not blocked by reality. It is not therapeutic, for example, to end the group with Sandra so upset that, functionally, she does not have an available Adult ego-state. That would be the equivalent of allowing the group members to "discover" that letting yourself feel things deeply ends with negative, if not destructive, consequences.

I would be noticing that Sandra's nonverbal behavior had been indicating her emotional responsiveness to the group. Noticing this behavior suggests that her feelings and reactions are likely to be related directly to script issues. The group situation always replicates at an emotional level the conflicts that a person experiences "on the outside." When someone resists getting effectively involved and talks about things outside the immediate situation, the way

Jonathan and Franklin do, we know they are resisting the involvement that would trigger the experience of the underlying conflict.

Most important, I would be diagnosing Sandra's ego-state. If she is in a Critical Parent ego-state, I would know I am seeing a picture of a parental influence that she dealt with as a child, probably her mother. I would then look for the Child feeling that was too frightening to experience directly and that led her, internally, to "run to her Parent" for protection and for a solution. If she is in an Adapted Child ego-state, then I would know that she is manifesting game behavior that reveals the nature of the underlying script. My hypothesis would be that she is in a racket because an emotional racket is by nature exploitative and the group members provide ample evidence that they have been effectively thrown into a guilty silence, feeling accused for not having given Sandra something that she had not been asking for. My guess would be that Sandra is programmed to do things for others and ends up depriving herself and then falling into an angry, resentful, accusatory racket, which results in giving herself sympathy and the implicit demand that others express sorrow over the deprivation and guilt over their insensitivity.

I would be diagnosing the others' ego-states, particularly Jonathan's because he has been specifically invited by Sandra both to feel guilty and to become more directly related. Therapy always occurs in relation to the Child, shifting the executive function from Adapted Child and Parent to Natural Child and Adult. If I see someone in a Parent ego-state, I want either to get at the underlying Child feeling or to wait until their ego-state has shifted. To invite someone in group to transact from a Parent ego-state is to pull for conflict or adaptation. If Jonathan is in his Parent state, he may accuse Sandra in retaliation and criticize her behavior. If he is in his Child state, it may be very therapeutic to get him to express his hurt feelings when Sandra accuses him of being insensitive to her.

I am also aware that if I do something that "takes care of" Sandra's upset and defuses her effect, I would run the danger of communicating to the members that intense feelings are "Not Okay" and should be suppressed and that when things seem to get out of hand I will rescue the group and handle the situation.

Thus, I would be likely to say something to Sandra, such as "I'm glad you're letting people know that you are wanting to be related to. How about letting someone know directly how you want them to respond to your feelings right now." This intervention would stroke Sandra for participating and would also let others in the group know they are not to blame for Sandra's plight and need not become immobilized by guilt.

In all likelihood, Sandra's response would be to respond directly to me, saying something like, "I just want them to understand that I have feelings, too," at which point I would suggest that she speak directly to Jonathan. Jonathan, as well as the other group members, would thus be released from paralysis and could begin the process of relating to Sandra's feelings and to the feelings generated by Sandra's blaming and challenging the members. I would likely end the session by encouraging Sandra to take the initiative in the next meeting and to talk about her feelings. I would also acknowledge that the other members had important feelings to explore in future sessions.

By demonstrating Sandra's characteristic patterns of relating and emotional responding in the here and now, this incident allows for the beginning of therapeutic analysis. Through identifying the sources of patterns in her past and seeing how she unwittingly participates in setting up situations that keep them intact, she can begin to experience options that avoid them. As other people transact with her, more of their patterns will emerge and be identified, analyzed, and altered.

Theoretical Practitioners' Congruence With Their Theory

CLIENT-CENTERED THERAPY

What behaviors, which were stimulated by this incident, might we expect our TP to engage in? Given the intensity of Sandra's emotional discharge, we look for behaviors reflecting therapist transparency, empathy, validation of Sandra, acceptance of Sandra, individual feedback to Sandra, and trusting group members to offer help. Once again, we expect to see evidence of his considering the three variables: external, group, and therapist.

The first we hear from our TP is when he discloses to us his self-talk, his first reaction to the incident. By being in touch with his feelings of the moment, he says he has a better sense of what the members may also be experiencing. In effect, he draws on the universality of human experience to a given stimulus or event that allows members to be joined together (i.e., makes them similar). He also lets us know that by being wholly present (human) he is less caught up in being role bound as a therapist. His open response to Sandra is one of understanding and empathy. By being with her, he is validating her; it is unconditional recognition of her as a human being. He also wants to draw help from the group as a whole by first building a "community," thereby divesting himself as being the seat of wisdom and allowing for members to share in the leadership. Because interpretation and analysis are not reinforced but feedback and self-disclosure are, members are then more likely to feel the urgency to be responsible for the group's direction. We hear our TP tell us he would listen closely and reflect Sandra's message to her in order to help "clear away the clutter of her feelings." We also learn that our TP is hopeful for the transfer of learning to take place (group member variable) so that the self-mastery members have acquired through the group experience will help them deal with similar experiences outside the group.

COGNITIVE–BEHAVIORAL THERAPY

Among the key concepts we were exposed to was that of learning. It is the position of cognitive–behavioral therapy (CBT) that all behavior is learned. Therefore, we can expect our TP to analyze Sandra's and other group members' behaviors. We might expect our TP to reinforce some behaviors and discourage others. We also want to see if our TP is monitoring member behaviors and how he addresses them. In this case we particularly want to see if he attempts to strengthen and equalize Sandra's participation by the way he deals with group structure. Finally, given the nature of this incident, let us see the attention our TP gives to pretraining of group members.

Once again, we are informed that this incident would be highly unlikely to occur in a CBT group. Explaining why it would not happen helps us learn that our TP would have used the pretraining period to have helped Sandra state clearly what she wished to change. He also tells us that, because of the group's structure, Sandra would have had to read her problem card. Though he dismisses the likelihood of this event ever occurring in a CBT group, he does see therapists disapproving of the behavior in which the group as a whole had engaged. The group had not listened to Samuel. Through their disapproval, therapists would be attending to the here and now. They also would address group procedures, which means the group would have to be more responsible and cooperative. In addition, the group had not been modeling helpful behavior and to some extent had been engaging in the very behavior that they needed to change (i.e., the behavior that brought them to the group). Certainly, our TP's intervention would eventually lead to building group cohesion. Sandra was reinforced for her courage. She had modeled behavior that perhaps was consistent with her problem card and certainly consistent with what the TP wishes the other members to follow. Our TP's focus on the avoidance behavior of the group as a whole is intended to break the avoidance cycle. Notice, this is done by having the members monitor themselves and then dialogue with one another regarding Sandra's statement. Thus, group interaction and responsible behavior was being encouraged.

FAMILY-CENTERED THERAPY

The nature of this incident might pose as an interesting event for family-centered therapy (FCT). Much as with some of the others we have studied, FCT is very interactive. The therapist's role is an active one, so we expect our TP to participate and offer process observations. We expect him to be the celebrant, go-between, and side taker at any given moment. We also expect to see him engaging in any or all of the seven skill areas ascribed to FCT therapists.

As our TP, with emphasis, explains why this incident would not have occurred under his leadership, we are made aware that his reasons include clearly stated goals and purposes for forming the group. Furthermore, he would have engaged the group through use of structured exercises. Sandra's age would have precluded her membership in the group because she was at a much different developmental stage than the other members, vis-à-vis her marriage and family. Our TP is quick to note Sandra's chronological age at marriage and with some simple arithmetic determines she may have possibly missed some developmental stages in her maturation process. The integratedness of various modalities is clear at this point, including an emphasis on family theory.

From a group therapy perspective, he is concerned with the contagion effect Sandra's disclosure will have upon the group and her emotional well-being. His intervention includes supporting her, offering her empathy, and using the group to provide her support. Interestingly, our TP adds that deep disclosures likely do occur at or near the end of sessions. He would recompose the member and the group and ask that the issue be presented at the next session. Thus, he is adhering to the group therapist's task of group maintenance.

Gestalt Therapy

A central construct in Gestalt therapy is for individuals to be aware of their feelings as they are occurring both in relation to themselves and in relation to others. Sandra's emotions are housed in much intensity. We want to see the extent to which our TP addresses this aspect of the incident. We want to see if she models effective living, if she is integrated, and if she takes responsibility for what is her part in this incident. Finally, we want to learn how she helps the members behave responsibly.

Our TP sees Sandra's pronouncement and denouncement of others as something that was to be welcomed and overdue. She refers to the Gestalt principle of contact and that perhaps there may have even been some risk for Sandra in her action. Our TP observes that Sandra's behavior not only as being in contact with herself but also as making contact with other members. This means she reached out to others and left the individualized state that she had been occupying for 6 weeks. Furthermore, our TP was willing to take ownership for the group's current state: "I have colluded in the noncontact atmosphere and, as leader, have contributed a lot toward setting up the apparent group expectation of 'hands-off,' which is a burlesque of the existential belief in self-determinism."

Take notice of our TP's way of listening and *focusing* on the behavior of individual members. She wants to encourage Sandra to be specific with her confrontation. Our TP focuses on Sandra's breathing, how she supports herself physically, and if she can support herself by what she knows. Our TP then plans to focus on Jonathon and eventually each of the others in the same way. The objective is to help them all be congruent (integrated) and self-reliant (responsible).

Individual Psychology

This is session 7, so we expect our TP to have taught members the fundamental principles of individual psychology by this point. So, we look to our TP to not only model Adlerian theory but also use interventions that will help members act according to those principles.

Our TP tells us that individual psychology's purposeful, functional view of behavior and emotions should have taken hold by this stage in the group. Thus, he opts to wait out the group. By choosing not to openly acknowledge the emotionally intense tone of the group, he hopes to appeal to the group members' intellect through his model, direct instruction, or both. This strategy appears to be most pronounced in the way he draws our attention to the fact that he is less interested in terminating on an emotionally positive note but is more concerned with teaching group members the ways to engage in purposeful behavior. Furthermore, our Adlerian TP "ups the ante" by purposefully engaging in a behavior that "teaches" the intended lesson. If his final intervention with Sandra appears paradoxical, it should, for Adlerian therapists are masters of paradoxical intervention.

Interpersonal Psychotherapy

As we consider our interpersonal psychotherapy TPs' management of this moment, keep in mind that therapist roles and techniques include culture building, activating the here and now, and attending to process. We have reached a point in our own development as students to understand that curative factors will be present. How and if our TPs consider them are of interest to us. Finally, we know that feedback and viewing the group as a social microcosm are standard fare for interpersonal psychotherapy.

Our TPs tell us that as part of their role, which is group maintenance, they would not have allowed 6 weeks to have passed without acknowledging Sandra. She was communicating through her nonverbal behaviors. Therefore, they would have intervened sooner. Even so, they are still willing to pick up where the incident places them. Once again, they engage in a maintenance intervention intended to support Sandra by offering her empathy and avoiding the possibility of her dropping out as a group casualty. Having supported Sandra, our TPs are also aware the group is in equal need of support, and they provide it by illuminating what happened and normalizing such occurrences. By so doing, our TPs also address process. They inform us that a number of group factors—such as stage of development and cohesion (i.e., weak bonds)—were considerations that influenced their intervention. Notice, though, that they view the incident as a nodal event in the group's history and believe that much more will be learned by the members. Further emphasis of the interpersonal dimension occurs when our TPs "carefully elicit feedback from the members" so that Sandra might learn about the affect she had on others. This form of consensual validation (curative factor) can be most powerful. The notion that the group is a social microcosm receives attention when our TPs suggest that Sandra's "experience in the group is indeed a reenactment of disappointing relationships or attempts at relationships. . . ." Finally, we are reminded that this event will have so affected other members that our TPs anticipate conflict, and its resolution will continue to receive focus. We are reminded, therefore, that group history will be very much a part of the here-and-now experience in future sessions and consequently cannot be ignored by our TPs. This focus is consistent with their theory.

Psychodynamic Therapy

The degree of intensity in the emotional pronouncement made by Sandra suggests to us that, of all the theories we have discussed, this incident would be greeted most favorably by our psychodynamic therapy TP, for a number of reasons. Sandra's outburst (behavior and emotional state) reflects the basic psychodynamic premise that all behavior and thought have purpose and are connected. The same can be said regarding the group as a whole. Recall that we said, that no matter how outlandish, behavior can be traced to insulating the person from pain and the task of the therapist is to empower the individual(s) through insight to more effectively manage the unconscious conflict between id, ego, and superego. This incident suggests that at least the two key concepts of regression and resistance may be operating, so we want to see how our TP intervenes. We might observe him employing interpretation, working through, allowing for ambiguity to continue, the here-and-now principle, and process.

We first observe what is not addressed, and understandably so. Our TP makes no mention of the low profile of the therapist. Thus, we can deduce that therapist behavior in this incident is consistent with psychodynamic therapy. We also learn that the rather unstructured nature of the group also fits the psychodynamic view. In both observations, the element of ambiguity is maintained in order to heighten anxiety. Recall, psychodynamic theory holds that only through the heightening of anxiety can unconscious processes be reached. It is no small wonder, then, that our TP believes that the "group has been moving along very nicely." He makes a subtle reference to stage of group development when he tells us that the level of group conversation should change as early as session 7. Thus, he attends to group-as-a-whole development. He also attends to process—that is, the motive behind Sandra's choosing to disclose near the end of the session—and views it is an unconscious protection against confronting the thing she and the others most want and fear.

Our TP's intervention does little to lessen the heightened anxiety level of group members. Not extending group time to deal with the incident *is* an intervention (i.e., to not do something *is* doing something). He employs the principle that group process is continual, which is the equivalent of all thoughts and feelings are connected over time. Therefore, he observes that Sandra's outburst at the end of the session was not a chance happening, meaning it has a history, is occurring now, and will continue into the future. Consequently, our TP's decision to end by telling the group it "will continue this next week" reflects the foregoing principle while still encouraging the maintenance of the affect level Sandra and the other group members had reached.

RATIONAL–EMOTIVE–BEHAVIORAL THERAPY

By this point in all of our reading, we have good reason to expect that this group event does not represent an REBT group, nor does the therapist's behavior. If the basic principles and concepts of REBT had been presented at the beginning of the group, Sandra, the group as a whole, and the therapist would have behaved differently. We would have expected the therapist to behave more actively and be more visible, periodically instructing the A-B-C-D-E construct and modeling the REBT approach to living. Paradoxically, however, we expect that this incident may provide the format for our TP to clearly demonstrate all these expectations.

With a certain degree of gratification, we learn that our suspicions are valid. Our TP immediately takes the group leader to task and proceeds to inform us why this event would not have occurred in his group. He quickly models the principles of REBT; in fact, he employs them on himself! He also moves very quickly in establishing rapport with his members who will sustain the confrontation they will eventually face. These objectives are achieved through instruction of basic REBT principles. In some respects we became his group members. He attacks our irrationality by allowing us to be privy to his innermost thoughts as they relate to his interpretation of each situation. We are challenged about how we might employ ourselves as a group therapist. For example, how many of us would openly state to our group members that our predecessor (previous therapist) was ineffective and the preceding sessions were wasteful? Perhaps we might have thought it but would not have considered stating it out loud. As we continue, we find our TP makes efforts to help members see how they are responsible for behaviors that evolve from unrealistic (irrational) directives, which ultimately lead to dysfunction. Our TP does not hesitate to be a living example of the person who follows the percepts of REBT.

REALITY THERAPY

As we watch our reality therapy TP's initial approach to this incident, we are reminded of a number of reality therapy principles and therapist roles and techniques that neither the therapist nor the group members represented. For instance, we see the lack of therapist involvement, and neither commitment nor positive, responsible behavior is evident from the therapist and members. The key concepts of the need to feel worthwhile and engaging in denial appear to be evident. Therefore, we can expect that our reality therapy TP will attempt to address each of these as he intervenes on this moment in the group.

We would expect nothing less of our TP than to make contact (become involved) with group members. He makes this his first order of business as he sets out to build a meaningful relationship with the members. By asking members to evaluate their behaviors and identify their concerns, he encourages them to develop positive, responsible behavior. He also works to identify a group concern in order to facilitate commitment through shared experiences and goals. The here and now receives focus, to hold members accountable for behaviors in which they are presently engaged. We witness how our TP becomes involved with Sandra. He does so by reinforcing her (helping her feel worthwhile) and then committing to work with her, provided he can help her commit to working through her concern. He encourages group member involvement (contact) by drawing from Sarah and Francine. He also notes that Sandra's current behavior in the group may also reflect how she has been with her family. This leads him to let us know how her age differential may have a here-and-now effect upon the others (e.g., the other members are the age of her college-graduated children). He makes her feel worthwhile by reframing her role in the group so that she may be viewed as a resource advocate, which in turn may help her be seen as an asset in her family.

Our TP informs us that he needs to take responsibility for the group ending on time. He does this by reinforcing the role Sandra is to take in the group and encouraging her to be helpful to Jonathon. His assigning Sarah the responsibility for the next session will reinforce her sense of feeling worthwhile. We see how he tries to facilitate everyone's involvement and witness his commitment to be involved with Francine and Janet.

SOLUTION-FOCUSED THERAPY

We are interested to find how our solution-focused therapy (SFT) TP approaches this incident because a number of pieces to this event strike us as not likely to occur in an SFT group. For example, members are permitted to focus on what they have not been successful at doing, and the leader neither helps members look for exceptions nor emphasizes such group processes as member-to-member interaction and getting acquainted. The leader does not use group therapy factors such as instillation of hope and cohesiveness. We also note that the leader in the incident, while encouraging members to seek solutions, does not invite feedback nor attends to making certain that language is clear so that absolutist or that categorical thinking is avoided. We expect that our TP's intervention will reflect her consideration of these concerns.

From the beginning, our TP attends to how language is used. She tells us that she reads Sandra's silence as conveying that Sandra had at least shared some things, including what she wants to change, her progress goal, and weekly updates. We also learn that our TP would have employed some sort of structured exercise designed to encourage member-to-member interaction that would facilitate group cohesiveness. Our TP asks the question of how Sandra could have gotten past her during the prescreening; she allows us to be privy to her assessment of Sandra, as well as the prescreening activity she will employ to address Sandra now. Our TP's self-talk addresses Sandra's absolutist talk (behavior), and she is persistent and insistent to have Sandra find a single moment, no matter how small, when she felt listened to. Thus, our TP employs the technique that tries to have a member identify *exceptions* to an absolutist view. Notice that even if Sandra chooses her outburst as the moment to enter the group, our TP, rather than reinforcing that, plans to turn to the group and use the power of feedback (the group process of consensual validation) to help Sandra learn about herself and find suggested solutions. We also learn of our TP's concern for terminating the group on time. Knowing that Sandra's and the group's work cannot be completed in the time remaining, our TP assigns Sandra homework that will have her practicing the exception position and then bringing to the group what she has learned about how her words and ways of behaving got others to listen to her. Here again, focus and reinforcement are on the member's strengths and abilities to find solutions to her problem.

SYSTEMS-CENTERED THERAPY

We find that from an SCT perspective this incident raises our awareness of virtually all of SCT's concepts: functional subgrouping, apprehension, comprehension, boundarying, phases of group development, centering, vectoring, partnership treatment plan, and resonance. How our TP will attend to them will be of interest, as well as seeing how she follows the three leader tasks.

Right from the start, our TP works to establish her partnership with Sandra. Because she has done this, she helps Sandra become centered, which involves vectoring energy toward her psychophysiological "center" in order to gain access to her apprehensive understanding of her relationship to her self and in the context of the group as a whole. Remember that centering, we are told, increases boundary permeability between what we know through our experiencing and feeling (apprehension) and what we know cognitively through words (comprehension). Our TP strives to contain Sandra's energy in order to help her reach a balance between comprehension and apprehension. She also employs eye contact as a means for moving Sandra from a complete self-focus to outside of self by being with our TP.

Our TP lets us know she is aware of the group's phase of development. Attending to the phase of group development will also influence her choice of intervention, because any stage of individual member or group development, cannot be skipped. Concurrently, we hear her refer regularly to the importance of containing Sandra's emotion. This focus on containment is intended to have Sandra increase her sense of herself by staying in resonance with herself until she can resonate with other group members. In other words, our TP wants Sandra to first experience congruence with herself (i.e., internal feelings) before she attempts experiencing an emotional congruence with her subgroup and the group as a whole. Currently, our TP sees her as containing the group's emotion as well as her own, which is partially the reason for her feeling and being so overwhelmed. Our TP works to have Sandra contain her own emotion first. Once Sandra has managed to be contained, we learn subgrouping can occur, which means that Sandra and the other group members can then address either side of the split.

We are also shown three contingency interventions if the member cannot be contained. The first is designed to move out into the group to shift the focus from Sandra to the group as a whole, and the second is to reestablish the partnership between her and our TP.

The third intervention would move to contain the energy in the group, provided Sandra agrees to allowing that to happen. We learn that our TP anticipates the possibility that Sandra may renege on her deal; therefore, our TP will have to reestablish her partnership and have Sandra in a position to contain the energy that is hers.

TRANSACTIONAL ANALYSIS

TA emphasizes behavior that is in the present. Thus, we expect that focus will be on what can be seen and heard. With this in mind, we want to see how our TP addresses this incident. We want to keep in mind TA's four views of life, the ways in which members seek to gain strokes, how scripts are played out, and member ego-states. We also want to see how our TP attends to the four forms of group processes.

We first learn from our TP that some aspects of this incident are not representative of a TA group. His interventions address structural concerns. He would have made certain that a clear contract with each member was established, the purpose of the group would have been changed to meet the needs of the individual, and individual responsibility taking would have been emphasized. He also tells us that this group has not enough time allotted to work. He says that this structural impediment will only serve to reinforce life scripts that "life and relationships do not work." He notes that the group is engaged in pastiming (i.e., looking for ways of gaining strokes). He lets us know that he would have addressed each individual differently and certainly would not have allowed any to have gone unacknowledged by him. Time plays a crucial part for him because it represents reality. He tells us that to end the group with Sandra not having access to an Adult ego-state would not only be countertherapeutic for her but also convey counterproductive messages to other members. He initiates a diagnosis of Sandra's ego-state at this moment and then hypothesizes that she is in a racket. However, before he determines his intervention, he diagnoses the ego-states of each of the other members. He allows us to hear his thoughts and concerns as he anticipates the consequences of his intervention. He takes into consideration the effect it will have on the other members. When he finally decides, he lets us know his plan is to stroke Sandra, while letting the members know they are okay and are blame free for Sandra's current emotional state. His plan is to have Sandra take responsible action for herself by initiating the next session. He expects to do the same with all the others. By his own admission, he will have identified, analyzed, and altered their patterns of behavior—how typical of TA therapy.

Theory Evaluation Form

1. Which theoretical practitioner do you most resemble? Why?

2. Which theoretical practitioner do you least resemble? Why?

3. What does your response to Question 1 tell you about yourself and your leadership style as a potential or present group therapist?

4. What does your response to Question 2 tell you about yourself and your leadership style as a potential or present group therapist?

5. After rereading how the theoretical practitioner of your choice responded to the incident, how would you modify your response?

CHAPTER EIGHTEEN

A Member Maintains Distance

In this situation the theoretical practitioners examine the ways of dealing with a group in which one member sets himself apart from the rest of the group. There are a number of ways to interpret the individual's behavior. Similarly, there are numerous ways to interpret the behavior of the other group members.

Critical Incident 6

This is a group of four women and three men. During your pregroup interview sessions, you discovered that all members had expressed a personal concern over their inability to be assertive. This prompted you to offer them an opportunity to deal with the issue in a group setting. The members are briefly described as follows:

> **Francie** is 35 years old and married. Her husband drives trailer trucks for long-distance hauling. She has two teenage daughters. When she first met with you, she explained that she had the primary responsibility of raising her children. She is having difficulty dealing with her parenting role and wants more active support from her husband.
>
> **Kathy** is 28 years old and employed as a librarian. She lives at home with her parents, both of whom are in their 70s. She is the youngest of five siblings. She would like to live a life of her own but feels obligated to take care of her parents. This situation has also caused her much consternation in other areas of her personal and professional life.
>
> **Michele** is 42 years old and has been married for 22 years. She has disclosed her dissatisfaction with spending the rest of her life as a homemaker, but

she has been under considerable pressure from her husband and children to remain at home.

Jackie is 30 years old, lives apart from her husband, and has custody of their 6-year-old son. Jackie is employed as an executive secretary for a large corporation. The job demands that she be decisive and work independently. She is experiencing a great deal of anxiety because her new boss has not acknowledged her abilities or defined her responsibilities, yet she fears confronting him. It seems this symptom is also appearing in other phases of her life, particularly with her husband.

Troy is 36 years old, single, and presently employed as a senior high school science teacher. He has tried, on a number of occasions, to obtain an administrative position and not succeeded. He says he seems and feels very inept at expressing himself, especially in areas where he must compete or take a stand on what he believes.

Jim is 28 years old, and has recently married. He sought you out because he feels he has always been taken advantage of; this is especially true with significant others in his life. He is very upset with himself for not being able to say *no* when others ask him to do things for them.

Joe is 33 years old and has been married for 6 years. A foreman at a local brewery, he has expressed discontent with himself and his job. He says he does not know whether he is "fish or fowl." His subordinates demand one thing of him and his superordinates another. He feels as though he must serve two masters.

This is session 7, and there has been a great deal of disclosure on the part of all members except Joe. In previous sessions, whenever the others would share their concern about being unable to speak out on their rights or their own mind, Joe would insist that he had no such problems. Now, it is the middle of the session, and the group has been grappling with the difficulty of holding different opinions and taking a personal stand on important issues. Joe again states that this is not the case for him. He no sooner completes his statement when the entire group attacks him and accuses him of not being honest. Jackie leads the attack by stating that people such as him scare her and that if she could she would not have anything to do with that kind of person. Jim follows by offering that he has taken some big risks in saying some of the things about himself; it is people like Joe who takes advantage of such information and makes it hard for Jim to be his own person. The interaction gains intensity, and the more the others accuse Joe, the more he states that he has no problems. This in turn only serves to increase their attack. Throughout this exchange, Joe has given no clues about how this whole series of events has affected him.

Client-Centered Therapy
Implemented by William R. Coulson

The group is working on Joe, and I am tempted to join in. I think I see an opening. He is saying he has none of the problems of the others—yet he wanted to join an assertiveness group. "Okay, Joe, why did you join the group if you don't have these problems?"

I don't say it.

I think of other ways to make Joe humble ("I think Joe wants our attention"), but again resist.

I never like it when I am argumentative, and I never like it when the group is working on somebody and I join in. It is tempting, to be sure. There is something Joe cannot see but that everybody else apparently can. Each, in turn, wants a crack at straightening him out. We are having a contest to see who can make Joe confess.

Working on somebody like that wastes group time. In that sense, Joe disrupts the group. My tendency when such things happen is to wait them out. I have said before that the leaders have a good deal of initial authority because of their title. If they do not play games, such as "Let's fix Joe," such activities tend to run out of gas on their own.

If group members persist in going after Joe, I might ask one of them about it: "It sounds like you want to get Joe to confess." And if the member agrees with me, I might say something like, "I thought so. I felt that way myself, until I realized we could have a group without having to make Joe the same as us." Maybe if Joe sees what a group is, he will want to join in. Maybe it just takes him longer than 7 weeks to feel safe.

By and large, I like to go around disruption. Dealing with it directly can add to the disruption: We are fighting over fighting. I have seen groups that were very slow to develop because they spent so much time arguing about how to be a good group. I would rather see if we can come to it without talking about it. I would trust it more if we discovered it rather than ordered it.

If we went on with the group without requiring Joe to confess, I think we just might find him joining in later. Generally, people do not change because of attack; they dig in and defend themselves.

"If sharing problems is a good thing to do, Joe will come around to it." That would be my attitude. I would also have considerable curiosity about Joe. I would assume he had joined the group for a good, even pressing reason, and I would find it interesting that he did not seem to want to reveal it. I might make a date with him (maybe just inside my own mind) to discuss this in the future, when the pressure is off. But I would not push it, even then. As far as I am concerned, he never has to tell. Sometimes people who participate very little say later that they got a lot out of the group. I believe them.

When I give in and push people, it is sometimes for my own sake. I want them to know I do good work. I make them cooperate so that I can help them. I would want to try to avoid doing this with Joe, or with anybody. I have made more mistakes in the name of "helping" people than in the name of being patient.

I can reach some people in therapy groups but not others. Some I cannot reach because I do not like them. I think I would like Joe, however. I would like his orneriness. In fact, I might say, "I kind of like your stubbornness, Joe. You seem like you're not going to let anybody make you say you're different than you want to be." That I cannot reach everybody in my groups does not matter at all if other members can reach them. Usually, someone in the group will be able to get through.

Cognitive–Behavioral Therapy
Implemented by John V. Flowers

This incident presents an area where behavioral group therapy greatly differs from the model represented in the incident. Behavioral group therapists would never face this problem because disclosure about assertive problems would not occur in a traditional group circle where people talk or not as the impulse struck them. Assertion training is one of the earliest contributions of behavior therapy to the group therapy literature, and it is titled "training" because the effective methodology proved to be psychoeducational, not merely group discussion.

What seems to have happened in this group is that the therapist's assumption that these members share a common assertion problem is agreed to by every member but Joe. The therapist has then placed Joe in this group without clearly specifying what theme the group is focused on. A skills-training group is no place to attempt problem recognition and attitude change. If Joe is not ready to acknowledge and change his assertion (presuming the therapist is correct), this group is not the place for him. Pretherapy discussion and a pretherapy contract should have either resulted in Joe ruling himself out of the group or in his tentative acknowledgment that assertion might be a problem he could work on.

Behavioral skills-training groups give homework. A common assignment for a group like this would be to keep track of any statements each client felt he or she should say during the week that were difficult or impossible to accomplish. Examples of requests, refusal expressions, giving or getting criticism, and giving or getting compliments would be shared in session 1, to help with the assignment. Role playing would occur from session 2 on. If Joe did not comply with homework assignments or avoided role play, it would be clear long before session 7. One therapist would have already discussed this with Joe privately, to determine what he wished to do.

If the incident as specified occurred, one therapist would go to Joe's aid by encouraging him to continue the interaction. The other therapist would slow down the group by asking, "Was what you just said assertive?" to any member who criticized Joe. The mass attack on Joe is an example of nonassertive behavior, a live example that can be used in the group to help with the training. Joe can be encouraged to learn how to defend himself when under attack. The group can be taught to assertively (not aggressively) ask for what they want. In an assertion-training group, the members would have already been coached by the therapists in role plays. A therapist intervening to elicit a more assertive and appropriate response would be seen as normal for the group.

Given that Joe is not alexithymic, which if true should have ruled him out of any assertion-training group, he does not seem to code or disclose emotions easily. Inspection of and practice in expressing even low-level emotions is part of assertion training. With his agreement, Joe's next homework assignment could be identification of any feeling experienced during the week, which he can share with the group. This assignment recasts the problem into a skill-based as opposed to resistance-based issue, which invariably diffuses the attack. Behavioral group assertion training works well precisely because the incident posed does not occur. Assertion is best taught in a collaborative skill-training model. Joe is clearly not yet a collaborator, and the group is discussing assertion—not role-playing how to be more assertive, less anxious, and more self-reinforcing. Both lead to the incident that should not occur in a group with assertion identified as the therapeutic goal.

Family-Centered Therapy
Implemented by James P. Trotzer

My view is that this group is thoroughly immersed in the work stage of the group process and that the incident reflects the problems that brought the members to the group, the purpose for which the group was formed, and the process by which individual issues are therapeutically addressed in the social laboratory of group therapy. The common theme of the problems that brought each member to the group was a lack of assertiveness. The purpose for which the group was formed was to help each member become more appropriately and effectively assertive. As the group process evolved, the norm of asserting oneself in the context of interpersonal pressure emerged, which subsequently granted members the opportunity to express themselves as individuals—including the confrontation that led to the attack described in this incident. My perspective is that all parties involved are engaged in this encounter because each participant is working on his or her own issues in the context of the group milieu. Joe, who purports to not knowing whether he is "fish or fowl," has been and is practicing taking a stand for himself, thereby setting himself apart from the group. This behavior in turn draws the attention and attack of the group, spearheaded by Jackie and Jim. For Jackie—who fears confronting her husband and her new boss—confronting Joe is a step in the right direction. For Jim—who feels he is always "taken advantage of" by significant others, possibly including his wife—disagreeing with Joe is also a new initiative. Consequently, I see this incident as an excellent opportunity to get some relevant and constructive work done on the very issues that brought the group together. In addition, my systemic orientation provides me with fertile resources as I facilitate the group in working through this incident. As group leader, my objective and task is to transform this attack on Joe into a conflict that can be resolved in a manner that enhances the individual ability of each group member to be more assertive in the face of differences in perception or opinion or in spite of group pressure to conform. To that end, my approach emphasizes working directly with the dynamics as manifested in the group and introducing systemic resources to reframe and resolve the current conflict, thereby improving the transferability of learning to the members' lives outside the group.

My first step would be to mentally create a tentative, potential agenda of the work that might be addressed as an outgrowth of this attack. Minimally, that agenda includes (1) the Jackie–Joe conflict; (2) the Jim–Joe conflict; (3) the spectator therapy dimension—that is, why other members chimed in on the attack; and (4) validating Joe's learning and value to the group. My intervention as leader is designed to contain the attack and reformulate it as a conflict that involves the agenda components just identified. My specific response is intended to celebrate the encounter and mobilize the dynamics of conflict for therapeutic purposes. I would side with Joe in the face of group pressure to conform and back down from his stated position that he doesn't have a problem taking a personal stand on important issues. I anticipate that my support of Joe would blunt the attack dimension of the group dynamics and introduce the norm dynamics that authenticate individual assertiveness. I might even state my view of the group norm if the group appears to be too confused or discomfited by my siding with Joe. That norm is "Assertiveness by individual members as an expression of their own reality rather than compliance of individual members to conform to the group's perspective of reality." To mobilize the conflict dynamics, I would have to walk the fine line between encouraging Joe to hold his position and encouraging the group, particularly Jackie and Jim, to hold their position. This is where the systemic perspective is vitally helpful and serves as a bridge to the work agenda noted above.

Conflicts between group members often reflect and enact problems and patterns members experience in their lives outside the group. Therefore, if they can learn different ways of responding in the group, they will likely transfer that learning to their relationships outside the group. In this case, I believe Jackie's and Jim's own issues are propelling their attack on Joe, just as Joe's own issues are setting himself up for the attack. Most likely, Joe represents in some relevant manner traits that Jackie, Jim, and possibly other group members (e.g., Francie) have difficulty dealing with outside the group (e.g., Jackie, with her husband and new boss; and Jim, with significant others, possibly including his wife). In addition, authority issues are also likely involved, reflective of unresolved family-of-origin experiences. Consequently, I would want to shift the focus of work in the group from Joe as the object of the attack to the conflict between Jackie and Joe.

Therefore, after siding with Joe directly, I would act to bring the Jackie–Joe dyadic conflict to the fore. For example, I would say to Jackie, "Something about Joe raises your ire, and in this case you risked speaking your mind. I'm wondering, who does Joe remind you of? In what other situations in your life do you have these kinds of feelings? And where did you find the courage to speak up?"

Assuming Jackie can respond to the introspective invitation, she would likely raise her relationship with her boss, her husband, or possibly an authority figure from her family of origin. With that background, I then would propose a fishbowl interaction involving Jackie and Joe, in which they talk out their issue with each other. This detaches the dyad from the group attack focus, defusing the destructive dynamics, and substitutes constructive interpersonal dynamics related to the theme of the group. The fishbowl is a here-and-now experience, but if their interaction is relevant, I might also suggest a role-play situation where Joe plays the role of Jackie's boss. Once this scenario has played itself out, I would ask for group input and feedback. Time permitting this session or the next, I would raise the Jim–Joe dyad in much the same manner. However, I would fully expect that spectator therapy dynamics will become operationalized and that this group will take over the work agenda with or without the help of leader-activated fishbowl or role-play techniques. For example, I would anticipate that Francie might see Joe as a resource in addressing her issue relative to involving her husband in the family.

I see this incident as propelling the group into an intense work agenda that could easily extend into several sessions. At some point, however (during a lull or at a transition point), I would ask group members to process the events leading up to and through the attack on Joe, to help them crystallize their own learning as well as validate their effective group process. A specific outcome of this processing would likely help group members differentiate between assertiveness and aggression, which is a useful concept to guide their advances in being assertive. I also would expect that Joe will be acknowledged as a resource in the group for having the courage to stand up under attack, just as Jackie and Jim will be affirmed for their risk taking in leading the attack. At the risk of being criticized for a "happily ever after" projection, I see this incident as fraught with therapeutic value and potential.

Gestalt Therapy
Implemented by Mirriam F. Polster

Joe appears to be doing pretty well with what the rest of the group have said they would like to do—namely, hold different opinions and take a personal stand on important issues. Here he is, holding all of them off and insisting that he has no problems in the face of a direct confrontation by two members of the group.

The possibilities for contact between the three main actors, Joe, Jim, and Jackie, are clear and arousing. The rest of the group, too, has some investment in what is going on here.

First, and most obvious, is Joe's insistence that he has no problems. However, in the pregroup interview, he did express some discontent with his life and his middle-management position at work. His present system of self-support requires that he deny and cover up what problems he may have, clearly deflecting contact with other members who have been admitting their difficulties. Several options are open to the group leader. I could point out, though other members may disagree with him, Joe is being assertive and standing up for himself. In confronting him, they too are being assertive. How do they feel to be doing this? Do they speak crisply, and are they stating their opinions clearly? What do they want from Joe?

I might ask Joe that, if his presence in the group signifies that he has identified some personal problems that he wants to work on, has anything anyone else has said meant anything to him personally? He is dealing right now in the group with some of the same pressures he may experience on his job, where people are demanding something from him that he may neither be ready nor willing to give. This might provide a chance for him to express some of the frustration he experiences when he tries to reconcile demands of others with his own needs. Previously, I speculate, he has handled such situations by clamming up and by not knowing whether he is "fish or fowl." Not supporting himself adequately and getting no support from his marginal position as foreman, he turns silent and puts up a good front. But now, I can ask, does he feel he is being attacked by the group? Does he feel he is being pushed prematurely into taking action?

Taking time for himself is a luxury that he presently does not claim for himself, which illustrates an important point about assertiveness. One of the most basic needs in assertiveness is to establish one's own pace and move when one chooses to move and not merely at the prodding of others. It is important to me that Joe not be made a scapegoat and that the members see his actions as an act of self-regulation and not capricious stubbornness. He has come to his predicament through a long and painful history of trying to do the best he could in the circumstances he was in.

The rest of the group members have much to learn in directly moving from their customary roles as victims to the unfamiliar opposite roles as bullies. How might they explore this?

Jim is telling Joe that Joe makes it difficult for him to be his own person, whatever that may mean. The underlying message is unclear and unspecified. He tells Joe that he believes he took great risks in saying some of the things about himself that he had just said. But is that not what being his own person means? Joe has given no indication that he is going to go around blabbing about what people have been saying. There is no indication that he disrespects the privacy of the group's communications with each other.

It seems likely to me that when I ask Jim to be more specific in his requirements from Joe, it would become more apparent that what he is seeking from Joe is easy agreement and confluence (Polster & Polster, 1973). For Jim to be his "own person," he may be saying that Joe has to be just like him! Joe has to "own up" to his problems at the same time that Jim does and to take risks in revealing himself—otherwise, Jim feels taken advantage of. Jim is scared that differing with others indicates that something is wrong with him. So, from his fright, he insists on similarity as the only way to reassure himself. This is both dangerous (because this kind of confluence is illusory and temporary) and presumptuous (because it compels another person to overlook some very real differences and bow to Jim's need for similarity).

I might ask Jim to expound on his wish from Joe by telling Joe how this silence hampers him in his search for assertiveness. If I wanted to heighten the drama of this interaction, I might ask Jim to deliver a lecture or sermon or a pep talk urging Joe to shape up. Perhaps when Jim starts to listen to himself telling Joe how important it is to him that Joe agree with him or be like him, he may also begin to recognize the absurdity, tyranny, and dependence of his own position.

Jim can, after all, do what he needs to do in the group, regardless of whether Joe conforms to his wishes. If this means revealing something about himself, so be it, without Joe's doing the same thing. It is quite possible that Jim's need to have the support of others, before he can stand up for himself, impedes him from doing it because it sets up an impossible situation. Here, in the group, he has the opportunity to begin to function independently, to go about the business of saying what he is moved to say and getting what he needs or wants, irrespective of whether the rest of the group supports and endorses him.

Jackie's spunky confrontation of Joe is somewhat different. I suspect that what she wants and finds supportive is Joe's approval. She doesn't know how to get it for herself and ends up scared, silent, and intimidated. She hears Joe's repeated insistence that he does not have any problems as an implicit statement about her own inferiority because she does have problems. She projects onto Joe her own doubts and disapproval of herself and then says that she is scared of him. She has given up ownership of her own low opinion of herself and of her discontent with the way she acts and inserts it into Joe's denial of his problems and, possibly, her boss's lack of acknowledgment of her job performance. This situation can be the cornerstone of movement out of her stuck position. I might direct Jackie to go over and stand behind Joe's chair and to speak for him and tell Jackie what (she imagines) he thinks of her. She may come up with harsher statements than Joe himself might make. She can check this out with Joe right there and determine if he is actually looking down on her as she fears. Or, instead of checking with Joe, Jackie could return to her chair and reply to the words she has put into Joe's mouth. When she does this, we have the beginning of a dialogue that is long overdue. Jackie may have been seeing her own self-disapproval in other people, such as her husband and her boss, for a long time. By having nothing to do with them, by remaining silent, she has refused to engage in dialogue with them and confront her fears. It is time for her to speak aloud in her own self-disparaging voice and to mobilize her response to this retroflected criticism (Perls, Hefferline, & Goodman, 1951; Polster & Polster, 1973). She has taken over the criticism that she dreads getting from someone else and redirected it toward herself. She does this selectively. After all, if she is projecting in the face of someone else's silence, she could conceivably imagine that they were approving of her. But this she does not do. In the dialogue we can begin to trace the one-sided nature of her self-doubt.

The reactions of the other group members is not made clear, and so I can only propose what I might do in principle, rather than a specific reaction about each of them. I would ask the rest of the group what they are feeling about the interactions among Joe, Jim, and Jackie. I would hope that there would be some support among them for Joe. He is accustomed to standing on his own, feeling isolated, and it could be a very warming experience to have an ally when he is feeling attacked. It may be that he needs this before he can admit to having difficulties.

Kathy, for example, might feel pleased that Joe can say no. She might express a wish that she could do likewise. Troy might identify with Joe's inability to express trouble and might recognize and identify with Joe's denial as an easy way out of trying to say something that is just too complicated for him to express. Francie may have something to say about the importance of getting support from someone when dealing with personal decisions.

Individual Psychology
Implemented by Guy J. Manaster

I have no more information about Joe than the brief description given and know no more about him than do the other group members. The group assumption, predicated on the reasons given for organizing the group, is that all members have "a personal concern over their inability to be assertive." The group's consternation at this point is over Joe not "fessing up," not acknowledging that he has this concern.

In my opinion, it is fallacious to assume homogeneity in a group designed to be "homogeneous"—that is, a single-problem group. As stated earlier, from an Adlerian position, people may appear similar and be categorized, labeled, and grouped together, but they are not the same—each person, personality, and lifestyle is unique.

At this point in the group, we know very little about Joe, but we do know something about the group process, and, in my opinion, both our knowledge and lack of knowledge lead to the same response—the leader had better step in and find out what is going on with Joe.

"Joe, may I ask something? It looks now, to me, as if everyone in the group feels like they have some things in common, some positive and some negative, and they are working together on the negatives. You have not been participating. Everyone wants you to. I guess I wonder how you feel about what's going on right now? And I also wonder what you want from the group—is there an issue or concern you have?"

Joe may be so entrenched in his "no problems" position that he cannot graciously express any concerns. So he may say, "This is all right. I'm all right," and nothing more.

If, in fact, I had more information from the pregroup interview with Joe, I might not draw on it. Nonetheless, I would press on, trying to read the goal of his behavior from the way he spoke and sat, trying to assess the reaction he wanted, not consciously, from his behavior.

"Joe, do you want to know what I think?"

I would expect an affirmative grunt.

"I think your problems are not the same as everyone else's. Is that right?"

(From this point on, I would go on as if Joe agrees. If and when he does not, I would try other tactics until I was correct, until he joined me in the effort or until I could not figure out what he was after, in which case I would probably say, "Joe, I don't think you want anyone to know what you are about," and then I would expect a smile of recognition.)

"Everyone in the group is unsure of what to do, but you know, don't you?"

"But you don't do what you know to do. Is that right, Joe?"

"What would happen if you did?"

If Joe agreed to this point, I would wait for his response, which would grudgingly reveal the essence of his fear and his reason for his "he-man" coverup.

This might look like a short one-to-one therapy interchange in the midst of a group therapy session. That is what it is. I think this is perfectly permissible and in this situation demanded. If we do not get to Joe so that he can begin to benefit from the group, we may lose him. Moreover, his obstinacy to the point of this incident shows great distancing, denial, and defense. Joe is not only not a part of this group, neither "fish nor fowl" at work, but also, I suspect, not a part of any group. His behavior and the attitude it reflects is quite worrisome. My immediate concern would be to give Joe a handle on his goals and an inkling of the warmth and joy of having others interested in you and you interested in them. Without a dynamic and dramatic intervention, the prognosis for Joe could be quite negative.

This instant in the group is critical for the group *and* Joe. The rest of the group has each other and, for the moment, their common anger at Joe. My regard for Joe, his feelings, and the compassion I show will be considered by the group and be part of the discussion, which I hope includes Joe, at the end of our one-to-one interlude.

The worst outcome of the exchange with Joe would be his agreement that he does not want anyone to know what he is about, followed by stony silence. I would try to get him to agree to a private session with me to see what he wants to do from here on.

A less drastic outcome would reveal some understanding of Joe, but it certainly might not include Joe's wholehearted support for the group's goals and further participation in the group. However, the group will also have learned something about Joe and in the process, learn about themselves. I would ask, "How do you feel about Joe now? How do you feel about what has happened?"

I would expect that someone, possibly Kathy whose life seems devoted to taking care of others, will say that she, or he, did not understand Joe and is now sorry for attacking him. Others would probably agree, but someone would still say, and I would if no one else does, that with the information we had, the way Joe was behaving, they had no choice, he was asking for it. "How?" The discussion might lead to the conclusion that seems warranted—he wasn't behaving according to the group norms that had developed—he wasn't behaving as he "should."

A number of "lessons" for the group should be clarified in a summary at the end of the session. Among these lessons are (1) people usually get what they want, and what their lifestyle, goals, and behaviors bring, from situations—Joe got what he wanted; (2) people often, maybe usually, do not consciously understand what they want, do not understand their goals—again, Joe did not; (3) but this understanding, although not conscious, is readily accessible, what Adler termed "dimly envisaged"—note Joe's recognition (which I must admit I confidently included); (4) other people react to you as you want and react in a group as the group wants, to the degree that it also suits their purpose; (5) the way one feels (emotions) depends on one's perspective on and understanding of a situation or another person—as when everyone was angry at Joe when they thought he obstinately would not behave as he "should" but felt differently, not angry, when they better understood his behavior and plight; and (6) sometimes people will go beyond their personal limits in emotional vehemence when they are part of a group (but that is probably for the next session).

Interpersonal Psychotherapy
Implemented by Victor Yalom and Mary Jean Paris

A group assault against a member can be quite unnerving for members and leaders alike. In an incident such as this, we would actively intervene, temporarily putting on the brakes before the cycle of attacks and defensiveness leads to further assault. We would empathize with Joe and acknowledge that it might be difficult for him to have so many members come at him at once. Although this has escalated to the point of attacks on Joe's character, we assume that underneath their attacks is a desire to get to know him, to connect with him on an emotional level. On some level, Joe undoubtedly wants this to happen as well, although the fear of such intimacy appears at the moment to be more pervasive. We would ask him for his permission to discuss some of the issues that came up in the pregroup interview. Why did he initially join the group, and what did he hope to gain? If under the spotlight he cannot articulate this, then we'll seek his permission to serve as his auxiliary memory and remind him and the group of his initial concerns.

Although this degree of focus on Joe might look a bit like a one-on-one therapy session, the situation warrants it. His back is against the wall, and if we can't help him see or at least imagine the benefits that the group has to offer, he may flee from therapy. Besides his lost opportunity for personal development, the other group members might get the wrong message: Confrontation in the group leads to ruptured relationships and should be avoided at all costs.

Rather than continue the group's direct quest to get Joe to open up and disclose his problems, we would invite him to talk about his experience in the group thus far, but particularly the latter part of the group today. Is he, for example, surprised by the intensity of the group's reactions? Is there anything that feels familiar about the experience in the group? Does he think there is any validity to the feedback, does any of it have a familiar ring, or are the group members just being irrational and caught up in an hysteria? If he acknowledges that this is in anyway familiar, then we could help him relate what happened in the group to his experiences at work where he is unable to express himself. At work he feels neither "fish nor fowl," and in group it appears that he feels neither in nor out; he has chosen by his free will to join, yet has not really joined in. At this point his inclination might be to take the safer route and talk further about his situation at work. This would be fine—anything that helped make him more of a member and less of a spectator would be welcomed. We might ask him to describe his work as foreman, especially the discomfort of serving two masters, and encourage other members to ask Joe specific questions, rather than attacking him.

Eventually, we would like to go back and have Joe and the group explore the dynamics that led up to the escalation in tension. Assuming that Joe had been able to be somewhat disclosing about his work situation, we would try to help him identify the conditions that led up to this. "It has not felt safe for you to share this in the past. Today, with some prompting, you chose to do so. What has happened in the group or your feelings toward the group today that has allowed you to do this? What were your fears about revealing to us in the past? What did you think would happen?" In answering these questions, he would begin to talk about his feelings toward other group members and his dilemma about being a participating member, which is particularly useful. This is horizontal disclosure, as opposed to vertical disclosure: disclosure about here-and-now feelings in the group, as opposed to personal historical information. Although both are important, it is the former that really energizes a psychotherapy group, facilitates interpersonal learning, and most distinguishes it from a support group.

An alternate way in which we might intervene would be to make a process comment about the dynamics that are presently occurring in the group. For example, we might say, "There are a lot of intense feelings in the group. We notice everyone is putting pressure on Joe. We detect some rising tension and anger toward Joe, yet the more people try to goad him, the more he resists. It seems pretty clear that the more you pressure Joe, the less likely he is going to want to join in the group." Our hope would be that this would cause the attacks to subside and that members could then take a look at their behavior and underlying motivation, rather than focus exclusively on Joe.

For example, we would want to explore with Jackie what it was about Joe that scares her. Can she talk more about her own experience of being afraid, rather than pouncing on Joe? What does she usually do when she is afraid, and how well does it work? And, similarly with Jim, what leads him to believe Joe will take advantage of his disclosures? And to other members of the group: How long had they been aware of their feelings? What kept them from speaking up sooner? As mentioned above, eventually we would go back to Joe and ask him if he has any reactions to all the feedback.

One of the ways group therapy is so powerful is that it provides a safe environment and sets up ideal conditions for individuals to experiment with new behaviors. The basic premise for the formation of this group was that all seven individuals expressed a concern about their inability to assert themselves. So, we would want to be sure to highlight the positive aspect of this uncomfortable episode: Members are beginning to manifest the very behavior—namely, assertiveness—they considered themselves incapable of doing. At the same time, we would also acknowledge that Joe did not submit to the pressure of the group and this was a different experience for him, compared with his behavior at his job.

As leaders, we make sure we do not miss an opportunity to acknowledge and reinforce successful attempts at using more adaptive interpersonal styles. We would ask questions regarding their new behavior: "How does it feel to assert yourself? How was it for other members to watch? Do they feel differently about some members? Do they want to approach or avoid some members? Do they feel they could deal with conflict this directly in other situations in their life?" As therapists we seem to be unduly focused on finding and endlessly exploring problems and need to remind ourselves to share with our clients the celebration of successes—for example, the enjoyment of discovering hidden strengths. Fortunately, a cohesive, well-functioning psychotherapy group often provides opportunities for therapists and members alike to laugh, rejoice, and appreciate the powerful and healing qualities of the entity that they have coconstructed.

Psychodynamic Therapy
Implemented by J. Scott Rutan

From a psychodynamic perspective, Joe represents a scapegoat. Scapegoats are individuals who can bring the ire of entire groups (or families) down upon them. The goal of treatment is to help Joe and the group understand how this behavior unconsciously serves both Joe and the entire group. The term *scapegoat* comes from the Bible.* Aaron confesses the sins of the children of Israel over the head of a goat, which was then driven into the wilderness. In other words, the "evil" of the entire tribe was placed into the goat and the goat was driven away *to protect the tribe.*

Joe came to the group because he did not know whether he was "fish or fowl." It would appear that he had the same style at work as is now evidenced in the group—he had become a target for both supervisors and subordinates. Dynamically, we would understand this to be behavior learned as a child in order to hold his family together. The "troublesome child" often distracts the family's attention from a much more disturbed family member.

This group came together because the individuals had difficulty being assertive. But it would appear that Joe has cured them of this problem! That is, he was willing (quite unconsciously) to be the target for their assertiveness.

I would likely say, "Joe, it would appear that you have been of great assistance in helping your colleagues express the assertiveness they have had such trouble in expressing. However, it appears to be quite costly to you. I wonder if this is a familiar situation for you—feeling yourself to be the target for angry feelings?"

My hope would be that ultimately Joe could connect this moment to his family of origin. We could then begin the process of helping him understand how his behavior as a child may have helped hold his family together. At the same time, it is hoped that as Joe speaks about his characteristic role it may provide the group with some empathy for his position and lessen the attacks. Finally, it is hoped that the other members could begin to explore what unacceptable parts of *themselves* they have projected into Joe.

*Leviticus 16.

Rational–Emotive–Behavioral Therapy

Implemented by Albert Ellis

I would assume, as usual in situations of this sort, that the group members are not merely healthfully confronting Joe (and trying to see that he admits to some of his major problems and tries to do something about them) but that they are also angry at him, they feel that he *has to* disclose himself to them and admit that he is holding back displaying his feelings, and he should do his best to change his ways. I would tell myself that they are quite probably correct about Joe's holding back and about his sabotaging himself in the process of doing so but that they are wrong about making themselves seriously upset about what he is doing or not doing.

I would also tell myself that, in accordance with rational–emotive–behavioral therapy (REBT) theory, their hostile and confrontative manner toward Joe will in all probability encourage him to be angry at them, to become more defensive, and to avoid, rather than to seek, looking more intently at his own problems. I would therefore first choose to talk with the group members about their anger and would try to get them to reduce it. I would keep in mind that helping them undo their anger might help Joe see more clearly some of his own problems. One advantage of group therapy is that people often understand others' problems more clearly than their own and, in getting them to do so and to work to help these others, they can frequently be persuaded to work, consciously or unconsciously, on their own emotional difficulties.

I would therefore first say to the group, or to one of the hostile members of the group, "I can see that you are quite upset about what you consider to be Joe's holding back and his refusal to acknowledge some of his deep-seated problems. And let's assume, for the moment, that you are right about him. Jackie, let's assume that Joe acts in a 'scary' manner and that people like him scare you and put you off, so you want nothing to do with them. Even if this is so, you are still condemning Joe for his holding back and for his scariness. Now, why *must* he not hold back and be unscary? And in what way does he become a louse or a rotten person if he continues to act the way that he does?"

I would try to show Jackie that, whatever Joe's deficiencies may be, she is commanding and demanding that he not have them and, by her unrealistic and irrational demands, she is foolishly upsetting herself, making herself exceptionally irate at him. I would first try to get her to give up her demands, while keeping her strong desire that Joe not act the way he is acting, and then try to help her work with Joe to get him to change some of his ways.

I would also try to show her that Joe's behavior may be bad or self-defeating and that it may be against the group's best interests, but it is not really "scary." She makes it scary by needlessly frightening herself about it—by contending, in her own head, that she cannot stand his acting that way and that she cannot allow herself to be comfortable and unscared if he continues to act that way.

I would work with Jackie, with the help of the other members of the group—whom I would induce to join in and to question and dispute Jackie's irrational beliefs about Joe's being "scary"—to give up frightening herself about his behavior and to stop blocking her own openness and honesty just because he chose to be closed. At the same time, I might get Jim into the center of the stage and show him that he, too, is taking Joe too seriously, is *making it harder for himself* to be his own person, and then assuming that Joe was making it hard for him to act openly. I might particularly try to help Jackie see that Jim is upsetting himself needlessly about Joe and help Jim see that Jackie is gratuitously upsetting herself about Joe. I would assume, while talking with both of them (and the other group members), that Joe really had a serious problem of defensively keeping himself closed; and I would show Jackie, Jim, and the group members that they viewed this problem in an overdramatic light and *made themselves* upset about it.

I would also try to show them that, if they really *wanted* (and not *needed*) Joe to be more open, they would hardly persuade him to act better by beating him over the head, complaining viciously about the way he is acting—thereby encouraging him to be even more defensive. If they are more open themselves, despite Joe's remaining closed, and if they mainly ignore his shut-off qualities for the moment, he may well take after their good modeling and make himself more open and honest.

In other words, I would show Jackie, Jim, and the other group members that, although their goals and desires (to have Joe be more open and to feel safe in opening up themselves) are highly desirable, their method of achieving these goals is not very effective or productive. They are really asking Joe to open up *first*, and then they will presumably begin to do so themselves. But they can make themselves open—as they actually had been doing up to now—whether or not Joe acts openly.

I would show the group members who complained about Joe that in some ways they are probably right, that he may well be defensive and may be doing himself little good by holding back, and that he may also be harming the group process. But I would also show them that he has a right to be wrong—as have all humans—and that, although his behavior may be "bad" or "harmful," *he* is not a *bad person.* I would try to show them that unless they accept this kind of philosophy about Joe and his errors they are unlikely to accept themselves when they do badly. I would try to get them, as well as Joe, to see that all humans are fallible. Most of us have a very difficult time opening ourselves to others and admitting that we have serious problems, but if we stop putting themselves down for *having* such problems (and stop denigrating others for having similar problems or for denying such problems), we will be able to face ourselves much more openly and successfully.

In the process of talking with members of the group, I might tell them something of myself and some of the difficulties I have had, to show them that I too am fallible and have screwed up during my lifetime. I might give them a specific self-disclosure exercise such as thinking of something secret they have not revealed to anyone in their entire lives and then revealing this secret to the group right now. I would show them that whatever they revealed there is nothing to feel ashamed of or to put themselves down for, even though their act may well have been immoral or reprehensible. And I would show them how not to feel ashamed or embarrassed, now that they have revealed this secret to the group. In the course of this exercise, I would especially try to induce Joe to reveal something "shameful" or "humiliating" and try to show him that he could do so without condemning himself for having done it or for revealing it.

I might also give all group members some kind of shame-attacking or self-disclosing homework exercise such as revealing some "shameful" act (including ones they have already revealed in the group) to an important person outside the group who might condemn them for this disclosure. If Joe, in particular, could not do this kind of thing, I would try to induce him to think, during the week, about something that he has not yet revealed to the group about himself that he would hesitate to reveal and then disclose it next week.

In various cognitive, emotive, and behavioral ways, such as those just listed, I would try to keep the group centered for awhile on this problem of disclosing oneself to others. I might even spend several sessions trying to help members see what they tell themselves to keep themselves closed up, how they can dispute their dysfunctional beliefs that make them secretive and defensive, and how they can actively push themselves to become more open with members of the group and with significant people outside the group.

Reality Therapy
Implemented by Thomas E. Bratter

I believe that the group experience can provide optimal conditions for individuals to experiment with new roles and concurrently become more self-confident and assertive. Because the group is a homogeneous group, whose members have similar presenting problems characteristic of their inability to be assertive, I would be prepared to use some newer and more innovative techniques to help them. I certainly would incorporate, at appropriate times, some behavior therapy and psychodrama techniques such as modeling, which has been described by Bandura (1969; 1971) and Rachman (1972); behavioral rehearsal, which has been described by Wagner (1968a; 1968b); and role playing, which has been described by Greenberg (1968). These are responsible and effective therapeutic adjuncts that can serve as catalysts to help people become more assertive. Besides the more traditional discussion and didactic group session format, for this specialized group I would adapt the four-phase process for problem solving developed by Siegel and Spivack (1976), which incorporates the major components of reality therapy:

1. The ability to recognize problems
2. The ability to define problems
3. The ability to think of alternative solutions
4. The ability to decide which of the alternative solutions is the best way to solve the problem

The objective of this approach is to help individuals solve problems by providing practice and reinforcement. This approach assumes that the desired behavior change can be achieved more effectively through planned therapeutic action rather than by the acquisition of insight.

The group leader in Critical Incident 6, however, appears to be unaware and may be unwilling to modify his or her approach to accommodate the group who individually has verbalized a desire to become more self-assertive. Unfortunately, the group leader apparently did not orient members before forming the group. Wolpe and Lazarus (1966) explore whether a person would be a good candidate for assertiveness training by asking the following questions:

1. Are you inclined to be overapologetic?
2. Can you contradict a domineering person? Can you openly express love and affection?
3. If a friend makes what you consider to be an unreasonable request, can you refuse?
4. Is it difficult for you to compliment and praise others?

Had these questions been specifically addressed to Joe, it is doubtful whether he would have refused to acknowledge a problem. Joe has in fact the insight to recognize his "problem"—that is, "he feels he must serve two masters"—but, though he may wish implicitly to change, the group leader never requests he make any commitment to change by becoming more assertive. Joe does not know whom to please. Rather than risking alienating either, he decides to do nothing. He thus becomes trapped in his own game and remains reluctant to change. Bugenthal (1965) would view Joe as saying, "Since I can't control everything that will determine what happens to me, I have no control at all." Experiencing the unpredictability of his life, Joe gives up and enacts this feeling of having no possibility of affecting what happens to him. He makes himself totally an object. Olden (1943), who writes from a psychoanalytic reference, has conceptualized a person who refuses to change as being obstinate, one whose efforts are to maintain feelings of supremacy even though such feelings may have no bases in reality.

The group leader in this situation may have inadvertently placed everyone in a no-win situation. Jackie and Jim have begun to assert themselves by confronting Joe about his denial of his problems. This confrontative behavior needs to be reinforced because it represents a significant and positive achievement. In contrast, Joe's refusal to be manipulated also shows assertion. Obviously, the group is correct by assessing that no one is problem free, yet the existence of the group is threatened by a power play. Apparently, the group leader has failed to create a climate where people can honestly relate to their vulnerability and contemplate adopting more self-fulfilling behavior.

In all probability, most reality therapists who work with unassertive individuals would avoid the potential dilemma of having one person adamantly deny having any problems while the group insists he does. The group would become frustrated with Joe's denial and condemn him for refusing to change. Even though Joe's assertion is less than positive for him, most mental health workers would agree the individual retains the right to select any lifestyle as long as it does not interfere with anyone else's attempts to be responsible and productive. Joe's decision, though annoying to the group, certainly harms no one but himself. As the leader, I would defend Joe's right not to change, which could of course provoke other members. I would try to maintain an atmosphere conducive to candid examination and creative change. I would take the opportunity to make the following points: "Joe, I respect your right to make a decision regarding which issues you wish to discuss and then determine whether or not you choose to change. People are basically accountable only to themselves. You do not owe us any explanations. Some members obviously are less than happy with your assertion that you do not feel as if you have any problems, which is their right. There is no reason why we need to achieve consensus. I would be interested to learn what caused you to join this group and also what your goals are."

If Joe continued to deny he has any problems, I would suggest that he spend the next week evaluating whether he could justify the expenditure of his time and money to continue with the group. I would hope to de-escalate the malignant and countertherapeutic *ad hominem* attacks by other members and give Joe some time without feeling pressured to make a decision. The only commitment I would attempt to get from Joe would be for him to return next week and share his thoughts with us. At this juncture, depending how much time remained, I would switch the focus to another member. I would try to reinforce the most rational and reasonable member who disagreed with Joe. I might say, "Gee, Jim, you shared with Joe some candid feelings. Maybe you can tell us your reaction to your comments. Do you think it will be easier for you to do this in the future and in different settings?"

In an effort to diffuse the tension, I would suggest that the members might wish to consider sharing with someone whom they trust and respect a not-so-pleasant opinion. They could report back to the group at the next meeting.

Before concluding the group, I would volunteer either to see or to speak with Joe, individually if he wanted. I would also point out, though I may disagree, that in his own way Joe was being assertive.

If Joe did not attend the next group, which might be likely, I would set aside 15 minutes of discussion time. I then would ask if anyone would volunteer to call Joe to invite him to return. I would do this in such a way that the person would become assertive in a protective way because it would help both the volunteer and Joe.

Assertiveness training and reality therapy are closely aligned.

Solution-Focused Therapy

Implemented by Rebecca LaFountain

I am having difficulty relating to this critical incident involving group members attacking Joe, who continues in session 7 to deny having any problems. Solution-focused therapy (SFT) groups often terminate by this time; therefore, it is unlikely that this context would tolerate members not yet disclosing their difficulty. Because this situation is not apt to happen, I would like to take the opportunity to create a scenario, based on the minimal amount of information I have about Joe, to illustrate the SFT group process that facilitates members to share their difficulties, state goals, and progress successfully.

I would meet with Joe for a pregroup interview to tell him more about the group, so that he can choose whether or not to join it, and to assess his appropriateness for the group. From the beginning, I would encourage solution-oriented talk, and I would ask him what he would like to change or do differently. When Joe begins to speak of his unhappiness with himself and his job, I would help him state what he *wants*, as opposed to what he *doesn't want*. Because it is clear to me that he wants to replace his discontent with a sense of peacefulness, I would help him restate this in his own words. In addition, I would prepare him for the first session where he is to share with the group what it is he would like to change.

In session 1, Joe concisely shared that he wants to feel less stressed at work. I then encouraged him to say what he wants to feel "more of" rather than "less of." He got my point but had difficulty putting it into words. So I asked him if he wasn't feeling stressed, how is he feeling? After a bit of thought he said, "a lot more comfortable." He restated for the group that he wants to feel more comfortable at work and then gave the group a little background information. Members usually like to tell a little of their story, which I concede to but do not focus on. As Joe shared about his discontentment at work and not knowing if he is "fish or fowl," I attended to his choice of words. I hypothesized that he doesn't really know his role or identity as it relates to work. I was curious about his specific analogy. He definitely mixed metaphors when he identified himself as a slave (since he feels he "is serving two masters"). I suspected that he feels overworked, either physically or emotionally, at work. Because I wanted the group members to begin to feel a sense of belonging and commonality with each other, I commented that both Joe and Troy are struggling with work issues of discomfort that involve components of leadership. I ended the group by asking them to notice in the upcoming week that which they would like to make happen more often.

In session 2, Joe provided the group with information that helped everyone better understand what he means by not knowing whether he is "fish or fowl." Joe told the other group participants that one of the fringe benefits of working in the brewery is that at the end of the workday employees are allowed to have a few beers in the hospitality room, where tour groups have sampled the product all day. He mentioned that he used to regularly stop into the hospitality room after work when he was "on the line," but since his promotion to foreman several months ago he rarely goes. He stated that, although he still wants to still feel like "one of the guys," they treat him differently because he is their immediate boss. He continued that he doesn't really feel like he belongs with management either. In response to the homework assignment, he reported that a few days before he went into the hospitality room after work and sat with just two other guys—rather than at a table occupied by a crowd of rowdy workers. They talked about everything but work, and he felt relatively comfortable. Troy responded to Joe by saying he can sort of relate. He said he hates going into the teachers' lounge where teachers often tear down the administration. He feels uncomfortable because he aspires to being an administrator.

I encouraged the group members to move into goal setting through the use of the miracle question: "Suppose that one night, while you were asleep, there was a miracle and this problem was solved. How would you know? What would be different?" (De Shazer, 1988, p. 5). Joe responded by saying, "I would feel comfortable at work. I could joke around with my subordinates yet still maintain their respect. I could walk into the hospitality room and have a good time sitting with 'the guys' if I wanted to. At the same time I would feel welcomed by the management, and occasionally one of the 'big guys' would ask me to join him for a beer after work."

As the group members shared their responses, I directed them to focus on what they would be *doing* differently. Most of them were very excited as they shared their best-case scenario. I jokingly apologized that I hated to burst their bubble but stated that it was unlikely that the miracle will happen. I brought them to reality by asking them what they could do to make those things happen that they experienced in their fantasy. Their responses laid the groundwork for the establishment of a process goal.

Joe stated that he knows his hard work and productivity are what got him promoted to the position of foreman. He said that he knew what was expected of him in his old job but doesn't really know what is required of him now. He shared some anger that management just assumed, because he was productive on the line, that he has the know-how to be a boss. He admitted that he went along with the charade and pretended he knew what he was supposed to do in an effort to be accepted and appear competent. He realized that ironically he is feeling isolated and incompetent. His process goal will be "I will talk to others to find out more about my role as foreman." He clarified his goal by stating he would talk to such persons as his former foreman, his immediate supervisor, and a guy in another department who got promoted about the same time he did.

Although members usually establish goals regarding difficulties outside the group, skilled SFT leaders use techniques to help clients practice solutions within the group and to generalize the successful solutions outside the group. For example, the counselor may ask, "Joe, you discovered that when you are confused in the group it is helpful for you to express your confusion—even though you risk looking foolish. How can that work for you in your place of employment?" Group members help each other come up with solutions, and participants borrow solutions from each other. This cocreation of solutions continues the group support and cohesiveness.

Sharing in SFT counseling groups is promoted in a number of ways, starting with the prescreening interview, where problems are normalized. In session 1, participants realize that everyone experiences difficulties, and they learn that difficulties become problems when individuals continue to use the same poor solutions. Because it is a given that all group members are striving for new solutions in areas that cause them difficulties, then it is unlikely that group members will insist that they have no problems, such as Joe did in the original scenario. SFT counselors encourage an atmosphere of belonging and commonality among group members as the leader helps the participants recognize their similarities. This process is facilitated further by the systematic steps employed by the group leader. This framework provides individuals direction and reinforces the expectation, established in the prescreening interview, that everyone is expected to share—thus promoting interchange and cohesiveness.

Systems-Centered Therapy
Implemented by Yvonne Agazarian

SCT INTERVENTION

The group is grappling with how difficult it is to be different—to stand up for oneself and what one believes in when it means taking a position that is different from everybody else. We have one of life's important paradoxes here. Group, do you notice that Joe is doing just that: standing up for himself and what he believes in, even though it means that he's taking a position that is different from everyone else in the group!

We are coming to a very important human problem in our group. We human beings all have an impulse to scapegoat difference. Whenever we meet something that is too different, we try to change it to something that is more comfortably similar. This impulse is so strong in us that even when a person (like Joe) is actually doing the very thing that we wish we could do, we are blind to anything except our impulse to attack. It is perhaps this tendency to scapegoat that we are acting out right now in the group that makes us also frightened of standing up for ourselves if we have to stand alone.

We are in fact fortunate to have the very issue alive for us right now in the group. We want to scapegoat Joe. This gives us an opportunity to explore all sides of the experience we are having right now: our impulse to attack, our impulse to avoid being attacked even if it means losing ourselves, and our impulse to speak out no matter what it costs.

In groups there is great resonance between the delegation of containing roles by the group (like the scapegoat) and the individual-member salience for playing the roles. Perhaps it has always been too much to expect individual group members to be able to contain, rather than act out, their own conflicts, when their own conflicts in development are being strongly stimulated by the conflicts in the developing group (see Chapter 11, Table 1). Scapegoating is the typical response in a group that is shifting from the flight phase (where the containing role is that of the identified patient) into the fight phase.

In systems-centered therapy (SCT) groups, subgroups, rather than individuals, contain different sides of predictable group splits around difference. When the group as a whole works to contain the conflict consciously as a working task, then it is no longer necessary to delegate conflicting differences to a scapegoat, an identified patient, or a deviant pair. In this way, the group learns to exploit the natural tendency to split the "like me and good" from the "not like me and bad." By *deliberately* containing the good–bad split in different subgroups, each side of the split can be explored with less conflict than when contained as different parts of the inner self. By employing the technique of functional subgrouping, the mechanisms of splitting and projection are utilized rather than pathologized. When these mechanisms are seen as functional, there is less pressure to deny or repress their manifestations.

In responding to this critical incident 1, find the ongoing dilemma that the group is not systems centered and therefore not aware of the predictable dynamics that occur in each phase and subphase of the developing group. The preceding intervention is designed to (1) stop the acting-out of the phase-specific dynamics of scapegoating; (2) use a "humanizing" and "universalizing" frame that will not humiliate or censure the group; (3) bring to the group's attention that the very issue they are trying to solve is being enacted in the here and now; and (3) encourage members to explore their experience. (The group is not given a choice between whether to explore or act out!)

In an SCT group, the intervention would have required members to pay attention to what is suspiciously absent in themselves that they are attacking in Joe's chair—and Joe, as a member, would be doing the same work. However, this intervention is predicated on the group already knowing that members tend to project onto others aspects of themselves that are too different from their existing organization to integrate within themselves.

SCT therapists talk, not in the language of pathology, but in terms of dynamics that are central to all human system development. It is also for this reason that the focus of attention is not on interpretation but on communication: not on content but on context. All of this requires the SCT therapist to learn both how (1) to relate to the group as a whole and the individual members and (2) to see in the mind's eye the dynamics of the communicating systems and subsystems in the context of the system hierarchy.

The consequences anticipated are that the members would (1) recognize that they were in fact attacking Joe for the very ability that they said they wished they had—and (2) become willing to explore what they are acting out. I would anticipate that it would be easier for these members to explore their fear of being attacked if they stand up for themselves and probably quite difficult for this group to explore the sadism that fuels the scapegoating in which they had been involved. For Joe to join the work, the therapist probably would have to give considerable encouragement so that he could explore his experience of standing up for himself in ways that tend to get him scapegoated. An individual-member intervention would be framed something like, "Joe, was this a familiar experience?"

The most glaring or outstanding condition of the incident is that the behavior and content in the group are congruent with the scapegoating that can be expected in all groups if they act out fight-phase dynamics. The subgrouping methodology is the conflict resolution technique that addresses the issue of projecting out and attacking differences that are too different to be integrated.

Thus, the management of scapegoating of members, and later scapegoating of the leader, is fundamental to the ability of all groups to be a therapeutic environment. Mismanagement of scapegoating is likely to fixate the group in a regression to flight. Mismanagement of scapegoating the leader is likely to fixate the group, either in a dependency relationship with an idealized leader or a contending relationship both with members and leader. The underlying dynamics of these issues are specifically addressed in SCT work through subgrouping and education. It is the denial and acting-out of the retaliatory impulse in intermember scapegoating that can precipitate depression in group members and, when mixed with guilt, precipitates a depressed group as a whole.

The SCT recognizes that the management of the sadism in the scapegoating of the therapist is fundamental if the negative transference is to be contained and worked and if the group is to develop past its first-phase preoccupation with authority to the separation and individuation dynamics that come to the surface in the intimacy phase.

Transactional Analysis
Implemented by Herbert Hampshire

Working with problems of assertiveness can be particularly tricky, if not treacherous. A lack of assertiveness functions as a racket, which with great effectiveness justifies a life of unwanted outcomes and avoids the direct experience of uncomfortable effects. The lack of assertiveness constellation is difficult to deal with because it has the illusion of being the problem when it is in fact not. When clients come in for treatment and say they want to be assertive, I always ask if they will be satisfied if that is all that happens. If they become assertive and nothing else changes, will they consider their goal accomplished? Would Francie be happy if she became assertive *and* her husband still supported her no more than he does now? Would Troy consider therapy successful if he became assertive and *still* did not get an administrative position?

Underneath the identification of the problem as one of assertiveness is the implicit assumption that the "real" problem (e.g., the lack of support from Francie's husband) will be cleared up simply by the acquisition of assertive behavior. If not very careful, the therapist will give tacit agreement to this assumption, often without being conscious of doing so. At the outset it is critical to determine if the client's analysis is correct. Does it appear the problems being encountered in the client's life would be resolved if a more assertive lifestyle were available? In my experience, this conclusion is unjustified and comes from a contamination of the Adult. Although definite advantages accrue from developing a more assertive style of relating, it seldom includes obtaining immediately what the client claims to want.

In arriving at a clear understanding of the underlying dynamics that hold the life pattern in place, one often sees the potential costs involved in cure. Philosophical and ethical problems are involved in proceeding with treatment when the client is unaware of these dynamics. There is a very real necessity for obtaining informed consent on the client's part. It is important, for example, that Francie's development of assertiveness in relation to her husband may undermine the stability of the marriage. The same holds true for Michele. When major changes in life circumstances of a client are possible, concomitants of a cure of the presenting problem, both therapist and client are well advised to enter the process with awareness and a specific contract around the issue.

These considerations arise particularly when problems presented initially by the client are obvious results of the client's behavior. Francie marries a man with a job that is likely to keep him away and relatively uninvolved in the family and ends up unhappy that he is not more actively supportive. Kathy stays at home with her parents and ends up feeling that she would like "a life of her own." Michele embeds herself in a stereotypically sexist marriage and, after 22 years, is unhappy at getting opposition to going out on her own. All are examples of problems resulting from operating within a self-defeating script. The rule of thumb for identifying script-driven behavior is that a problem is set up by someone who, if observing another person, would clearly be able to identify the inevitability of the undesirable outcome. Thus, to deal with the overt problems is to confront the script, it is therefore essential to know all elements of the matrix, including what clients are likely to do to themselves if they defy the injunctions of the script.

Joe is the member in this group who evidences the greatest degree of connectedness to the underlying anxiety associated with breaking out of the scripted patterns. His resistance to even acknowledging the existence of the conditions bringing him to treatment is indicative of a great deal of fear. At the outset I would want to be sensitively aware of his level of affect. This concern is augmented by his denial of the effect that group members' attacks are having on him.

When a group member is being attacked and does not have the available resources to effectively handle either the attack or the feelings generated, my priority becomes that of defusing or de-escalating the situation before significant damage is done to the individual, the relationships, or the context of therapy. This can often be done by recontextualizing the interactions.

One possibility is to stroke Joe for not submitting to the group pressure—evidencing the kind of power that he does not experience at his job. It is also possible to focus on Jackie or Jim, who are responding with great force and assertiveness (if not aggressiveness). It is often useful to point out to clients that they are manifesting the very behavior that they consider themselves incapable of doing. They are so accustomed to thinking about themselves in a particular way that they tend to ignore inconsistent observations. Jim is doing a good job of relating directly to "being taken advantage of," one of his presenting complaints. I might ask if he was aware that he was dealing with Joe more directly than he typically dealt with people who "took advantage of him." He might also be focused on his feelings in the process of confrontation to get him to shift toward acknowledging his own experience rather than continuing to relate to Joe as his persecutor, thereby maintaining his own position as victim. Were it not for the importance of keeping the attention of the group on the volatile situation within the session, it would be possible to ask Jim if he ever talked to others—his boss or his wife, for example—the way he was talking to Joe.

As usual, my underlying motive would be to foster interaction that produces contextual shifts through the meshing of issues and programming. Michele is likely to be a caretaker for her family, as well as for others, so I would be watching her for signs of discomfort at open conflict; the same would be true for Kathy. It is also an opportunity to work with Troy on his ability to express himself in the midst of an affect-laden circumstance.

In the final analysis, my response would be determined in this circumstance by my awareness that the situation had developed to this point out of my at least passive collusion. Optimistically, Joe would have been invited much earlier than session 7 to relate to his resistance to becoming involved with the group and to deal more openly with his anxieties about sharing his problems. Thus, I would be likely to say something to him, such as "You're under a lot of pressure now. Is this the way it feels for you at work?"

This intervention would, first, acknowledge the reality of what was going on and, second, create a context in which Joe could begin to verbalize his feelings and be involved, admitting to the problem he was having right then, without either submitting to or rebelling against Jackie or Jim. My intention would be to get him to relate directly to the "problem" and to his feelings and then move him toward transacting directly with the group members. At that point, it would become possible to begin to relate the experience to the programming and issues of the others in the group.

Theoretical Practitioners' Congruence With Their Theory

CLIENT-CENTERED THERAPY

At this juncture in our following of client-centered therapy, we are familiar with its key concepts: therapist roles and techniques and group processes. Now we want to see what of each of these areas our TP will demonstrate; because this is session 7, the stage of group development may enter in as factor. Of the eight group member variables, feedback looms as the one that could receive emphasis. Therapist roles and techniques probably will include acceptance of the group, acceptance of the individual, empathy, therapist self-disclosure, feedback, and avoidance of interpretation or process comments. A number of group processes are activated by this incident, including resistance to personal expression or exploration expression of negative feelings and cracking of facades.

Once more, our TP allows us to hear his thoughts. He wants to join in the attack. He is leveling with us, and he wants to humble Joe. He has allowed us to see him as a member and, as such, how he is experiencing and responding to Joe. He demonstrates trust in the collective power of the group. He is going to wait the moment out, unless the attack continues. Here he uses his leader role and offers a form of feedback to a member that has its genesis in his own feelings for Joe. He self-discloses and simultaneously adds that *he believes* in Joe's ability to come around, which communicates his acceptance of Joe. He tells us that he believes in and trusts the *process* and is less concerned if Joe ever capitulates. In Joe's case, he chooses not to press him; some member, he trusts, will eventually reach him. This means Joe's facade will be cracked even though for the time being he has engaged in what is resistance of self-expression, which our TP reframes as stubbornness. This reframing of resistance in a positive light actually is paradoxical, for it prescribes stubbornness as the means for being assertive!

Cognitive Behavioral Therapy

We first need to ask ourselves if our TP would have formed a group in this way, and could we have expected that a member would have continued without a much earlier intervention by our TP. Since this group did continue as it did over seven sessions, what our TP might do raises our interest. We do know there are key concepts we can look for, such as learning, here and now, and self-efficacy. We are aware of therapist roles and techniques such as evaluation, assessment, monitoring, feedback, assignment of homework, role playing, and contracts—to name but a few.

Our question is answered when our TP tells us that his groups are not formed as the one in the incident. He even relabels the group according to the cognitive–behavioral view of the purpose for forming as assertion training. The group is psychoeducational, which will affect to some extent the interventions he implements. We learn that every member, including Joe, needed to learn during pretraining the theme or purpose for the group forming. Failure to do so led to Joe being improperly placed in the group. We also find that our TP would have assigned homework and used role playing, thereby discovering early on if Joe were appropriately placed in this group. Our TP refers to a here-and-now intervention when he considers using the group's attack on Joe as an example of nonassertive behavior as a means of helping with the training. Coaching is another technique our TP employs in helping members in the role plays. We also know how important group interaction and cohesiveness is to cognitive–behavioral therapy. Our TP informs us that assertion is best taught through collaboration (i.e., member to member and group to member). By using this approach he is encouraging group interaction and would build group cohesiveness around a goal of assertion training.

Family-Centered Therapy

Considering this to be a family-centered therapy (FCT) group, the fact that the incident occurred in session 7 probably is important. Remember, our TP will invariably be calling on the integrated knowledge he has drawn from a variety of disciplines, but central to his approach is group therapy and family theory. So, among the multitude of concepts he may consider and for which we look include group development, family and individual development, curative factors, and roles and techniques in which he will engage (e.g., roles of director? participator? expert? go-between? which reaching skills? interaction skills? action skills? modeling?). Very important to FCT is attention to group process. Therefore, we want to see how our TP addresses the needs of members, such as safety, love and belonging, and self-worth.

Our TP's first observation is to note the level of interpersonal interaction of the members, from which he determines its stage of development. He also keeps in mind the purpose for which the group was formed. He lets us know that individual-member and Joe's behaviors reflect the goal of learning to be assertive. He employs the here-and-now concept as he plans to take advantage of the incident to get "relevant and constructive work done." The way he envisions his task suggests to us that the roles of celebrant and go-between will be played, given the emotionally charged nature of the group. We hear his thoughts as he analyzes each member; not surprisingly, he includes in his analysis that family-of-origin experiences have generated issues with authority. In many ways his desire to contain and refocus the conflict suggests how he plans to direct the power of the group in a productive direction. He implies a psychodynamic concept is operating when he asks Jackie for the source of her projection onto Joe. His intervention with Joe tends to normalize his behavior (i.e., he is being assertive). We note his sequencing of interventions that keeps the focus on the group goal of assertiveness development. Our TP considers a structured exercise such as the fishbowl and role playing, which would diffuse the group attack. Again, he infuses the here and now, not only for the role players but also for the "spectators." He trusts that the self-correcting and self-monitoring processes of the group will operate, meaning members will actively take part with or without his structured interventions. We learn that process illumination by the group members is another part of his plan. Our TP's intention for doing this is consistent with the goals of group therapy: Members will realize that the skills and knowledge they have learned will enable them to make the transition from the group to their other social settings.

GESTALT THERAPY

Very early we learned, according to Gestalt therapy, that the way people view the world is what blocks or impedes achievement of growth and experiencing life. It is Gestalt therapy's goal to free a person from these barriers to effective living. Because this group formed to help its members learn to be assertive, we conclude our TP's objective fits nicely with the foregoing statement regarding the purpose of Gestalt therapy. We want to see her activating the principles with which we have become familiar: the here and now, introjection or projection, responsibility taking, experiments drawn from the ongoing interactions of members, individual member work and vicarious learning, therapist focusing, and helping members to be authentic.

Our TP's goal clearly is to free the members from their impediments so that they can live and experience life fully. From the beginning she employs the here-and-now principle, using the interactions of Joe and other members. Reframing Joe's and the group members' behaviors as being assertive, she moves to hold them responsible by asking them questions that are designed to have members be specific. This questioning clears away the underbrush of emotional barriers and makes members accountable. Clear evidence shows that our TP focuses on member behavior. A good example is with Jim, when she tells us the underlying message his behavior is communicating. She plans to help Jim be self-responsible. To do so, she will employ role play that will have Jim learn of his introjections: topdog or underdog. Thus, he will reveal to himself how he views himself in relation to others; by doing so, the first step is taken to removing a barrier to his living life effectively. Similarly, with Jackie, our TP has her get in touch with her projections and plans to help her to become responsible for developing self-esteem. Her technique evolves from the moment. Our TP plans to have Jackie engage in a game of dialogue, which will help her get a clear view of how she blocks herself from being self-confident. While all of this work (and experimentation) is occurring with individual members, our TP is aware of the vicarious learning that is being experienced by other members. Thus, she informs us of the individual work she plans to do with each of them, drawing on their experiences from observing the works of Jim, Joe, and Jackie.

INDIVIDUAL PSYCHOLOGY

According to individual psychology, individuals are creators of their world-view and lifestyle and therefore are capable of changing and developing their own destiny. We need to keep this in mind as we watch our TP at work. In addition, the key principle of social interest should be his primary concern. How he helps members through this event will call upon his creative instincts. We know he is free to employ what works. We know that self-esteem and equality are important for members to develop. Let us see if how he addresses this incident takes all these constructs into consideration.

Strong evidence shows that our TP adheres to the theoretical principles that emphasize the development of member self-esteem and equality. For instance, he helps Joe establish (clarify) the goal of his behaviors. We see how he pays close attention to the social interest concept. He does so by being spontaneous and creative in the way he engages in individual therapy. His analysis of the situation justifies his conducting individual therapy with Joe. By so doing, our TP hopes to help Joe establish his sense of dignity, self-worth, and belonging-ness in the group. This is not at the expense of the other members.

He does not want to lose Joe, but he also tells us he is aware of the lessons the others will learn from witnessing his work with him. He informs us that he expects members will achieve an objective: They will learn more about Joe, including that he was behaving according to the group's norms, not as they expected him to behave. Having choice is implied here, so it is consistent with the Adlerian position regarding individuals, which was cited at the beginning of our summary.

INTERPERSONAL PSYCHOTHERAPY

The title of this form of group therapy underscores the expectation it holds out for its members and its process. Therefore, we have come to expect that our TPs will use such events as this to help members learn about themselves through the interpersonal interaction that has occurred. Activating the principle of here and now, use of the curative (group) factors, process illumination, and feedback are but some of the principles and concepts we want to see demonstrated. In addition, we expect our TPs to engage in building and reinforcing group norms and culture and attending to group process.

Our TPs attend very carefully to the way Joe and the other members are communicating. They let us know that they are listening to their metacom-munication. We are told the group members, in this attack, really want to get to know and connect with him, and likewise for Joe, but that right now intimacy is too frightening for him. Our TPs concern for the impact of Joe's flight behavior upon the group lets us know of their desire to shape the norms and culture of the group. They want to encourage conflict and confrontation but make certain it can be viewed as facilitative, not damaging, to relationships.

Their action to diffuse the attack on Joe by working with him individually has a familiar ring to it. They activate the here and now, while helping him become self-aware as they process his group experience. Sensitive to his possible need for emotional safety, they allow for him to engage in then-and-now sharing. The objective is to encourage him to talk, to interact at some level; this position is a *must* for interpersonal group psychotherapy. Once Joe feels reasonably safe in his sharing, our TPs can move him back to the here and now of his experiences within the group.

We learn of another possible intervention: a group-as-a-whole process comment. Again, this is intended to diffuse the intensity of the attack and to refocus members on their interactive behaviors so that they understand more about themselves. Our TPs underscore the need to make certain that group therapy provides a safe environment in which members can freely experiment with new behaviors. Their concluding remarks are particularly noteworthy. They emphasize that they include reinforcing members' successes, including considering termination-type questions that ask members how they might use what they have learned in the group in other life settings. Certainly, transitioning to other life settings is the ultimate goal of interpersonal group therapy.

PSYCHODYNAMIC THERAPY

What might we look for from our TP as we consider this incident from a psychodynamic position? We have members attacking a member and a member remaining resolute (i.e., that he is fine). What strikes us first is to consider what defense mechanisms are evidenced here. Following this, we consider the role our TP will assume and on which aspect(s) of this event he will focus. We also want to see him try to employ techniques that will bring the unconscious to conscious awareness.

Our TP interprets from the outset that Joe is the scapegoat and identifies this as one of the forms that resistance takes. The group members (and even Joe) appear to be defending against being exposed and changing. He likens Joe's behavior and role as the family's "troublesome child." The family (group) members are struggling with their own disturbances regarding lack of assertiveness (psychodynamic analysis), and his behavior unconsciously draws them out to be assertive. Our TP's role at this juncture is to be active. He focuses on the process and less on content. He attempts to help Joe understand the underlying motives for his behavior. Our TP is also aware of the group as a whole as he intervenes at the individual-member level. He hopes to help members explore and understand their projections onto Joe—that is, the motives for their own resistance. We conclude that our TP has interpreted member and group-as-a-whole behavior, saw resistance as an opportunity for gaining entrance into the unconscious, and encouraged members to work through their issue with assertiveness. It is important to close with underscoring the fact that our TP does not accuse Joe or the members of resisting. If he had, it would not have been available for him to use it as he did. Instead, the resistance would in all probability have raised group's resolve to defend itself.

RATIONAL–EMOTIVE–BEHAVIORAL THERAPY

Once again, we expect to find our TP central in the group. He will also be the teacher, perhaps by employing the A-B-C-D-E construct, using himself as a model, working with individual members to make new self-statements and be more rational, having member attack their shame, and assigning homework.

Without a doubt, our TP has taken a very central position. His words throughout the session indicate he wants to teach (show) each of them how their behavior was ineffective and not rational. However, given the purpose of the group's forming, he avoids any language that would appear belittling. He instructs the members on the A-B-C-D-E construct of REBT, but it is less direct than in previous incidents. He models how they do not have to feel ashamed when he discloses his own imperfection. He plans to assign shame-attacking homework. We view his work with different individual members, like Jackie and Jim, as helping them make new self-statements and be more rational. Our TP clearly shows congruence with his theory.

REALITY THERAPY

From a reality therapy perspective, our approach to viewing our TP needs to keep in mind the various roles and techniques available to him. We want to see how involved he gets, how he develops member commitment, his focus on the here and now, and how he reinforces—as opposed to punishes—behaviors. Of course, we want to see how he helps members feel worthwhile and develop a success identity.

Our TP tells us that as a therapist he plans to be more involved than the therapist in the incident. Moreover, he would have demonstrated this during the pregroup-screening process by giving them a "proper orientation." His assessment of Joe is that Joe is into denial and that he will take an individual approach with him. Our TP's approach to Joe takes the position of helping him to become more responsible and to determine if he really wants to make the commitment necessary for him to address the changes he seeks. He assesses the situation involving Jim, Jackie, and Joe and determines that he wants to turn it into a win-win versus a no-win situation. He would accomplish this objective by first defending Joe's right not to change (even though he disagrees with Joe), and he in turn would be diffusing the tension—power play—that threatens the group's existence. In other words, he wants to create an atmosphere where it is safe for members to participate.

We conclude that we saw therapist involvement, that he tried to develop member commitment, and that his focus was on present behavior. Though he avoided punishment, our TP anticipated the likelihood that Joe might not return, which may come as a result of confronting Joe to be responsible.

SOLUTION-FOCUSED THERAPY

We know that the prescreening interview is a very significant part of group process. It is then when potential members are determined to have the (1) characteristics of being amenable to change and (2) of being able to articulate an attainable goal for themselves. It is also the case that the therapist looks for potential underlying themes. This incident certainly raises our attention in relation to the prescreening process. Other concerns that receive our focus are our TP's attention to member strengths, process goals, and keys. We also want to see how our TP encourages universality, hope, and cohesiveness.

Our TP wastes no time telling us that this event would not occur in an SFT group. From that moment, she proceeds to emphasize the prescreening interview process she would go through with Joe. This includes having him make specific what he wants to achieve in the group, and he is informed that he will be asked to state his desire in the group during session 1. Our TP's scenario includes her using encouragement with Joe to help him restate his goal clearly. She also focuses on his use of words and how he uses them. These leader interventions are designed to help her understand him in order to assist him to continue working toward his goal. She also invites group member contributions and interaction. Remember, this is an important dimension of SFT. Our TP uses the familiar technique of the miracle question to encourage group members to join in goal setting, ultimately leading them to develop a process goal. We notice that all during this period, our TP's focus is on members' strengths—what they can do versus what they cannot. Known as the search for keys to solutions, she helps Joe find the exception—that is, where he was successful despite his circumstances. Throughout the scenario, our TP encourages members, strives to build group involvement, and establishes group cohesiveness.

SYSTEMS-CENTERED THERAPY

Well, if we learned one thing at all from SCT, it is that scapegoating is not allowed to continue! Scapegoating means that the individual subsystem is not functioning in a healthy way, so our plan is to see how our TP manages this moment. Concurrently, we want to see how quickly she moves to create functional subgroups to contain the split this incident has reflected. The scapegoating of Joe emphasizes the group's differences with him, which will change as subgroups are formed around members' similarities with each other. We know that to form a subgroup one must face the fork in the road. Let's see how our TP implements the technique. We look for such concepts as boundarying, centering, balancing apprehension and comprehension, phase-appropriate interventions, partnership, member resonance, and resonating. This moment almost sounds ideal for our SCT TP's approach.

Our TP moves quickly to have the members face the fork in the road and decide which side of the split they wish to explore. Establishing the subgroups to contain the split, moving out of and away from it being contained in Joe (the scapegoat), is crucial. We cannot help but notice how rapidly she establishes a partnership with the members. She does this by making a process observation and uses the collective first-person plural "we," she includes herself with them. She invokes the here-and-now principle, which makes the moment more meaningful for all. We learn that SCT therapists encourage feelings and emotion but do not want it to reach a level that immobilizes a member or the group; so, by lessening the conflict via the formation of subgroups, members are freer to explore their intrapersonal individual system. Our TP makes clear reference to the phase of the group's development and that her intervention is designed accordingly (i.e., to stop the acting-out of phase-specific scapegoating, members must explore). She also is concerned not to humiliate the members, even though she expects scapegoating to occur (i.e., it's normal) as part of acting-out the fight-phase dynamics. Notice how knowledge and understanding of group development assists our TP in technique selection. Once again, we have evidence of how systematic the SCT approach is.

TRANSACTIONAL ANALYSIS

When a group attacks one of its members and the member does as Joe has done, we expect our TP to be drawing on the key concepts of member ego-states, transactions engaged in to receive strokes, and scripts. We can expect to see our TP showing his skill at listening beyond the surface messages and analyzing ego-states, transactions, games, and scripts. We hope to see him teach these skills to the members so that they may help each other and eventually reach their Adult state.

Analysis and interpretation seem to be the first order of business for our TP. He tells us that we should look at the lack of assertiveness as though it were the life view "I'm Not Okay—You're Okay," which "justifies a life of unwanted outcomes. . . ." He questions members in order to get to what is behind their desire to be assertive. In other words, how one's life will improve is called into question. He is unwilling to accept members' self-analysis as valid, to the extent that therapists run the risk of questionable ethical practice. Contracts, he urges, need to be written that spell out clearly that members understand the full consequences of their changed life pattern. He almost sounds relentless and insensitive in his pursuit of making certain that members are made fully aware that their present life circumstances are due to their current behaviors, which are associated with self-defeating scripts. His message to us is clear: We better know what we are doing if we decide to help members. The presenting problem is really a cover for the member's life script; this means that changing behavior has complex ramifications. Having presented us with an *honest* view of the group as a whole, he explains how he will work with each member. His initial concern is to diffuse the event so that no harm will come to Joe and the others. He calls it "recontextualizing the interactions"; in the past, we have referred to this as reframing. Rather than dealing with Joe as resistant, he chooses to stroke him for behaving in a way he has not managed to in his workplace. He does the same for Jackie and Jim, eventually getting around to each of the other members.

Our TP offers us an alternative approach. He invokes the here and now with Joe, acknowledging his current feelings in the group and asking if they are like what he experiences at work. No deep analysis is offered; instead, communication is clear and straight. It is intended to lead Joe to address his problem of the moment, his transactions with Jim and Jackie. While other members observe him teaching Joe, he eventually plans to transition to them, they will be ready to receive his teaching.

Theory Evaluation Form

1. Which theoretical practitioner do you most resemble? Why?

2. Which theoretical practitioner do you least resemble? Why?

3. What does your response to Question 1 tell you about yourself and your leadership style as a potential or present group therapist?

4. What does your response to Question 2 tell you about yourself and your leadership style as a potential or present group therapist?

5. After rereading how the theoretical practitioner of your choice responded to the incident, how would you modify your response?

Conclusion

At this juncture, we can conclude that each of our TPs adhered to their respective theories. More important, however, we need to note how much significance can be placed on not only what I. Yalom (1995) had referred to as the *core* of group therapy but also the *front*. In our efforts to determine the degree of congruence therapists had with their theories, the personhood of each of our TPs seemed to emerge with a degree of frequency. In virtually every instance, the way each theory was applied was determined as a matter of how the TPs chose to make their theory "fit" their personal style, thereby giving us subtle yet significant variations between theory and practice. This suggests that therapists' rigid adherence to theoretical principles not only may be unrealistic to expect but also would be restrictive to the development and implementation of interventions needed to deal with the moment-to-moment interactions in a group.

PART THREE

WHERE HAVE WE COME?

CHAPTER NINETEEN

Comparing the Theoretical Practitioners' Interventions

Historically, practitioners have been faced with the question of whether one theoretical approach is better than another. In Chapter 18 we concluded that there is a degree of variability between theory and practice, which in large measure is attributable to the characteristics of the therapist. We had an opportunity to explore this issue within the context of how our theoretical practitioners (TPs) have presented themselves. What we set out to emphasize in this chapter is that effective leadership is more a matter of choice and blend, rather than determining which theoretical intervention is the best. The manner in which we address this task is to introduce briefly the central issues elicited by each critical incident, comparing similarities and differences among TP interventions by identifying specific group therapy concepts or procedures and concluding with an assessment of the primary intervention emphasis of our 12 TPs and a brief synthesis of what we have learned about effective leadership as suggested by our TPs' interventions.

Critical Incident 1

Critical Incident 1 addresses the issue of beginning a therapy group with brief introductions, which was then followed by an initial silence.

With the exception of the client-centered and transactional analysis (TA) approaches, all TPs initially address the group silence with varying amounts of structured comments aimed at "getting started," "setting ground rules," or exploring "how members feel about the silence." Our rational–emotive–behavioral therapy (REBT) TP is the most explicit in outlining his goals, motives, and REBT theory and in determining whether members could commit themselves to his therapy group. In a similar but briefer fashion, the Adlerian (individual psychology) TP informs members why they were there, particularly emphasizing the need to belong. The Gestalt TP, like the Adlerian TP, believes members were reluctant to talk because they felt their concerns were different or unique, but she does not verbalize them as does the Adlerian TP. She asks the group, "What pleases them?" and "Who do they miss?" and the like, whereas the Adlerian TP asks them to specify their concerns. The Adlerian, Gestalt, and solution-focused therapy (SFT) TPs focus on the "universality" of concerns of group members and the importance of cohesion (camaraderie for the Adlerian TP or environmental support for the Gestalt TP). The SFT TP uses the linking of similarities to enhance universality and the development of cohesion. Our Gestalt TP, however, emphasizes the importance of balancing "individual differences" with environmental support. The reality therapy TP self-discloses his experiences and feelings as a new college student as a means of facilitating disclosures regarding similar experiences and feelings that the members of this group might have.

Several TPs observe that pretherapy training would have reduced the likelihood of silence following the introductions. For example, the cognitive–behavioral therapy (CBT) TP asks members in the prescreening meeting to develop "problem cards" to bring with them to the first group meeting. With these instructions, "disclosure becomes a group norm prior to the group." Member interaction is also facilitated by the SFT TP who uses the prescreening to set expectations of both the content (working on solutions) and the process (interacting with others using clear I-language). The interpersonal psychotherapy (referred to in this chapter as IGP, or interpersonal group psychotherapy) TPs use the pregroup interview to explain the interpersonal model and prepare members for the here-and-now interactive approach. In a similar manner, the SFT TP uses a welcome, introductions, and the linking of the introductions to set a tone of member involvement in the group. She makes a point of teaching I-statements and clarifying the goals of SFT.

The psychodynamic therapy and family-centered therapy (FCT) TPs view the silence as an assessment device. From the psychodynamic perspective, members' behavioral reactions to silence become important information to use in the group. The psychodynamic therapy TP would not interrupt the silence; his attention is directed to *how* members cope with silence, who breaks the silence, and how the group begins to develop. For the FCT TP, silence is viewed as a normal event; he pays attention to how members work with the silence in the first 20–30 minutes in order to decide on his intervention. He is likely to use structured group activities designed to address individual needs, the interactions among members, and the group's purpose.

The systems-centered therapy (SCT) TP joins with the IGP TPs in focusing on the member's experience of silence in the here and now. The SCT TP believes that anxiety is an expected response to the silence, and she seeks to normalize the anxiety while inviting members to examine the experience that all are having at that time. The IGP TPs want their members to (1) reflect on how they feel in the group, (2) engage with each other, and (3) then through reflection and discussion, understand their experience so that they can generalize their experience to life outside the group.

The client-centered and psychodynamic therapy TPs treat silence with silence, which in effect is a group-as-a-whole intervention, eliciting ambiguity and individual member's tolerance for ambiguity. The client-centered TP believes "not talking will give us something to talk about later." Assumption of responsibility for involvement is therefore left to group members. Similarly, the psychodynamic therapy TP views the group as "a laboratory for exploring how the members cope with this new experience." By taking this quiet, unintrusive role, he hopes to enhance the development of transference and promote members' ability to "think psychodynamically" about their behaviors, feelings, expectations, and perceptions. In contrast, the TA TP begins by giving his name and, sequentially, notes members' discomfort (body language) in response to the silence and invites them to verbalize their feelings. Contracting with individual members begins immediately to define *what* aspect of behavior they want to change. He requires clarity and specificity of concerns in these individuals transactions; consequently, "contract negotiations" could take up most of the beginning session because members' concerns are often unclear. His approach is similar to the CBT and SFT approaches that emphasize up front the setting of clear, obtainable goals. The Gestalt TP, like our TA, SFT, and IGP TPs, stresses clarity of communication ("sharpening their language"), *how* members listen and express themselves (body language), and "saying clearly what they want." The SCT TP has members face the fork in the road. The intention is to have members choose which side of the issue each wishes to address. By choosing, members would then be in a position to explore their defenses or explore that which their defenses are defending against.

Both Gestalt and REBT TPs utilize role playing as an intervention during the latter portion of their sessions, although the methods and purposes differ. The Gestalt TP employs role playing as "experiments" in interpersonal transactions with others to make individuals more aware of their behaviors. In contrast, the REBT TP selects a member who presents a concern and, in a fashion similar to the TA TP, conducts an individual transaction with the member. He demonstrates, however, the process of REBT problem solving with this member to the group (imitative learning) as opposed to the TA TP's contracting process. The REBT TP involves other members to challenge and question the problem-solving member and to involve themselves in REBT problem solving. The SFT and the CBT TPs also use members as resources to one another in the problem-solving process. Therefore, the REBT TP employs the universality of experience around the process of problem solving; further, he and the SFT and CBT TPs are the only ones who require homework assignments for their group members for purposes of practicing new behaviors.

SUMMARY OF CRITICAL INCIDENT 1

Clearly, all TPs are interested in having members talk or participate in the beginning group session. With the exception of the client-centered and psychodynamic therapy TPs, all others are active in providing varying amounts of structure or direction to get group members talking. The crucial difference among TPs is *how* and *when* they decide to involve group members. For instance, the REBT TP demonstrates the most explicit form of structuring, whereas the client-centered and psychodynamic therapy TPs demonstrate the least amount of structuring. It might be inferred that these two interventions reflect the extremes of *therapist-centered* (REBT) and *group-centered* (client-centered) intervention styles.

Specific TP similarities are the Gestalt, TA, IGP, SCT, FCT, and SFT TPs who emphasize specific member concerns and the identification of member feelings in the here and now of the group. Other similarities include the REBT and Gestalt TPs' uses of role playing and the Adlerian, Gestalt, REBT, IGP, SCT, and SFT TPs' emphases on cohesion and universality (group processes). Specific differences among TPs are the introduction of contracting (TA and CBT), homework (REBT, CBT, and SFT), and group-as-a-whole intervention (client-centered and psychodynamic).

Critical Incident 2

Critical Incident 2 addresses the issues of group members' views and complaints regarding the therapists' competency to conduct the therapy group.

To varying degrees, the client-centered, reality therapy, Adlerian, REBT, IGT, and SCT TPs openly acknowledge some responsibility for having been uncaring, cold, and distant toward the group, whereas the TA and Gestalt TPs initiate interventions at slightly different rates and styles toward members expressing the most intense affect. The CBT TP departs from the others by discussing the importance of coleadership in cases where the therapist is attacked. The IGP TPs also support the use of coleaders to assist the leader being challenged to respond in a way that models an effective way to receive feedback. The SFT TP provides a response that elicits member participation and ownership in the process. She invites members to consider what they would like to do more of and whether they have any negative reaction to the way she is structuring the group. The FCT TP is likely to move the conversation to a discussion about role differentiation. He hopes that the members will be able to use their reactions to him "as a springboard" before working on their reactions to one another. The psychodynamic therapy TP prefers to go with the resistance of members discussing "safer issues" and uses that opportunity to help members see the relationship between feelings from the previous session and those expressed in the present moment.

The client-centered TP clearly assumes the most responsibility by disclosing ineptness in previous sessions and contributing to the current state of affairs (self-disclosure). He invites criticism from the group and views it as an opportunity for learning about his errors. Implicit in the invitation, he uses himself as a model so that "criticism eventually shifts to group members as we move to higher forms of individuality." He implies by his statement his collusion (group process) with the group in avoiding more important interactions. Apart from disclosing substantially less responsibility for the "group's floundering," the Adlerian TP, like the client-centered TP, invites group criticism to "learn about myself and how I come across as a leader" and views the incident as an opportunity for group development. In a similar way, the SCT TP addresses the members' feedback directly; however, unlike the client-centered response, she moves the group into a discussion of how she might be behaving in ways to help or hinder the work in the group. Her response is similar to the SFT TP in that both are trying to include all members in providing feedback and making next steps toward more effective group functioning. The Adlerian TP differs from the client-centered TP by structuring group feedback, asking what he should be doing and what would a real therapist be doing. Clearly, his structuring comments, along with those of the SCT and SFT TPs serve to dilute the affective components of members' complaints, whereas the client-centered TP's "open invitation" allows for affective components to be expressed.

Our REBT and reality therapy TPs use self-disclosures that assume "half of the responsibility for the group's floundering." The reality therapy TP validates, "in part," the group's reaction and recommits himself to contribute more but is curious about *why* the group "wants me to run the show." The REBT TP views the group as "copping out," admitting he "didn't structure the process well enough," and going on to reeducate the group on the purposes of REBT; unlike the reality therapy TP, however, he explains the *why* of their avoidance.

Unlike the other TPs, the Gestalt, and TA TPs do not disclose responsibility and discount the group's attack. The Gestalt TP views the group's waiting for a member to present a therapeutic "opening" in the present session; she invites responses to "unfinished business" or addresses a member with "spoken vehemence" from the previous session. The client-centered, Adlerian, reality therapy, IGP, SCT, FCT, SFT, and Gestalt TPs view the incident as an opportunity for group movement or "new emotional territory" (norm development).

The TA TP, like the Gestalt TP, views the group's "small talk" as a continuation of "revealing client's programming" and attends to those members displaying the most intense affect in either the current or previous session. Both TA and Gestalt TPs, in terms of shaping and initiating their interventions, acknowledge the importance of the group's history (previous sessions) and of members who display the most intense affect. In addition, the Gestalt, TA, and REBT TPs focus on individual transactions between leader and member to demonstrate their therapeutic expertise and discount attending to group processes, which are more characteristic of the client-centered, Adlerian, reality therapy, IGP, SCT, FCT, and SFT TPs.

Our TA and FCT TPs are the only ones who address the issue of extra-group socializing and how the interaction outside the group influences subsequent group behavior in the form of a subgroup. The TA TP also notes the importance of "end programming" this subgroup with the larger group.

The emphasis on understanding the causes of the flare-up is articulated by the IGP TPs. They encourage members to "describe their experience in getting angry." The expression of angry feelings in this intervention is coupled with the opportunity for members to understand their experience. Similarly, the psychodynamic therapy TP wants members to express their feelings and to "understand that the feelings they have are not random or chaotic, but rather reasonable and understandable." This focus on meaning attribution is also expressed by the SFT TP. Both the SFT and SCT TPs utilize group-as-a-whole interventions.

Of all the TPs, the CBT TP demonstrates most clearly how a coleadership model would be effective in this particular incident. He provides the example of how one leader could receive the feedback while the other could "slow down the process" in order for the feedback to be heard and for therapeutic learning to take place. His focus is on making sure that both the group and the leader would not be damaged. Once the criterion "do no harm," is in place, the group can attend to "the therapeutic meaning of the attack," and then learning for group leaders and members can occur. The emphasis on coleadership is central to this particular intervention.

SUMMARY OF CRITICAL INCIDENT 2

Six of our TPs (client-centered, Adlerian, reality, REBT, SCT, and SFT) utilize varying amounts of therapist self-disclosure to account for ineptness in conducting prior group sessions in order to dilute the growing attack (emotional contagion) in the current group session. In contrast, the Gestalt and TA TPs covertly acknowledge the influence of group history (group processes) on the current session but choose to attend to those members displaying the most intense affect.

The SFT, SCT, FCT, IGP, and psychodynamic therapy TPs utilize the group as a whole to begin exploring the feelings and reactions to the therapist. These therapists invite discussion at the group level. The Adlerian and REBT TPs exhibit control over the amount of affect expressed in the group by their structuring comments. The CBT and IGP TPs emphasize the therapeutic role of coleaders to facilitate the giving and receiving of feedback to the leader.

Most of the TPs view the incident as an opportunity to shape new norms and enhance group movement. Interestingly, the TA and FCT TPs introduce the possible existence and influence of two group processes—extragroup socializing and subgrouping—evolving in the current incident.

Critical Incident 3

Critical Incident 3 addresses the issue of group denial in response to a member's discussion about death.

All TPs agree that the issue of death, as verbalized by Jean, must not be avoided (denied) by the group, and all view Jean as needing support. In dealing with the group's denial, the Gestalt and client-centered TPs focus primarily on Jean; the Adlerian, reality, psychodynamic therapy, and SCT TPs focus largely on the group; the REBT, TA, IGP, SFT, and FCT TPs attend both to the group and Jean. The CBT TP brings in the issue of "voluntary collaboration" and the larger issue of ethics. He is concerned that the group may not be ready for the discussion that is being avoided.

Although both the Gestalt and client-centered TPs attend primarily to Jean's distress and have similar outcomes for the session, the manner in which they intervene varies significantly. Both are intent on serving as *the* providers of support for Jean because the group appears immobilized or traumatized at the time, and both are concerned with creating group support and reducing fear in members by means of their individual interactions with Jean (imitative learning).

The Gestalt TP goes through a series of confronting interventions with Jean, which attends to Jean's feelings about the group's response to her sadness. Her interventions require Jean to disclose her feelings, by having her fantasize and dialogue with the dead boy, while the therapist observes her body movements. She views this intense encounter (emotional stimulation) as "support generation momentum" (instillation of hope) in having provided other group members with the ability to face the issue of death.

The client-centered TP sees Jean as a "human in pain" and becomes "absorbed" in her pain by means of empathic interventions and models to the group (imitative learning) appropriate responses to help members overcome their fears (instillation of hope). Unlike the Gestalt TP, he does not attend to Jean's body movements; but similar to the Gestalt TP, he offers no guidance other than modeling for the group members. The client-centered TP, in contrast to the other TPs, talks about this desire to cry and why he decided to avoid it.

Although the reality therapy, Adlerian, SCT, and psychodynamic therapy TPs direct their interventions primarily toward the group, the way they view and treat the group is quite different. The reality therapy TP, in conceptualizing his interventions, considers the "formation history" of the group in that nurses were "told" to attend; consequently, individual differences exist among nurses regarding their expectations of group. He emphasizes the therapist's ability to recall personal history (recall of pain) in dealing with issues of death. In sum, the therapist must respect individual differences among members.

In contrast, the Adlerian TP confronts the denying group by the use of paradox, with little concern for group history or individual differences among the nurses. He confronts the group as a whole by describing their avoidance and states the paradox "Why not work at figuring how we can be nurses who only work with well people?" (emotional stimulation). He continues the paradoxical intervention using provocative statements until, hopefully, a member recognizes the paradox and the denial subsides. If, even after repeated interventions, the group still does not recognize the paradox, he would dismiss the group, leaving them with a final paradox to discuss the next session, but would invite Jean to meet with him privately. The reality therapy TP, in contrast, invites the group as a whole to focus on what Jean said, acknowledges their pain, and asks members what "we can do to help Jean deal with her grief." Clearly, his intent is similar to the Gestalt and client-centered TPs. The REBT and TA TPs also elicit support for Jean by means of generating immediate group support, as opposed to therapist support. The Adlerian TP, in contrast, tries to evoke (provoke) group support for Jean.

Both the REBT and TA TPs initially address the group as a whole, as do the reality therapy, Adlerian, psychodynamic therapy, and SCT TPs. However, the TA TP quickly refocuses the group from safer responses by joining Jean's feelings, ignores any group comments, and begins working with Jean. The REBT TP, in contrast to the TA TP, first spends time interpreting the group's resistance ("unconscious cop-out") and subsequently attempts to link members with Jean (universality). "I wonder if you, like Jean, have some real problems, when one of your patients dies like hers did." He continues to prod members to question the *whys* of their fears and "overconcern with death" at the expense of more personal issues. Thus, he creates a form of "environmental support" similar to the Gestalt, TA, reality therapy, client-centered, psychodynamic therapy, SCT, IGP, SFT, and FCT TPs, but by addressing the group. Once support is mobilized, he directs his attention to Jean.

Taking the involuntary membership situation into account, the CBT TP raises the issue of ethics and reiterates that "voluntary collaboration" is at the heart of CBT therapy. If the entire group is avoiding, then the question arises about whether clients are willing or unwilling. In the view of the CBT TP, the client is the head nurse who sets up the group to accomplish a task but is not present in the group. He points out that a contract and a discussion of norms, goals, and ground rules may not work well in the current situation where the members have not been given a choice about whether to be in the group. He is further concerned about Jean and addresses her feelings while pointing out that Jean's feelings of despair might not be shared by others in the group, so he invites members to leave if they so desire. If members stay, then they are exerting their decision to remain in the group; thus, the intervention offers members an opportunity to take some ownership in a group that was planned ahead for them. We are left at the end of this intervention with the question of whether group therapy can be effective with unwilling clients.

In her response to this critical incident, the SFT TP reiterates the value of forming groups with heterogeneous concerns and points out that the group formation is a very important group leader intervention. Groups formed in this way are likely to have members who have coping skills in dealing with death, whereas others have strengths in different areas. As she notes, both the issues of maternity and death deal with loss. In a group organized by heterogeneous concerns, she would look for ways to help one participant discuss her loss about not being able to have children, while she could focus on Jean, who in this incident feels despair and loss regarding the death of a boy. The SFT TP focuses on action, not feelings, and structures some questioning to "encourage movement and energy." This approach is needed because SFT groups are only six sessions in length. She closes with a homework assignment to help members express their fears and wishes to avoid certain topics. She strongly believes that the group process only works when people are involved and can serve as models to one another on a range of issues.

The psychodynamic therapy TP views the statement "there is some hope" as a group-coping statement—a statement that reflects the best way that the group can cope in the moment. In his intervention, he links the hopeful statement with Jean's earlier comment. For him, what followed Jean's comment is not a change of subject but an elaboration of the same subject. His intervention links Jean's despair with the group's comments about hope, thus creating a both or and experience. Perhaps through this intervention, Jean will feel less excluded, and the group as a whole might be more ready to tackle the painful feelings. The SCT TP takes a similar approach in that she embraces both or and in her intervention when she states, "Jean, today is the group voice of despair and anguish, Diane and Tom and Julie are voicing the group hope." Her intervention addresses the group as a whole and engages a discussion that taps both voices. She wants members to confront a reality that contains living as well as dying; thus, members are helped to recognize and value both sides of nursing.

The IGP and FCT TPs choose to address the denial directly and broaden the discussion to include other members of the group. The here-and-now emphasis is evident when the IGP TPs invite members to reflect on "the way they backed away from Jean's emotional expression, and how they use denial in their daily work." In this instance, members have the opportunity to learn how their denial can be a helpful or problematic behavior. The FCT TP recognizes the coping response in the group but views it as avoiding. He makes a comment that also broadens the discussion of death. He hopes to support Jean and provide some common ground for members to discuss the issue of death. His homework assignment gives members the chance to continue their focus on death and to discover the personal and systemic implication of death in their lives.

The REBT and psychodynamic therapy TPs acknowledge the role of the unconscious and subconscious in influencing group behavior.

SUMMARY OF CRITICAL INCIDENT 3

All TPs believe the issue of death, as expressed by Jean, should not be avoided (denied) and that she requires support. The critical difference among TP interventions is *how* they choose to provide support for Jean. Specifically, support for Jean is provided by the therapists (client-centered, Gestalt, reality), by the group (Adlerian, psychodynamic therapy, SCT), and by both the therapist and the group (REBT, TA, CBT, FCT, and SFT). Interestingly, all TPs believe their respective interventions would simultaneously reduce group members' fears of talking about death while providing support for Jean.

Many of Yalom's (1995) curative factors are noticeable in these interventions: universality, instillation of hope, imitative learning, interpersonal learning, and existential issues. Lieberman, Yalom, and Miles's (1973) findings regarding effective leadership are also present: high levels of caring and meaning attribution and moderate levels of emotional stimulation and executive function.

Unique procedures suggested by the TPs in this incident are fantasy and dialogue (Gestalt), group interpretation of unconscious behavior (psychodynamic and REBT), a private therapy session with Jean (Adlerian and CBT), and the discussion on the ethics of involuntary clients (CBT).

Critical Incident 4

Critical Incident 4 addresses three issues: (1) a member announcing departure from the group in the beginning moments of session 5; (2) the resulting group silence; (3) the decision-making process regarding termination or continuation in the group.

The client-centered and TA TPs' initial response to John's announced departure and consequent group silence is their own silence. The client-centered TP uses the silence to internally diagnose his feelings regarding the announcement, assumes that a group response will eventually occur, but is unclear what he would do if the group remains silent. The TA TP uses the silence to conduct an internal diagnosis of those members exhibiting "intense ego-states" in response to John and what they mean theoretically. In sum, for the TA TP, the *why* of member behavior is important to the group therapist, whereas the *how* is important for the members. The TA TP's subsequent strategies, unlike those of the client-centered TP, call for inviting John to tell members "how he wants them to respond" and for members to respond to John (feedback).

Our Gestalt, reality therapy, psychodynamic therapy, IGP, FCT, SCT, SFT, and CBT TPs bypass the silence and initiate action with John. The Gestalt TP, unlike the TA TP, wants to know specifically *why* John was leaving, for his benefit as well as the group's, and wonders whether John thinks "Since I cannot such and such in this group, I feel like leaving." Similar to the TA TP, the Gestalt TP is concerned with the intense member reactions to John's announcement, but more in terms of their identifying those feelings (helplessness, sadness) that were similar to John's (universality).

The reality therapy TP initiates action with John by self-disclosure, "I feel sad to hear you're leaving," and showing caring, "because I like you and think you can contribute something important." He continues working with John by stressing the crucialness of the decision to leave the group and how it relates to doubts regarding his second marriage (insight). The reality therapy TP, unlike the other TPs, views it as imperative that John express his feelings and see the correlation between action and feelings with the group "waiting in the wings" until John saw the *why* of his behavior.

The psychodynamic therapy TP sees John's behavior as consistent with his presenting problem. Insight is a major ingredient in psychodynamic therapy; thus, the psychodynamic therapy TP's direct and immediate intervention is directed to John with the hope that he can help John see "how his wish to leave the group he agreed to join fits into his characteristic style of coping." His intervention, though directed to John, enlists the curiosity of other members to examine what lay beneath behaviors and feelings.

The IGP TPs continue the theme of exploring the *why* of John's behavior. They wonder about "why he has decided to leave, what he hoped to get from the group that he was not getting, and whether he has any understanding of what has contributed to his disappointing experience." Like the psychodynamic therapy TP, they see John's behavior in the group as a representative indicator of his present interpersonal difficulties. In extending the conversation to group members, the IGP TPs teach members how to work in the here and now. If John states that he feels as if he does not fit in, then members would be asked to state whether they agree with his perception of himself in relation to the group. These TPs recognize that, as they reinforce the norms of working in the here and now, they can also teach members to function more effectively in the group therapy setting.

The FCT TP is joined by the CBT and SFT TPs in recognizing that, as the CBT TP stated, "therapy is neither long term or a single-unit process." All believe that the door can remain open for John to continue at a later time. The FCT TP focuses on how to take John's statement of departure from the group and help it become a therapeutic event for John and the group. "Since John has dropped the bomb, how can the group help him go out with a bang?" He recognizes that both John and the group are on the brink of John learning about "his pattern of getting lost and leaving" and the group in terms of "moving into purposeful work or losing its sense of purpose and direction." He uses an adaptation of the miracle question. By inviting John to brainstorm in the here and now of the group, he works with John and helps other members provide input and feedback to John. He also reminds the group that they will process this activity and John's leaving at the next session. In summary then, the FCT TP gives John and the group members something to take with them to reflect on and possibly propel the group further into the working stage of group therapy.

The SFT TP also leaves the door open for John. Her initial response to the incident is to reiterate the importance of pretraining and preparing members for successful experiences. In John's case, she recognizes that he has not really been able to articulate a goal; thus, his feelings of helplessness are not good signs for success in an SFT group. She uses the incident to describe how to better prepare a member, like John, so that he can reframe his feelings into a workable goal. She invites the members to "react and respond in ways that they choose." She stays tuned to the process by watching carefully for the impact of the group's feedback on John. Her tone is upbeat as she shares with John her appreciation for his presence and the gains he has made. In sum, she views this event as a chance for John to go out and try the behaviors and language he has learned in the group and perhaps return at a later date to another group. She states, "When a group member prematurely decides to leave a group, it is a reminder that people change at different rates and need different levels of support."

The CBT TP initially focuses on John. He then extends the focus to the group for a discussion on such issues as appreciations, needs, hopes, and wishes for the departing member. The focus on John and then the group is shared by the psychodynamic therapy, IGP, SFT, and FCT TPs. The CBT TP brings up the point of having a balance between the here-and-now events in the group and the relationship of the events to the group's agenda. He is sensitive to John and the departure issue but at the same time directs his interventions to the purpose of the group. He once again emphasizes the importance of having a coleader to maximize that the balance between process and content occurs and that the content stays connected to the purpose of the group.

The SCT TP chooses to use the group-as-a-whole energy to help clarify John's concerns. This alternative to reacting at the individual level expands the focus to larger questions and issues to which all members could relate. Her intervention diffuses "taking things personally" and provides grist for the therapeutic mill that could benefit all members. In addition, it avoids having the group scapegoat John.

Both the REBT, Adlerian, and SCT TPs direct their interventions to the group. The REBT TP wants details regarding members' feelings about John's departure for purposes of identifying their self-blaming and hopeless feelings and teaching them not to "illegitimately rate themselves." Unwittingly, later in the session, when the REBT TP focuses on John's "self-blaming behaviors," he also initiates the process of universality, as does the Gestalt TP. The REBT TP is similar to the Gestalt TP in attempting to elicit the *why* of members' behavior, but different from the Gestalt TP in that he explains the why (imparting information) by means of REBT theory. The Gestalt TP generates the *why* from John. Both the REBT and Gestalt TPs also rely on the use of specific exercises (imagery and dialoguing) for members to dispute faulty thinking, as well as a means of clarifying John's faulty thinking.

The Adlerian TP asks the group, "Does anyone here like John, want him in the group? How would you see him helping the group, helping you?" His group intervention parallels the REBT TP's by having members present feedback to John regarding his behavior and simultaneously relieving members from being responsible or blaming themselves for John's departure. This intervention also gives John the opportunity of seeing what was and was not likable about him so that he could make a responsible decision regarding termination. Being placed in the position of being responsible appears to correlate with the TA TP's notion of John being in an Adult ego-state when making his decision to leave group.

ISSUE OF DEALING WITH MEMBER TERMINATION

The reality therapy TP stands alone in having asked John to *think* about his decision to leave group for 1 week and to return for the following session before making his final decision. In contrast, the client-centered TP appears to leave or "trust" the decision to John. Several of the TPs (CBT, SFT, and FCT) recognize that therapy is not a single-unit process and are willing to keep the door open for John. The remaining TPs seem to take a middle-of-the-road position by initiating process either toward John (Gestalt and reality), toward John and the group (SFT, FCT, psychodynamic, CBT, IGP), or toward the group (REBT, TA, Adlerian, and SCT), for purposes of helping him make a responsible decision in the current session. At varying degrees, all TPs are concerned that the remaining group members *not* feel a sense of being responsible if John chooses to leave.

SUMMARY OF CRITICAL INCIDENT 4

The outstanding similarity among five of the TPs in Critical Incident 4, with the exception of the client-centered TP, is their concern with the *why* of John's behavior or the group's behavior (silence) and *how* they employ or discount the group silence in making their interventions.

The Gestalt, reality therapy, Adlerian, IGP, and psychodynamic therapy TPs are concerned that John *discover* the why of his behavior, although their strategies differ. In contrast, the REBT TP *explains* the way to John, whereas the TA TP *internally diagnoses* the why and is more interested in John knowing the *how* of his behavior. Interestingly, the client-centered TP internally diagnosed the why of his *personal reaction* to John.

Both the TA and client-centered TPs use the silence to complete their internal diagnosis, whereas the remaining TPs bypass the silence to work on the why of John's announced departure by attending to the group, to John, or both.

Unlike the other TPs, the TA and Gestalt TPs confront these members who show the greatest discomfort with John's behavior, even though the TPs' view of why was different. Both REBT and Gestalt TPs employ specific exercises to clarify John's faulty thinking.

With regard to John's termination, most TPs leave the decision to him. The reality therapy TP differs by asking John to attend one more session before making a final decision to leave the group.

Critical Incident 5

Critical Incident 5 deals with issues concerning an emotional outburst, with 15 minutes remaining in session 7 of a therapy group, as well as group closure within the prescribed time limits of the group.

With regard to the emotional outburst, *all* TPs acknowledge the importance of Sandra's outburst by attending to her directly. Four TPs (Gestalt, REBT, TA, and reality) specifically choose to reward Sandra for her expression of feeling.

The Adlerian and client-centered TPs choose not to reward Sandra's behavior. However, all TPs encourage Sandra to continue verbalizing and exploring her thoughts and feelings to the group, to specific members, or to the therapist. The client-centered TP encourages Sandra to continue exploring her thoughts and feelings (self-exploration) and rewards continual exploration. He appears content to allow members to respond "at will," without direction, hoping that some "bridge building" (linking or identification) will occur naturally among members. The Adlerian TP assumes a similar approach to focusing on Sandra's outburst but differs from the client-centered TP by summarizing Sandra's behavior and providing a framework (framing) for purposes of having Sandra compare her current group behavior with similar behavior with her husband outside the therapy group (insight). The REBT TP assumes a similar posture to the Adlerian TP in that he provides a framework for explaining and educating Sandra about the why of her behavior according to the A-B-C-D-E construct of personality. However, he chooses to involve group members in helping Sandra, by answering some questions he poses to her or Jonathan. Therefore, he elicits group involvement at a cognitive level, unlike the client-centered and Adlerian TPs, and also indoctrinates or teaches members to understand and apply principles of REBT theory. The TA TP, like the Adlerian and REBT TPs, has an internal framework for understanding Sandra's and members' behavior (ego-states) but does *not* employ his internal framework to explain member behavior, as does the REBT TP. Rather, he has Sandra act on the framework by suggesting she let Jonathan and other members know specifically "how you want them to respond to your feelings right now." The TA TP, like the client-centered TP, assumes that member involvement might occur without direction, but unlike the client-centered TP, he acknowledges that "members has important feelings to explore in future sessions."

The Gestalt TP, like the TA TP, encourages Sandra to make specific statements to Jonathan (feedback) and other members of the group by confronting them directly with her complaints, as opposed to asking them to respond to what she wants them to acknowledge. The Gestalt, IGP, SCT, psychodynamic therapy, CBT, SFT, and FCT TPs, unlike the client-centered TA, and Adlerian TPs, facilitate member involvement *after* dealing with Sandra by asking Jonathan and other members to verbalize their feelings regarding Sandra's outburst.

In contrast to other TPs, the reality therapy TP acknowledges Sandra's pain (empathy) and subsequently utilizes self-disclosure about himself as a means of providing a framework for Sandra to understand her current behavior. Unlike other TPs, our reality therapy TP poses two alternatives, from which Sandra and the group can choose, to pursue examination of her behavior. In addition, he first solicits Sandra and Jonathan's permission (consent) and, subsequently, other group members' input regarding their desire to participate in examining Sandra's behavior. In making the statement "If the group wishes . . . ," the reality therapy TP employs a group-as-a-whole intervention, as opposed to the primary emphasis on intrapsychic interventions and to a very lesser degree interpersonal interventions by other TPs. The reality therapy TP clearly tends to emphasize the importance of group involvement by actively soliciting members' input.

The IGP TPs are concerned about "containing the affect" and "protecting Sandra." Their usual approach might be to help express the affect, but in this case, given the early development of the group, the lack of Sandra's participation, the weak bonds between members, and the limited time, they choose to intervene first, to acknowledge Sandra's feelings and to invite others to share their feelings in response to anger. The IGP TPs want Sandra to feel heard and at the same time provide her with some content on which to reflect—if not in the moment, then over the next week. The idea that there must be something to learn from this situation might "moderate her discomfort and encourage her to return to the next session." They would likely phone her the next day to see how she is doing and to reinforce the messages they made in the group. The TPs then shift the focus to the other group members and their discomfort. Their hope is that, by addressing the feelings of Sandra and the group members and returning to the topic in future weeks, both Sandra and the other members will heighten their awareness of how they affect others, how they respond to conflict, and how they respond to anger. Implied in their intervention is the opportunity for interpersonal learning that will transcend the actual group experience (corrective emotional experience).

The SCT TP starts with Sandra, in order to give her some room for her feelings, hoping that she can take care of Sandra, prepare the group to end, and prepare the group for work in the next session. The TP is clear that she would stay within the 15-minute time frame. She also presents a skillful strategy for attending to Sandra and attending to the group. The here-and-now focus allows her to reframe Sandra's expressions so that those expressions are connected to Sandra, to other members, and to the goals of the group. Her interventions are similar to the IGP TPs in that she needs to contain Sandra's emotions in order to come to some therapeutic closure for the group. As she states, "No one can do their work if they are not in a state to work." Her interventions convey caring, meaning attribution, emotional stimulation, and executive function.

In the psychodynamic therapy intervention, the TP has three goals: (1) Support the expression of affect ("we seem to have an opportunity for the very type of authentic, 'nonshallow' interactions that each of you came to learn more about"); (2) make the point that the group process is continual ("we will continue this next week"); and (3) point out that present interactions parallel the presenting problems that members brought to the group ("pay careful attention to what you are feeling at this moment"). He focuses on the group as a whole and sees the therapeutic possibilities that derive from the group interactions. In this intervention, the psychodynamic therapy TP does not extend the group time, believing that Sandra's emotional statement near the end of the group was made for a reason: It perfectly highlights what she and the other group members most feared—"an intense, deep, and authentic encounter." With this intervention, he communicates that the group is the agent of change.

The CBT TP reinforces the value of coleadership and flexible ending times; he also recognizes how "unresolved unexpected attacks are dangerous to all group members." Thus, his intervention is active and direct in nature. With two leaders present, one leader can support Sandra, thanking her for her courage, and the other leader can help the remaining group members listen and attend more actively. For him, the silence is a crucial issue, and if members are not looking at Sandra, he will have moved in quickly and started a discussion about their avoidance behavior. If his group-as-a-whole intervention does not succeed, he will then invite each member to look directly at Sandra and talk to her about the feelings her statement aroused. His goal is to break the avoidance cycle. He makes the point that Sandra's behavior will be reinforced only if it is "rare, difficult, and potentially profitable." If he assesses that Sandra's behavior is "common, easy, and disrupts the group for no good reason," he will ignore, confront, or perhaps exclude the member.

In the SFT model, the TP begins by wondering what her role has been in this "eruption," while also musing about whether Sandra's behavior is "just another example of her attempt to apply more of a poor solution to the relationships in life . . . resulting in shallowness with her significant others." This latter observation is made because of Sandra's use of absolutes and labels. The SFT TP breaks the silence by reframing her statements from absolutes into qualifiers. For example, she states, "Much of the time you feel that the group members aren't listening to you. When is a time you felt listened to in here?" or "When is a time you were listened to *just a little bit?*" By using the here and now, she responds as do the CBT, IGP, psychodynamic therapy, and FCT TPs. Her inclusion of polyocularity provides Sandra with the opportunity to receive members' viewpoints, suggestions, and feedback. Along with CBT, IGP, and FCT TPs, SFT TPs share the collective view that this type of silence would not have occurred in their groups for this long a period of time. The FCT TP raises other issues, therapeutic and ethical. In his view, Sandra's outburst is "not a usual deep disclosure." He expresses his concern that Sandra is not appropriate for this group. In his view, ineffective screening and placement, coupled with inappropriate group leadership and process, precipitate the depth, direction, and impact of her affective statement in the group. Given his grave concerns, he immediately seeks to comfort Sandra, and he is prepared to extend the group time to do so. Thus, his intervention is at the individual level, bringing in the other group members if their assistance is needed. He uses the additional strategies of a contract and possible referral to individual therapy or another group.

SESSION CLOSURE AND PREPARATION FOR THE SUBSEQUENT SESSION

Closing a session within a short period of time following an emotional outburst by a group member is dealt with in several ways by the TPs.

Clearly, the REBT, reality therapy, TA, Gestalt, FCT, SCT, SFT, psychodynamic therapy, and IGP TPs explicitly note the need to give closure to the group and some direction (structuring for the subsequent session).

Both the TA and Gestalt TPs encourage Sandra to initiate the next session by addressing her feelings, whereas the TA TP emphasizes the importance of ending the current group by having an available Adult ego-state or some control over her behavior instead of her present Child ego-state. The reality therapy TP and, particularly, the REBT and SCT TPs are more explicit with regard to preparing *all* group members for the subsequent session by giving them homework assignments. Sandra is asked by the SFT TP to "notice those times when others listen to her." The IGP, SCT, and psychodynamic therapy TPs attend to the here and now of the reactions to the outburst as grist for the therapeutic mill not only in future sessions but also for life outside the group. Inherent in these TPs' approaches is a concern with ambiguity reduction for Sandra during the closing 15 minutes and varying amounts of direction for members during and following this session. The CBT TP would have extended the group time in order to accommodate Sandra's needs, whereas the psychodynamic therapy TP emphasizes that he would not extend the time. The Adlerian TP takes a different position from many of the others but similar to the psychodynamic therapy TP, in that he views the closing 15 minutes as a "beginning" for this group and that "important and personal work" has only begun. The SCT TP thinks that the 15 minutes could be used effectively to "prepare ourselves to work next week." Therefore, closure is not necessary at this time, and a state of disequilibrium among members is a prerequisite for "some hard self-analysis" between sessions. The client-centered TP, like the Adlerian TP, does not provide direction for the subsequent session but assumes that members will learn to respond to each other as a function of witnessing his interaction with Sandra (modeling). The FCT TP is primarily concerned with his analysis that this particular disclosure is not of the usual type, and he focuses more on screening and ethical issues.

SUMMARY OF CRITICAL INCIDENT 5

Clearly, all TPs agree that Sandra's emotional outburst, with 15 minutes remaining in group, must be attended to. *How* they choose to involve her participation in exploring her thoughts and feelings demonstrate both intervention similarities and differences. More specifically, the TPs' interventions are directed either to the group (REBT, reality, psychodynamic, SCT), to specific members (TA, Gestalt), or to the therapist (client-centered, reality). Our TP strategies for involving Sandra's participation include self-exploration and reward (client-centered), behavior summarization and framing (Adlerian), questioning and education (REBT), group-as-a-whole intervention and leader self-disclosure (reality and SCT), and confrontation (Gestalt and TA). The IGP, FCT, SFT, and CBT TPs focus on Sandra first and then bring in other members for their reactions and feedback.

With regard to closure of the group session, the REBT, reality therapy, TA, FCT, SCT, psychodynamic therapy, SFT, IGP, CBT, and Gestalt TPs agree that some closure or preparation for the subsequent session is necessary, whereas the Adlerian and client-centered TPs view closure and preparation for the subsequent session as unnecessary.

Critical Incident 6

Critical Incident 6 addresses the issue of a group attack on a denying member during the middle of the group session.

All TPs seem to agree that Joe (denying member) is being scapegoated and needs support and protection. Further, they think that the group attack on his behavior should be diluted or de-escalated because the attack will only increase his denying behavior.

To dilute or de-escalate the group attack, the TA, Gestalt, Adlerian, reality therapy, FCT, CBT, SFT, psychodynamic therapy, and IGT TPs focus initially on Joe, for varying periods of time, before attending to group members, whereas the client-centered, REBT, and SCT TPs direct their early interventions toward the group.

Both the TA and Gestalt TPs view Joe's behavior as assertive (more than the group members) and attempt to define reality or provide a framework for Joe by means of comparing the group's demands with demands he experienced in his work setting (insight). Similarly, the SCT, psychodynamic therapy, and IGP TPs wonder if there might be a "familiar ring" to the feedback Joe is hearing. The psychodynamic therapy TP is interested in promoting insight into the connection between Joe's style at work and what he had learned as a child. The TA TP assumes a more protective role for Joe than does the Gestalt TP because he believes he had colluded with the group (group history) by not inviting Joe to work on resistances in previous sessions. The IGP TPs' initial protective stance comes from their view that Joe's "back is against the wall." Whereas the TA TP focuses on defining reality, helping Joe express himself more openly and subsequently interacting with other members, the Gestalt TP assumes that Jim and Jackie (two intense reactors) were *not* as open as Joe and confronts them to be specific about *what* Joe did that frightens them (feedback).

The here-and-now focus is shared by a number of TPs. The SCT TP focuses on differences in her group-as-a-whole intervention. She believes that the group is grappling with "how difficult it is to be different—to stand up for oneself and what one believes even when it means taking a position that is different from everybody else." She hopes that the group can go beyond acting-out in order to "take this opportunity to explore all sides of the issue: the impulse to attack, the impulse to avoid being attacked even if it means losing ourselves, and the impulse to seek out no matter what it costs." The FCT TP continues the focus on differences in the here and now by devising a fishbowl exercise and role playing to walk that fine line between "encouraging Joe to hold his position and encouraging the group, particularly Jackie and Jim, to hold their position." He views these conflicts as reflective of problems and patterns that members are experiencing in their daily lives. The use of here-and-now work is aimed at helping all members develop strategies for addressing conflict in their lives outside the group setting. In their here-and-now interventions, the IGP TPs want to focus on the strengths expressed as members try new assertive behaviors, even if the behaviors are not completely successful. For example, Joe could be acknowledged for the fact that his response in this group (he did not submit to the group's pressure) is different from his usual response at work. The IGP TPs want us to expand our response options beyond a focus on problems to "discovering hidden strengths."

The psychodynamic therapy TP uses the here and now to help "create meaning." He wants to help Joe connect his family-of-origin issues to what is happening at that moment in the group. Through that discussion, he hopes that members will develop some empathy for Joe and recognize that they may have projected their own needs onto Joe. The CBT TP sees the incident as a here-and-now example of the issue for which the group was formed (lack of assertiveness). In the CBT framework, collaboration is a key for change. He hopes that, by recasting the problem into a skill and through using homework assignments, he can strengthen the impact of this collaborative skill-training model. He asks Joe to consider identifying any feelings experienced over the week and to bring them to the next group. The main goal is to teach Joe to appreciate the collaborative learning process. Finally, he reminds us again of the value of coleadership: One leader can encourage Joe to continue his interaction and the other leader can slow down the group by asking, "Was what you just said and did assertive?" to any member who criticized Joe. Both Joe and the group have great potential for learning new adaptive behaviors.

Similar to the CBT TP, the SFT TP does not believe that this type of incident would occur in her group. Part of the prescreening process is to teach members the language of SFT and to understand, like the CBT TP, that everyone is expected to share in this type of group. She chooses to respond to this incident by developing her own scenario, illustrating how Joe might be screened and prepared for the group in order to effectively learn in an "atmosphere of belonging and commonality." The process of identifying and practicing solutions is a collaborative one; thus, her view is similar to the ones expressed by the CBT, IGP, and SCT TPs. She demonstrates the use of solution-focused language, linking statements, homework, the miracle question, and the connection between work in the group to life outside the group.

Our Adlerian and reality therapy TPs conduct "individual therapy" with Joe, apparently seeking causes (why) for his behavior in group. The Adlerian TP spends time explaining and interpreting the goals of Joe's behavior, until Joe "agrees," which in turn would elicit different responses than anger from group members. The reality therapy TP, in contrast, asks Joe *why* he joined the group and *what* his goals were. Continual denial would have led the TP to ask Joe to evaluate his decision to stay in the group but also to commit himself to returning the following week.

The Adlerian, reality therapy, and client-centered TPs advocate an individual or private session outside of group to assess Joe's current group behavior, whereas the Gestalt, TA, and REBT TPs do not view an outside session as necessary or his behavior as requiring special attention.

Like the other TPs, client-centered and REBT TPs direct their primary attention to the group, but their strategies differ. The client-centered TP initially conducts an internal dialogue to avoid colluding with the group attack on Jim. His strategy is to wait, believing that "disruptions are a waste of time," and he does not want to "fix Joe." However, if the attack increases (emotional contagion), he will interpret the group's behavior by saying, "It sounds as if you want Joe to confess!" Later, he acknowledges Joe's right to his behavior: "Maybe it takes him longer than seven weeks to feel safe." In contrast, the REBT TP views the group as "not healthfully confronting Joe?" and asks them to "surrender their anger." He, like the Gestalt TP, focuses on those two members (Jackie and Jim) who display their disturbance, although he works with Jackie first. However, although their leadership behaviors differ, the REBT TP, like the Adlerian TP, explains the why of Jackie's behavior as self-defeating and then describes Jim's behavior as self-defeating, thus attempting to address Jackie's and Jim's fears while attempting to reduce Joe's fears. Unlike the other TPs, the REBT TP invites group members to challenge and question Jackie and Jim.

The REBT, reality therapy, CBT, and SFT TPs assign homework to Joe and group members, related to their current behavior. The Gestalt TP, in contrast, has group members do homework in the group, by means of various verbal and nonverbal techniques.

Summary of Critical Incident 6

All TPs agree that Joe is being scapegoated and needs both support and protection. The critical issue is *how* the TPs choose to de-escalate the attack on Joe and move the group in a more productive direction.

Most TPs work initially with Joe before focusing on other members. The client-centered, REBT, and SCT TPs direct their interventions to the group but vary in the degree of structure they provide for the group. There is ample use of the here and now by the SCT, FCT, IGP, CBT, psychoanalytic, and SFT TPs as they seek to provide meaning attribution and to generate a collaborative atmosphere for learning that can be helpful for both Joe and the rest of the group. The TA TP intervenes by helping Joe express himself more openly.

Interestingly, the TA, Gestalt, and SCT TPs view Joe's behavior as assertive, whereas the remaining TPs view his behavior as either defensive or his best shot at behaving, given his family of origin. Many TPs see this incident as an opportunity to bring to life a real example of the struggle to be assertive and to use the moment for everyone's benefit.

Conclusion

The central task of this chapter was to emphasize that effective leadership is more of a choice and blend rather than a determination of which theoretical intervention is best. In comparing and contrasting the 72 TP responses to the six critical incidents, our TPs have clearly provided us with some important learnings regarding effective leadership and have demonstrated that effective leadership is more of a choice and blend. The following are some of the learnings that stood out for us. Others certainly may have been found by you as you compared and contrasted the responses made by our TPs.

1. TPs of differing orientations intervene in a similar fashion.
2. TPs of differing orientations focus their interventions on one of the following: the leader, the member(s), the group, or the group processes.
3. TPs of differing orientations vary their interventions on the leader, member, group, or group processes during a specific critical incident.
4. TPs of differing orientations employ a series, or sequence, of interventions during a specific critical incident.
5. TPs of differing orientations may base their current interventions on the basis of previous group sessions (group history).
6. TPs of differing orientations may intervene to generate affect (emotional contagion) or dilute affect in a therapy group.
7. TPs of differing orientations conduct individual therapy with group members during or between group sessions.
8. TPs of differing orientations educate members regarding the *why* of their behavior, through a variety of strategies.
9. TPs of differing orientations differ more in terms of how and when they intervene than why they intervene.
10. TPs of differing orientations conceptualize the existence and influence of a group process but may or may not acknowledge its existence in their intervention to the group.
11. TPs of differing orientations employ individual therapy interventions in therapy groups.
12. TPs of differing orientations may employ interventions based on members' physical responses (body language).
13. TPs of differing orientations give greater or lesser degrees of attention to activating member-to-member interaction.
14. TPs of differing orientations vary in their emphasis on pregroup preparation.
15. TPs of differing orientation vary in their emphasis of activating and utilizing the here and now.

16. TPs of differing orientations vary in their view of using and working with coleaders.
17. TPs, in their discussion of ethics, vary in their ways of highlighting ethical concerns in their approach to group therapy.
18. TPs of differing orientations vary in their emphasis on member selection and screening.
19. TPs of differing orientations vary in their approaches to the use of time, both in terms of beginning and ending the group.

CHAPTER TWENTY

Considerations in Developing Your Theory of Group Therapy

Just as we began this text by explaining the reasons we believed a theory of group therapy was important, we can now address how a beginning group therapist might undertake the development of his or her own theory and rationale of group therapy. In this final chapter we provide you with some of the primary elements that you should consider fundamental to an evolving theory of group therapy.

Steps to Developing a Theory

In developing a theory of group therapy, the first step is to define what group therapy is and how it differs from other systems of therapy, such as individual or family therapy. In other words, it is necessary (1) to determine what is unique about group therapy as a therapeutic system that sets it apart from other therapeutic models and (2) to ask "What characteristics or properties of a therapy group do not exist in other therapeutic modalities that contribute to therapeutic change?" More simply stated, we need to understand why it may be more beneficial to place clients in a therapy group instead of individual or family therapy.

In defining group therapy, the fact that five to ten people are meeting with a therapist suggests an inherently different system for conducting therapy, understanding client behavior, and generating therapeutic change than does a system that employs a two-person interaction.

A group provides the therapist an opportunity to *see* how group members interact with each other, as opposed to just interacting with the therapist in individual counseling. More specifically, the group therapist can see what clients do and how they behave in their relationships with others. In other words, the process of group therapy provides the group therapist with behavioral data on member interactions that are unavailable in individual therapy. This behavioral laboratory provides data on verbal and nonverbal behaviors emitted by members in response to each other, the therapist, and the group. An adequate definition of group therapy must take into account the unique contributions of the group as a whole, the therapist, and the group members and the way each affects the therapeutic process.

Properties unique to groups—such as cohesiveness, "group-generated affect" (emotional contagion), power distribution and influence, proxemics, subgroups, group development, and norms and standards—have been identified as evolving or existing processes within the group system. The question arises about how these processes interfere with or contribute to changes in a therapy group, group development, the learning of new behaviors, and the success or failure of the therapist's interventions. The group therapist's theory of group therapy must account for these unique processes in order to understand, control, and predict group movement and member behavior (Donigian & Malnati, 1997).

Besides defining what group therapy is and what those properties are that make group therapy a unique system of change, a theory of group therapy must address three elements: the therapist, the member, and the group. To ignore one or more of these elements is to neglect a potential explanation for unexplained occurrences or events during the course of group therapy (Donigian & Malnati, 1997).

Among the group therapists presented in this text, it can be said that only the psychodynamic therapy, family-centered, interpersonal psychotherapy, and systems-centered therapists explicitly address the contribution of group dynamics to therapeutic change. Also, with the exception of the systems-centered therapist, the other TPs primarily focus on the characteristics of the leader, member, or both. It is our position that all three elements must be given equal attention when formulating a theory of group therapy (Donigian & Malnati, 1997). We have therefore developed a series of questions that should help you identify features of the three elements, which will guide you when establishing a theoretical "map" of group therapy. Keep in mind, however, that all three elements are interdependent and are not to be thought of as in isolation of one another (i.e., they are isomorphically related). So, as you undertake answering the questions, try to think of the elements in a systemic context.

ELEMENTS OF GROUP BEHAVIOR

1. How does group therapy differ from individual therapy?
2. How do nontherapeutic groups (support groups) differ from therapeutic groups?
3. How do groups go through specific stages, and how do the stages (phases) of groups reoccur?
4. How does the history of the group affect its current operation and future development?

5. How do norms and standards influence *what* is talked about (content) and *how* it is talked about (process)?
6. How do emotional issues exist in groups, and how are they manifested by the group process?
7. How do group processes interfere with or contribute to therapeutic change in a group?
8. How do group processes contribute to helping determine a member's readiness to leave group therapy?

ELEMENTS OF MEMBER BEHAVIOR

1. How does group member behavior differ in group therapy versus individual therapy?
2. How does group member behavior differ in nontherapeutic groups (support groups) versus therapeutic groups?
3. How do group members' pregroup histories influence how they experience the group process?
4. How do the members' historical behaviors in groups affect their current behavior in the therapy group?
5. How do the group members' behaviors influence *what* is talked about (content) and *how* it is talked about (process)?
6. How do group members' behaviors elicit emotional issues in the group, and how are they manifested by the group process?
7. How do group members' behaviors contribute to therapeutic change, and how do group members' behaviors interfere with therapeutic change?
8. How do group members' behaviors determine their readiness to leave group therapy?

ELEMENTS OF THERAPIST BEHAVIOR

1. How does the therapist's behavior differ in group therapy versus individual therapy?
2. How does the therapist's behavior differ in nontherapeutic groups (support groups) versus therapeutic groups?
3. How do group therapists' pregroup histories influence the way they experience the group process?
4. How does the therapist's historical behavior influence the group's current operation and future development?
5. How does the therapist's behavior influence *what* is talked about (content) and *how* it is talked about (process)?
6. How does the therapist's behavior elicit emotional issues in a group, and how are they manifested by the group process?
7. How does the group therapist contribute to therapeutic change, and how does the group therapist interfere with therapeutic change?
8. How does the group therapist determine a member's readiness to leave group therapy?

Conclusion

From the beginning we have emphasized the need to observe the value of the *core* of the therapist. That is, we have argued for the value of each individual developing his or her own theory. Our primary mission was to urge you to demystify this phenomenon called *group process* by placing it in your terms. Our intention has been to underscore the fact that reasons exist for all events that occur in groups, and the way you choose to experience and interpret them will be determined by the theoretical reference point on which you rely. Furthermore, your choice of leader response (intervention) will also depend on this theoretical frame of reference.

As a result of witnessing our TPs' approaches to each critical incident, we hope you have come to realize that effectiveness may well be a matter of choice and blend of concepts as opposed to trying to find which theory is better. We also hope that you have come to recognize the flexibility and imaginative fluidity in each of our TPs' particular approach. We hope that you have observed how their particular interventions of choice evolved from their *core*. In other words, a theoretical framework guided their perception of a given event, which subsequently determined the technique they employed to manage the event.

We see the development of your personal conceptual framework of group dynamics as analogous to Yalom's (1995) core concept. Taking it a step further, we contend that techniques evolving from one's core will tend to be more effective than those applied in a serendipitous fashion. It therefore follows that it will be to your disadvantage to enter group therapy with simply a kit bag of procedures and techniques, as opposed to a formalized theoretical perspective.

REFERENCES

ADLER, A. (1956). *The individual psychology of Alfred Adler.* New York: Basic Books.

AGAZARIAN, Y. M., & JANOFF, S. (1993). Systems theory and small groups. In H. I. Kaplan & B. J. Saddock (Eds.), *Comprehensive group psychotherapy* (3rd ed.). Baltimore: Williams & Wilkins.

AGAZARIAN, Y. M. (1994). The phases of development and the systems-centered group. In M. Pines & V. Schermer (Eds.), *Ring of fire: Primitive object relations and affect in group psychotherapy.* London: Routledge, Chapman & Hall.

———. (1997a). *Systems-centered therapy for groups.* New York: Guilford.

———. (1997b). Notes included in manuscript to *Critical Incidents in Group Therapy* (2nd ed.).

AGAZARIAN, Y. M. & PETERS, R. (1981). *The visible and invisible group: Two perspectives on group psychotherapy and group process.* London: Routlege & Kegan Paul.

ALLEN, T. (1971a). The individual psychology of Alfred Adler: An item of history and a promise of a revolution. *The Counseling Psychologist, 3*(1), 3–24.

ALLEN, T. (1971b). Adlerian interview strategies for behavior change. *The Counseling Psychologist, 3*(1), 40–48.

BANDURA, A. (1969). *Principles of behavior modification.* New York: Holt.

———. (1971). Psychotherapy based on modeling principles. In A. E. Bergin and S. L. Garfield (Eds.), *Handbook of psychotherapy and behavior change.* New York: Wiley.

———. (1977). *Social learning theory.* Englewood Cliffs, NJ: Prentice Hall.

BARNES, G. (Ed.). (1977). *Transactional analysis after Eric Berne.* New York: Harper's College Press.

BECK, A. T. (1976). *Cognitive therapy and the emotional disorders.* New York: International Universities Press.

BECKER, B. J. (1972). The psychology names of analytic group psychotherapy. *The American Journal of Psychoanalysis, 32*(2), 181.

BERNE, E. (1964). *Games people play.* New York: Grove Press.

———. (1966). *Principles of group treatment.* New York: Oxford University Press.

————. (1976). *Beyond games and scripts.* New York: Grove Press.

BICKHARD, M., & FORD, B. (1976, May). Adler's concept of social interest: A critical explication. *Journal of Individual Psychology, 27–49.*

BION, W. R. (1959). *Experiences in groups.* London: Tavistock.

BLAKENEY, R. (1977). *Current issues in transactional analysis.* New York: Brunner/Mazel.

BOWEN, M. (1977). Family systems theory and society. In J. B. Lorio & L. McClenathan, (Eds.), *Georgetown family symposium: Volume 2* (1973–1974). Washington, DC: Georgetown Family Center.

BRATTER, T. E. (1975a). Group psychotherapy: A restructuring of the probation process. *Corrective and Social Psychology, 22*(1), 1–5.

————. (1975b). Responsible therapeutic eros: The psychotherapist who cares enough to define and enforce behavior limits with potentially suicidal adolescents. *The Counseling Psychologist, 5*(4), 97–104.

BUBER, M. (1967). *A believing humanism.* New York: Simon & Schuster.

BUGENTHAL, J. F. T. (1965). *The search for authenticity.* New York: Holt, Rinehart & Winston.

————. (Ed.). (1967). *Challenges of humanistic psychology.* New York: McGraw-Hill.

CHASIDIC RABBI. (1970). *Words on his death bed.* Winter Park, FL: Dare to Be Great.

CLEVENGER, C. (1982). *A middle range theory of power in universities.* Unpublished dissertation. State University of New York at Buffalo.

COULSON, W. R. (1972). *Groups, gimmicks, and instant gurus.* New York: Harper & Row.

————. (1974). *A sense of community.* Columbus, OH: Merrill.

————. (1977). *The foreignness of feelings.* In D. A. L. Coulson & B. S. Meador (Eds.), *The La Jolla experiment: Eight personal views,* pp. 45–58. La Jolla, CA: Landmark Press.

————. (in press). *The Socratic inquiry in medical school.* La Jolla, CA: Helicon House.

DE SHAZER, S. (1985). *Keys to solutions in brief therapy.* New York: Norton.

————. (1988). *Clues: Investigating solutions in brief therapy.* New York: Norton.

DINKMEYER, D., PEW, W., & DINKMEYER, D., Jr. (1979). *Adlerian counseling and psychotherapy.* Monterey, CA: Brooks/Cole.

DONIGIAN, J., & MALNATI, R. (1997). *Systemic group therapy: A triadic model.* Pacific Grove, CA: Brooks/Cole.

DREIKURS, R. (1950). *Fundamentals of Adlerian psychology.* New York: Greenberg.

————. (1957). Group psychotherapy from the points of view of various schools of psychology: I. Group psychotherapy from the point of view of Adlerian psychology. *International Journal of Group Psychotherapy, 7,* 363–375.

————. (1971). An interview with Rudolph Dreikurs. *The Counseling Psychologist, 3*(1), 49–54.

DREIKURS, R., & SONSTEGARD, M. (1967). *The teleoanalytic approach to group counseling.* Chicago: Alfred Adler Institute.

DURKIN, H. (1964). *The group in depth.* New York: International Universities Press.

DURKIN, H. (1981). The group therapies and general systems theory as an integrative structure. In J. Durkin (Ed.), *Living groups.* New York: Brunner/Mazel.

DUSAY, J., & STEINER, C. (1971). Transactional analysis in group. In H. I. Kaplan & B. J. Sadock (Eds.), *Comprehensive group psychotherapy.* Baltimore: Williams & Wilkins.

ELLIS, A. (1962). *Reason and emotion in psychotherapy.* New York: Lyle Stuart.

————. (1969). A weekend of rational encounter. In A. Burton (Ed.), *Encounter.* San Francisco: Jossey-Bass.

————. (1974a). Rational–emotive therapy in groups. *Rational Living, 1,* 15–22.

————. (1974b). The group as agent in facilitating change toward rational thinking and appropriate emoting. In A. Jacobs & W. Spradlin (Eds.), *The group as agent of change.* New York: Behavioral Publications.

————. (1975). *Reason and emotion in psychotherapy.* Secaucus, NJ: Lyle Stuart.

————. (1993). Changing rational–emotive therapy (RET) to rational–emotive–behavior therapy (REBT). *Behavior Therapist, 16,* 257–258.

ELLIS, A., & HARPER, R. A. (1975). *New guide to rational living.* Englewood Cliffs, NJ: Prentice Hall.

ELLIS, A., & WHITELEY, J. (1979). *Theoretical and empirical foundations of rational-emotive therapy.* Monterey, CA: Brooks/Cole.

FAGAN, J., & SHEPHERD, I. L. (1970). *Gestalt therapy now.* Palo Alto, CA: Science and Behavior Books.

FESTINGER, L. (1957). *A theory of cognitive dissonance.* Evanston, IL: Raw, Peterson.

FORER, L. (1977). Use of birth order information in psychotherapy. *Journal of Individual Psychology, 33,* 105–113.

FREUD, S. (1921). Group psychology and the analysis of the ego. In *Standard edition of the complete psychological works of Sigmund Freud* (Vol. 18, p. 67). London: Hogarth Press.

GLASSER, W. (1961). *Mental health or mental illness?* New York: Harper & Row.

————. (1965). *Reality therapy: A new approach to psychiatry.* New York: Harper & Row.

————. (1969). *Schools without failure.* New York: Harper & Row.

GLASSER, W., & ZUNIN, L. M. (1979). Reality therapy. In R. Corsini (Ed.), *Current psychotherapies* (2nd ed.). Itasca, IL: Peacock.

GOLDHABER, G., & GOLDHABER, M. (1976). *Transactional analysis: Principles and applications.* Boston: Allyn & Bacon.

GREENBERG, I. A. (1968). *Psychodrama and audience attitude change.* Beverly Hills: Behavioral Studies Press.

GREENSON, R. (1978). *Explorations in psychoanalysis.* New York: International Universities Press.

GUSHURST, R. (1971). The technique, utility, and validity of life style analysis. *The Counseling Psychologist, 3*(1), 30–40.

HANSEN, J., WARNER, R., & SMITH, E. (1976). *Group counseling: Theory and process.* Chicago: Rand McNally.

HANSEN, J. C., STEVIC, R. R., & WARNER, R. W. (1977). *Counseling theory and process.* Boston: Allyn & Bacon.

HARRIS, T. (1969). *I'm okay you're okay: A practical guide to transactional analysis.* New York: Harper & Row.

HOROWITZ, L. (1993). Group-centered models of group psychotherapy. In H. I. Kaplan & B. J. Saddock (Eds.), *Comprehensive group psychotherapy* (3rd ed.). Baltimore: Williams & Wilkins.

HOWARD, A., & SCOTT, R. A. (1965). A proposed framework for the analysis of stress in the human organism. *Journal of Applied Behavioral Science, 10,* 141.

HUBER, C. H., & BACKLUND, B. A. (1991). *The twenty minute counselor.* New York: Continuum.

JAMES, M., et al. (1977). *Techniques in transactional analysis.* Reading, MA: Addison-Wesley.

KIEFER, H. (1980). *Some reflections on the philosophy of education.* Unpublished paper presented at a meeting of the Center for Philosophic Exchange. State University of New York, College at Brockport.

KOCH, S. (1969). *Psychology: A study of a science: Vol. 3. Formulation of the person and the social context.* New York: McGraw-Hill.

KUTASH, I. L. & WOLF, A. (1993). Psychoanalysis in groups. In H. I. Kaplan & B. J. Saddock (Eds.), *Comprehensive group psychotherapy* (3rd ed.). Baltimore: Williams & Wilkins.

LA FOUNTAIN, R. M., & GARNER, N. E. (1996). Solution-focused counseling groups: The results are in. *The Journal for Specialists in Group Work, 21*(2), 128–143.

LA FOUNTAIN, R. M., GARNER, N. E., & ELIASON, G. T. (1996). Solution-focused counseling groups: A key for school counselors. *The School Counselor, 43,* 243–267.

LESHAN, L. (1959). Psychological states as factors in the development of malignant disease: A critical review. *Journal of the National Cancer Institute, 22,* 1–19.

———. (1966). An emotional life-history pattern associated with neoplastic disease. *Annals of the New York Academy of Sciences, 125,* 780–793.

———. (1968). Psychotherapy and the dying patient. In L. Peerson (Ed.), *Death and dying.* New York: Macmillan.

LEVITSKY, A., & PERLS, F. S. (1970). The rules and games of gestalt therapy. In J. Fagan & I. L. Shepherd (Eds.), *Gestalt therapy now.* Palo Alto, CA: Science and Behavior Books.

LEVITSKY, A., & SIMKIN, J. S. (1972). Gestalt therapy. In L. N. Solomon & B. Berzon, (Eds.), *New perspectives on encounter groups.* New York: Jossey-Bass.

LEWIN, K. (1935). *Dynamic theory of personality.* New York: McGraw-Hill.

LIEBERMAN, YALOM, I., & MILES, M. (1973). *Encounter groups: First facts.* New York: Basic Books.

MAHONEY, M. J. (1977). Reflections on the cognitive learning trend in psychotherapy. *American Psychologist, 32,* 5-13.

MANASTER, G. (1977). Birth order—An overview. *Journal of Individual Psychology, 33,* 3–8.

MEICHENBAUM, D. (1977). *Cognitive behavioral modification.* New York: Plenum.

MINUCHIN, S. (1974). *Families and family therapy.* Cambridge, MA: Harvard University Press.

MOSAK, H., & MOSAK, B. (1975). *A bibliography for Adlerian psychology.* Washington, DC: Hemisphere.

O'CONNELL, W. (1971). Sensitivity training and Adlerian theory. *Journal of Individual Psychology, 31,* 65–72.

O'HANLON, W. H., & Weiner-Davis, M. (1989). *In search of solutions.* New York: Norton.

OLDEN, C. (1943). The psychology of obstinancy. *Psychoanalytic Quarterly, 12,* 252.

OSIPOW, S. H. (1973). *Theories of career development* (2nd ed.). New York: Appleton-Century-Crofts.

PAPANEK, H. (1964, May). Bridging dichotomies through group psychotherapy. *Journal of Individual Psychology,* 38–47.

PERLS, F. S. (1969a). *In and out of the garbage pail.* Lafayette, CA: Real People Press.

———. (1969b). *Gestalt therapy verbatim.* Lafayette, CA: Real People Press.

———. (1969c). *Ego, hunger, and aggression.* New York: Random House.

———. (1978). Concepts and misconceptions of gestalt therapy. *Voices, 14*(3), 31–36.

PERLS, F. S., HEFFERLINE, R. R., & GOODMAN, P. (1951). *Gestalt therapy.* New York: Julian Press.

POLSTER, E., & POLSTER, M. (1973). *Gestalt therapy integrated.* New York: Brunner / Mazel.

RACHMAN, S. (1972). Clinical applications of observational learning, imitation and modeling. *Behavior Therapy, 3*(2), 379–397.

RAUBOLT, R. R., & BRATTER, T. E. (1976). Beyond adolescent group psychotherapy: The caring community. *The Addiction Therapist, 1*(4), 10–17.

REISSMAN, F. (1965). The helper therapy principle. *Social Work, 10*(2), 27–32.

RICHARDS, I. A. (1942). *Principles of literary criticism.* New York: Harcourt Brace.

ROGERS, C. R. (1942). *Counseling and psychotherapy.* New York: Houghton Mifflin.

———. (1951). *Client-centered therapy.* Boston: Houghton Mifflin.

————. (1959). A theory of therapy, personality and interpersonal relationships, as developed in the client-centered framework. In S. Koch (Ed.), *Psychology: A study of a science. Vol. 3, Formulation of the person and the social context*. New York: McGraw-Hill.

————. (1961). *On becoming a person*. New York: Houghton Mifflin.

————. (1965). *Client-centered therapy*. New York: Houghton Mifflin.

————. (1967). The process of the basic encounter group. In J. F. T. Bugenthal (Ed.), *Challenges of humanistic psychology*. New York: McGraw-Hill.

————. (1970). *Carl Rogers on encounter groups*. New York: Harper & Row.

ROSE, S. D. (1977). *Group therapy: A behavioral approach*. Englewood Cliffs, NJ: Prentice Hall.

————. (1993). Cognitive–behavioral group therapy. In H. I. Kaplan & B. J. Saddock (Eds.). *Comprehensive group psychotherapy* (3rd ed.). Baltimore: Williams & Wilkins.

ROSENBERG, J. B. (1983). Structural family therapy. In B. J. Wolman & G. Striker (Eds.), *Handbook of family and marital therapy*. New York: Plenum.

ROSENTHAL, L. (1993). Resistance in group psychotherapy. In H. I. Kaplan & B. J. Saddock (Eds.), *Comprehensive group psychotherapy* (3rd ed.). Baltimore: Williams & Wilkins.

ROTH, B. E. (1993). Freud: The group psychologist and group leader. In H. I. Kaplan & B. J. Saddock (Eds.), *Comprehensive group psychotherapy* (4th ed.). Baltimore: Williams & Wilkins.

RUTAN, J. S. (1993). Psychoanalytic group psychotherapy. In H. I. Kaplan & B. J. Saddock (Eds.), *Comprehensive group therapy* (3rd ed.). Baltimore: Williams & Wilkins.

RUTAN, J. S., & STONE, W. N. (1993). *Psychodynamic group therapy* (2nd ed.). New York: Guilford Press.

SHANNON, C. E., & WEAVER, W. (1964). *The mathematical theory of communication*. Urbana: University of Illinois Press.

SHEEHY, G. (1976). *Passages*. New York: Dutton.

SHULMAN, B., & MOSAK, H. (1977). Birth order and ordinal position: Two Adlerian views. *Journal of Individual Psychology, 33,* 114–121.

SIEGEL, J. M., & SPIVACK, G. (1976). Problem-solving therapy: The description of a new program for chronic psychiatric patients. *Psychotherapy: Theory, Research, and Practice, 13*(4), 368–374.

SIMKIN, J. (1974). *Mini lectures in Gestalt therapy*. Albany, GA: Woodpress.

SOLOMON, L. N., & BERZON, B. (Eds.). (1972). *New perspectives on encounter groups*. San Francisco: Jossey-Bass.

SULLIVAN, H. (1955). *Conceptions of modern psychiatry*. London: Tavistock.

TROTZER, J. P. (1989). *The counselor and the group*. Muncie, IN: Accelerated Development.

TROTZER, J. P., & TROTZER, T. B. (1986). *Marriage and family better ready than not*. Muncie, IN: Accelerated Development.

TUTTMAN, S. (1993). Countertransference and transference in groups. In H. I. Kaplan & B. J. Saddock (Eds.), *Comprehensive group psychotherapy* (3rd ed.). Baltimore: Williams & Wilkins.

VON BERTALANTY, L. (1968). *General systems theory: Foundations, development, application*. New York: Braziller.

WAGNER, M. K. (1968a). Comparative effectiveness of behavioral rehearsal and verbal reinforcement for effecting anger expressiveness. *Psychological Reports, 22,* 1079–1080.

————. (1968b). Reinforcement of the expression of anger through role playing. *Behavior Research and Therapy, 2,* 91–95.

WALLEN, R. (1970). Gestalt therapy and Gestalt psychology. In J. Fagan, & I. L. Shepherd (Eds.), *Gestalt therapy now*. Palo Alto, CA: Science and Behavior Books.

WALTER, J., & PELLER, J. (1992). *Becoming solution-focused in brief therapy*. New York: Brunner/Mazel.

WEINER, M. F. (1993). Role of the leader in group therapy. In H. I. Kaplan & B. J. Saddock (Eds.), *Comprehensive group psychotherapy* (3rd ed.). Baltimore: Williams & Wilkins.

WIENER, N. (1948). *Cybernetics*. Wiley. New York.

WOLF, A. (1949). The psychoanalysis of groups. *American Journal of Psychotherapy, 4,* 16.

WOLPE, J., & LAZARUS, A. A. (1966). *Behavior therapy techniques: A guide to the treatment of neurosis*. New York: Pergamon Press.

YALOM, I. (1983). *Inpatient group psychotherapy*. New York: Basic Books.

———. (1989). *Love's executioner & other tales of psychotherapy*. New York: Basic Books.

———. (1995). *The theory and practice of group psychotherapy* (4th ed.). New York: Basic Books.

YALOM, V. & VENOGRADOV, S. (1993). Interpersonal group psychotherapy. In H. I. Kaplan & B. J. Saddock (Eds.), *Comprehensive group psychotherapy* (3rd ed.). Baltimore: Williams & Wilkins.

ZINKER, J. (1977). *Creative process in Gestalt therapy*. New York: Brunner/Mazel.

ZUCK, G. H. (1981). *Family therapy: A triadic based approach* (Rev. ed.). New York: Human Services Press.

I N D E X